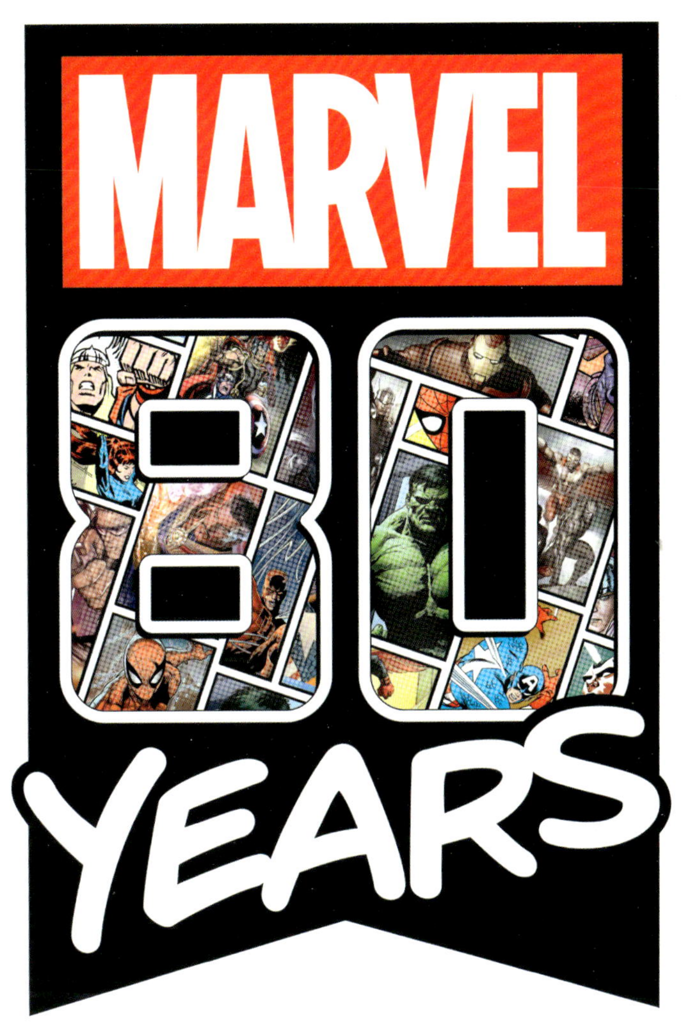
MARVEL
80
YEARS

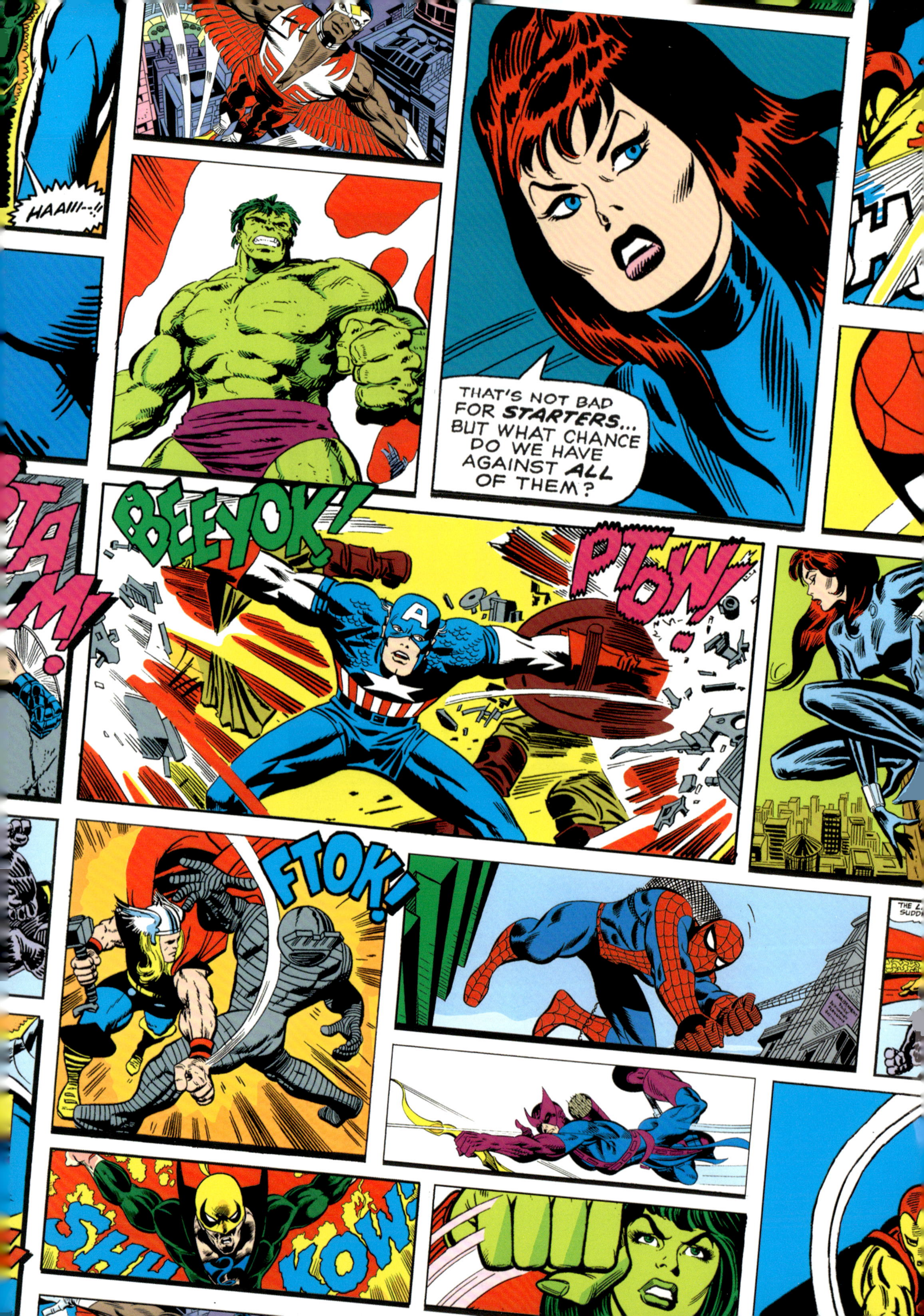
HAAIII--!!
THAT'S NOT BAD FOR STARTERS... BUT WHAT CHANCE DO WE HAVE AGAINST ALL OF THEM?
BEEYOK!
PTOW!
FTOK!
SHU KOW!

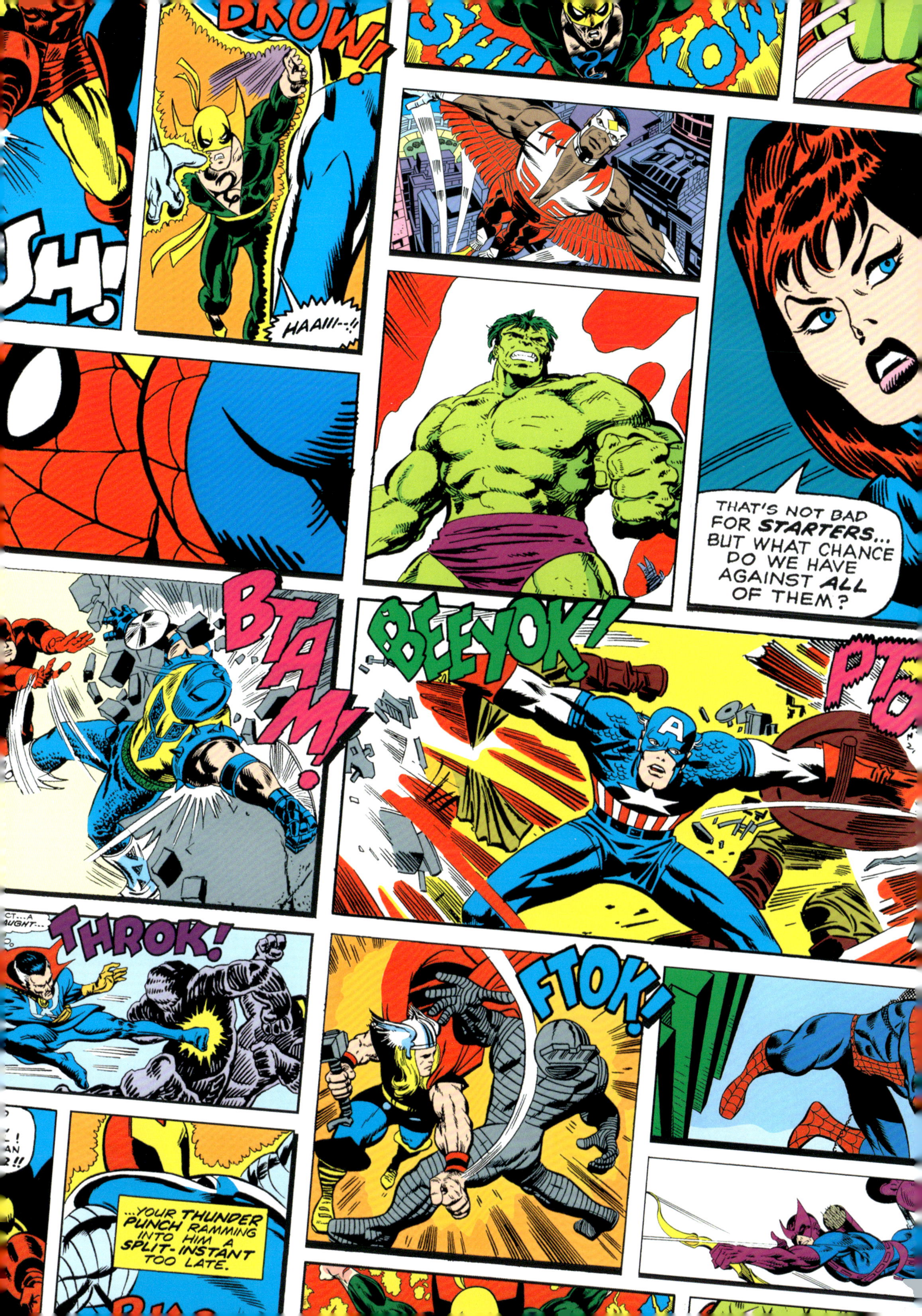

HAAIII--!!
THAT'S NOT BAD FOR **STARTERS...** BUT WHAT CHANCE DO WE HAVE AGAINST **ALL** OF THEM?
BTAM!
BEEYOK!
THROK!
FTOK!
...YOUR **THUNDER PUNCH** RAMMING INTO HIM A **SPLIT-INSTANT** TOO LATE.

TABLE OF CONTENTS

Introduction

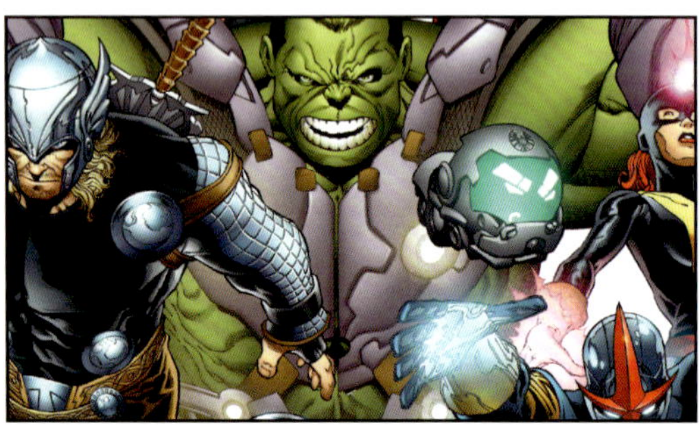

The 1930s 1940s

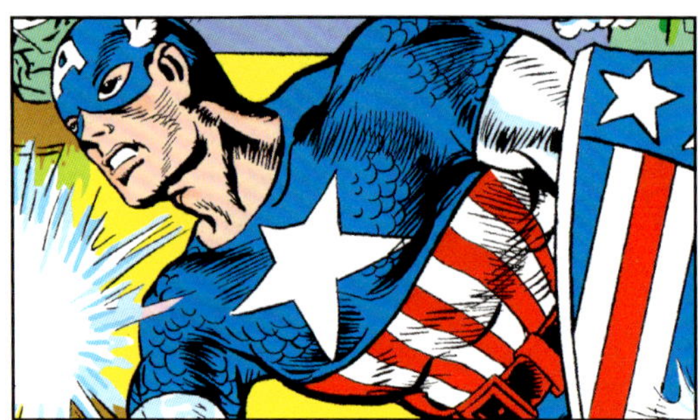

The 1950s

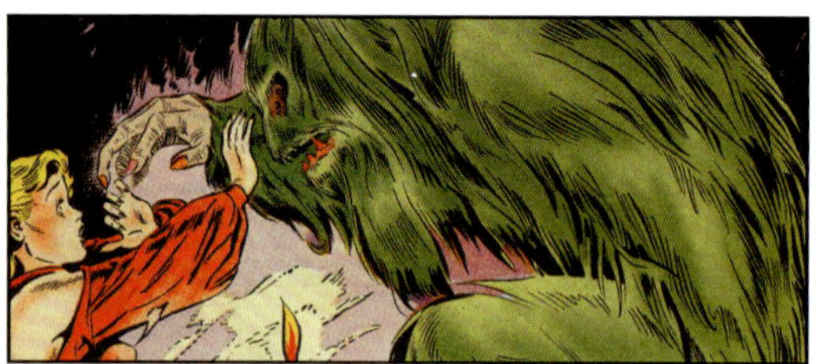

The 1960s

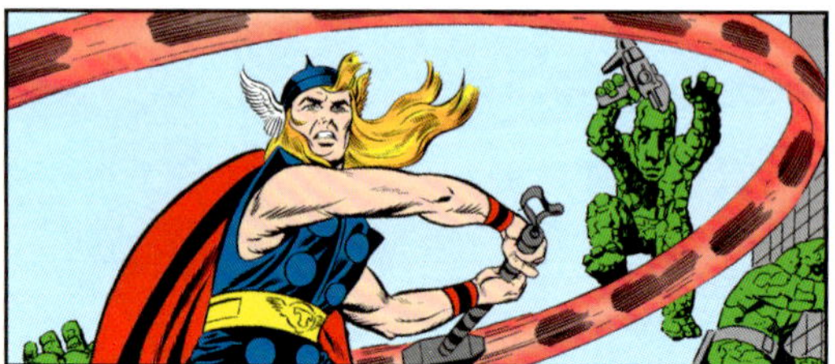

The 1970s

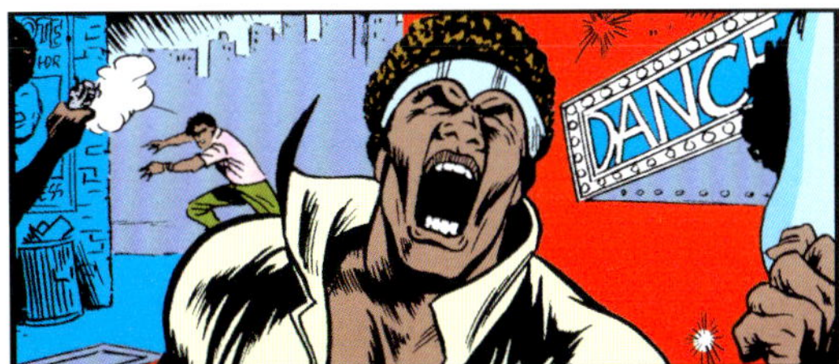

The 1980s

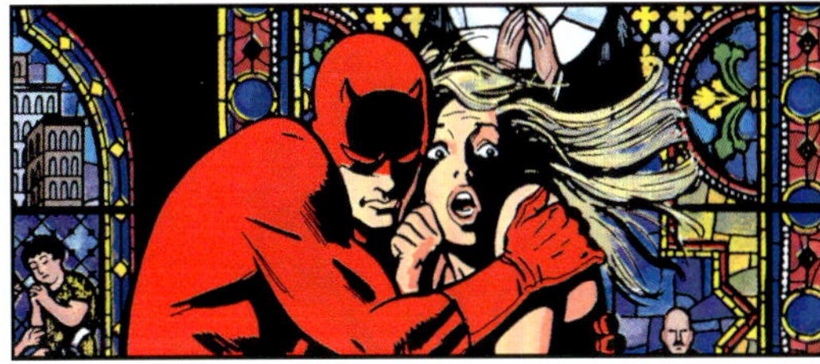

The 1990s

The 2000s

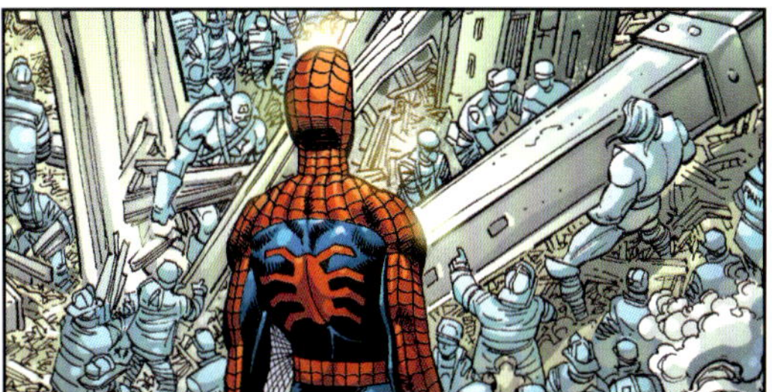

The 2010s

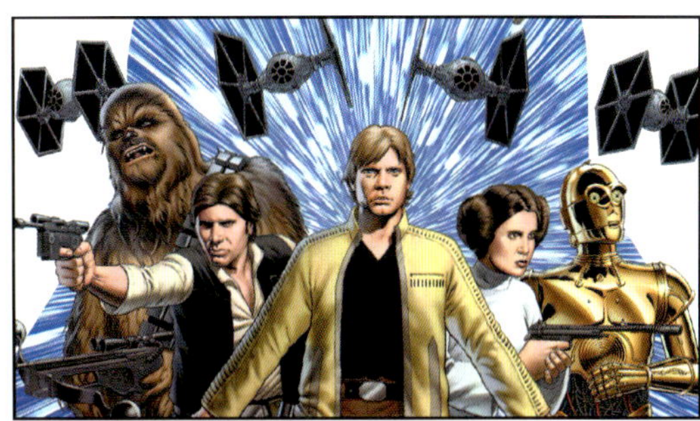

Index & Credits

 Published by Panini Publishing, a division of Panini UK Limited. Mike Riddell, Managing Director. Alan O'Keefe, Managing Editor. Mark Irvine, Production Manager. Marco M. Lupoi, Publishing Director Europe. Simon Frith, Senior Editor. Ed Hammond, Editor. Samantha Hammond, Editorial Assistant. Barry Spiers, Designer. Office of publication: Brockbourne House, 77 Mount Ephraim, Tunbridge Wells, Kent TN4 8BS. Printed in the UK by Zenith Media.

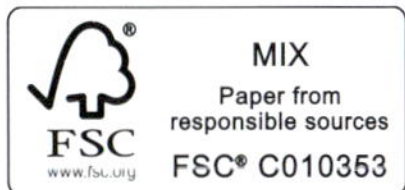

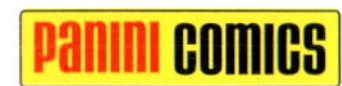

Introduction

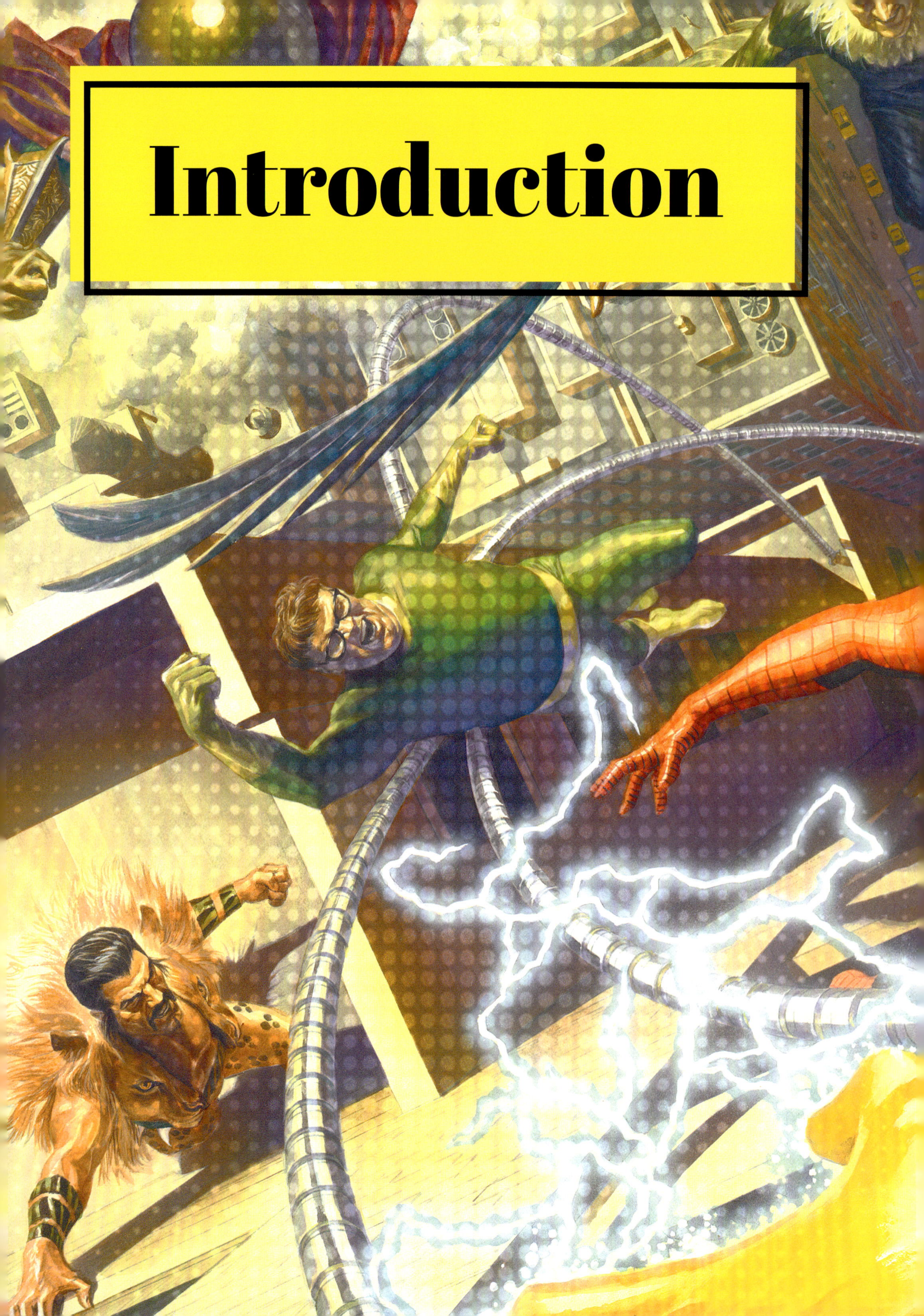

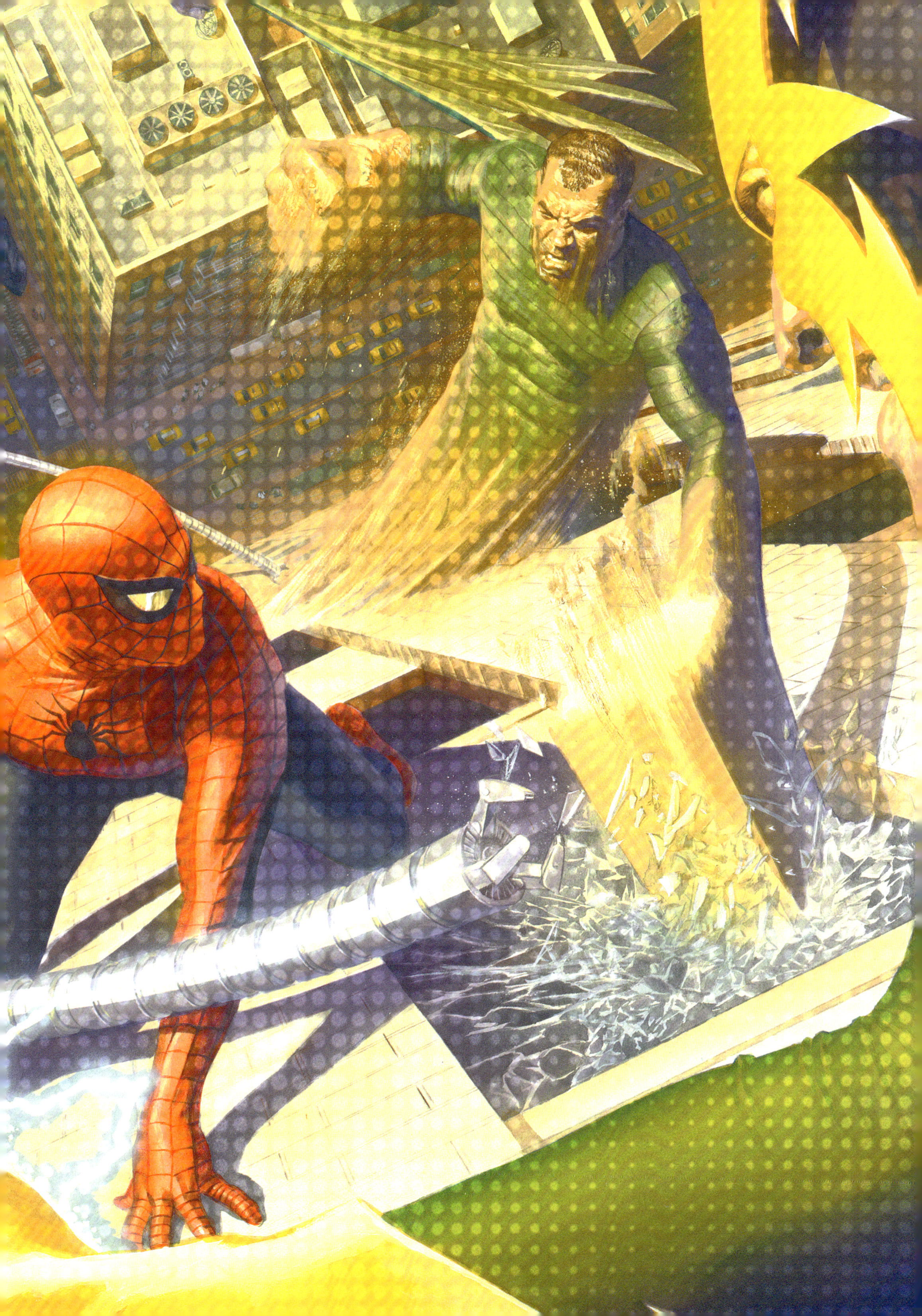

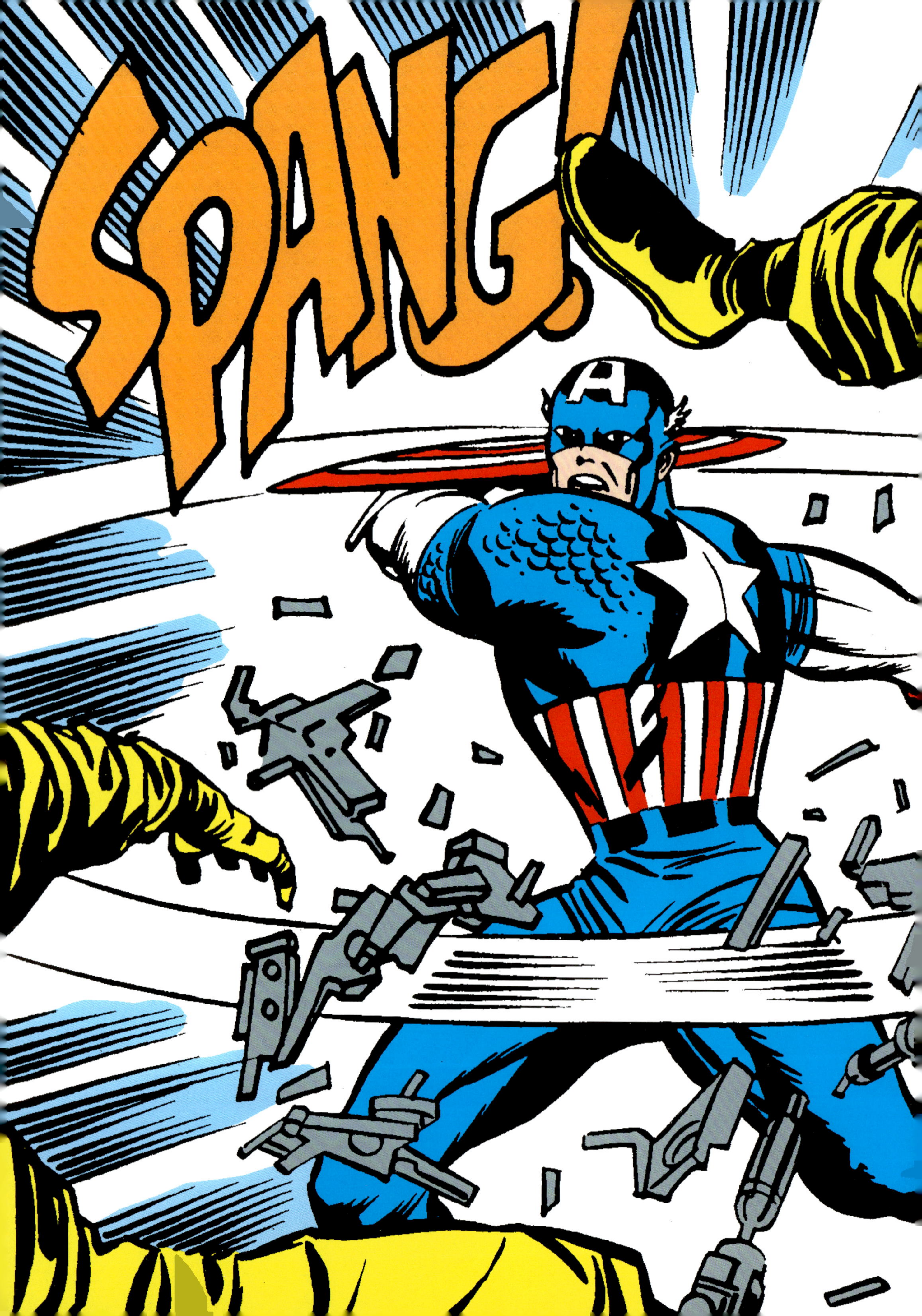
SPANG!

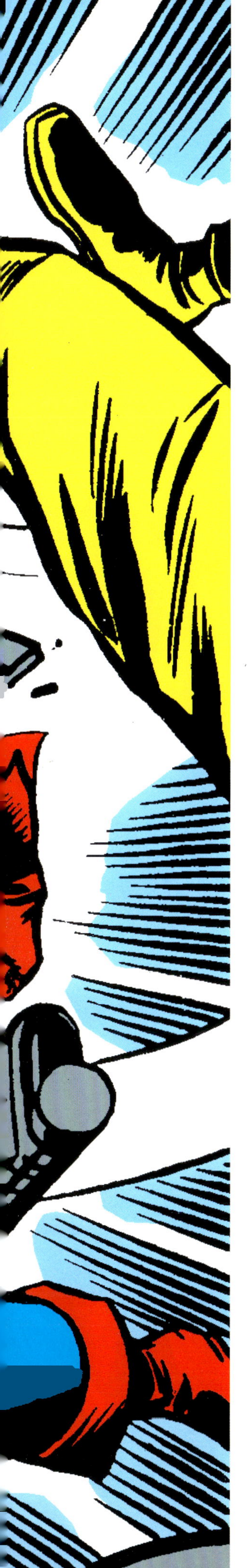

80 AMAZING YEARS

I've often asked myself why. Why, after poring over my very first Marvel comic book, with its dazzling colours and winning stories, I got hooked. Why my house quickly turned into a veritable library of comics featuring Super Heroes with super problems, leaving room for little else. Why Spider-Man became my friend right off the bat, a brother, someone I could share joy and pain with, an alter ego I could identify with. Why I cried out with rage when the Green Goblin threw Spidey's girlfriend off the Brooklyn Bridge. Why I suffered when J.J.J. unjustly, compulsively accused the wall-crawler of being a criminal; when Peter was forced to blow off his date; when his friends teased him; when Aunt May was lying in a hospital bed. Why, at the end of each story, victory had the bitter aftertaste of defeat.

Ultimately, I gave up looking for logical explanations. Until I realised that Marvel's power lies in the human qualities displayed by its pantheon of comic-book characters, in the spirit of the stories they star in, in the realism they're part of. What really throws you for a loop is that millions upon millions of readers the world over must have realised the same thing; caught up, to their great delight, in a virtual community whose epicentre is a universe of fictional characters that are as realistic and credible as they are super powerful. Marvel is modern-day mythology, a parallel dimension that is as close to everyday life as it comes. Art, literature, and legend all bundled up into one. No doubt, Marvel will have the same allure for scholars of the future as ancient Greek mythology has on today's minds.

The Marvel Universe is populated by a cast of all-too-human, fragile, weak, hysterical, unlucky, petty, and courageous Super Heroes who were born amid a series of chance circumstances—the

Cold War, the Space Race, the threat of nuclear war—in the offices of a tiny publishing house in Manhattan. Thanks to the intuition of a hard-nosed, highly skilled publisher, Martin Goodman, and his team of imaginative, all-too-human writers and artists, led by Stan Lee, Jack Kirby, and Steve Ditko. A swarm of talent. The masterminds behind the Marvel we know and love today, a compendium of Super Heroes and Super Villains that has become the 21st century's emblem of entertainment worldwide. It all started with Timely Comics back in 1939, when the world was on the verge of the most devastating and tragic of all wars, and in dire need of hope for a brighter future.

The earliest Super Heroes—the Human Torch, the Sub-Mariner, Captain America—made their first appearances at a time when comic book genres like suspense, romance, Westerns, sci-fi, and horror were in full swing. Following a long swathe of ups and downs came a burst of creativity in the 1960s, when Goodman ordered his editor in chief Stan Lee to come up with a team of Super Heroes that could vie for the success already achieved by the Distinguished Competition. It proved to be the spark of life, the mysterious event that brought into existence an entire world out of the proverbial primordial soup.

Marvel is a universe unto itself, one that exists parallel to our own, where real-life events unfold and famous personages play out their roles alongside fictional characters. Here lies its greatness. It is not an assemblage of individual, disconnected stories, but rather a single grand adventure in which all the chapters are connected. One might call it the true Great American Novel that so many authors dream of writing—a feat Marvel managed to pull off in a brilliant display of coherence and imagination through works of collective genius. In the Marvel Universe nothing is static or immutable. Characters are caught up in the flow of time (which is somewhat slower than real time), thus they grow, change, die, betray one another, love, get married, break up. Their actions and slang-studded speech reflect our own, their relationships and interpersonal dynamics are credible to the highest degree, while the whole is enshrined by spectacular, incomparable esthetics.

Such a unique approach is matchless in the history of comics. Actually, as a pop culture phenomenon, Marvel transcends comics, having left its mark in the realms of cinema, television and radio, graphics and design, art and literature. We ourselves have become Spider-Man and the Hulk, Wolverine and Thor, Iron Man and Captain America, while they have become universal icons. That's the magic of Marvel—any other explanation will leave you high and dry. Join us, then, on a journey back in time, as we revel in the wonders of the first 80 years of Marvel.

Fabio Licari

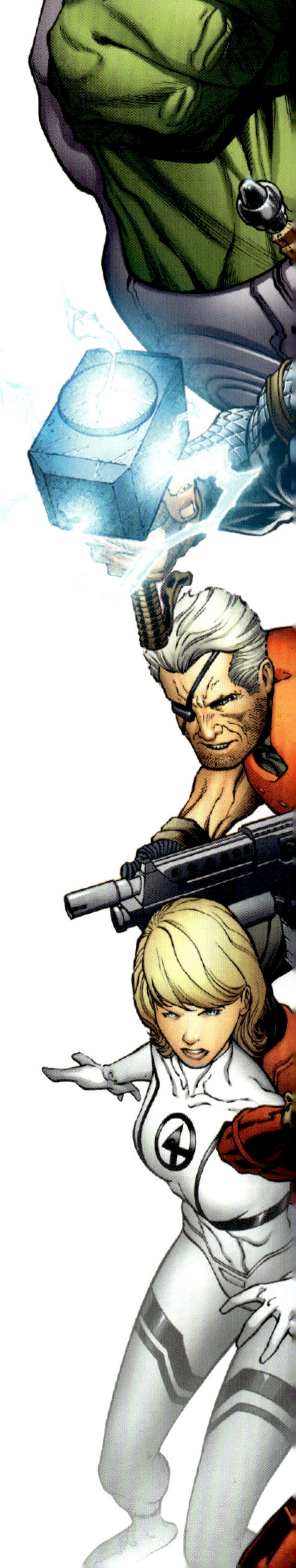

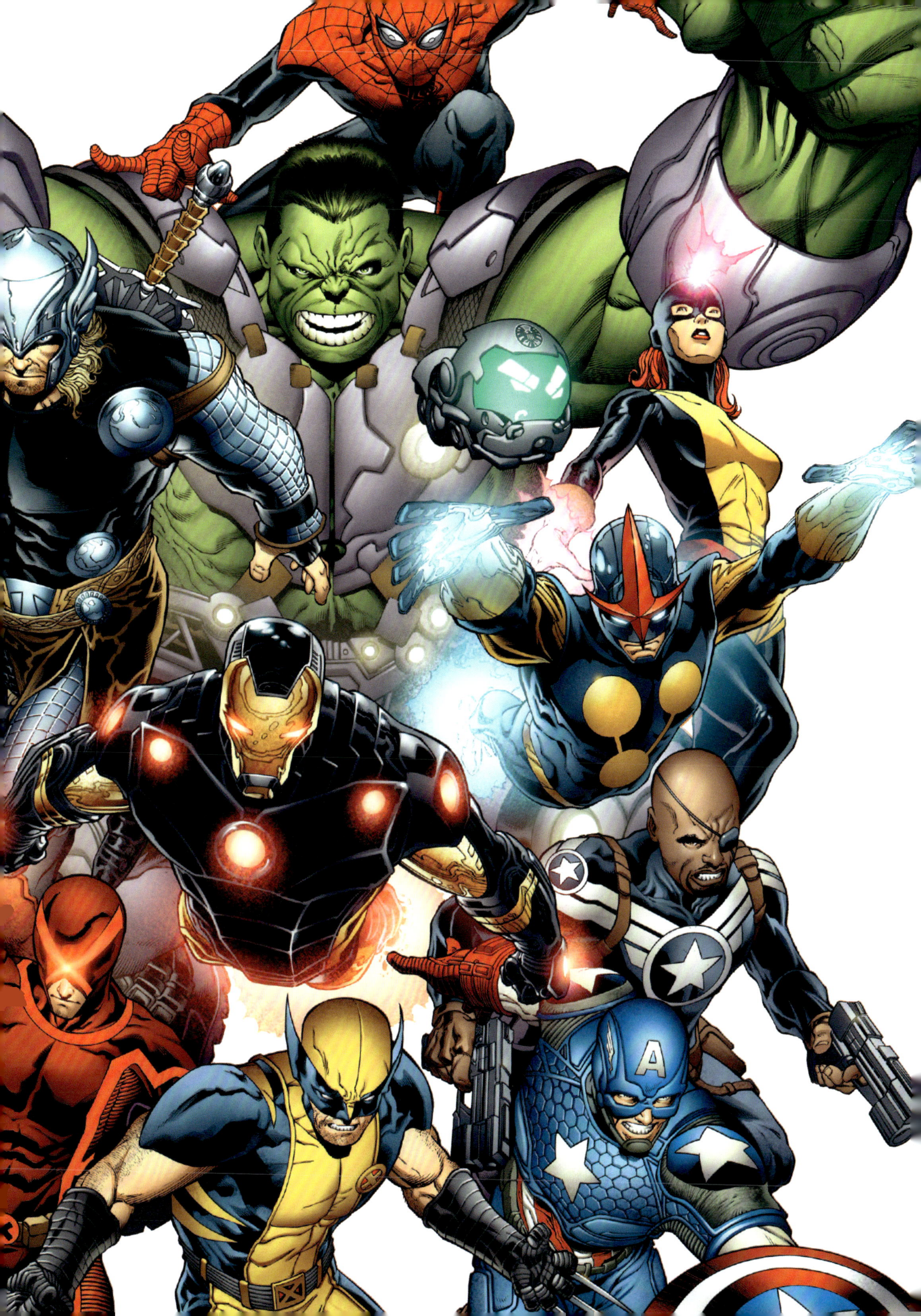

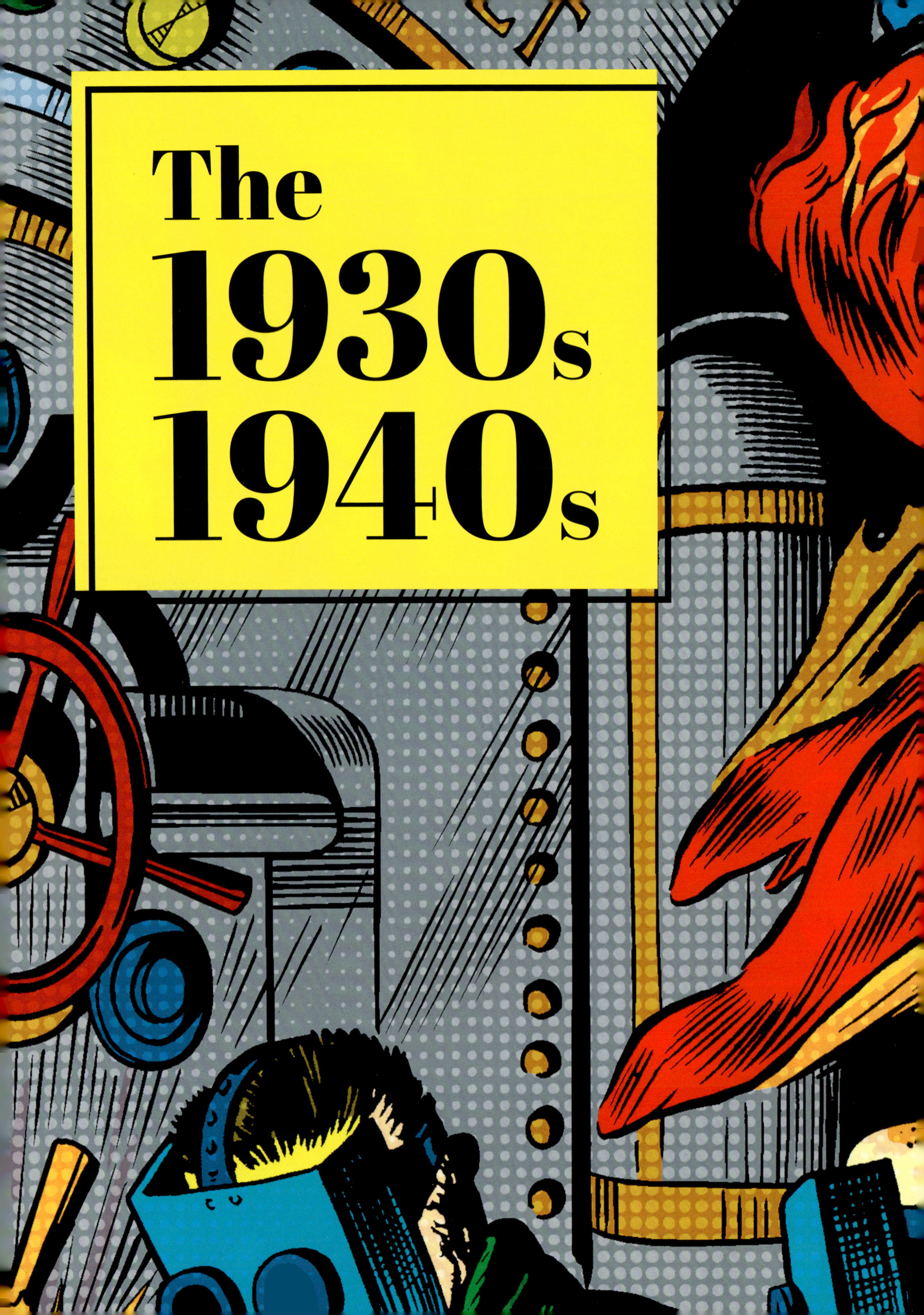
The
1930s
1940s

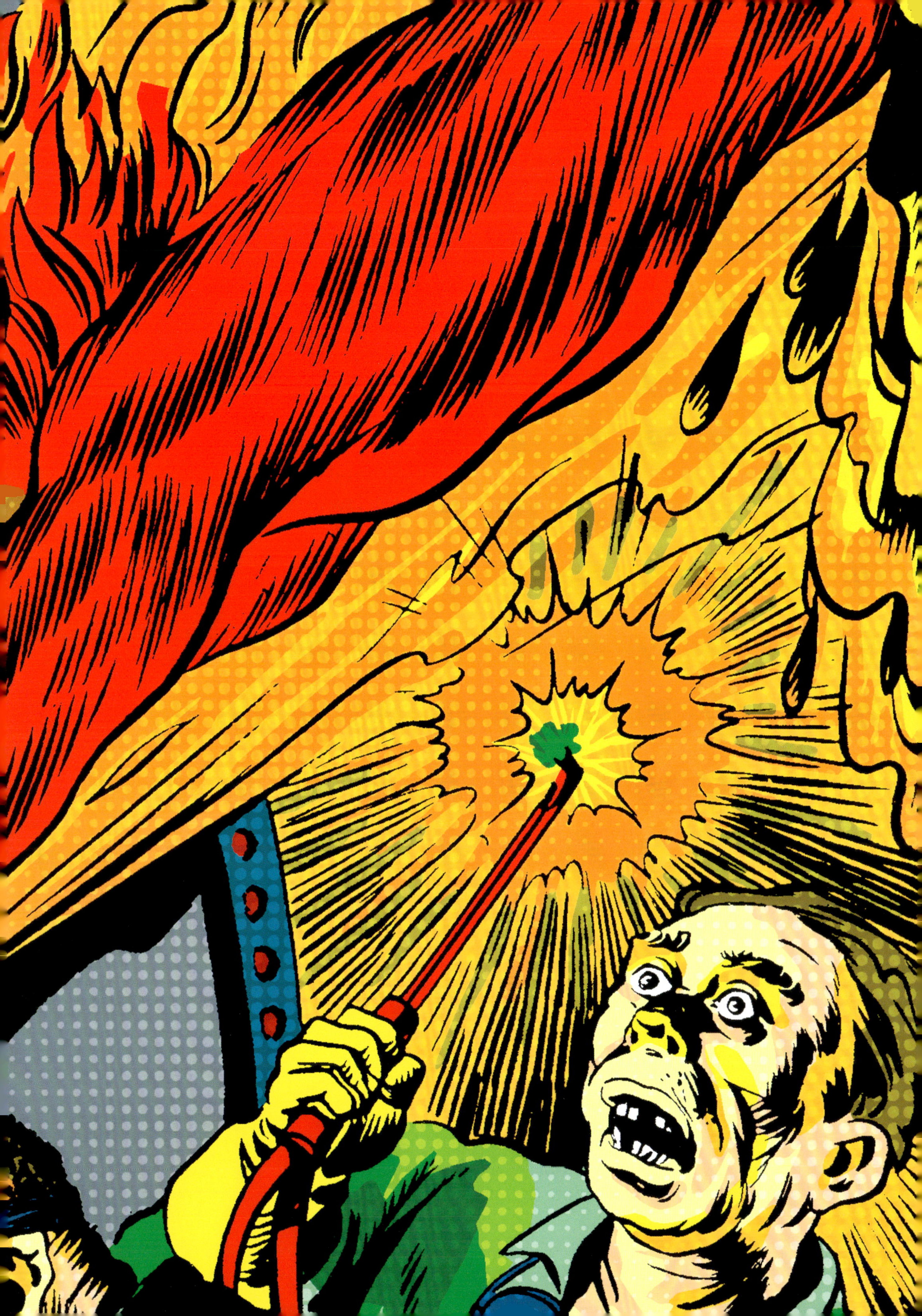

WHEN IT ALL BEGAN

A man, draped in the patriotic colours of the United States of America, delivering a crushing right to the jaw of the Nazi dictator Adolf Hitler. The image was indelible, instantly unforgettable.

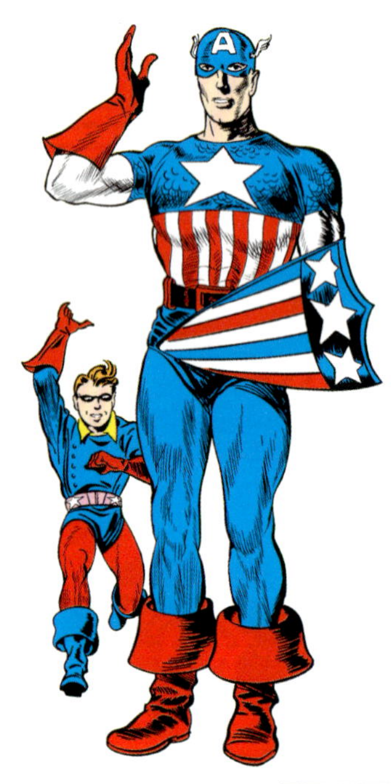

Bucky (left) and Captain America, from the splash page to *Captain America Comics #1* (March 1941). Art by Jack Kirby and Joe Simon.

Nestled in that punishing blow dealt to Hitler was a dream: a free world where America would send the latest Super Villain packing for good, a Doctor Doom (another nasty chap in dictator mode and the Fantastic Four's most dreaded enemy) who unfortunately was no pen-and-ink creation, but an enemy in the flesh. *Der Führer* would be made sport of, yes, to the applause of some readers, while others were moved to tears. The slipstream effect of that blow, the movement, even the 'sound' that resonated made it so palpable that it transcended what was simply the cover of a comic book, *Captain America Comics #1*. But what a cover it was!

The year was 1940, and Captain America, the new red-white-and-blue Super Hero, burst onto the scene, waylaying the world's archenemy. But such bravado alone wouldn't have been enough to win the hearts of a million readers without the eerily compelling stories that revealed the talent of a pair of iconic artists like Joe Simon and Jack Kirby, who in the process made comic-book history. It was a combination of emotion, emphasis, action and narrative flair that encapsulated what was to come, in the form of Marvel Comics, then known as Timely Comics.

Captain America Comics #1, however, was not Timely's first comic book. It all started with *Marvel Comics #1*, which debuted on 31 August 1939.

Captain America Comics #1 (March 1941). Cover by Jack Kirby and Joe Simon.

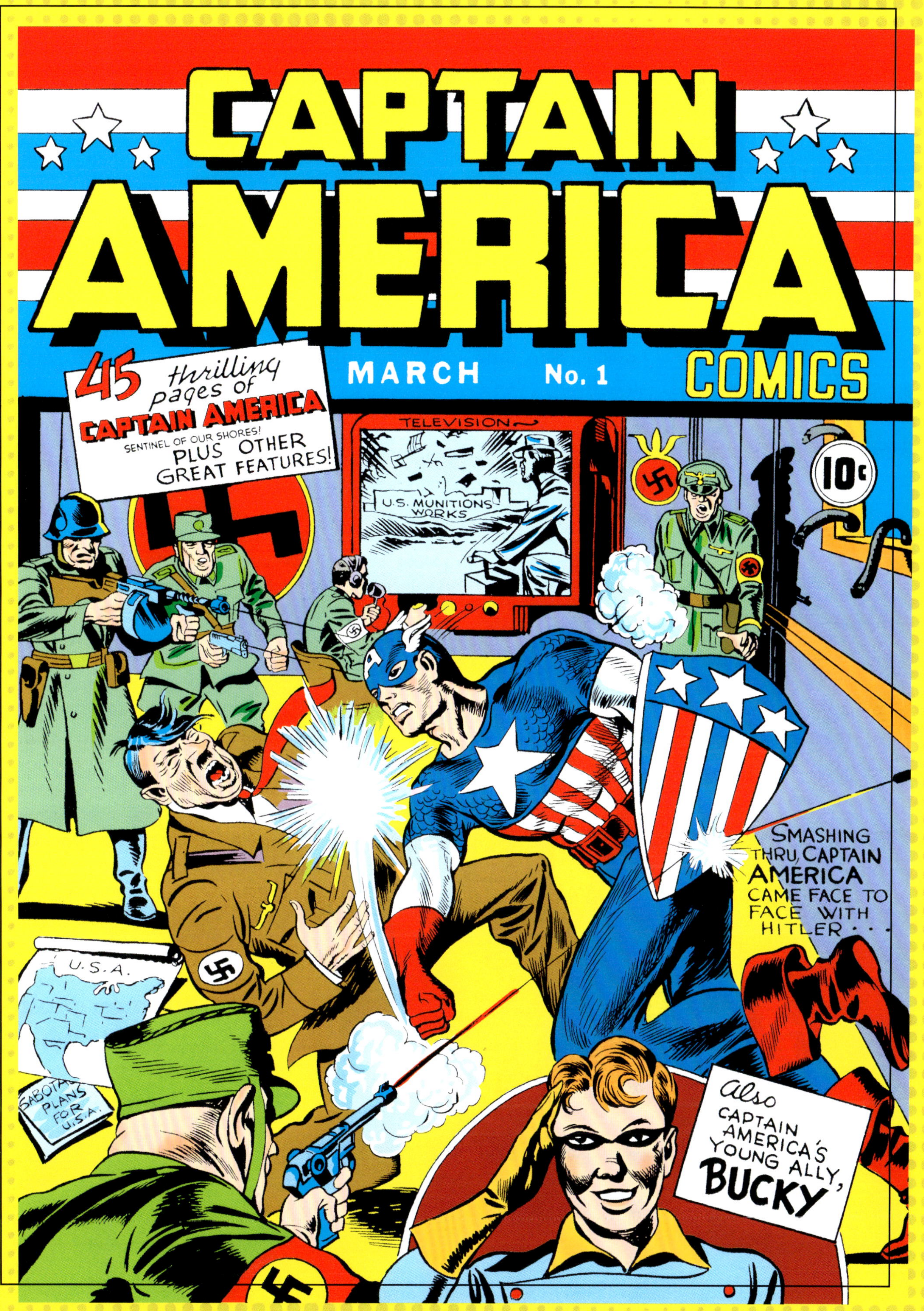
CAPTAIN AMERICA
COMICS
45 thrilling pages of CAPTAIN AMERICA
SENTINEL OF OUR SHORES!
PLUS OTHER GREAT FEATURES!
MARCH
No. 1
10¢
TELEVISION
U.S. MUNITIONS WORKS
SMASHING THRU, CAPTAIN AMERICA CAME FACE TO FACE WITH HITLER . . .
U.S.A.
SABOTAGE PLANS FOR U.S.A.
Also CAPTAIN AMERICA'S YOUNG ALLY, BUCKY

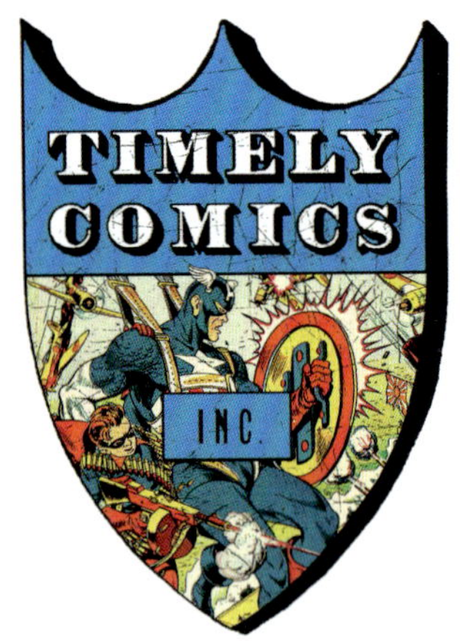

A shield emblem bearing the Timely Comics logo, early 1940s.

America had just shrugged off the Great Depression, which first reared its ugly head in 1929 and left millions of people grappling with poverty. The attack on Pearl Harbor in 1941 propelled America into World War II.

But even at the time, a 10-cent comic book was accessible to nearly everyone: kids and their families with little money to be spared on 'extravagances' like movies, soldiers heading off to this or that front. And comic books were something new. Until then, there were only the syndicated comic strips that appeared in newspapers by renowned artists like Alex Raymond and Hal Foster, who indeed considered their work an art form.

But in 1934 Max 'Charlie' Gaines came up with the brilliant idea of publishing those strips in a new format, the size of a newspaper folded twice over—and thus the birth of comic book that we know and love to this day, give or take a few millimetres. Reprinted comic strips would soon give way to all-new original stories and characters.

One of the most active publishers at that time was Martin Goodman, a tireless workhorse in his own right with a masterful editorial instinct. Goodman could sense what markets were longing for, and doggedly sought to hone in on the latest trends. His endeavours were not limited to comics—Timely Publications, the publishing house he launched in 1939, was also involved in pulp fiction that featured Westerns, sci-fi, horror, mysteries, romance, and detective and adventure stories.

Sales boomed. But it would have been hard for him to imagine that one day Timely would spawn what turned out to be the world's premier publisher of comic books, Marvel Comics. So that's how it all started, in those wonder-filled years that would come to be known as the Golden Age of Comic Books.

BELOW
Marvel Science Stories vol. 1 #1 (August 1938), the first Timely publication to bear the name 'Marvel'.

RIGHT
Marvel Tales vol. 1 #6 (December 1939).

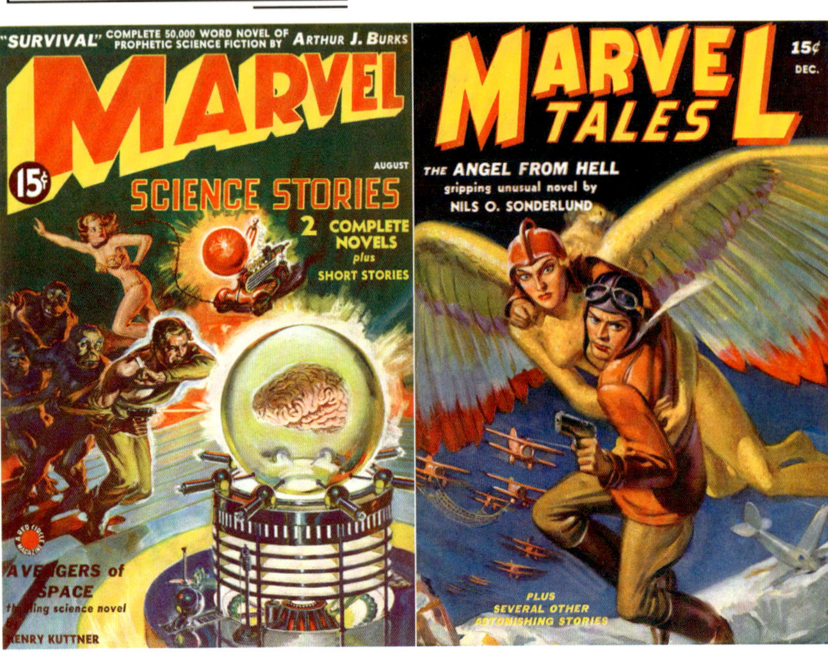

Goodman could sense what markets were longing for...

Marvel Comics #1 (October 1939). Art by Frank Paul.

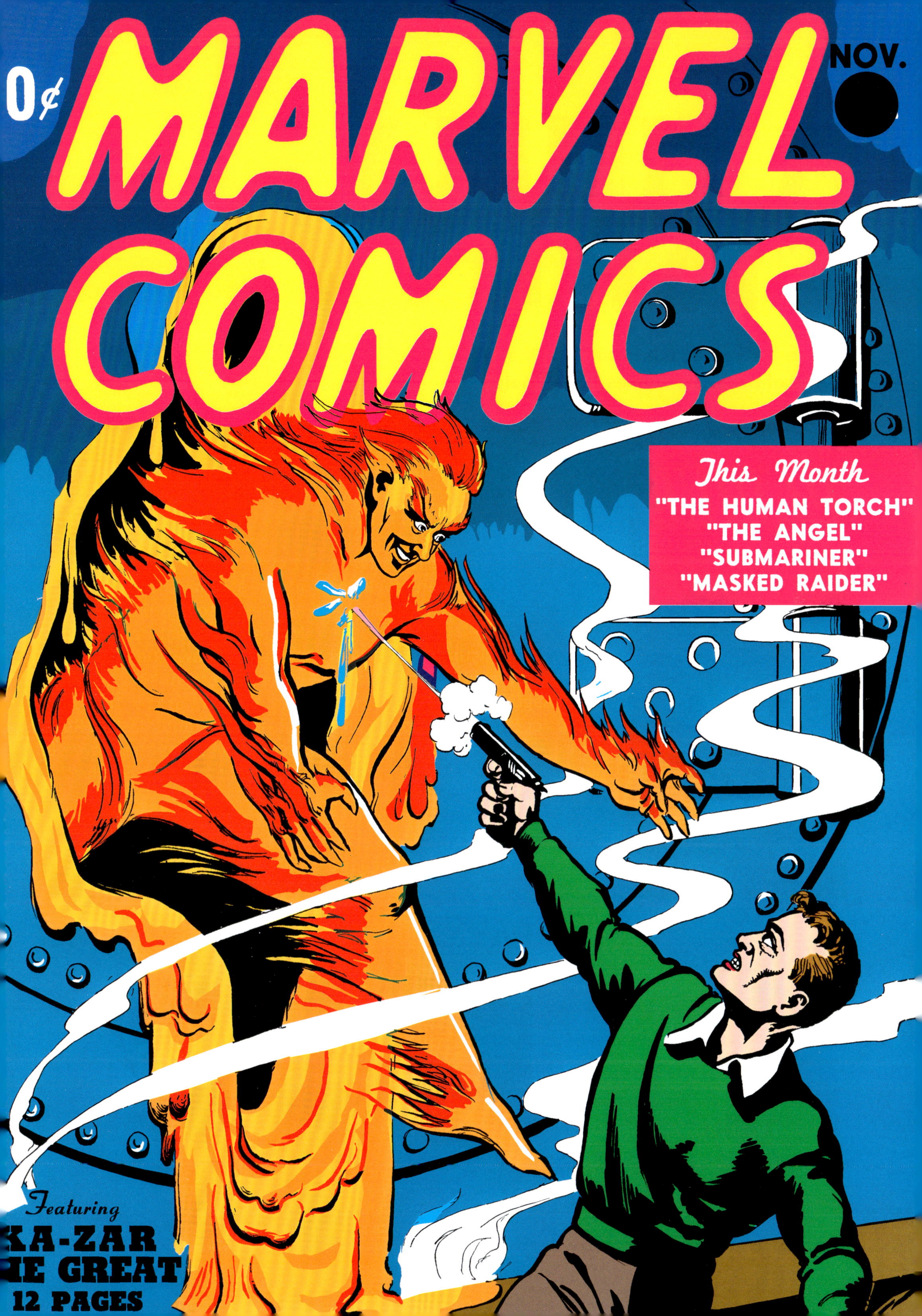
0¢
MARVEL COMICS
NOV.
This Month
"THE HUMAN TORCH"
"THE ANGEL"
"SUBMARINER"
"MASKED RAIDER"
Featuring
KA-ZAR
HE GREAT
12 PAGES

A TIMELY START

Before the world could marvel at Marvel, they would be in awe of the Super Heroes from Timely.

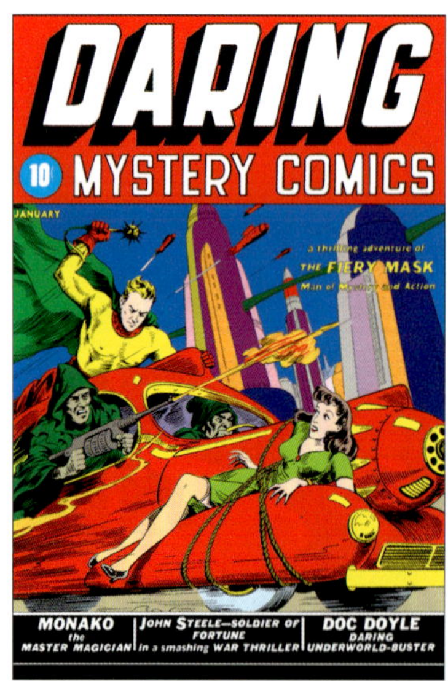

Daring Mystery Comics #1 (January 1940). Art by Alex Schomburg.

Timely's first comic-book release featuring Super Heroes was *Marvel Comics #1*. In the upper right corner of the cover—sporting extraordinarily powerful artwork by Frank R. Paul—there appeared the month of publication, "Oct."

However, historians consider the official publication date to be 31 August 1939, inasmuch as comic book publication dates were always (and still are) postdated, for reasons linked to distribution.

By postdating their releases, comic books had a longer shelf life at newsstands. As for the artwork, the scenic impact is riveting. It shows a flaming android bursting through a steel wall and attacking a man who in vain fires a pistol at his assailant. The red banner at the bottom promises "Action Mystery Adventure". The top screamer shows the names of the issue's protagonists in quotes: the Human Torch, the Angel, Sub-Mariner and Masked Raider; the screamer in the lower left corner presents Ka-Zar the Great in bold.

The issue was reprinted the following month and sold some

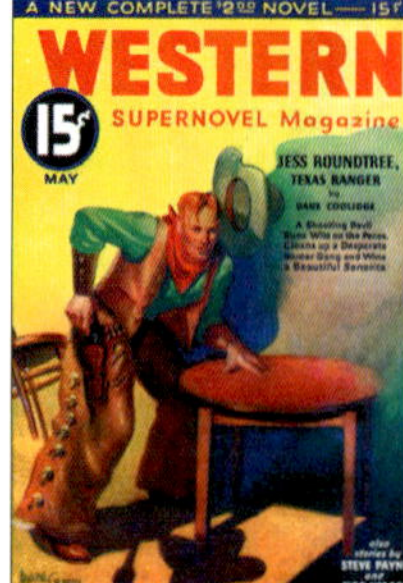

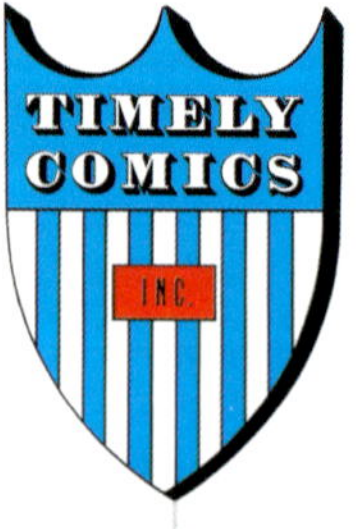

1930

MAY 1933
It all begins with *Western Supernovel Magazine*, the first pulp magazine published by Martin Goodman, future head of Timely Comics, which would go on to become Marvel Comics.

JANUARY 1939
Timely Comics is officially founded on 12 January 1939. Its logo: a blue-and-white shield. Offices were initially located in Manhattan's McGraw-Hill Building.

900,000 copies all told. A huge hit. Timely Publications, with offices at 330 West 42nd Street in Manhattan, had opened its doors in 1933 with the release of the pulp collection *Complete Western Book Magazine*. *Marvel Comics #1* was Goodman's very first comic-book release. Beginning with issue #2, which hit newsstands two months later, *Marvel Comics* became *Marvel Mystery Comics*, which continued until 1949, amassing a total of 92 issues before morphing into *Marvel Tales*, which kept up the pace throughout most of the 1950s.

It was clear to Goodman that comic books were potentially big business, and he wasted no time in setting up his own staff of writers and illustrators, headed by Joe Simon and Jack Kirby, two emerging artists who worked in tandem. Simon became Timely's editor in chief, and together with Kirby created the Captain America character for the imprint that bore his name, *Captain America Comics*. The first issue, dated March 1941, hit newsstands on 20 December 1940, and sold for 10 cents. It sold a million copies, Goodman's biggest seller to date. Legend has it that the publisher quaked at the thought of Hitler's untimely death as the issue went into print. "What if *Der Führer* is killed in the meantime?" he reportedly wondered.

His fear was that the artwork for the cover might be obsolete before readers could get their hands on it. That first issue contained half a dozen stories: four starring Captain America, one featuring Hurricane, and the last turning the spotlight on Tuk the Caveboy.

Meanwhile, by 1940 The Human Torch had gotten his own comic book, dubbed *Human Torch Comics*, which began with issue #2, since it followed in the wake of the short-lived *Red Raven Comics*, yet another Timely publication. In the years 1940–42, Goodman's young publishing house had flooded the market with a host of new titles, including *All Select Comics*, *Daring Mystery Comics*, *Mystic Comics*, *Sub-Mariner Comics*, *Young Allies Comics*, and *All Winners Comics*.

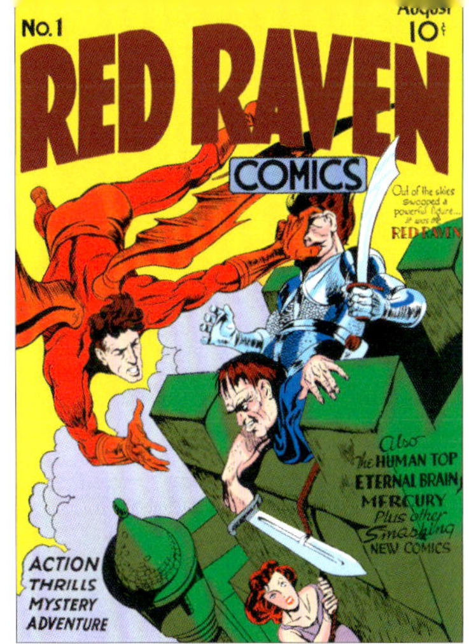

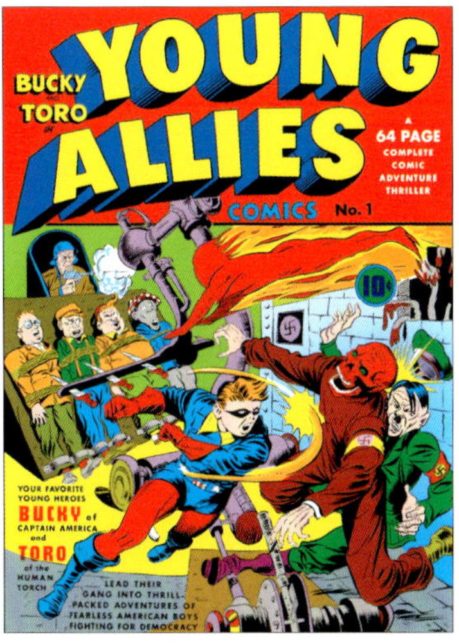

TOP
Red Raven Comics #1 (August 1940). Art by Jack Kirby and Joe Simon.

BOTTOM
Young Allies Comics #1 (Summer 1941). Art by Jack Kirby.

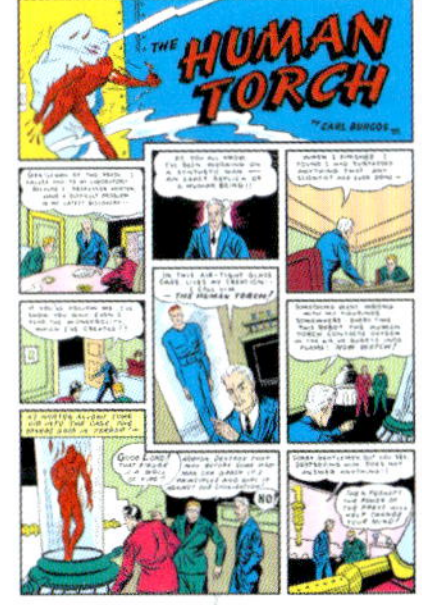

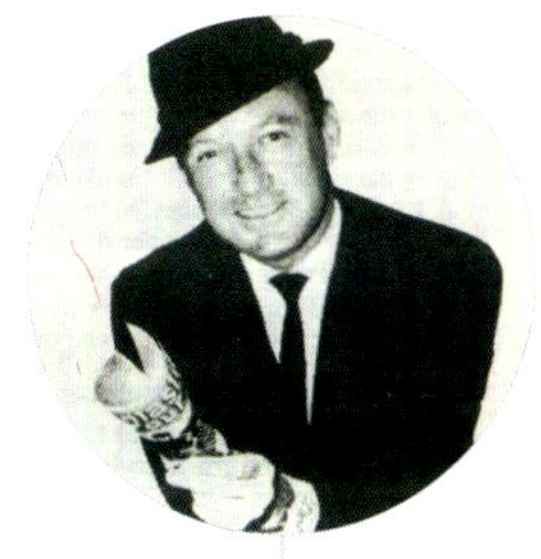

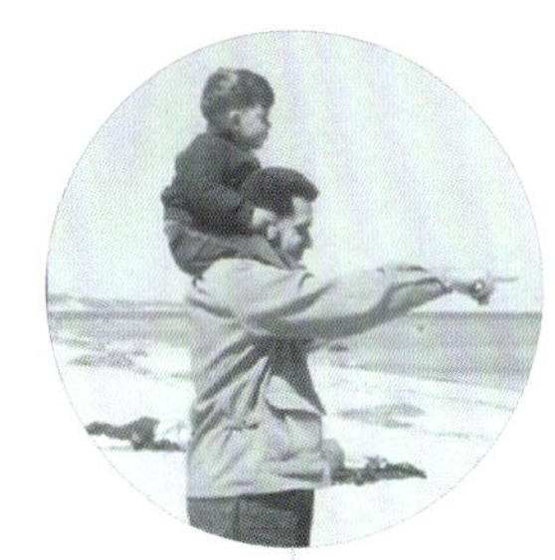

AUGUST 1939
Timely's first comic book featuring Super Heroes, *Marvel Comics #1*, hits the newsstands. It stars Carl Burgos's Human Torch, Bill Everett's Sub-Mariner, and Ka-Zar.

1939
Seventeen-year-old Stanley Lieber, better known as Stan Lee, is hired by Goodman as an assistant to Simon and Kirby. His first published story appeared in *Captain America Comics #3* in 1941.

1940
Jack Kirby joins the staff of Timely Comics invited by Joe Simon, previously hired by Goodman. The team of Simon and Kirby became legendary in the annals of comic-book storytelling.

SUPER HEROES AMONG US

They were dark, desperate times, and the call for heroes had never been stronger. Timely was ready to answer that call.

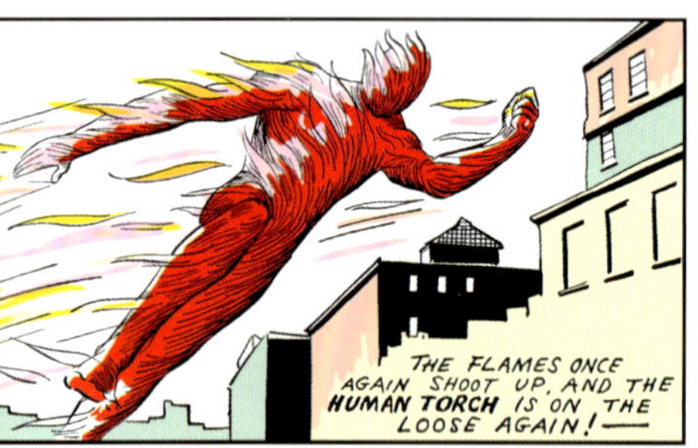

The Human Torch (October 1939). Script, pencils, and inks by Carl Burgos.

The key to Marvel's greatness has always been the humanity of its protagonists. There are no invincible, perfect, immaculate heroes among its ranks. Instead, they tend to be human beings much like us, possessed of commonplace weaknesses and fragility. They reveal contradiction after contradiction, focusing on characters who may lose even when they win, and often wind up being defeated by life. From the very beginning the seeds of restlessness, incompatibility with the world, diversity and solitude had already been sown, especially when it came to the three big names from Timely's Golden Age: Captain America, the Sub-Mariner, and the Human Torch.

Indeed, they have remained household names even today. Captain America is a living legend straight out of World War II, who after a period of hibernation, sprung back into action in the 21st century. Namor the Sub-Mariner, a

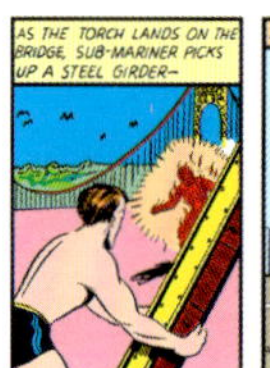

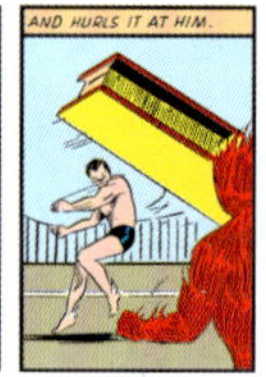

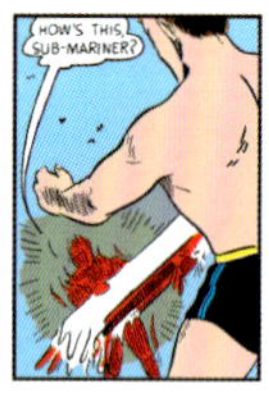

JUNE 1940
Timely's first crossover appears in *Marvel Mystery Comics #8* featuring a clash between the Sub-Mariner and the Human Torch. The battle rages on in #9 and #10.

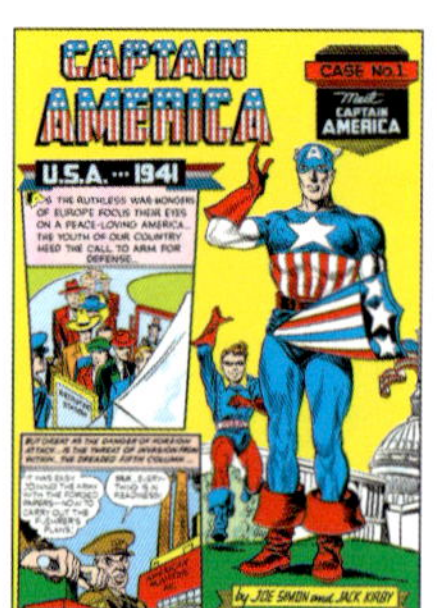

DECEMBER 1940
Captain America, created by Simon and Kirby, makes his debut in *Captain America Comics #1*. The Super-Soldier sends Hitler reeling and declares war against the Nazis.

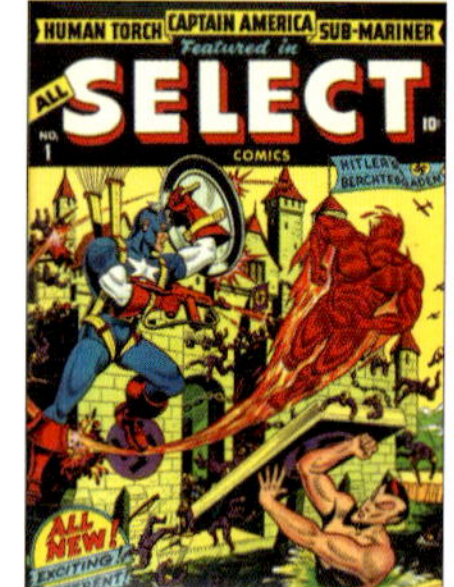

AUTUMN 1943
The release of *All-Select Comics*, a comic book featuring the adventures of Timely's top three Super Heroes: Captain America, the Human Torch and the Sub-Mariner.

deep-sea prodigy, tends to be scornful and resentful in his dealings with humans; his hybrid nature allows him to age at a snail's pace. Lee and Kirby revamped him in stories that date to the 1960s. In the 1940s the Human Torch was depicted as a heroic android (i.e., an automaton with human features) created in a laboratory. In the 1960s, a hero with the same name joined the Fantastic Four, while the original would later be reworked.

The original Human Torch, created by Carl Burgos, was a creature born in scientist Phineas Horton's laboratory. Misunderstood, he would initially terrorise the denizens of New York, where he had been created, because he was not yet able to control his fiery flare-ups. But soon he convinced people he was on their side in the fight against evil. He enrolled in the police academy and was often helped by his sidekick, Toro.

Namor the Sub-Mariner, a character conceived by artist Bill Everett, was half human with Atlantean blood coursing through his veins. His mother, Princess Fen, daughter of the Emperor of Atlantis, fell in love with Leonard McKenzie,

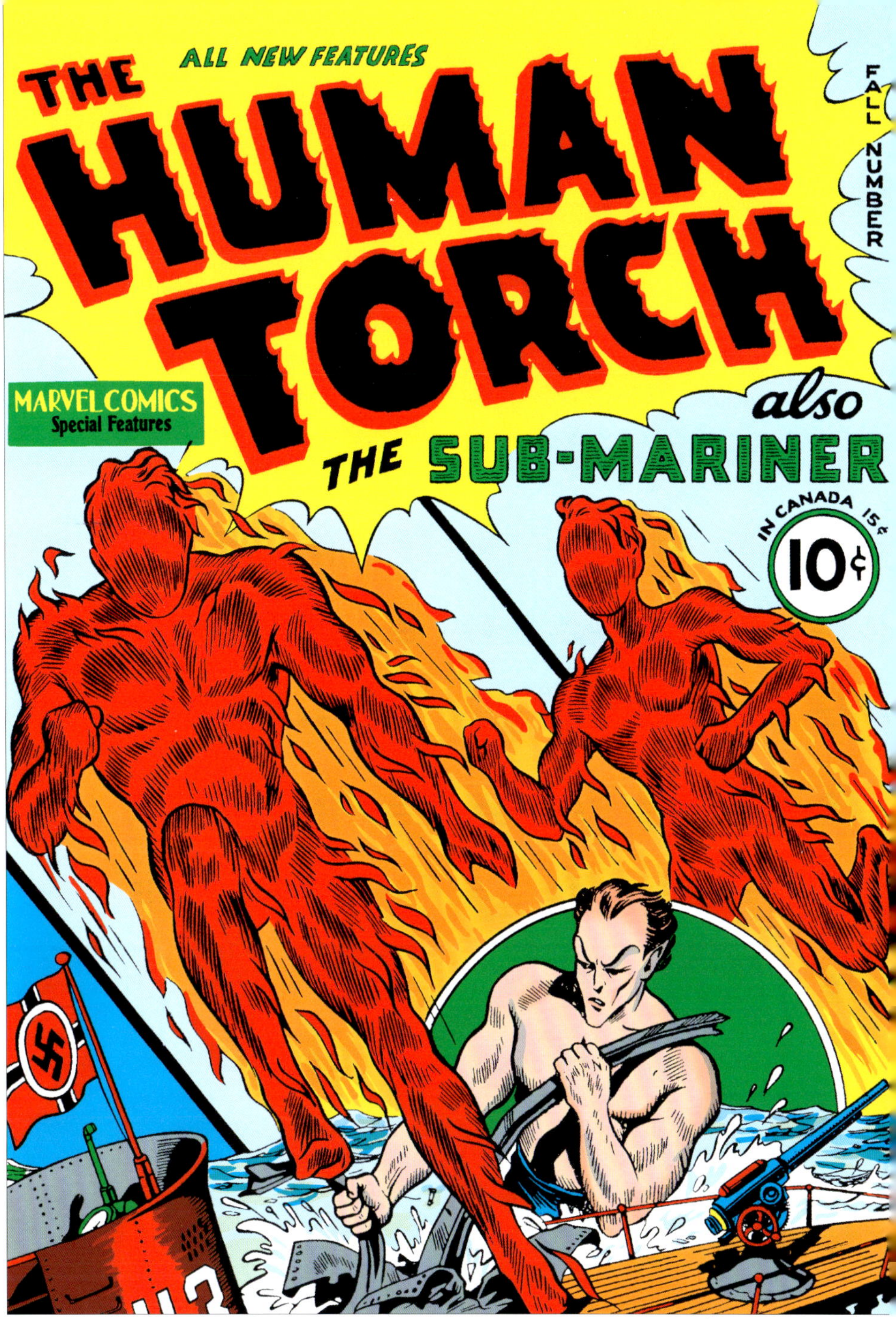

The Human Torch Comics #2 (October 1940). Art by Alex Schomburg.

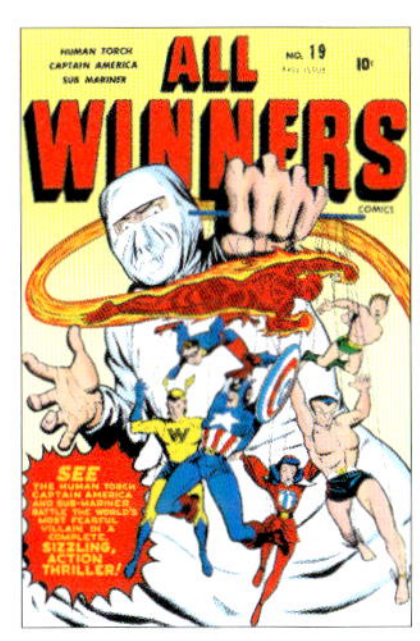

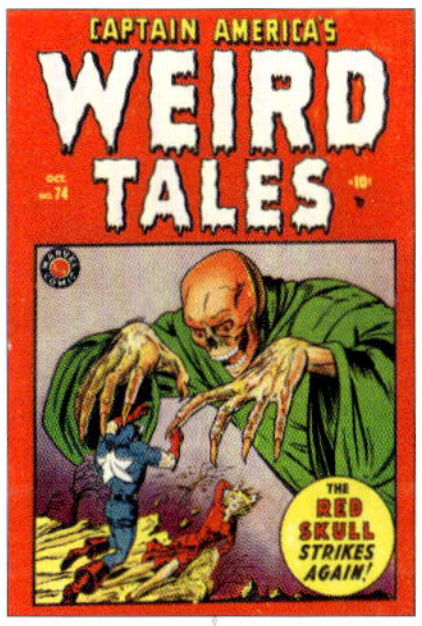

1950

AUTUMN 1946

All-Winners Comics #19 contains the first story featuring the All-Winners Squad, a team with Captain America, Bucky, the Human Torch, Toro, the Sub-Mariner, Whizzer, and Miss America.

OCTOBER 1949

For Timely, the end of the Golden Age of Comic Books is generally thought to coincide with the release of *Captain America #74*. After, the comic had been retitled *Captain America's Weird Tales*.

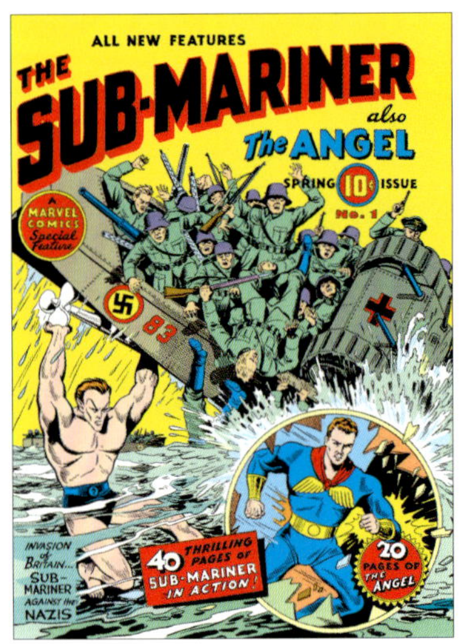

The Sub-Mariner Comics #1 (April 1941). Art by Alex Schomburg.

a surface dweller. Theirs was a strained romance which came to an end with Fen's forced return to Atlantis, along with her son, Namor. As Prince of Atlantis, Namor would have many an occasion to unleash his ire against the surface dwellers. He came off as haughty and presumptuous but, like the Human Torch and Toro, joined the fight against the Nazi war machine, together with Captain America and his sidekick, Bucky. Later on, Namor would often find himself straddling that thin, barely perceptible line that separates the good guys from the villains.

Then there's Captain America—the young and unassuming Steve Rogers, an illustrator deemed physically unfit to serve in the army. His dogged spirit and sense of patriotism were unmatched. Steve signed on to take part in an experiment whose outcome had the potential to turn the tide of the war. It involved receiving massive doses of the Super-Soldier Serum that had been perfected by Dr. Erskine (called Dr. Reinstein in the early stories). The experiment was a success—Steve was transformed into a superhuman, although shortly thereafter Erskine was murdered by a Nazi spy and took his secret formula with him to the grave. Captain America was born and, with his young sidekick Bucky, took on the Axis powers in Simon and Kirby's never-ending saga.

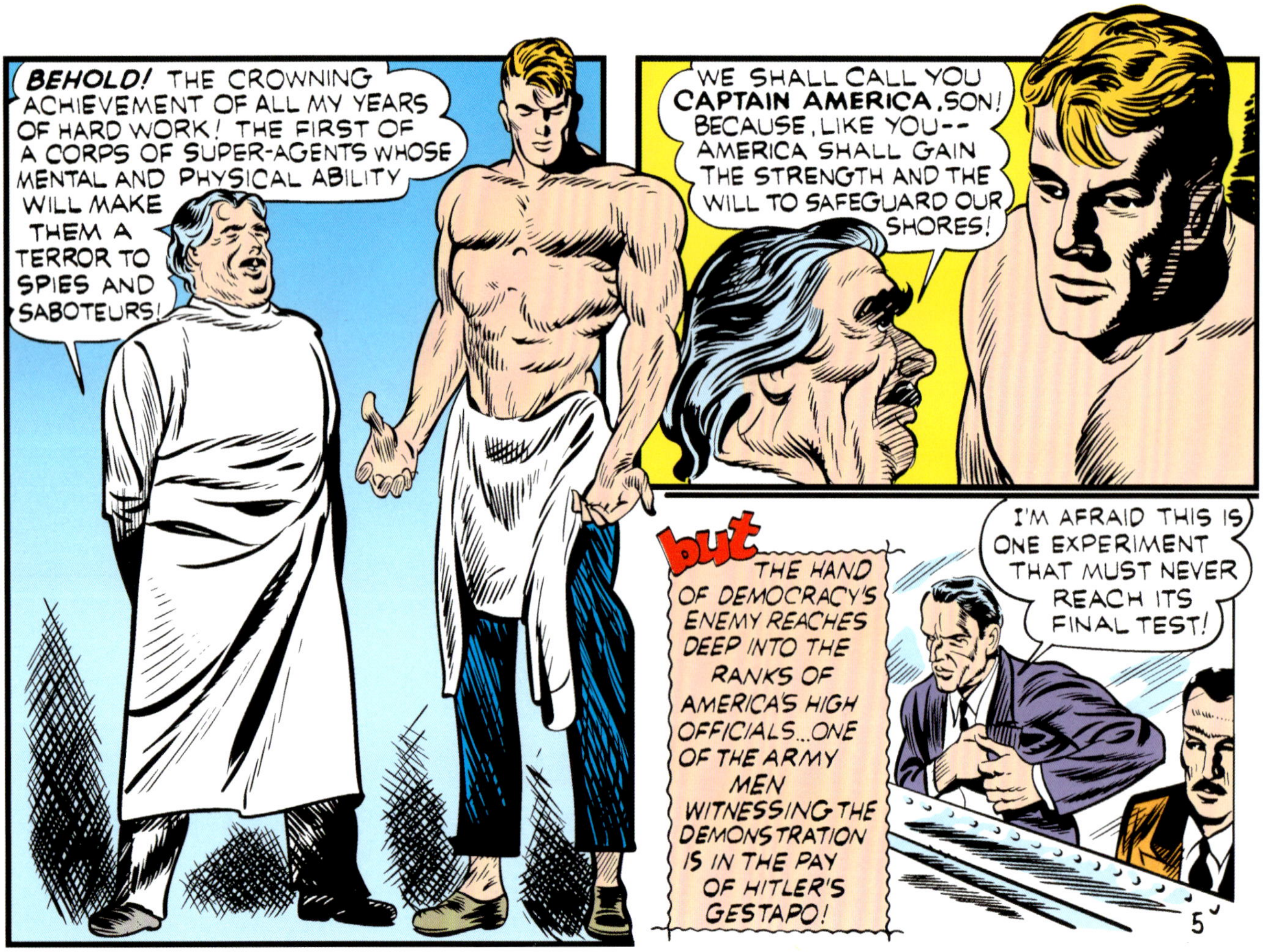

THE MEN BEHIND THE MAGIC

It took a team of brazen young men with brash ideas and bold pencils to bring the new Timely Super Heroes to life.

The history of a publishing house and its characters is inevitably the history of the creative minds behind the scenes, especially in an age when being a comic-book artist was neither a stepping stone toward social and cultural respectability, nor a way to get rich. But now that they were stars in the world of comic books, Joe Simon and Jack Kirby weren't doing so bad for themselves. Simon was born in 1913 in Rochester, New York. His passion for drawing was matched by a keen sense of business acumen. He went to work straight out of high school, and was eventually recommended to Lloyd Jacquet, head of Funnies, Inc., which Timely Publications had commissioned to create another flaming Super Hero along the lines of the Human Torch.

Soon Simon would meet up with another young comic-art prodigy, Jack Kirby (born Jacob Kurtzberg, 1917–1994), who, like Simon, was the son of an immigrant tailor. Kirby grew up on Manhattan's Lower East Side, the same working-class neighbourhood where Steve Rogers (A.K.A. Captain America) was from. What a coincidence! Simon took an immediate liking to Kirby—who in all likelihood had grown up in circumstances even more humble than his own—and his artistry. Looking at them, this dynamic duo made an odd match: Joe was a tall, handsome young man with a certain *savoir faire* about him, while Jack was a scrappy little fellow who took no lip from anyone.

Many years later, people still remembered the day when Kirby literally kicked a messenger from the mob out of the publisher's offices when the punk showed up to 'ask' whether Goodman and company might be interested in using suppliers affiliated with the underworld. Almost as if Kirby had been one of the Super Heroes that

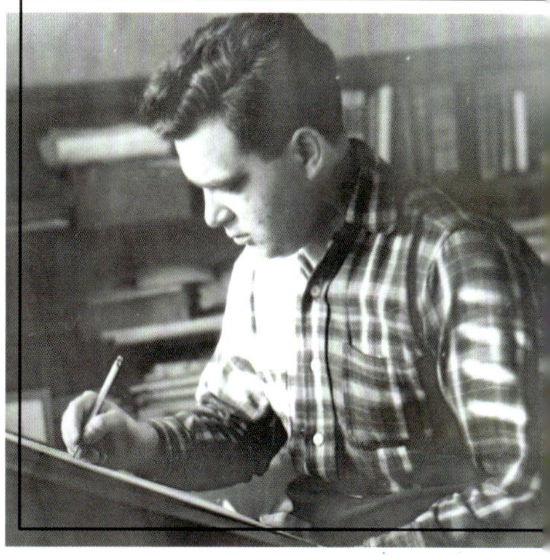

Jack Kirby unleashes his imagination, circa 1949/ early 1950.

OPPOSITE PAGE
The results of the Super-Soldier Serum are revealed. *Captain America Comics #1* (dated March 1941, released 20 December 1940).
Script by Joe Simon and Jack Kirby. Art by Joe Simon and Jack Kirby (pencils), and Al Liederman (inks).

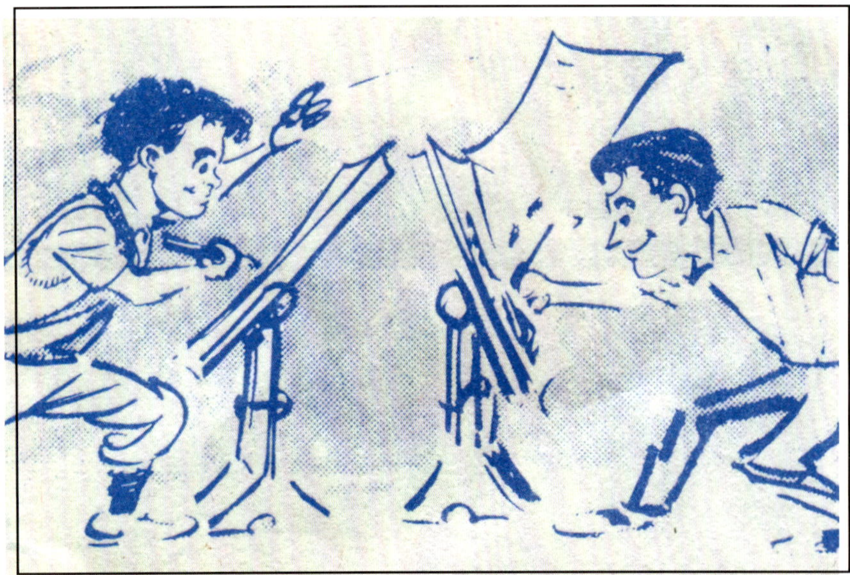

Illustration featuring Jack Kirby (left) and Joe Simon at work in the 1940s, from Marvel's in-house fan magazine *FOOM #8* (1973). *FOOM* stood for Friends of Ol' Marvel.

"I was 11 when the first issue was published. My friends in Brooklyn, all comics traders, were unaware that it was not the usual Super Hero book. My own reactions foreshadowed my future in comics. I showed them how different it was from all the others they had seen, and noticed the figures leaping out of the panels making every page so exciting. It was clear to me this 'Simon and Kirby' were not doing the ordinary comics we'd known."

—John Romita, Sr.

he himself had created. Captain America was their biggest hit at Timely, where Simon had become editor in chief (the very first at Goodman's storied publishing house) and Kirby worked as art director. Before moving on, the two had been responsible for Captain America's first 10 issues, and continued working together for a decade and a half. It was hard to tell where one's work finished and the other's began. Kirby would later return to the Marvel Comics fold for a stint in the 1960s and again in the 1970s.

It so happened that in those days another young hopeful began working for Timely, a distant relative of Goodman's by the name of Stanley Martin Lieber (1922–2018). He too was the son of European immigrants, and dreamed of becoming an acclaimed novelist. He worked under the pen name of Stan Lee, figuring he'd save his real name for the novel that, alas, never got written (though at the time he hardly realised that the Marvel odyssey itself would become akin to a Great American novel). Once Simon and Kirby set out on their own, Goodman made Lieber his editor in chief, even though he was only 19 years old. A move Goodman would never regret.

In those days, more great talent had come to the fore. Besides Simon and Kirby, A-list comic-book artists included the likes of Carl Burgos and Bill Everett. Both worked for Funnies, Inc. Burgos (whose real name was Max Finkelstein) had created the first Marvel Super Hero ever to appear on a comic-book cover, the Human Torch, which of course had been a tremendous success right off the bat. Burgos got his start at what had been dubbed Harry 'A' Chesler's studio, where he specialised in drawing backgrounds and inking, but soon evolved into an artist with his own very distinct personality. Everett's art was even more celebrated.

A virtuoso illustrator, Everett also had an eye for humour (among his many collaborations, he worked for *Cracked* magazine), although he would go down in history as one of the greatest Silver Age comic-book artists. In 1964, he co-created Daredevil with Stan Lee. Unfortunately, Everett met an untimely end in 1973.

Interior page from *Marvel Mystery Comics #8* (June 1940). Script by Bill Everett, art by Bill Everett and Carl Burgos.

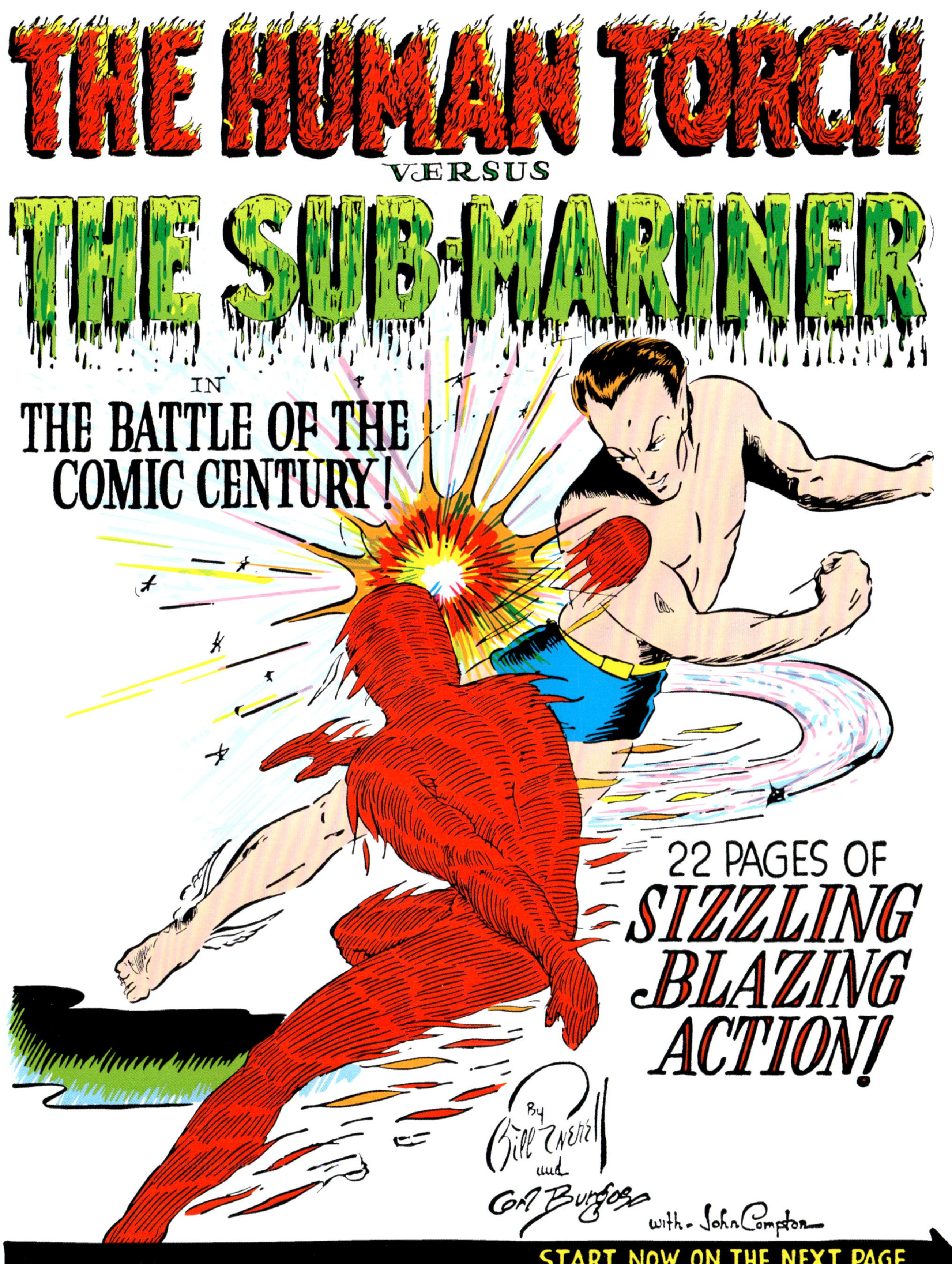
MARVEL COMICS
Presents
THE HUMAN TORCH
VERSUS
THE SUB-MARINER
IN
THE BATTLE OF THE COMIC CENTURY!
22 PAGES OF
SIZZLING
BLAZING
ACTION!
By
with- John Compton
START NOW ON THE NEXT PAGE

OUTSIDE INFLUENCES

The characters and stories of Timely Comics were swayed by the sentiments of the era—and almost immediately, they affected the world of popular culture. The image was indelible, instantly unforgettable.

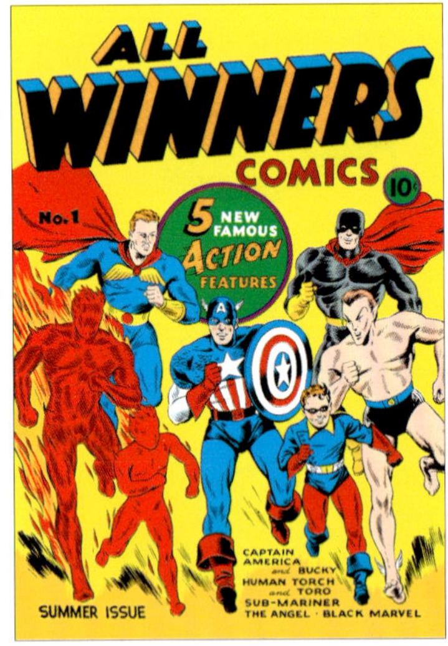

ABOVE
All Winners Comics #1 (dated June 1941, released 10 July 1941). Cover by Alex Schomburg.

RIGHT
Readers who joined Captain America's Sentinels of Liberty club in 1941 could receive this badge, along with a membership card.

Martin Goodman's comic books spoke his readers' language, providing precious minutes of escape from the harshness that plagued their existences and a promise of deliverance. On an emotional level, this was something readers could identify with. That's why the first issue of *Captain America Comics* sold a million copies, and the year before *Marvel Comics #1* had hit the 900,000 mark. In 1941, 30 U.S. publishers cranked out 150 comic books, with some 15 million copies sold to 50–60 million loyal readers—an immense market, the likes of which had never been dreamed of in the burgeoning comic-book sector.

Targeting younger readers, comic books were the heirs of pulp literature—pop culture stories and novels usually on the lower end of the quality spectrum, whose authors were paid by the word, which often attained best-seller status. The 'pulp' moniker took its cue from the cheap paper used to print them, which was made from low-grade pulpwood. The soon-to-yellow pages featured the debuts of characters like the Shadow and Doc Savage, who would go on to become comic-book staples, even if pulp fiction's content was more adult-oriented.

By the 1940s radio and film adaptations had made their way onto the scene, which meant that

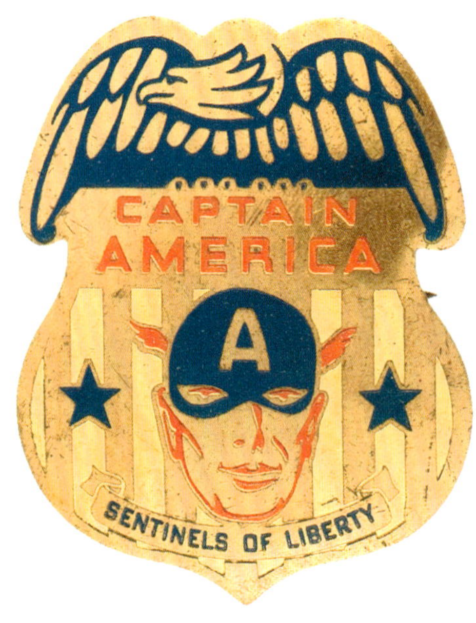

Timely's Super Heroes played their part in pioneering the latest developments in mass entertainment.

once again Timely's Super Heroes played their part in pioneering the latest developments in mass entertainment. In 1944, with the defeat of the Axis powers on the horizon, Republic Pictures created the *Captain America* movie serial. The record-breaking budget for the 15 black-and-white episodes, each of which ran approximately 15 minutes (except for the first, which was 25 minutes long), skyrocketed to over $200,000, a whopping figure for that time.

In reality, the series featured a Captain America different from Timely's Cap, even though his costume (minus the shield) was nearly identical to the one worn by his comics counterpart. Instead of Army Private Steve Rogers, Cap's secret identity was District Attorney Grant Gardner, who had no Super-Soldier Serum–induced super powers and never fought against the Nazis.

By the second half of the 1940s, America was on the eve of its post-war economic boom. The days of Super Heroes bashing enemies like Adolf Hitler had come to an end. Comic-book print runs began to shrink, forcing Timely to come up with new formulas for success. Dangers of a different kind lurked just around the corner, and the comic-book industry was already gearing up to meet the challenges of the next decade.

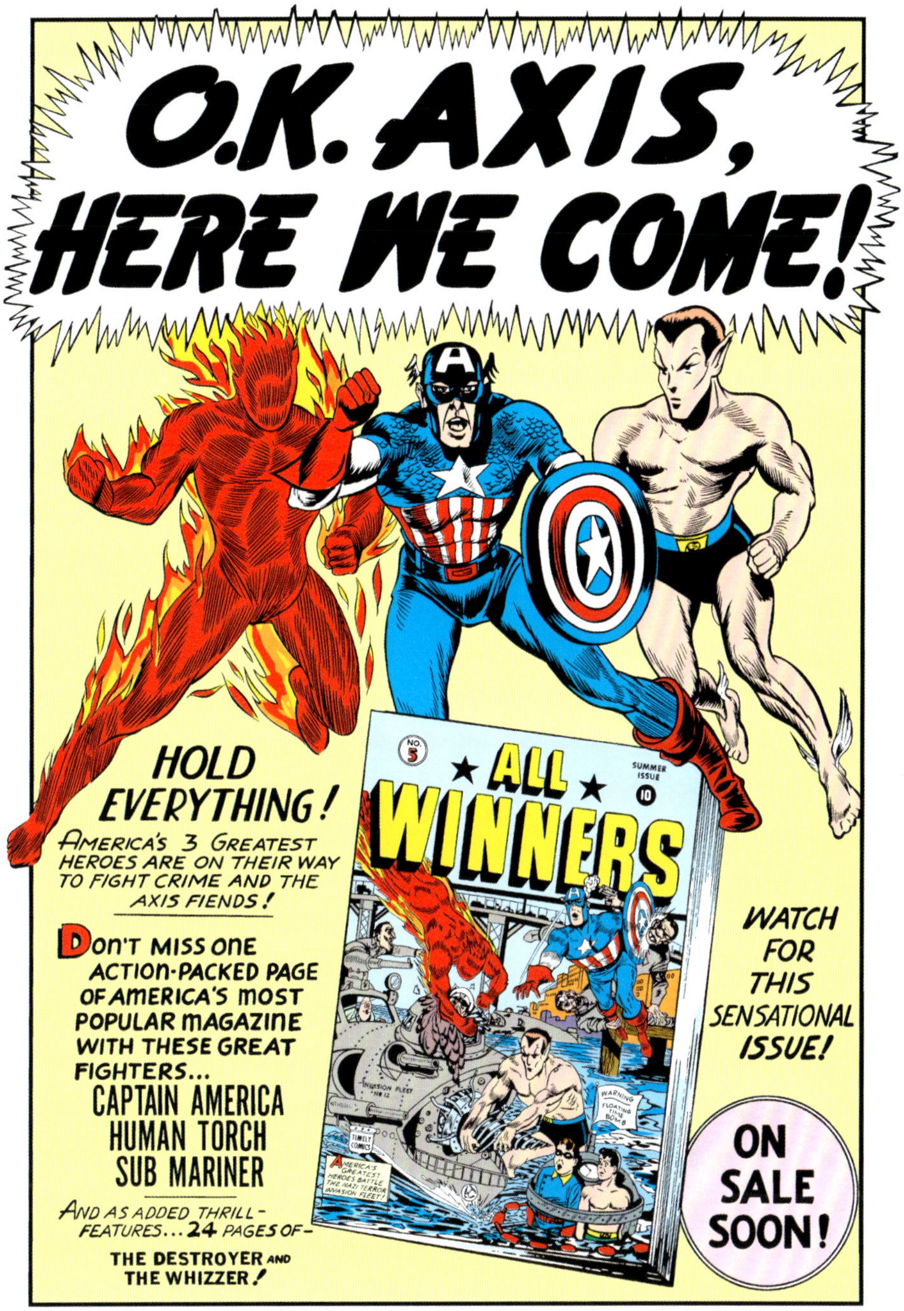

The Human Torch, Captain America, and Sub-Mariner get ready to take on the Axis Powers in a house ad for *All-Winners Comics #5* (featured in *Marvel Mystery Comics #34*, August 1942).

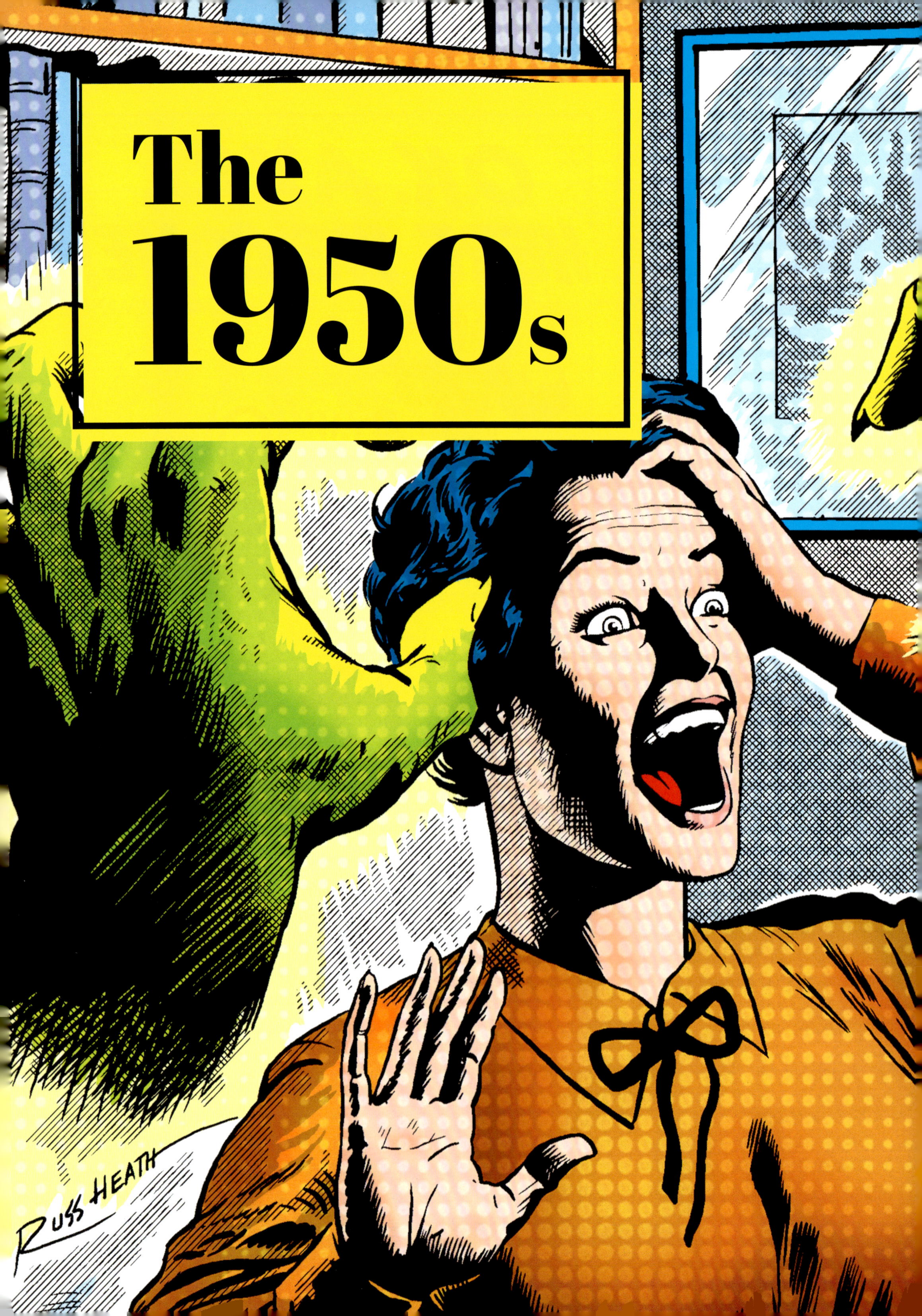
The
1950s
RUSS HEATH

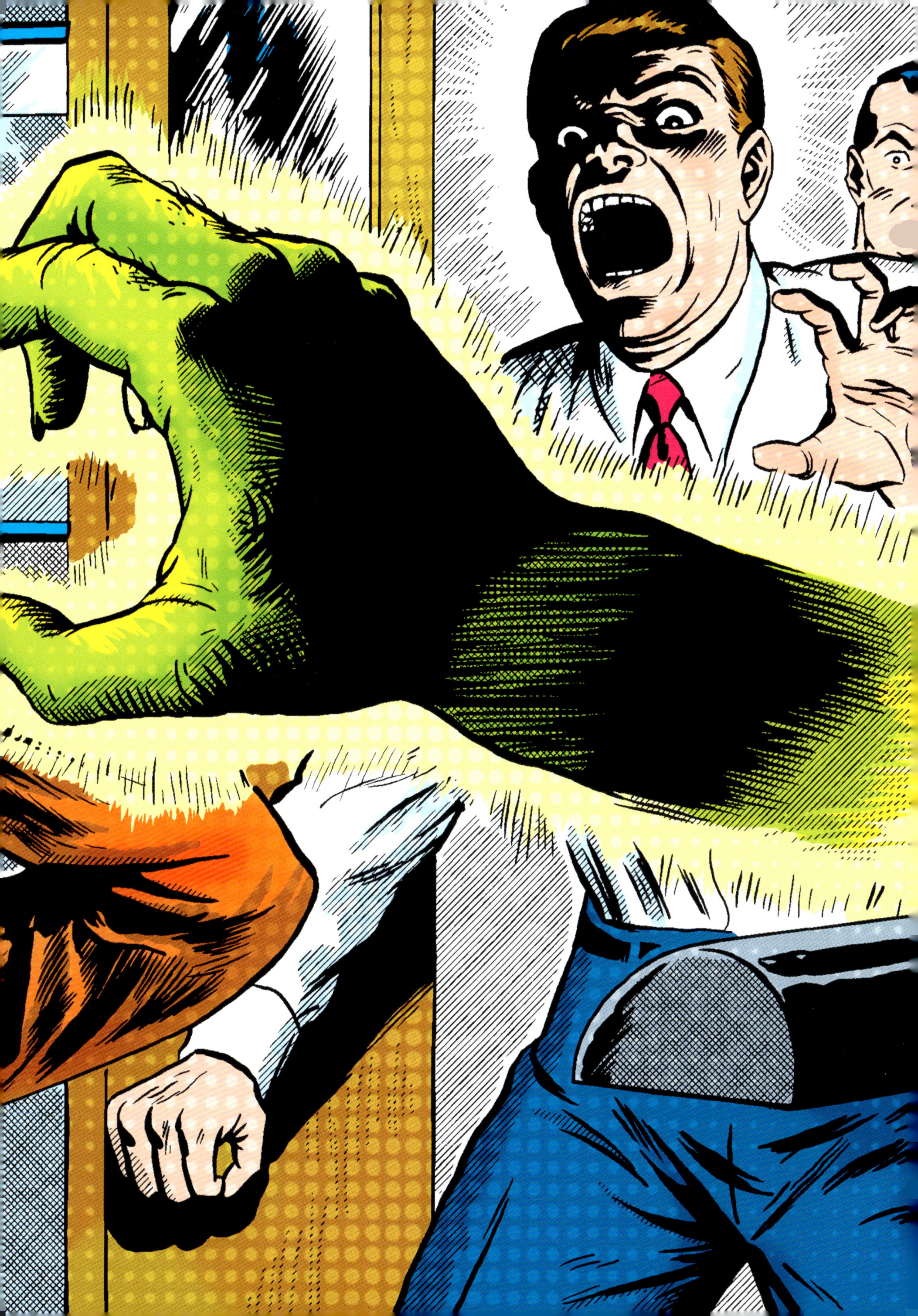

NEW THREATS

By the dawn of the 1950s, new and complex scenarios were coming into play that would be of concern not only to nations, but to the publishers of comic books as well. Among them, Martin Goodman's Timely Publications.

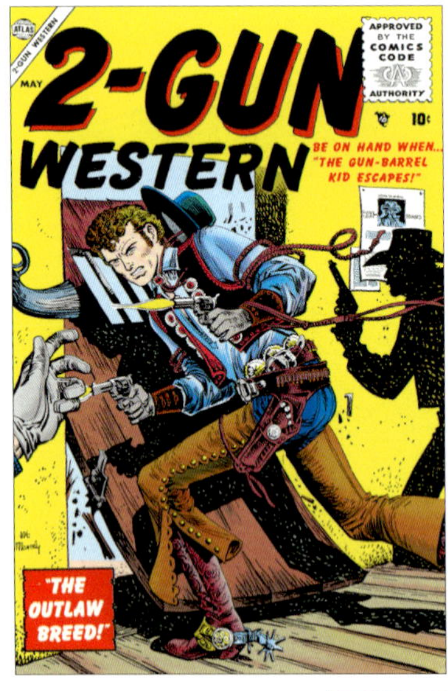

2-Gun Western #4 (May 1956). Art by Joe Maneely (pencils, inks).

Mankind was gripped by fears that unbridled progress in atomic energy would go unchecked, with potentially disastrous consequences, while tensions escalated between the United States and the Soviet Union (already engaged in the Cold War). It was hardly a time when people could rest easy. But as the events unfolded, they provided new angles for the creators of comic-book stories.

Other factors threatened the very existence of comic books, even if they were by no means on a par with the arms race. Enter: Dr. Fredric Wertham, a child psychiatrist and author of a 1954 study on comic books and their presumed negative influence on young readers.

In America, his *Seduction of the Innocent* sparked an ethical and moral crusade that, as we shall see, pretty much held the entire industry hostage, forcing publishers to adopt a code of self-regulation to keep from going under.

Not even Goodman and company could eschew this sudden and violent about-face. Meanwhile, beginning with comic books cover-dated November 1951, the old Timely shield was replaced with a new logo, Atlas. The logo—a white globe crisscrossed by black lines indicating longitude and latitude—belonged to Martin Goodman's own distribution company. The logo appeared on most of the company's comic books during this time, and it came to be known as the Atlas era.

What's more, by this time Super Heroes were on their way out. Readers were now more interested in romance, Westerns, horror, war, crime, and humour. Soon they'd also be turning their attention to adventures featuring aliens and monsters, as an all-new genre was about to embark upon its own Golden Age: science-fiction.

Astonishing #30 (Feb. 1954). Art by Joe Maneely and Stan Goldberg.

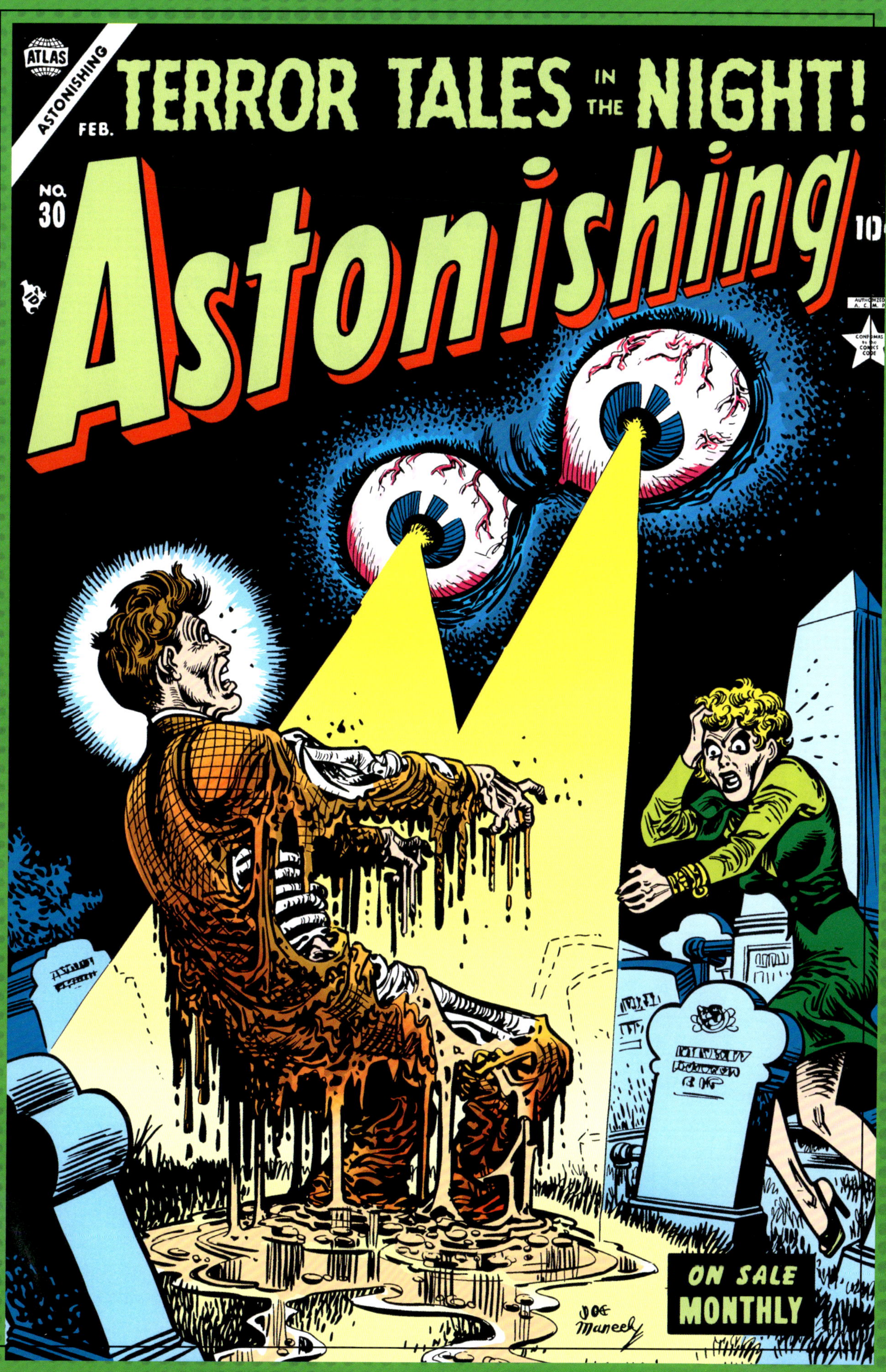
ATLAS
ASTONISHING
FEB.
TERROR TALES IN THE NIGHT!
NO. 30
Astonishing
10¢
ON SALE
MONTHLY
Joe Maneely

MODELS, MONSTERS, AND BLACK KNIGHTS

As the popularity of Super Heroes waned in the 1950s, other genres came to the forefront—with a vengeance.

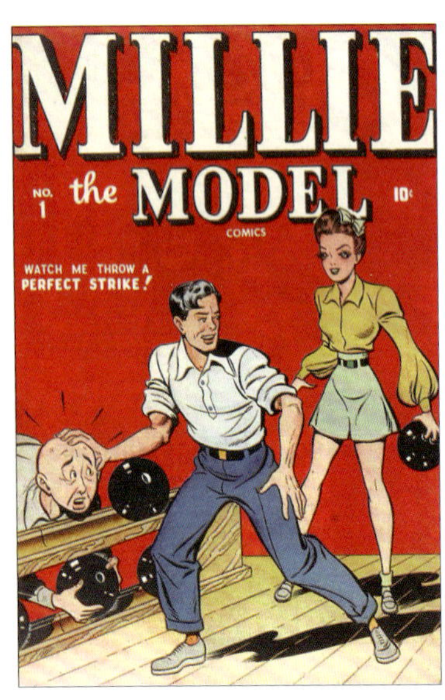

Millie the Model #1 (December 1945). Written by Stan Lee, art and cover by Stan Goldberg.

The last of Timely's Super Hero titles, *Captain America Comics*, came to an end with issue #75, cover-dated February 1950. An entire fictional universe had disappeared, although characters with super-powers, dressed in tight suits, would be making a comeback soon enough.

Atlas began releasing a diversified array of comic-book genres in an attempt to win over new audiences. They targeted girls with *Millie the Model*, a series that reached its height in popularity during the 1950s (though it had been created in the 1940s).

Among the hundreds of titles churned out at this time, four played a crucial role in expanding Goodman's empire, and continued until the 1960s, when they helped to launch a handful of Lee, Kirby, and Ditko's Super Heroes with super problems. The first of these was *Strange Tales* (#1 cover-dated June 1951), a monthly horror show featuring creepy monsters with outrageous names like Fin Fang Foom and Orrgo. *Journey into Mystery* was next. It debuted in June 1952 and featured more monsters and scary stories.

Then came the sci-fi titles *Tales of Suspense* and *Tales to Astonish*, both of which hit newsstands in June 1959. The wild names and the imaginative cover art sparked audiences' curiosity. Other titles from that time, including *Jungle Action, Black Knight, Love*

Romances, *War Comics*, *Kid Colt*, and *Rawhide Kid*, reveal the depth of genres then available.

But that didn't mean it was all over for the Super Heroes. In 1954, Goodman opted for a relaunch. He put Stan Lee in charge of writing and editing new stories. Short runs featured old favourites like the Human Torch (three issues), Captain America (three issues), and the Sub-Mariner (10 issues). But readers weren't hooked the way they had been in the 1930s and '40s, and it looked like this chapter in comic-book history had come to an end for the moment.

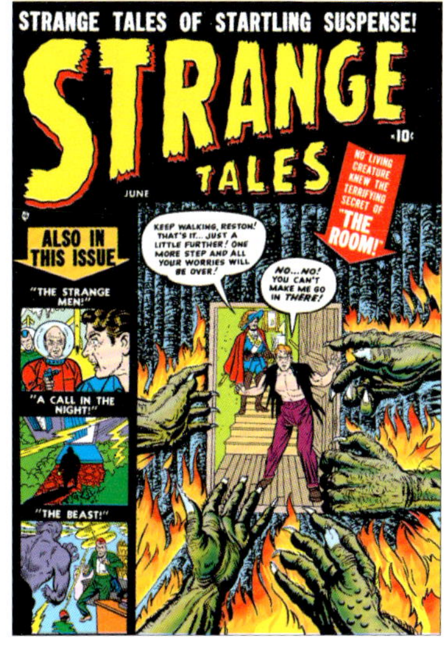

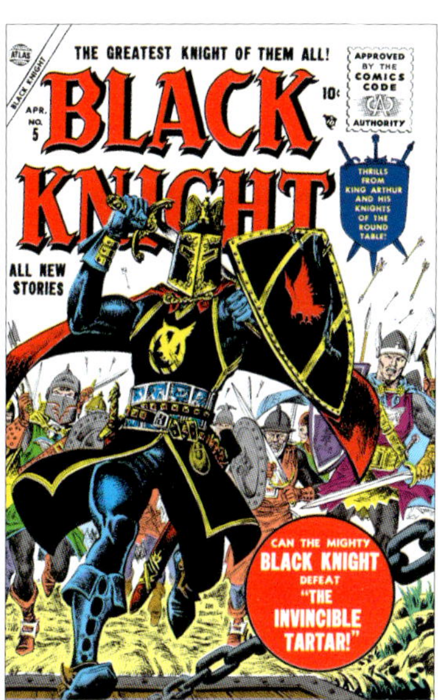

TOP
Strange Tales #1 (June 1951). Art by Carl Burgos (pencils).

BOTTOM
Black Knight #5 (April 1956). Art by Joe Maneely (pencils).

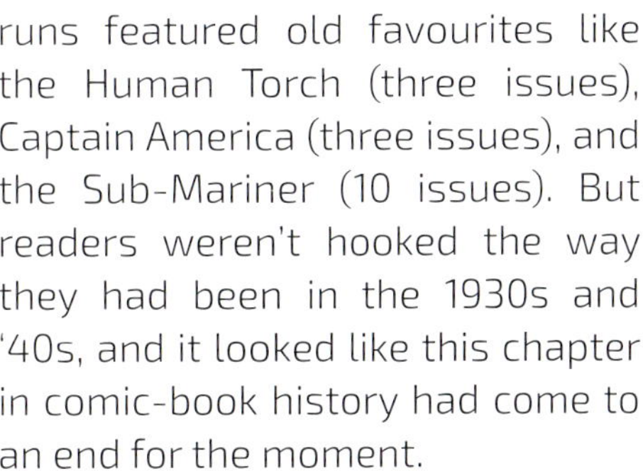

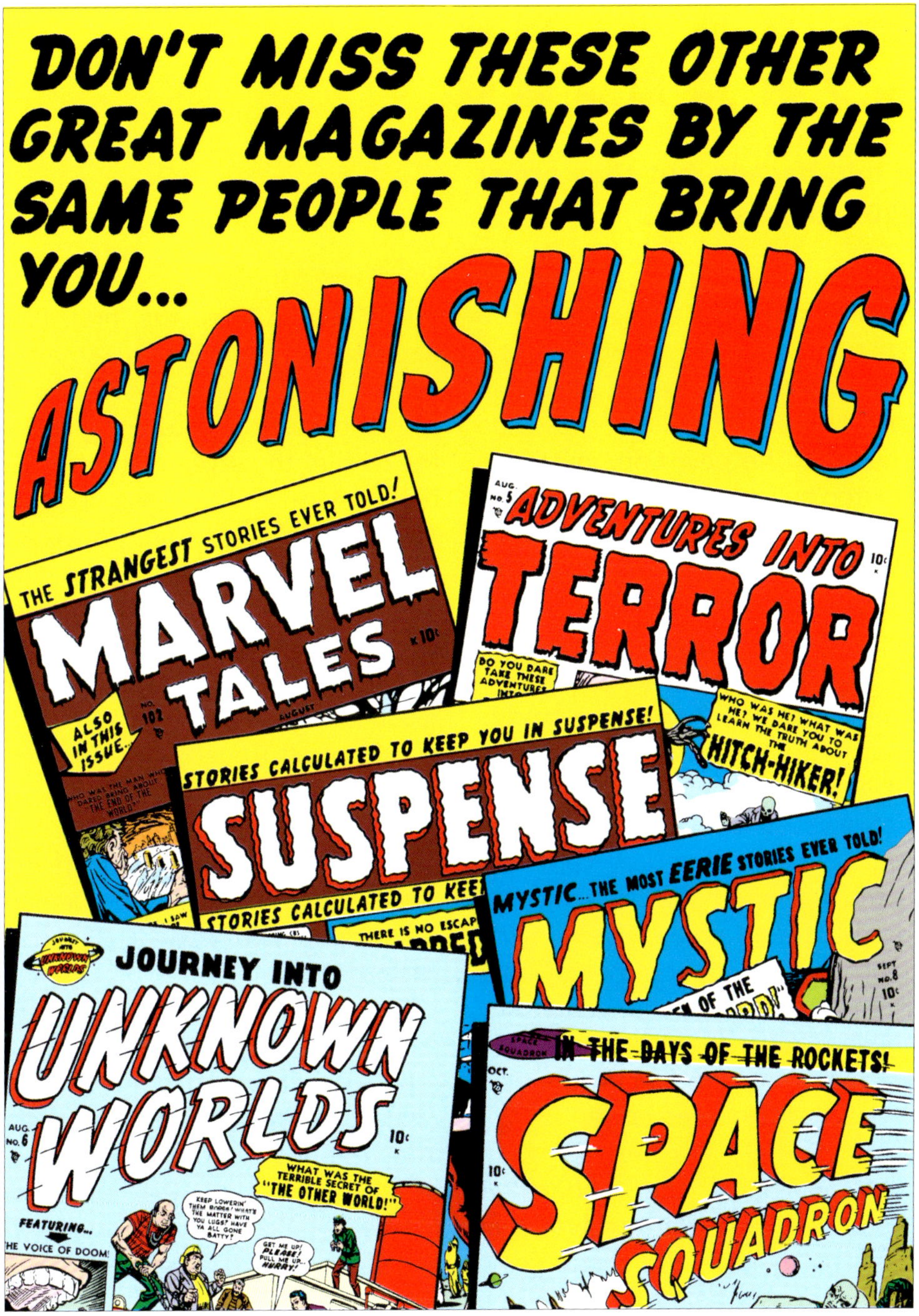

An assortment of Atlas comic-book offerings from 1951.

CAP, COMMIE SMASHER

The Super Heroes reappear mid-decade, but they aren't exactly the same as their 1940s counterparts.

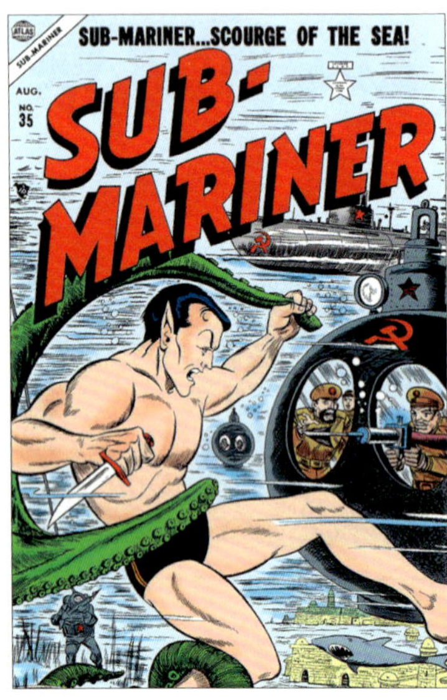

ABOVE
Sub-Mariner Comics #35 (August 1954). Art by Russ Heath.

OPPOSITE PAGE
Captain America #78 (September 1954). Art by John Romita, Sr. (pencils).

The return of Captain America excited readers who still remembered his feats of World War II heroism. But times had changed. The new Cap, in stories written by Stan Lee and illustrated by the young artist John Romita, Sr.—about whom we'll be hearing a lot more—was a man of the 1950s, fighting the Red Menace instead of the Nazis. He had become a "commie smasher" in stories that Marvel would later decide to attribute to another character entirely. At any rate, the Cold War Captain America came to symbolise an age whose concerns proved long lasting. Even in the stories starring the new Super Heroes of the 1960s, especially those revolving around the Avengers and Iron Man, the Red Menace still loomed large.

Meanwhile, the character from this 'Super Hero revival' that seemed to have the most going for it was none other than the Sub-Mariner. After the first film appearance by Captain America in the 1940s, it was very nearly the Sub-Mariner's turn to make the leap to the screen. But not the big screen—in this case, certain producers figured the Prince of Atlantis would be perfect for a new TV series. They had even chosen actor Richard Egan (of *Love Me Tender* fame), for the part. But for reasons lost to time, the project never got off the ground (not even a pilot was made).

Millie the Model, however, remained a hit. One reason behind her continued success was cartoonist Dan DeCarlo. Besides Millie, another female star had joined the ranks—the pretty young redhead Patsy Walker, who, like Millie, often found herself involved in love stories with comic overtones. In the decades that followed, Marvel would revamp Patsy and transform her in ways that 1950s Patsy could only imagine.

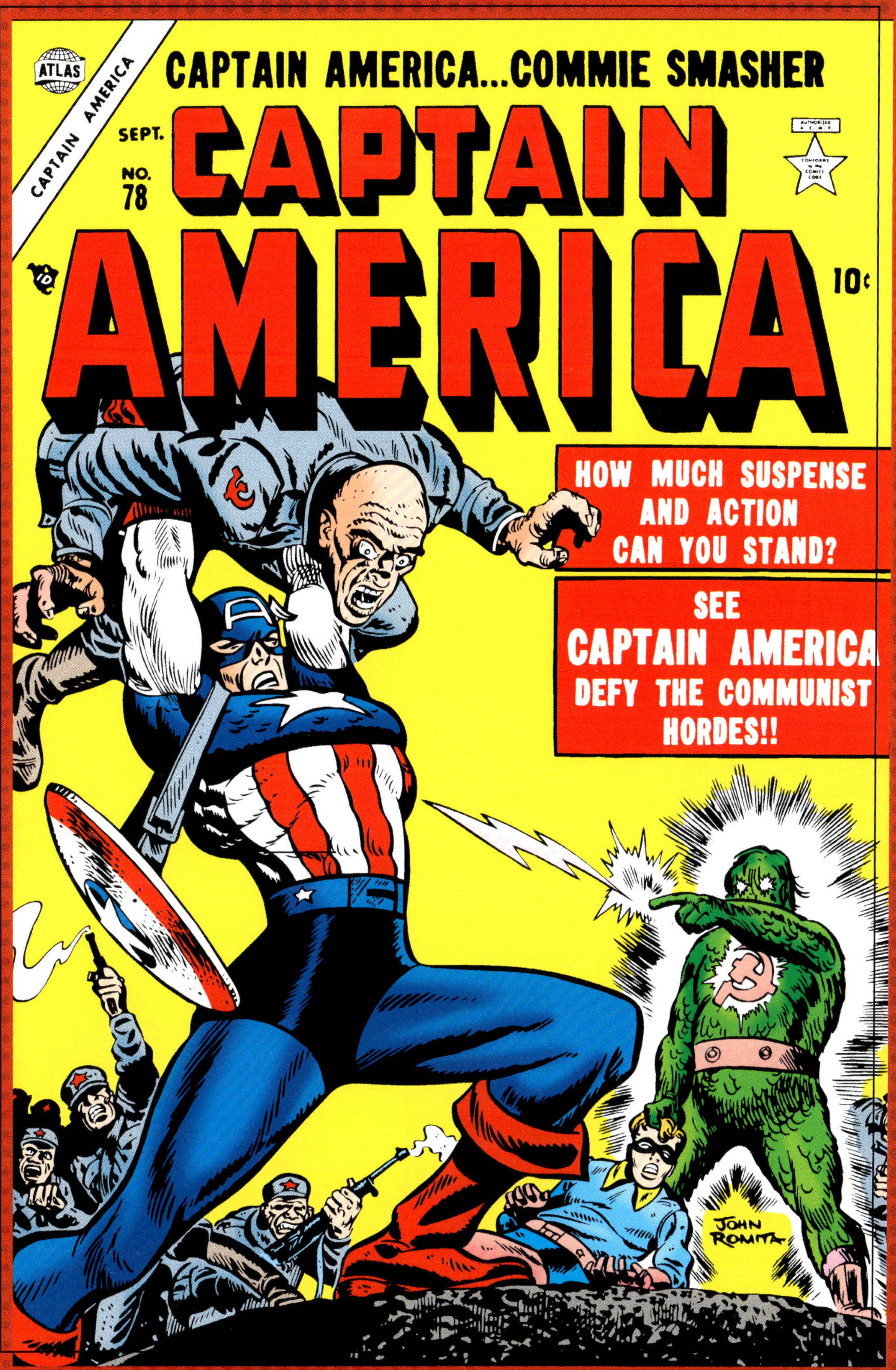
ATLAS
CAPTAIN AMERICA
CAPTAIN AMERICA...COMMIE SMASHER
SEPT.
NO. 78
CAPTAIN AMERICA
10¢
HOW MUCH SUSPENSE AND ACTION CAN YOU STAND?
SEE CAPTAIN AMERICA DEFY THE COMMUNIST HORDES!!
JOHN ROMITA

A FALLEN STAR

Joe Maneely was among Atlas' stable of amazing artists in the 1950s—but his career would be cut short by tragedy.

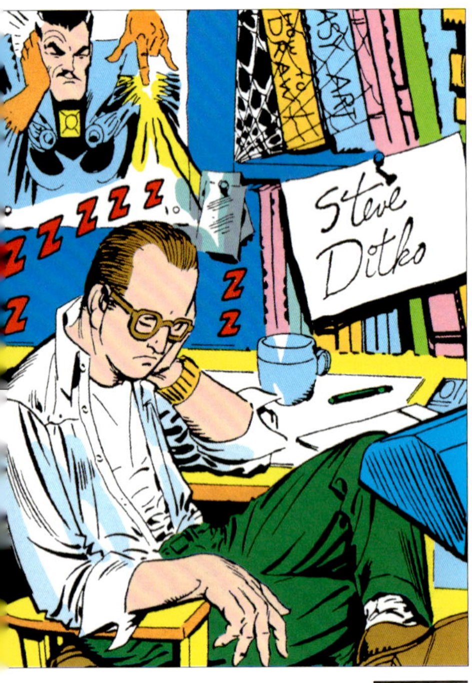

A self portrait of Steve Ditko "hard at work" from the featurette, "How Stan Lee and Steve Ditko Create Spider-Man!" (*The Amazing Spider-Man Annual #1*, October 1964). Script by Stan Lee. Art by Steve Ditko (pencils and inks).

Stan Lee remained as editor in chief at Atlas Comics, Martin Goodman's small but feisty publishing outfit, where he scripted most of the stories. As a writer, Lee had an uncanny knack for changing gears, and could move from Super Heroes to Westerns and beyond with ease. He had an inborn talent for dialogue, and brilliantly moulded his characters' often slangy speech patterns.

Lee worked alongside three artists who themselves epitomised comic-book creativity. One was Jack Kirby, who in the late 1950s returned to Atlas after setting out on his own a few years prior. Next was Steve Ditko, an amazing visual storyteller with just the right touch of weirdness for the times. Together, Kirby and Ditko illustrated hundreds of stories for Atlas Comics in genres that included horror, adventure, and sci-fi.

Then there was Joe Maneely, arguably Stan Lee's favourite collaborator of the era. An extremely talented artist, Maneely was known to work without pencils, and inked right off the bat. As Lee was fond of saying, "He could draw anything." With Maneely's fine lines,

1950

FEBRUARY 1950
Captain America's Weird Tales #75 marks the end of the series dedicated to the Super Hero created by Joe Simon and Jack Kirby.

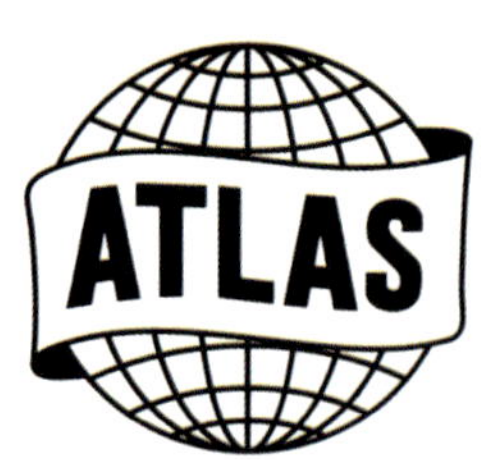

NOVEMBER 1951
The official debut of Atlas Comics, whose name was taken from Goodman's own distribution company. The name would change to Marvel Comics in 1961.

speed, and versatility, he might very well have gone on to become a key member in the Super Hero boom of the 1960s. Sadly, a tragic accident ended his young life at the age of 32. While returning to New Jersey after a dinner in Manhattan with fellow artists on the night of 7 June 1958, Maneely was struck by a commuter train, and was killed.

Other artists worked with Lee as well. They included Bill Everett, who returned to work on horror comics and the Sub-Mariner following the glory days of the Golden Age, as well as Wally Wood, Syd Shores, Paul Reinman, Dick Ayers, Larry Lieber (Stan's younger brother), Don Heck, George Tuska, and Gene Colan, who were all future stars of the Marvel Age.

By the late 1950s, Atlas Comics was in trouble. Comic-book sales across the board had dropped. Martin Goodman had shut down his distributorship in 1956, and struck a deal with the American News Company, which, however, soon closed its doors. The upshot: Goodman was forced to sign a distribution deal with the 'Distinguished Competition', rival National Periodical Publications (the future DC Comics), which drastically cut the number of Goodman's monthly comic-book releases. Ultimately, Goodman would opt to sift through the Atlas archives and use the wealth of previously unpublished stories and artwork he found there, ordering Lee to hold off on buying any new material. Staff were laid off. Disheartened, Lee was left to hold down the fort.

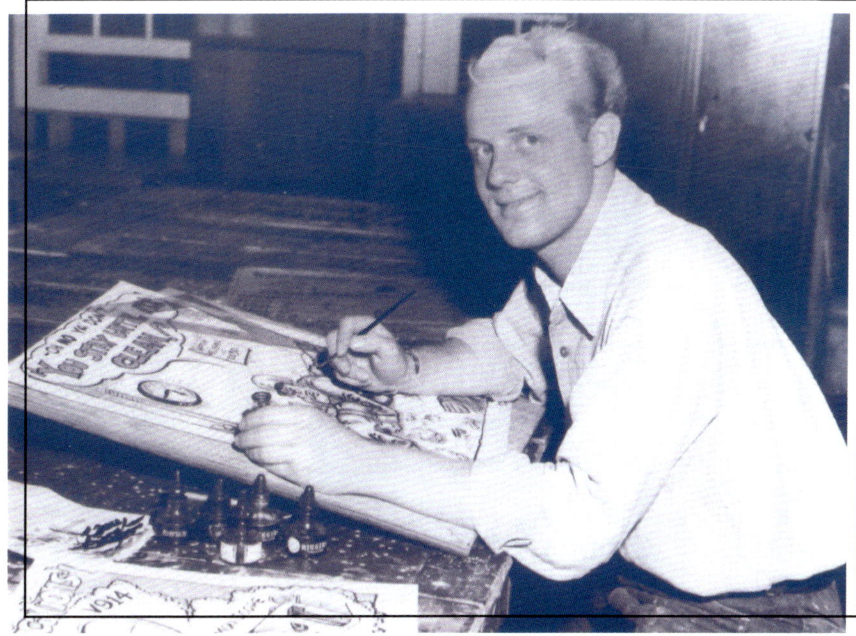

Artist Joe Maneely at the drawing board in San Francisco, California, 1945.

Artist Joe Maneely was one of Stan Lee's favourite collaborators.

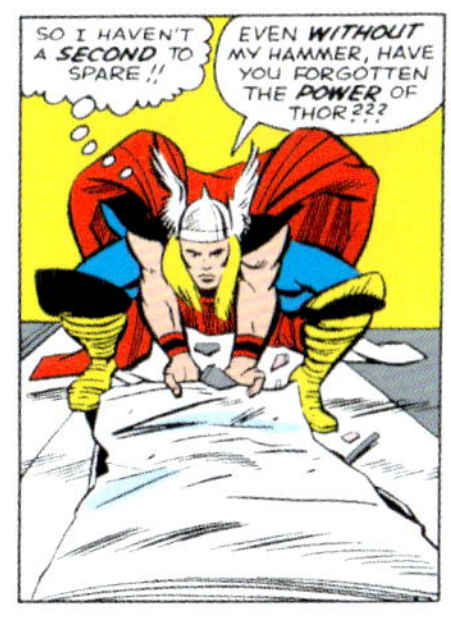

JUNE 1952
The horror and suspense series *Journey into Mystery* is released, following 1951's *Strange Tales*. Thor would make his first appearance in the August 1962 issue.

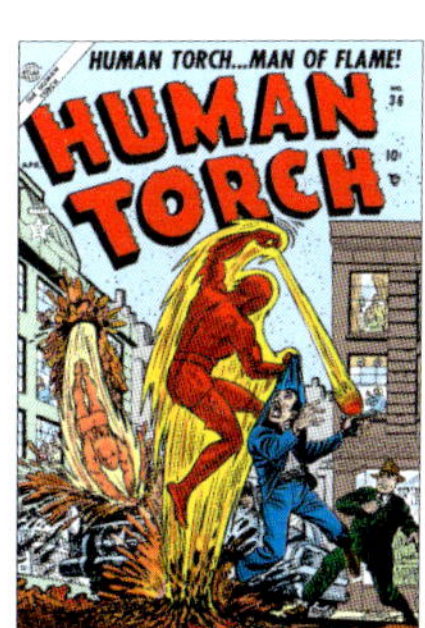

APRIL 1954
The Human Torch, the Sub-Mariner and Captain America returned in *Young Men #24* (December 1953). The heroes would appear in their own short-lived titles as well.

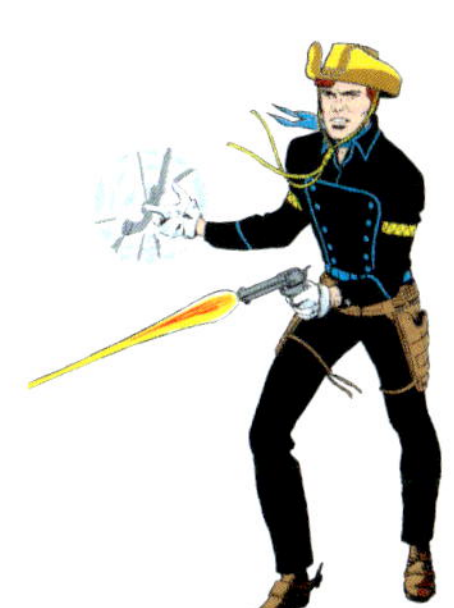

SPRING 1955
Rawhide Kid, one of Marvel's most celebrated Western heroes, debuts. The series would become even more popular in the 1960s, along with other Western heroes like Kid Colt.

U.S. VS. THE COMICS INDUSTRY

In the 1950s, comics came to symbolise a new type of menace for some—but how would comics respond to this attack?

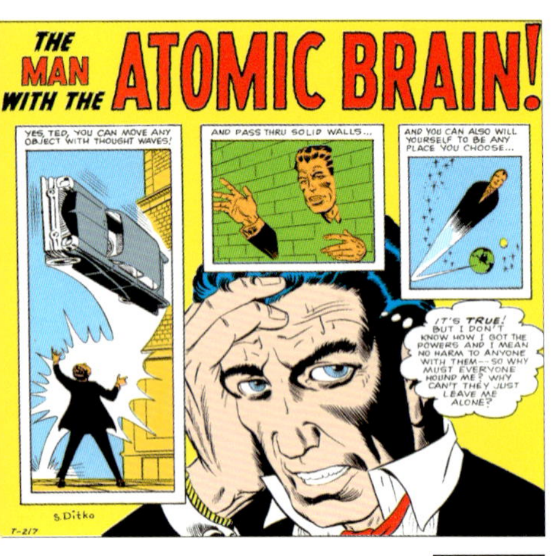

'The Man With the Atomic Brain!' from *Journey Into Mystery* #52 (May 1959). Script by Stan Lee. Art by Steve Ditko (pencils, inks), Stan Goldberg (colours).

The 1950s would also go down in history as the era of McCarthyism, a term denoting the witch hunt led by Republican senator Joseph McCarthy that targeted so-called communist sympathisers, who were considered a threat to national security at a time of all-out opposition to the Soviet Union. Accusations roiled politics, the motion picture industry, literature, and even everyday life, as many wound up paying the price for what were, in numerous instances, false allegations. A similar bane would plague the world of comic books.

Psychiatrist Fredric Wertham claimed that comics exerted a deleterious influence over the youth of America. According to Wertham, kids who read comic books—which at that time sold millions of copies each month—

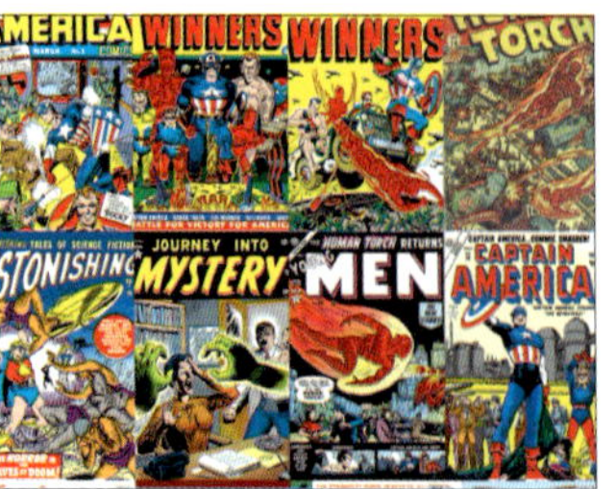

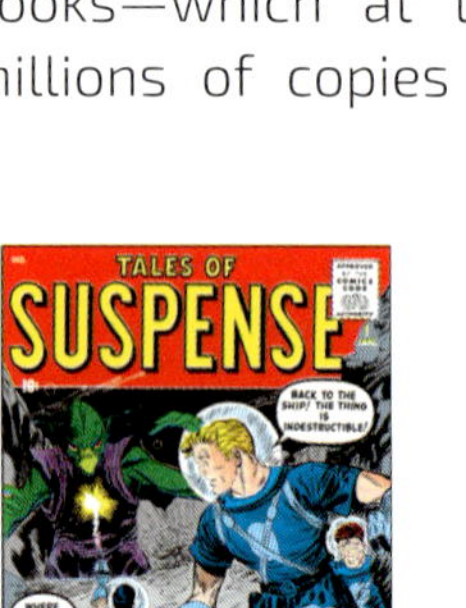

1957
Goodman had made a deal with the distributor American News, but it shut down in May, which meant he would have to come to terms with DC-owned Independent News.

1959
Atlas launches *Tales of Suspense* and *Tales to Astonish* in January, featuring monster stories drawn by Jack Kirby. Both titles would feature Super Heroes in the 1960s.

1960

ran serious risks of becoming criminals. There was no scientific proof behind such claims, which, nonetheless, took hold among certain segments of society at that time. The consequences proved devastating—from the burning of comic books in town squares, to investigations carried out against newspapers, magazines, and television broadcasters.

The frenzy reached its height on 4 June 1954 when Bill Gaines, owner of EC Comics, appeared before a U.S. Senate subcommittee at a hearing broadcast on live TV. His publishing outfit, famous for its unconventional, cutting-edge tales of horror steeped in violence, was at the eye of the storm of accusations. Gaines found himself at a loss when it came to defending his brand in the face of Senator Estes Kefauver's baited questioning, and, in fact, his answers served to make things worse. Subsequently, comic-book publishers banded together to self-regulate the industry, tantamount to censorship, in order to placate public opinion. The Comics Code Authority, established in 1954, set strict limits on comic book content: no blood, no positive representation of evil, no more vampires and zombies, and so on. To be sure, the police would be depicted as good guys, always on the winning side.

This sanitisation of comic-book stories and artwork would condition the work of the creators and force them to come up with new solutions. Naturally, Atlas was forced to comply and, as a result, began publishing stories and series that featured monsters from outer space, menaces from other planets, and forays into bygone eras like the Middle Ages, the Wild West, and the days when pirates roamed the seas. But the revolution that would change comic-book culture the world over was within sight, and Goodman's publishing house, soon to be known as Marvel Comics, would lead the charge.

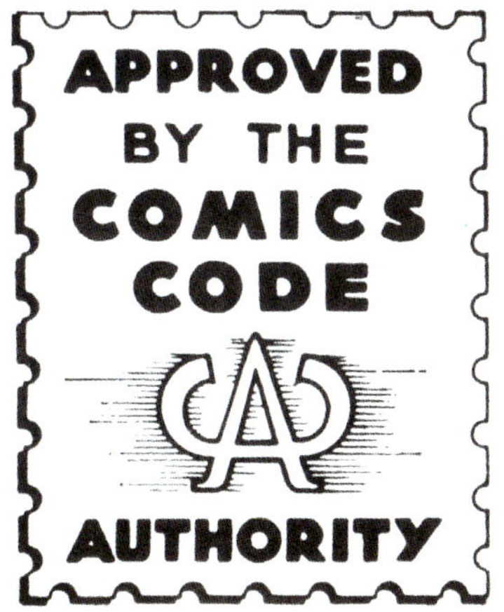

The seal of the 'Comics Code Authority,' part of the Comics Magazine Association of America formed in 1954.

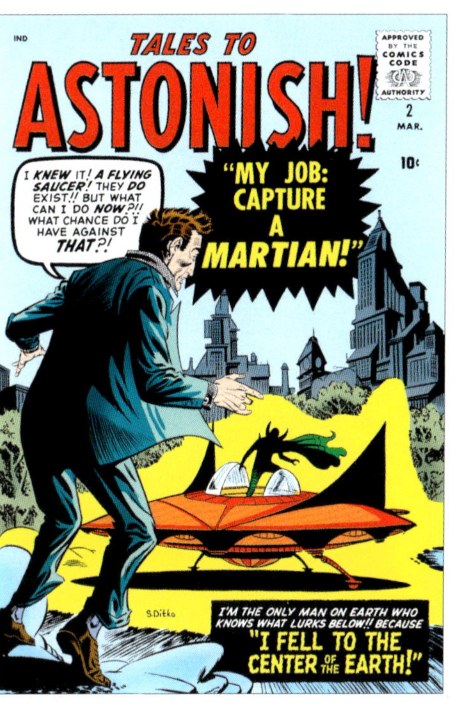

LEFT
Tales to Astonish #2 (March 1959). Art by Steve Ditko and Stan Goldberg. Letters by Artie Simek.

BELOW
Panel detail from "I Unleashed Monstro on the World!" *Journey Into Mystery #54* (September 1959). Script by Stan Lee. Art by Steve Ditko (pencils, inks).

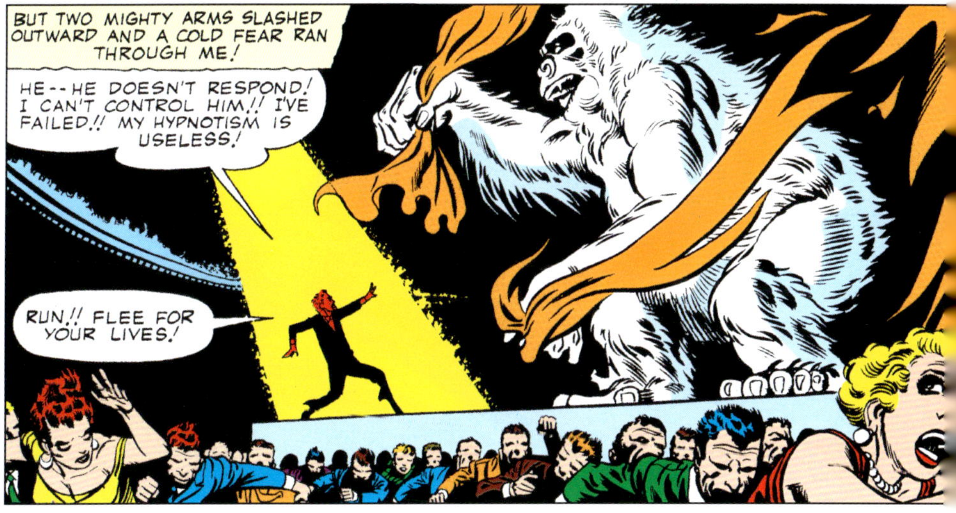

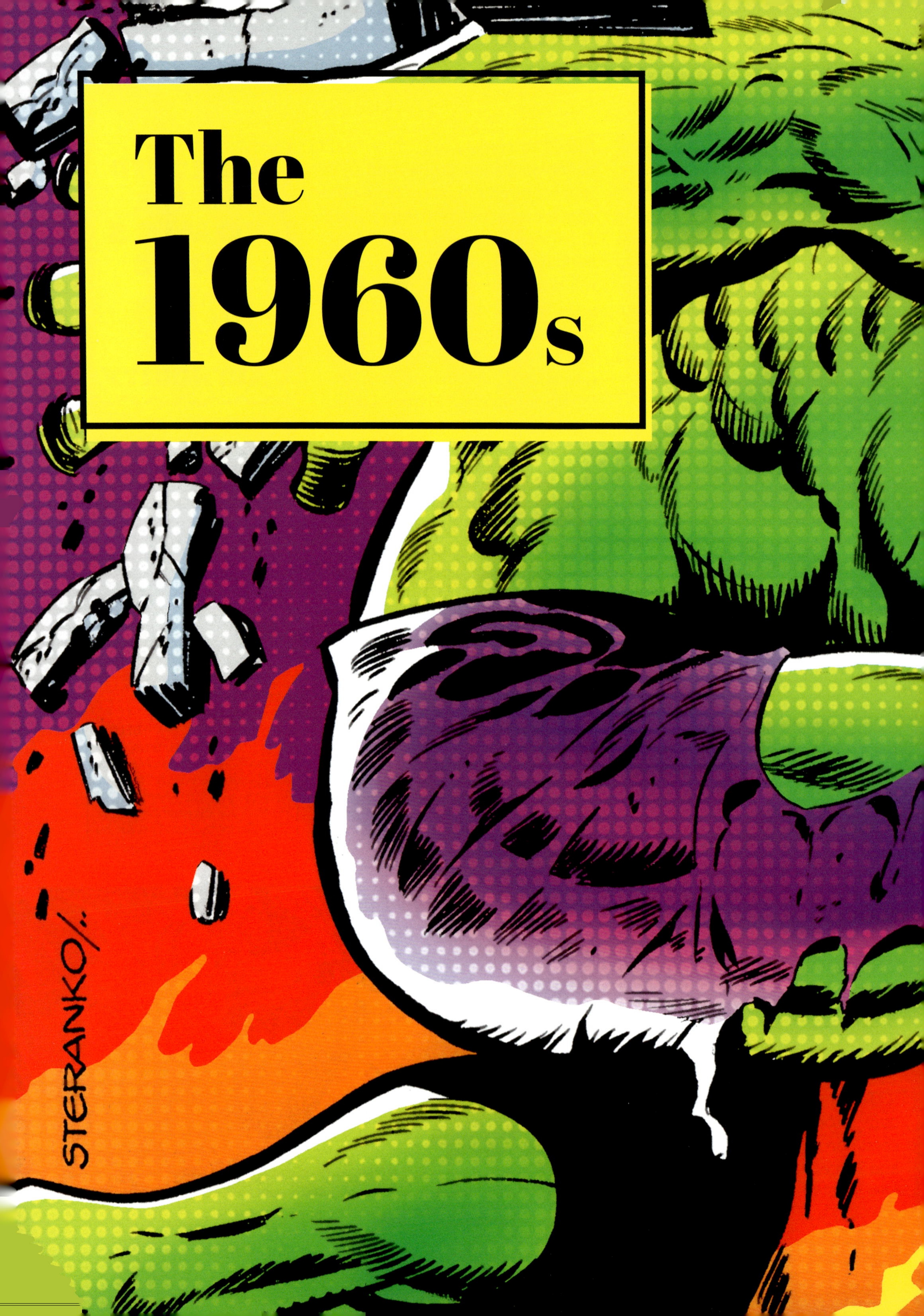
The 1960s
STERANKO

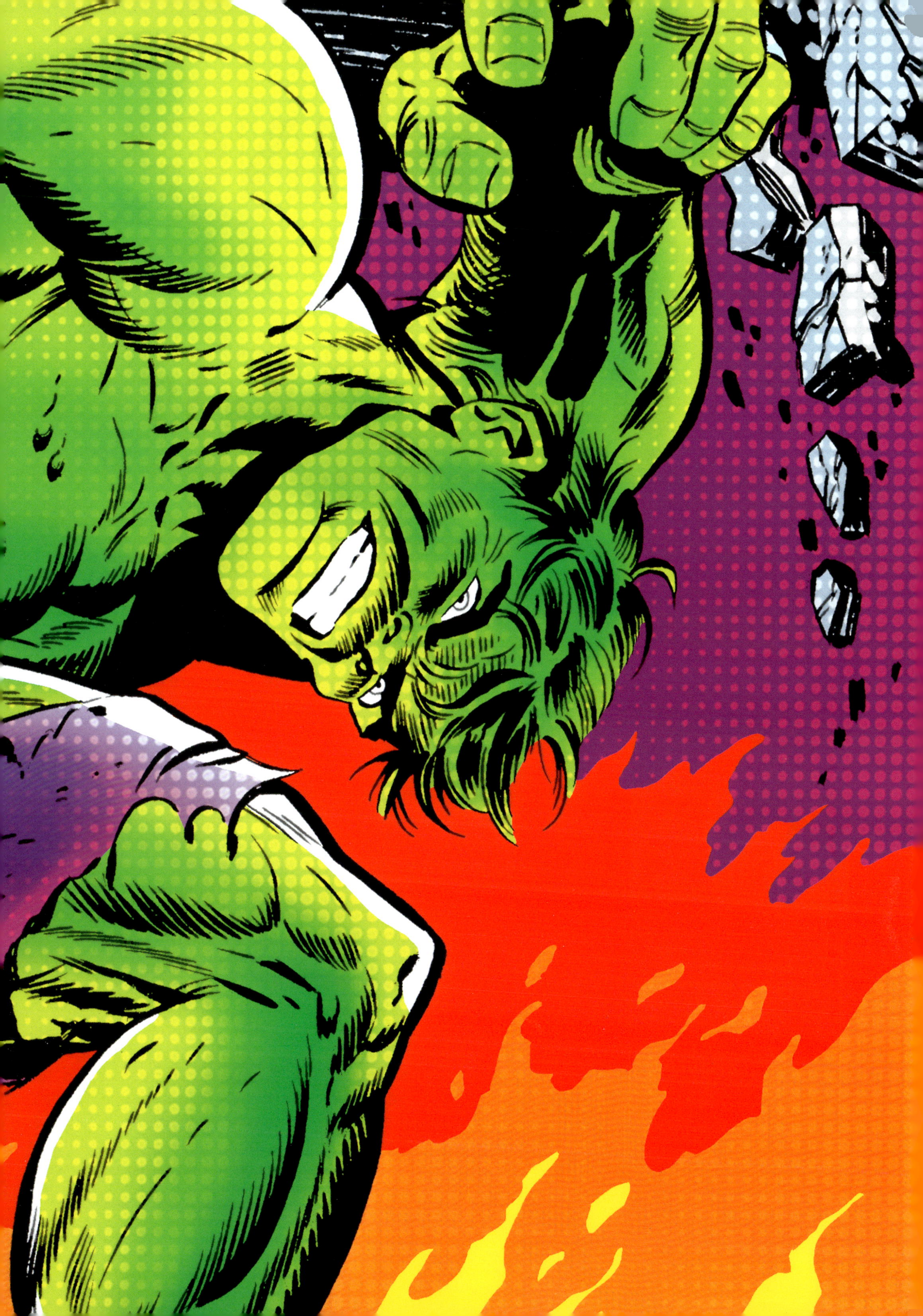

THE COMING OF THE MARVEL AGE

The 1960s would see a real atomic explosion of creativity from the mighty halls of Marvel.

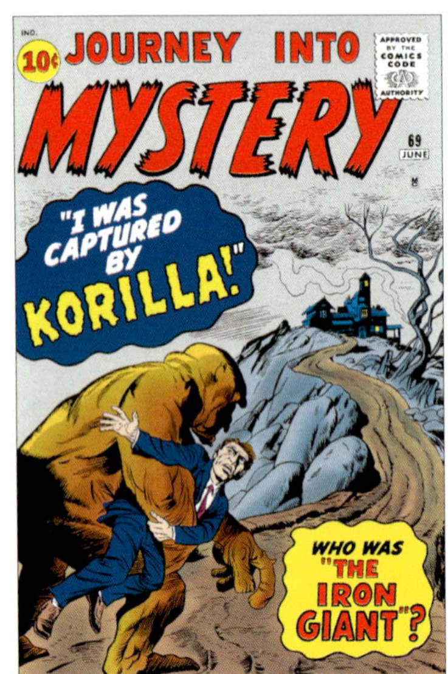

ABOVE
At the dawn of the decade, the company was producing monster stories like "I Was Captured By Korilla!" (*Journey into Mystery* #69, June 1961).

OPPOSITE PAGE
Pin-up from *The Avengers Annual* #2 (Sept. 1968). Art by John Buscema (pencils), Bill Everett (inks), Joe Rosen (letters).

The new frontier, the civil rights struggle, the conquest of space, the collapse of the myth of invincibility. The stage was set for the creation of the greatest comic book universe ever.

Comic-book creator Stan Lee was fed up with the old routine. He'd been working for Timely/Atlas for over 20 years, joining when he was just 17, and was appointed editor shortly thereafter. He had a knack for handling writers and artists, choosing covers, assigning stories and, most of all, for writing stories in an incredibly wide range of genres. He had no problem typing out an episode about a Wild West gunslinger and a few minutes later detail the invasion of monsters from outer space. But he was burned out. He felt as though his dreams were slipping away, and that he might not ever write that Great American Novel he'd been saving his real last name for. So he thought about walking into publisher Martin Goodman's office, and telling him he'd be moving on in search of a new path in life. But before he could do that, something... happened.

In 1956, National Comics (soon to be called DC) published their first story starring a new version of the 1940s character the Flash. National was hoping to bring back the glory days of their first Super Heroes (Superman, Batman, Wonder Woman, and others). Legend has it, National publisher Jack Liebowitz and Martin Goodman played golf together one morning. Liebowitz had been bragging about skyrocketing sales of the *Justice League*, a new series that teamed up his company's greatest Super Heroes. Goodman returned to his office, and called in Lee, asking him to devise a series featuring a team of Super Heroes.

Lee had a dilemma. He went home and talked with his wife Joan. She had a good head on her shoulders and was able to view the situation from a more detached perspective. Her advice? Why not put all his creative energy into this assignment, just to see what he could really do?

Stan took those words to heart, and immediately began exploring ideas for a new story that would be completely different and original. One that featured Super Heroes, only not in the classic mould, not the invincible, perfect kind. Not the ones who encountered their enemies at the start of a story, wound up defeating them over the course of 20 pages, and stood there all smiles in the final panel. No. Lee was after a story about real people. They would have super-powers, yes, but they would also be vulnerable, subject to disappointments, losers even. Then Lee worked out the story with Jack Kirby.

Kirby had made his way back to Goodman's fold in the late 1950s, where he, Steve Ditko, and a few other artists drew the short stories—mainly thrillers and horror—which filled Atlas comic books at that time. And truth be told, there weren't all that many comic books coming out.

After the decision to shut down Atlas's own distribution company and put distribution in the hands of the American News Company, which soon folded, Goodman was forced to strike a deal with National's distributor to get his comic books to

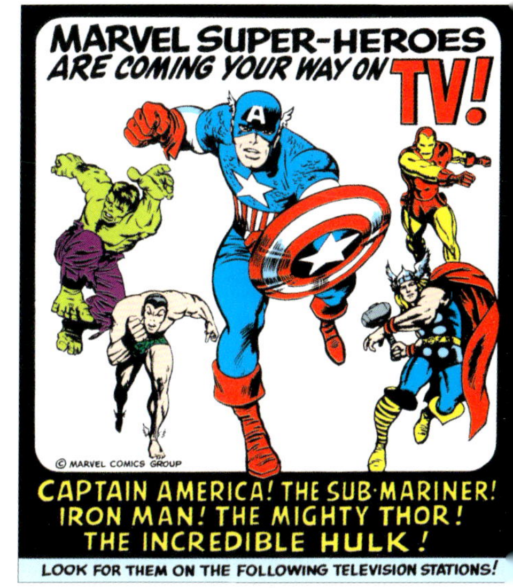

House ad heralding the arrival of the 1966 animated series *Marvel Super Heroes*.

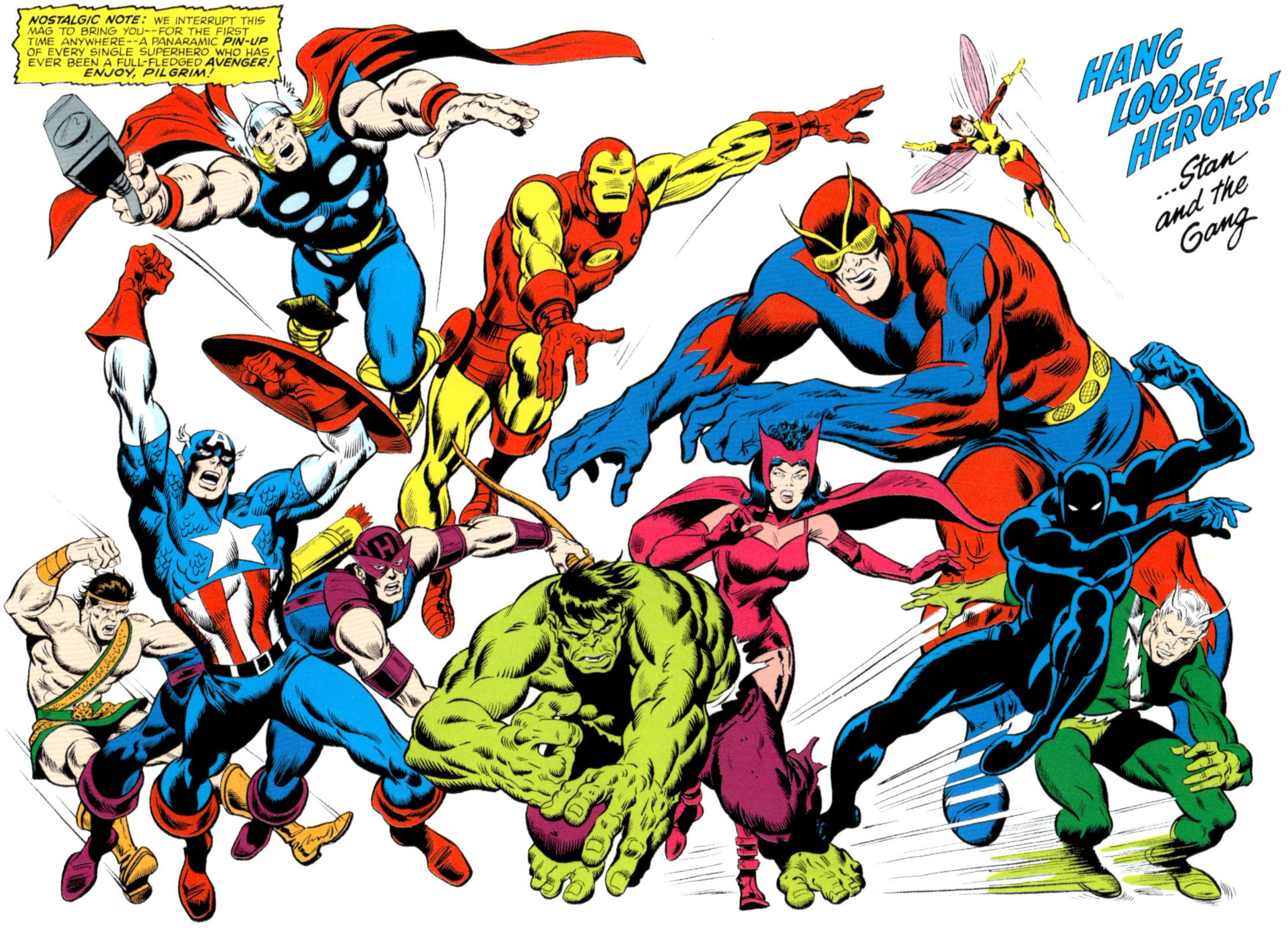

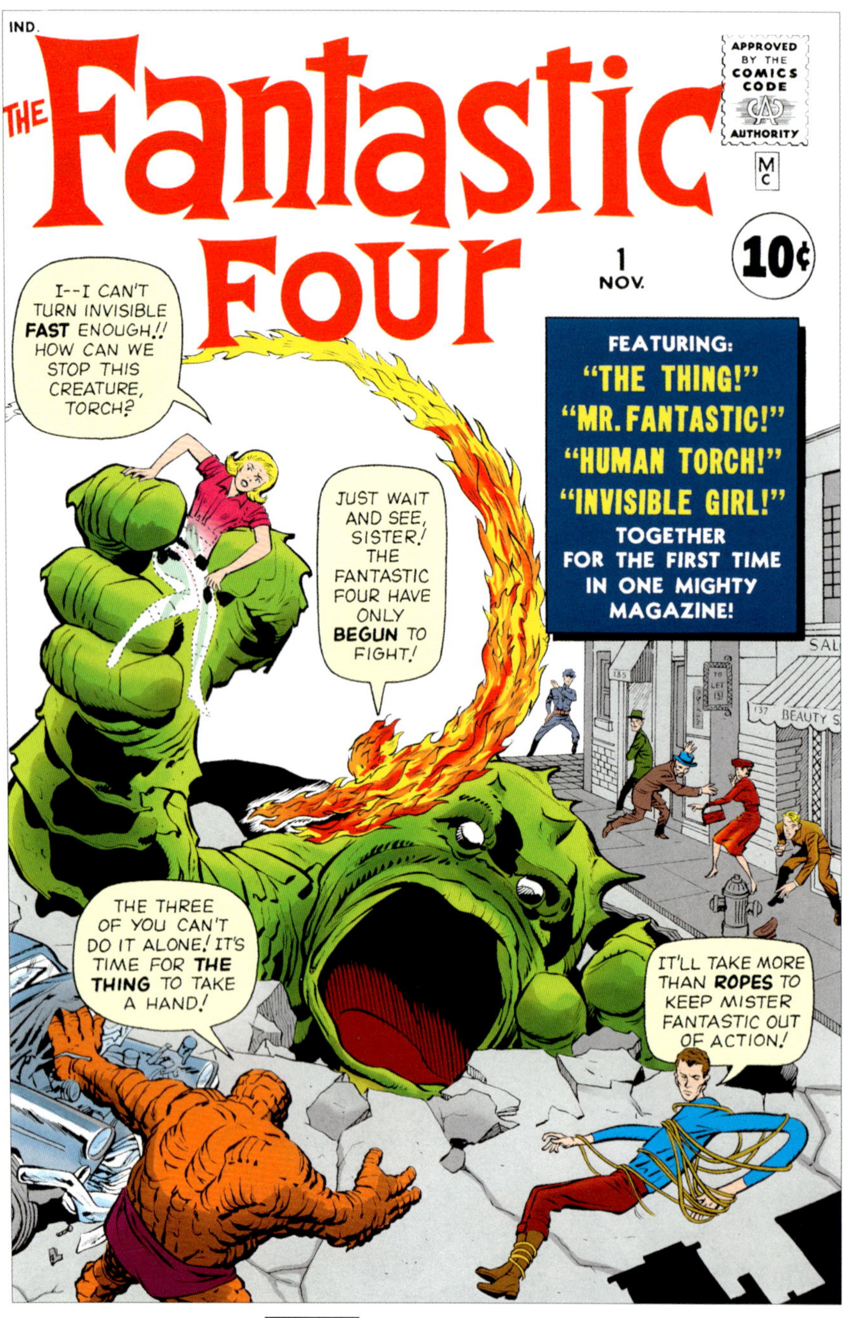

The Fantastic Four #1 (November 1961). Cover art by Jack Kirby (pencils) and Dick Ayers (inks).

newsstands—a deal that allowed for no more than eight comics a month. To get around this snag, Goodman began putting out bi-monthly issues, which allowed him to have 16 different comic books on newsstands in any given month.

Lee and Kirby worked out a plot featuring the new Super Heroes. It detailed their origins and main characteristics. There was the scientist, the girlfriend, the 'hot-headed' brother, the grumpy pilot friend. The four of them would challenge destiny and set out for space, on a mission to beat the Soviet Union, who at that time was leading the United States in the space race. Only these Americans hadn't taken into account the cosmic rays that would zap them as soon as they left Earth's atmosphere. A dose of radiation that would change not only their lives, but the lives of Marvel fans as well. Lee would script over Kirby's art.

The Fantastic Four #1 (cover-dated November 1961) hit newsstands on 8 August 1961. Nothing quite like it had ever been published. Its release marked the start of the Marvel Age in comics—a period when the creators would become as famous as the Super Heroes they wrote about and drew. Now characters would be loved more for the human adventures they embarked upon, their romances, the drama and tragedy in their personal lives, than the battles against their foes.

Lee, Kirby, Ditko, and later on John Buscema, John Romita, Sr., Bill Everett, Larry Lieber (Stan's brother), Gene Colan, Don Heck, Dick Ayers, Roy Thomas, Jim Steranko, and others worked as if they'd been possessed by the demon of creativity. It was a decade that saw the birth of Spider-Man and Thor, Ant-Man and the Avengers, Daredevil and the X-Men, Iron Man and the Hulk, Black Panther and the Silver Surfer, while Super Heroes like Captain America and the Sub-Mariner would be reborn.

THE MARVEL SUPER HEROES HAVE ARRIVED

From 1961 through 1964, Marvel brought some of the most beloved Super Heroes to life.

With the release of *The Fantastic Four #1* in 1961, through April 1964 (the cover date for *Daredevil #1*), Lee and his team created some of the greatest characters of all time—fuelled in part by the daunting competition from Batman and Superman, and distribution constraints that plagued Atlas (which would soon become Marvel, taken from the title of the first Timely comic book to feature Super Heroes way back in 1939).

The success of the Fantastic Four was unexpected. Mister Fantastic, the Invisible Girl (later known as the Invisible Woman), the Human Torch (a tribute to the Golden Age Super Hero of the same name), and the Thing all spoke the same language as their readers, so it was easy to identify with them. Goodman wasted no time in ordering Lee to forge ahead.

Cover-dated May 1962—but released on 1 March—*The Incredible Hulk #1* marked the introduction of a monstrous creature. Initially grey in colour, later green, possessed of uncontrollable brute strength, the Hulk was the scientist Bruce Banner, victim of a gamma-ray accident. The series, created by Lee and Kirby, was soon folded into the anthology title *Tales to Astonish*, a comic-book series with no fixed main character and focused on horror and suspense. Before that, issue #35 (cover-dated September 1962) had featured another new, highly original Super Hero: Ant-Man (created by Lee, Lieber, and Kirby), whose alter ego was again a scientist, Hank Pym, who devised a formula that allowed him to shrink to the size of an insect and communicate with ants.

Two more all-time greats were on their way: Thor and Spider-Man.

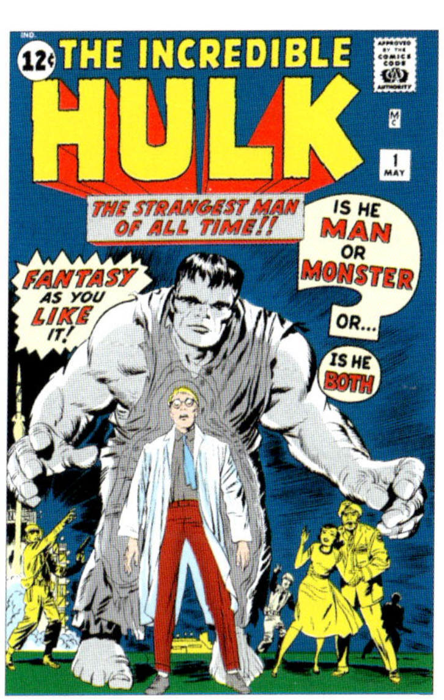

The Incredible Hulk #1 (May 1962). Cover art by Jack Kirby (pencils) and George Roussos (inks).

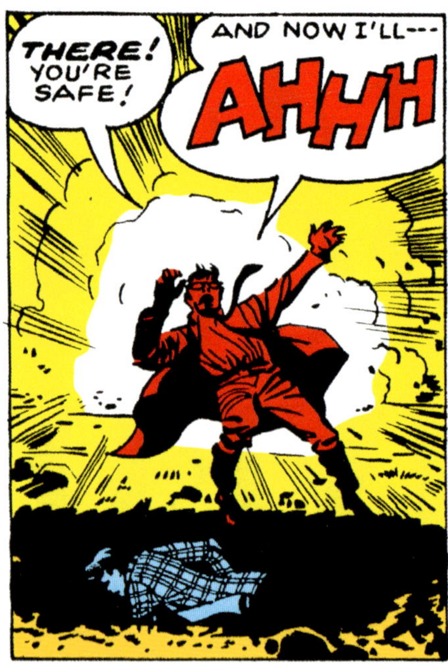

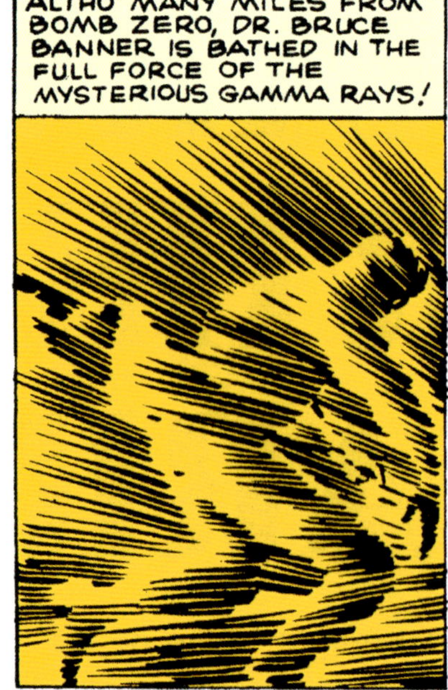

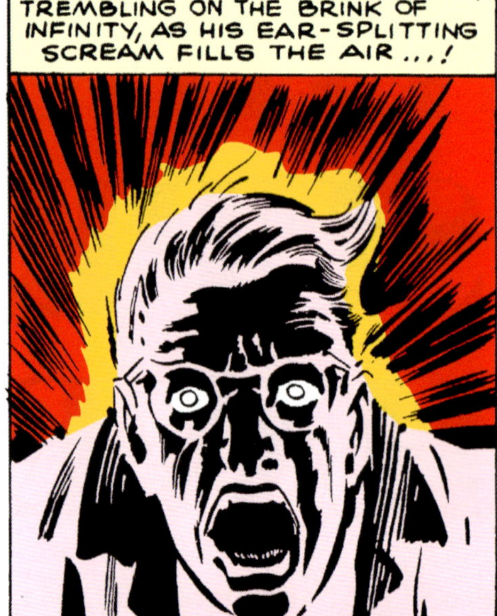

Bruce Banner is caught in the blast of the gamma bomb in *The Incredible Hulk #1*. Script by Stan Lee. Art by Jack Kirby (pencils), Paul Reinman (inks), and Artie Simek (letters).

Their respective first appearances were made in comic books cover-dated August 1962, but they must certainly have been released before that. Spider-Man made his first appearance in *Amazing Fantasy #15*, the last issue in an anthology series. It contained an unforgettable 11-page story, written by Lee and drawn by Steve Ditko, starring a high-school kid from Queens, New York, who gets bitten by a radioactive spider. He would receive astonishing powers. However, tragedy would strike, and young Peter Parker's life would never be the same.

But getting that first Spider-Man story published was no easy task. Lee has said that Goodman reacted poorly to the idea. "People don't like spiders!" he commented drily. Lee wound up including the story in the last issue of a series that was headed for cancellation. But lo and behold, that issue turned out to be a big seller, and Marvel received lots of letters from fans overflowing with praise.

With *Amazing Fantasy* out of the picture, the only viable solution was... *The Amazing Spider-Man #1* (cover-dated March 1963), the first comic book centred around the wall-crawler.

The other momentous debut saw Thor springing into action in *Journey into Mystery #83*, another anthology series without a fixed protagonist, which was mostly focused on mystery and suspense. Lee, Lieber, Kirby, and inker Joe Sinnott came up with the 13-page adventure that laid the foundations for the comic-book version of the God of Thunder, an immortal from Asgard who was cast among mankind by his father as punishment for his youthful arrogance. With issue #126, the series was renamed *The Mighty Thor*.

Journey into Mystery #83 (August 1962). Art by Jack Kirby (pencils) and Joe Sinnott (inks).

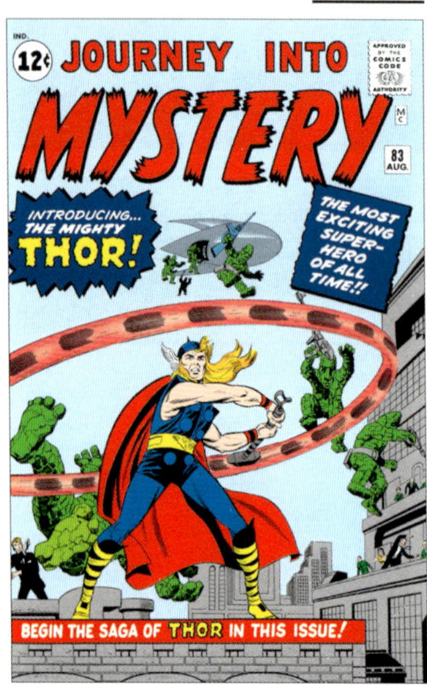

Amazing Fantasy #15 (August 1962). Art by Jack Kirby (pencils) and Steve Ditko (inks).

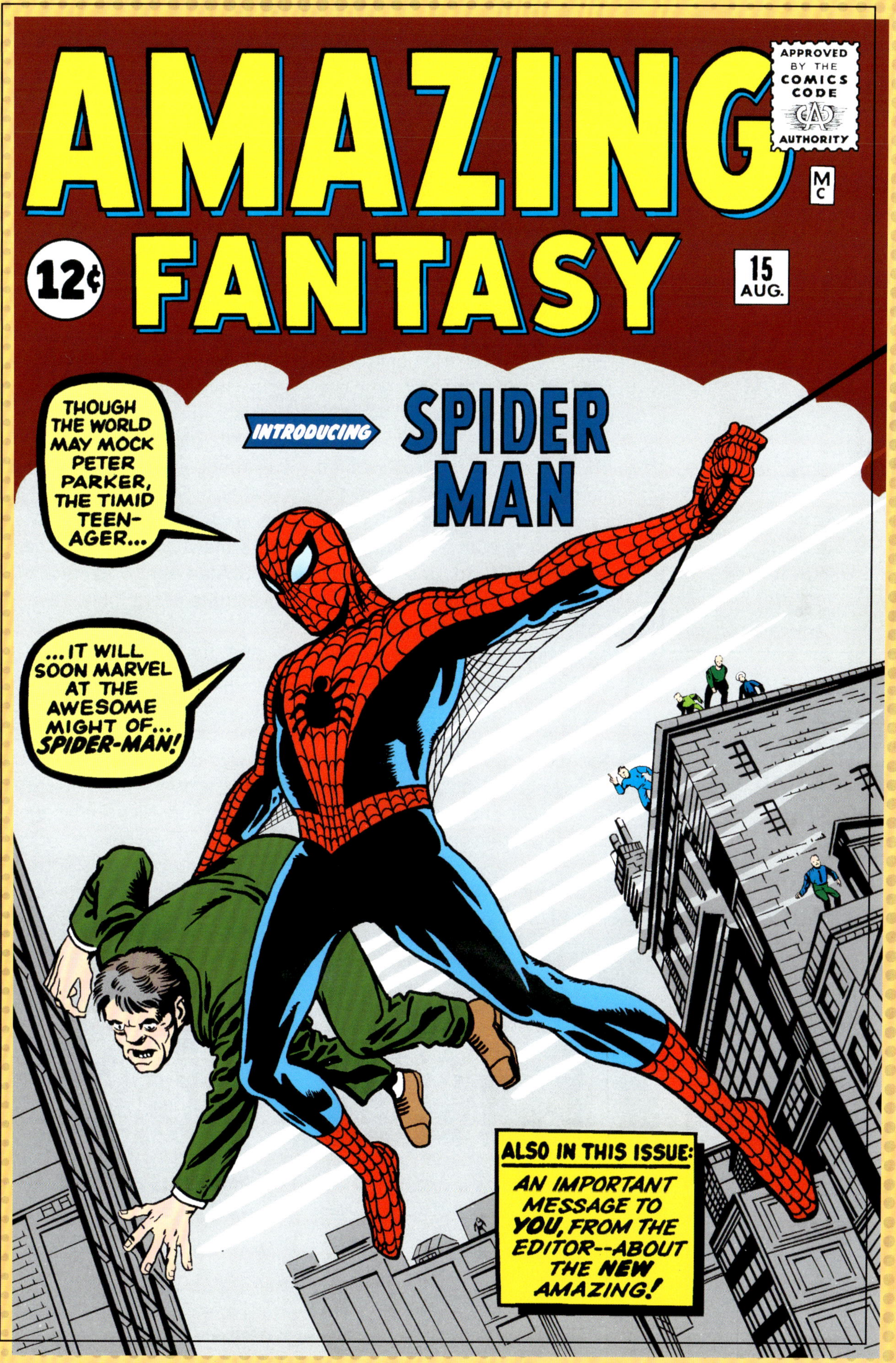
AMAZING
APPROVED BY THE COMICS CODE AUTHORITY
MC
12¢
FANTASY
15
AUG.
THOUGH THE WORLD MAY MOCK PETER PARKER, THE TIMID TEEN-AGER...
INTRODUCING
SPIDER MAN
...IT WILL SOON MARVEL AT THE AWESOME MIGHT OF... SPIDER-MAN!
ALSO IN THIS ISSUE:
AN IMPORTANT MESSAGE TO YOU, FROM THE EDITOR--ABOUT THE NEW AMAZING!

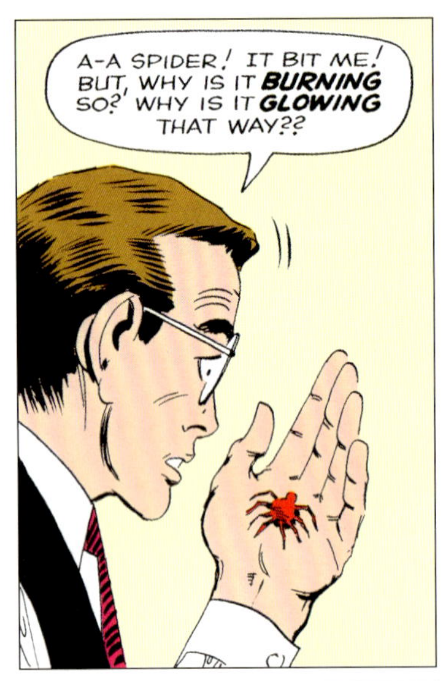

Peter Parker is bitten by the radioactive spider in *Amazing Fantasy #15*. Script by Stan Lee. Art by Steve Ditko (pencils, inks), Stan Goldberg (colours), Artie Simek (letters).

Marvel's new breed of Super Heroes had quirks and problems to spare—just like their readership.

Intent on launching more new Super Heroes, Lee and his brother Larry, this time along with Don Heck, created Iron Man, who first appeared in the science-fiction and horror anthology series *Tales of Suspense #39* (March 1963, with a cover by Jack Kirby). His alter ego was the billionaire industrialist Tony Stark, who during the Vietnam War donned a suit of iron armour in order to fend off a life-threatening piece of shrapnel lodged near his heart.

The Avengers #1 (cover-dated September 1963) marked the start of a new comic-book series featuring a second supergroup. Thor, Iron Man, Ant-Man, the Wasp, and the Hulk were the founding members. It was clear from the start that Marvel wasn't going to rest on its laurels. In issue #2, the Hulk left the team, and became their enemy. Then, in issue #4, Captain America returned to the modern world, found frozen in the North Atlantic and brought back to life from a state of suspended animation.

September 1963 witnessed the arrival of a unique supergroup—a bizarre collection of individuals called the X-Men. Another product of Lee's and Kirby's fervid imaginations, the series featured a cast of young Super Heroes born with genetic mutations and trained by their mentor Charles Xavier, A.K.A. Professor X.

And then came Daredevil, A.K.A. young Matt Murdock, who'd gone blind following an act of heroism, acquiring a 'radar sense' that allowed him to envision his surroundings. Daredevil was the creation of Stan Lee and Bill Everett, the artist behind the Sub-Mariner for Timely Publications back in the Golden Age. *Daredevil #1* was cover-dated April 1964.

And the new characters kept on coming. In another anthology series, *Strange Tales*, the Human Torch appeared in solo stories, followed by the appearance of the Master of the Mystic Arts, Doctor Strange, and Nick Fury, agent of S.H.I.E.L.D. Then there were all-new protagonists introduced within the pages of *The Fantastic Four*, like the cosmic Silver Surfer,

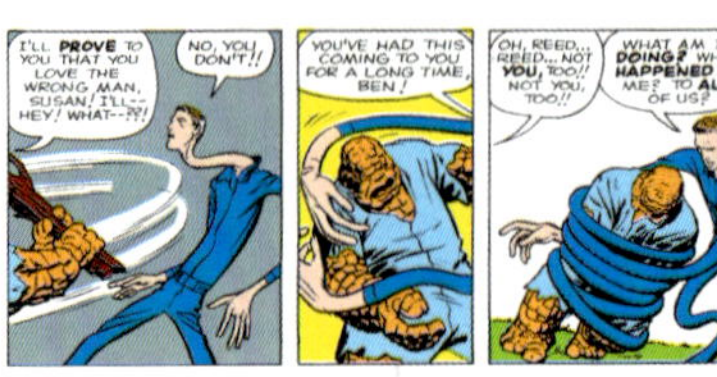

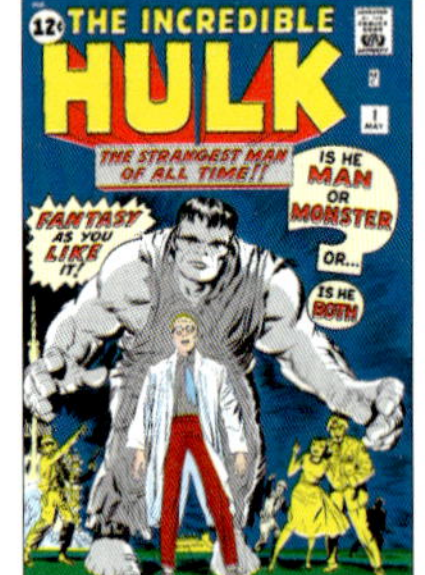

1960

8 AUGUST 1961
Although the cover date says November, historians date the start of the Marvel Age as 8 August 1961, with the release of *The Fantastic Four #1* by Lee and Kirby.

MAY 1962
The Incredible Hulk #1 hits the newsstands. This was the second big gun for the Marvel Universe, featuring Kirby's beautiful cover, inked by George Roussos.

the incredible Inhumans, and the ground-breaking Black Panther, adding to the ever-expanding Marvel Comics universe that told the story of 1960s America.

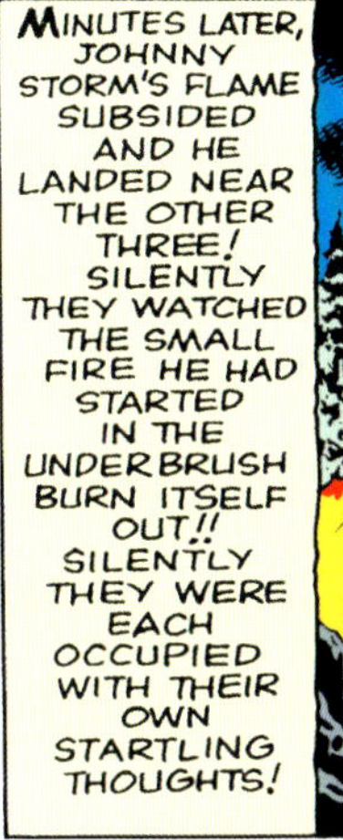

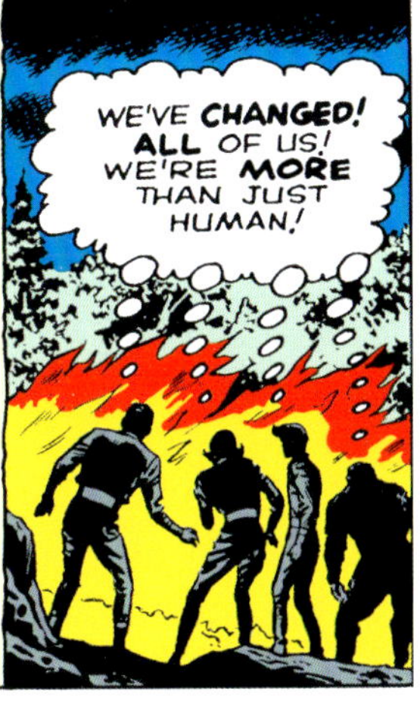

ABOVE
The Fantastic Four are born, *The Fantastic Four #1*. Script by Stan Lee. Art by Jack Kirby (pencils), George Klein/Christopher Rule (inks), Stan Goldberg (colours), Artie Simek (letters).

RIGHT
The Avengers #1 (September 1963). Art by Jack Kirby (pencils) and Dick Ayers (inks).

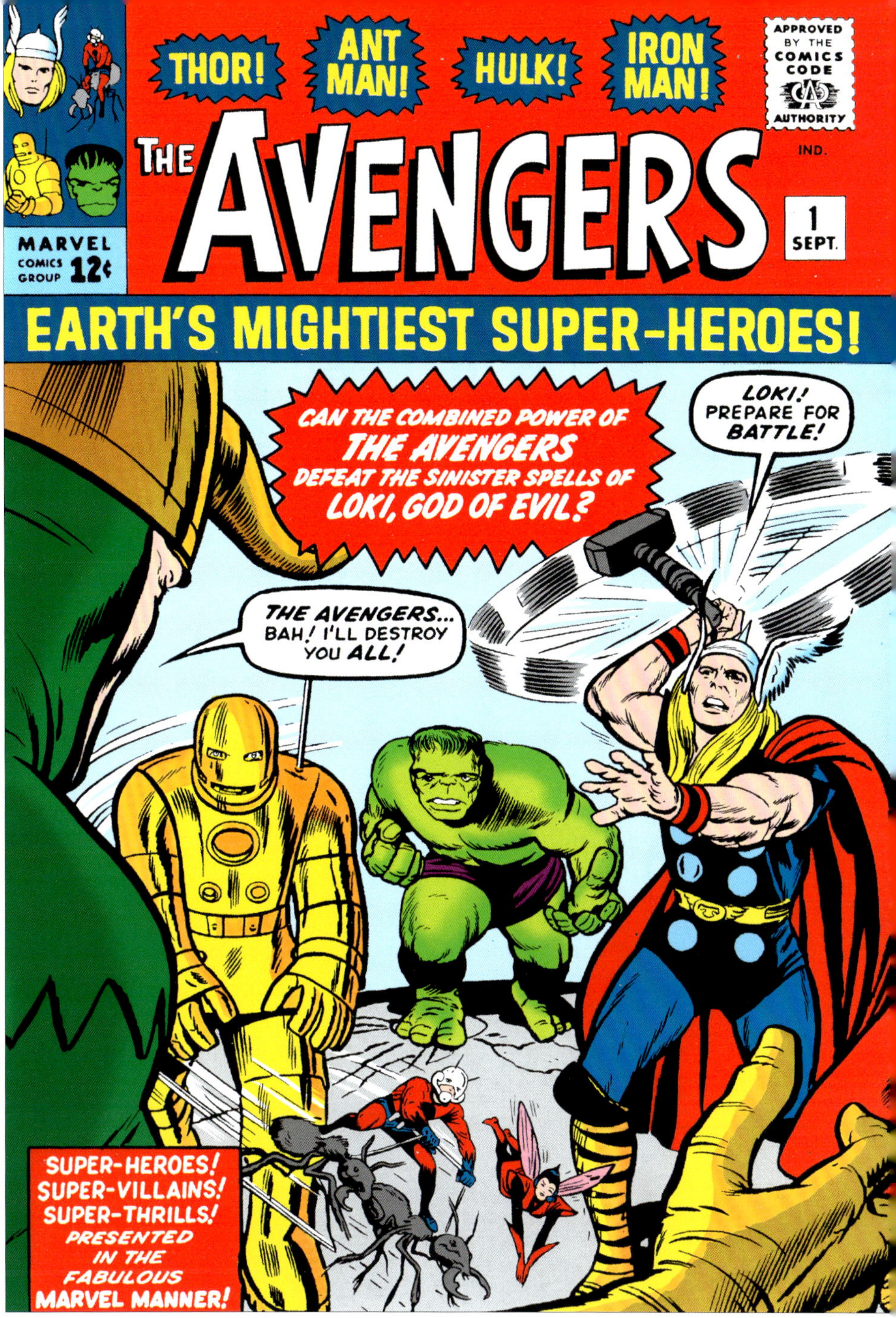

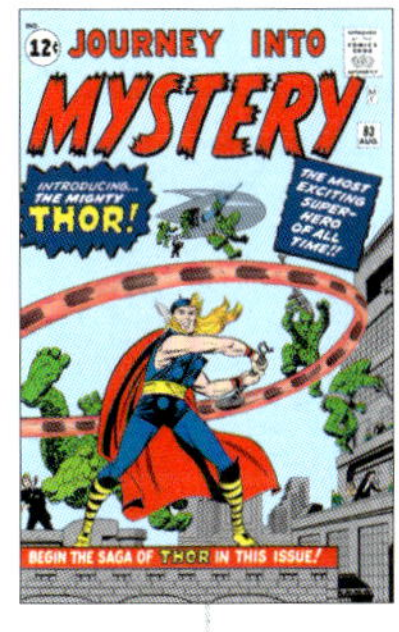

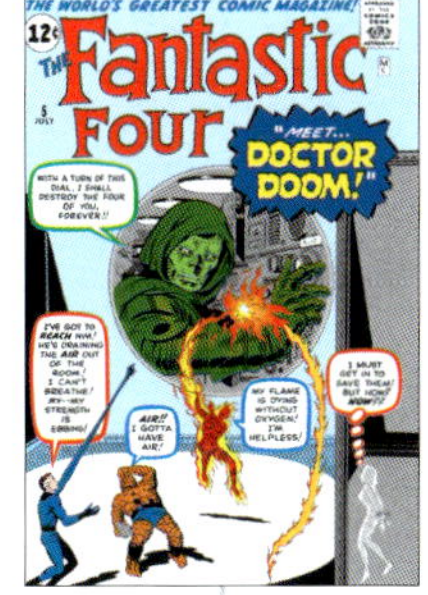

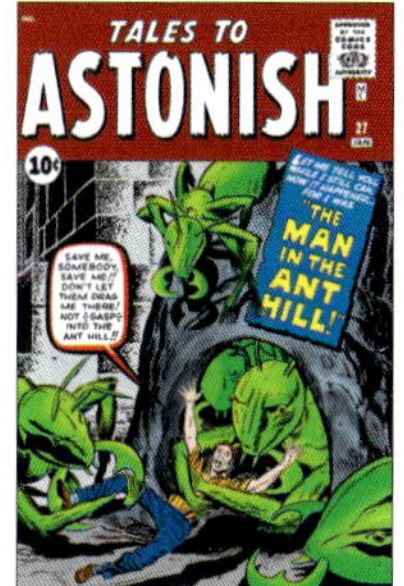

5 JUNE 1962
June 1962 marked the debut of two Marvel mainstays. *Amazing Fantasy #15* featured the origin of Spider-Man, while *Journey into Mystery #83* saw the first appearance of Thor.

JULY 1962
Doctor Doom made his debut in *The Fantastic Four #5*. The FF's worst enemy, Doom, went to college with Mr. Fantastic, then went on to rule the tiny nation of Latveria.

SEPTEMBER 1962
Following his appearance in a self-contained story in *Tales to Astonish #27*, by the time #35 rolled around Ant-Man had become a full-fledged member of the Marvel Universe.

FLAWS AND ALL

Driven by endless creative fury, Stan Lee—with Jack Kirby, Steve Ditko, and a host of others—really was writing the Great American Novel.

The space race between the U.S. and the U.S.S.R. is highlighted in *The Fantastic Four #1*. Script by Stan Lee. Art by Jack Kirby (pencils), George Klein/Christopher Rule (inks),Stan Goldberg (colours), Artie Simek (letters).

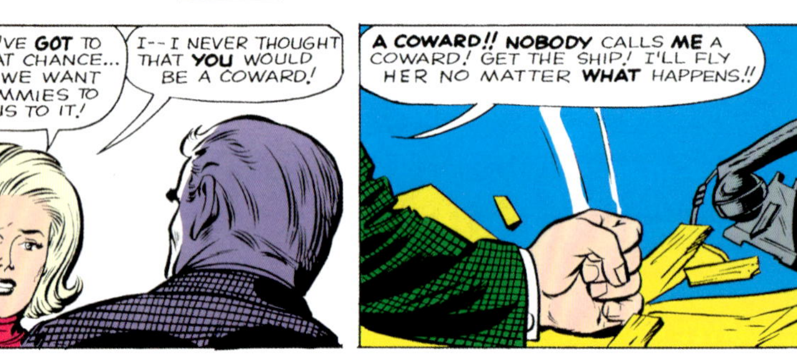

Only this story wasn't told in prose, but in comic books. A long coming-of-age novel in which characters are born, evolve, change, die... and along the way they argue, fight, lie, cheat, and let the insults fly. They seemed to be people just like us, hardly specimens of perfection that could do no wrong. That was the kind of stuff Lee had always wanted to write about. It was also the kind of material that series after series, origin after origin, won over readers across the globe.

Marvel characters could lose even when they won. They were constantly faced with trying dilemmas, forever forced to cope with the latest tragedy. Wasn't it that way for the Fantastic Four? True, they may have been a family, but a dysfunctional one, not the kind they showed in TV commercials. They bickered from

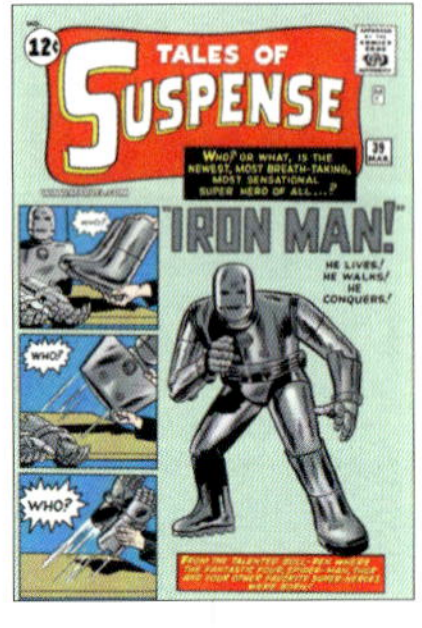

MARCH 1963
Tales of Suspense #39 unveils Iron Man, A.K.A. industrialist Tony Stark, an arms dealer who sells weaponry to the U.S. government.

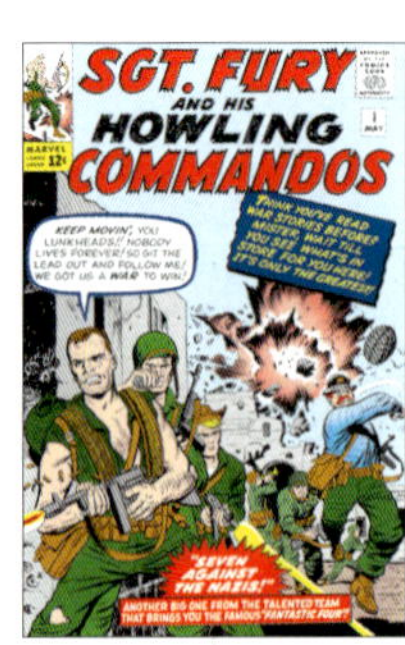

MAY 1963
Lee and Kirby come out with *Sgt. Fury and His Howling Commandos*. The war is on, and Fury would see continued action in the Marvel Universe as head of S.H.I.E.L.D.

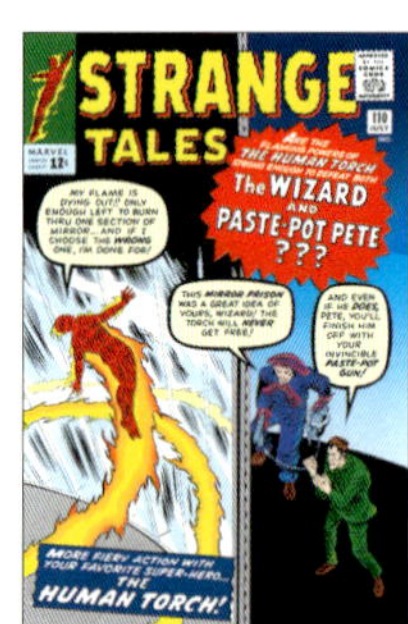

JULY 1963
Strange Tales #110 sees the debut of the counterculture hero, Doctor Strange. Stan Lee and Steve Ditko came up with the character and wrote and drew the character's early stories.

the very first panels. They arranged a trip to the Moon and would waste no time getting there—after all, the United States ran the risk of being overtaken by the Soviet Union. And when they set out, they broke the rules—ultimately to their own detriment, since they had not taken into account a host of variables and wound up paying the price.

Sue Storm criticised Ben Grimm for being a coward because he was afraid something bad might happen on their flight into the unknown—of course, he was right. Their leader, the scientist Reed Richards, who was Sue's boyfriend and Ben's pal, put new conquests and discoveries above all else—an attitude that would cost him dearly. Then there was Johnny Storm, Sue's little brother, who was fiery and impulsive. Cosmic rays turned the four of them into 'elemental' characters: Johnny became the Human Torch (fire); Ben morphed into the Thing (earth, which is to say, rock); Reed would be Mister Fantastic, so stretchable that he appeared to be almost liquid (water); and Sue turned into the Invisible Girl (air). A sense of guilt would loom large over the scenario, beginning with the first Fantastic Four story. Ben, the most tortured and best-loved character among readers, who wound up paying more dearly than anyone when he became more monster than man, would be a constant reminder for Reed of the mistake he made. And there was no lack of awesome Super Villains in their epic adventures, with Doctor Doom and Galactus standing out among them.

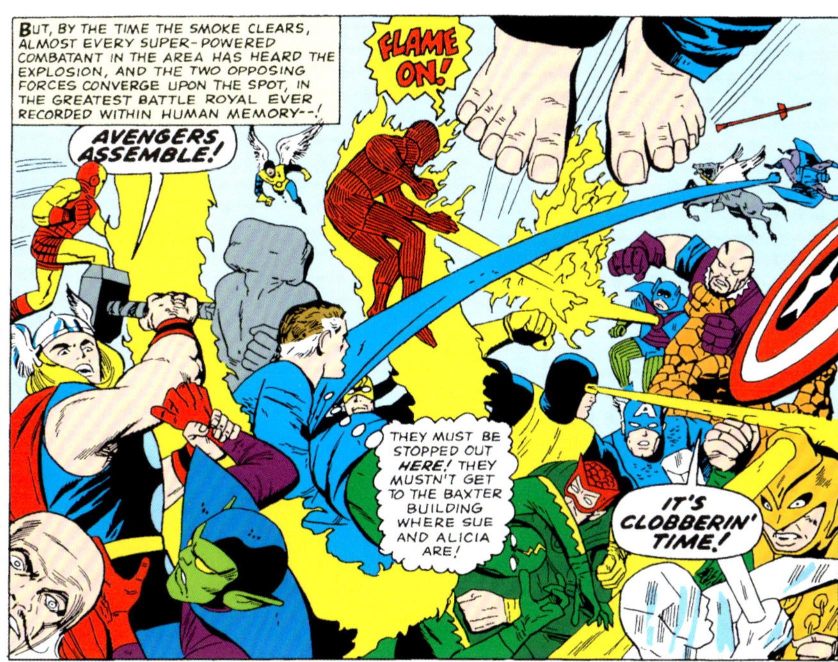

Reed Richard and Sue Storm fight off a host of Marvel villains before they can tie the knot in *The Fantastic Four Annual #3* (October 1965). Script by Stan Lee. Art by Jack Kirby (pencils), Vince Colletta (inks), Stan Goldberg (colours), Artie Simek (letters).

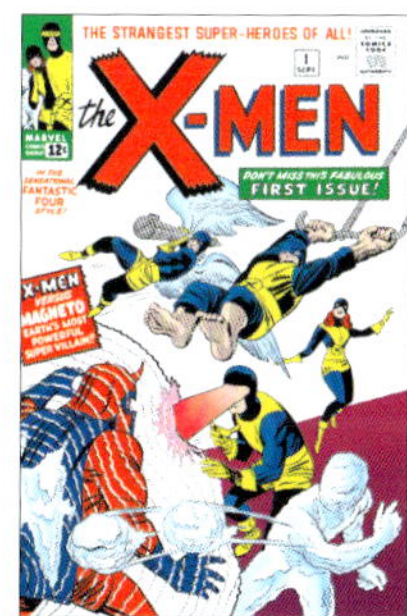

SEPTEMBER 1963
The Avengers and the X-Men, both by Lee and Kirby, make the scene. The former assembled a team of preexisting heroes; the latter showcased a new concept: mutants.

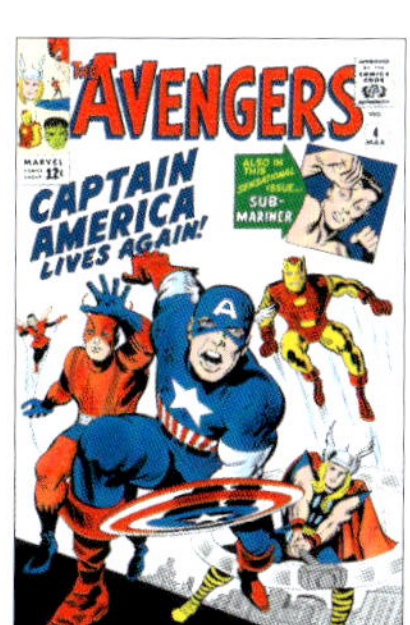

MARCH 1964
A flashback from the Golden Age: In *The Avengers #4* Lee and Kirby bring back Captain America, who had been frozen in the North Atlantic Ocean since World War II. A new Avenger!

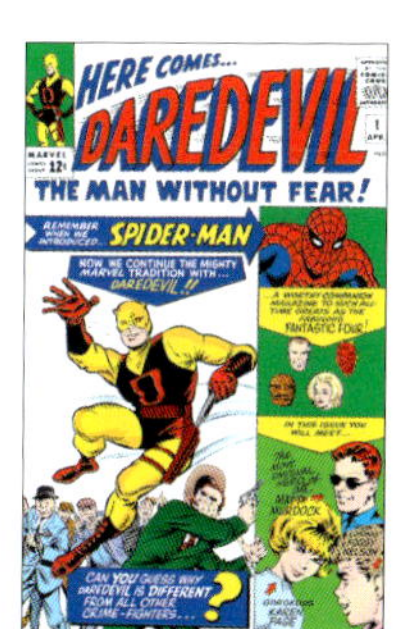

APRIL 1964
The dynamic Daredevil made his debut in his own series, written by Lee and illustrated by Bill Everett (of Sub-Mariner fame). Note Daredevil's original red-and-yellow costume.

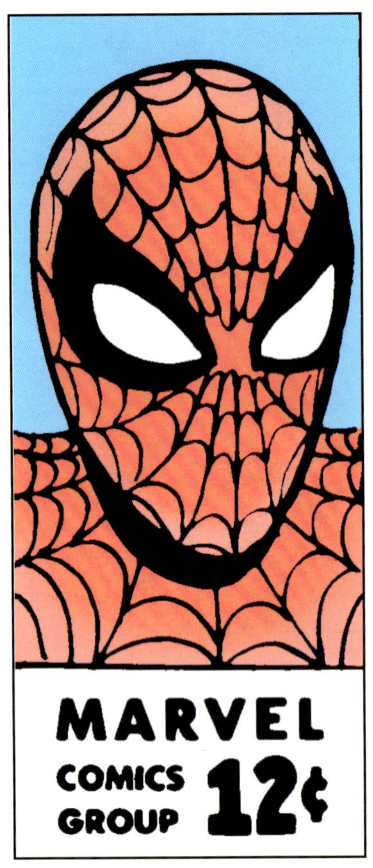

One of the corner boxes that adorned Marvel covers throughout the 1960s. Art by Steve Ditko.

While the Fantastic Four laid the foundations for what would become known as the Marvel Universe, the most popular Super Hero of all—the very symbol of Marvel Comics—would be Spider-Man. Perhaps no other character could claim origins as poetic and intense.

Peter Parker was a nerdy high-school kid. An ace science student, he never fit in and had no friends. His classmates considered him a bookworm, and on top of it all, his parents had died and he lived with his aunt and uncle, his elderly guardians Ben and May. Peter got his super-powers during an experiment, from the bite of a radioactive spider. Peter's new powers were proportional to those of a spider, and like any teenager, he thought only of taking advantage of his 'good luck' and sought to parlay it into some cash in order to help out his poor aunt and uncle. His hubris would cost him dearly, however. Cynical and indifferent, Peter let a thief get away from the scene of a crime he witnessed—little knowing that the same man would wind up killing his uncle during another robbery.

That proved to be Spider-Man's original sin, responsible for the feelings of guilt that would haunt Peter for the rest of his days. Lesson learned, as Lee wrote in the last panel, "With great power there must also come—great responsibility!" Those words summed up the philosophy of a comic-book series that would go on to become a cartoon, a TV series, a live-action movie, an animated movie, a Broadway musical, and an eternal icon of the tragic, losing hero.

The Peter Parker/Spider-Man saga would count on a cast of unparalleled supporting characters. Like J.J. Jameson, publisher of the *Daily Bugle*, who despises Spidey, but buys photos of the hero taken by Parker himself. Then came his friends, like Betty Brant, Gwen Stacy, Mary Jane Watson, Flash Thompson, and Harry Osborn, a melodrama tinged with tragedy, where mourning someone's death turns into a lifelong dedication to helping others.

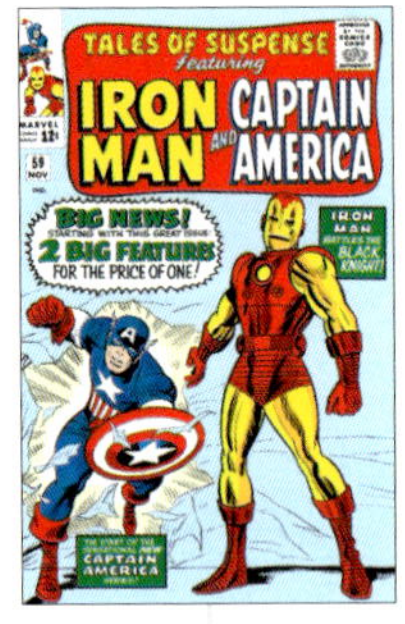

NOVEMBER 1964
Captain America gets his own series, which was actually *Tales of Suspense*, beginning with issue #59, in tandem with Iron Man. Soon each would be headliners.

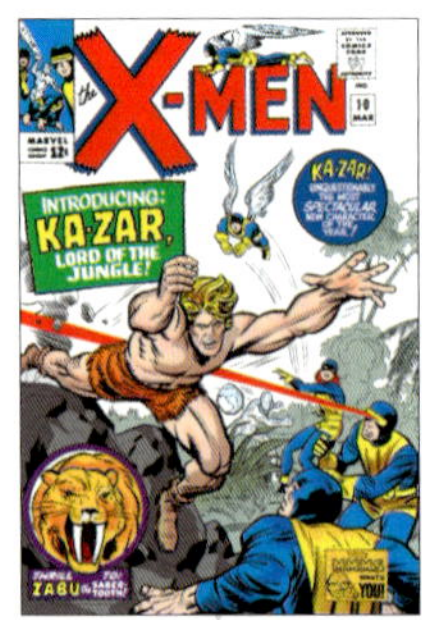

MARCH 1965
Ka-Zar returns from the Golden Age in *X-Men #10*. In the 1930s, this pulp creation appeared in *Marvel Comics #1* with the Human Torch and the Sub-Mariner.

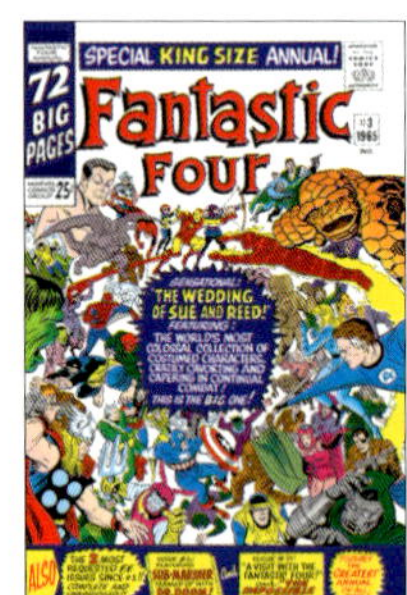

NOVEMBER 1965
In *Fantastic Four Annual #3* Marvel celebrates Reed and Sue's wedding. The happy couple is cheered on by plenty of heroes, but sinister Super Villains also lurk in their midst.

To some extent there is a focus on society's fear of the unpredictable developments in science, as symbolised by the appearance of the radioactive spider. Nuclear radiation would be found at the origin of another legendary Marvel character, the Hulk, along with Cold War and literary influences. Bruce Banner was the scientist who morphed into the musclebound green monster (who at first was grey, a colour that in print did not do justice to this Super Hero, forcing a change). During a military experiment, which went awry thanks to Soviet spy Igor Starsky, Banner was caught in the blast of a gamma bomb while successfully rescuing Rick Jones, a distracted teenager wandering around the New Mexico desert. At night, he transformed into the ornery, super-strong creature known as the Hulk, in a tug of war between split personalities that recalled Robert Louis Stevenson's Dr. Jekyll and Mr. Hyde, with a dash of Boris Karloff's Frankenstein's monster.

But science wasn't always to be feared. Dr. Henry 'Hank' Pym's scientific experiments were portrayed in a positive light. The 'Pym Particles' he discovered had the power to shrink him to almost microscopic dimensions and, later on, to increase his size dramatically. Introducing: Ant-Man, the Super Hero who could 'talk' to ants. Hank teamed up with a rich young heiress, Janet Van Dyne, who became his partner, the Wasp. But life for the scientific genius was torment that

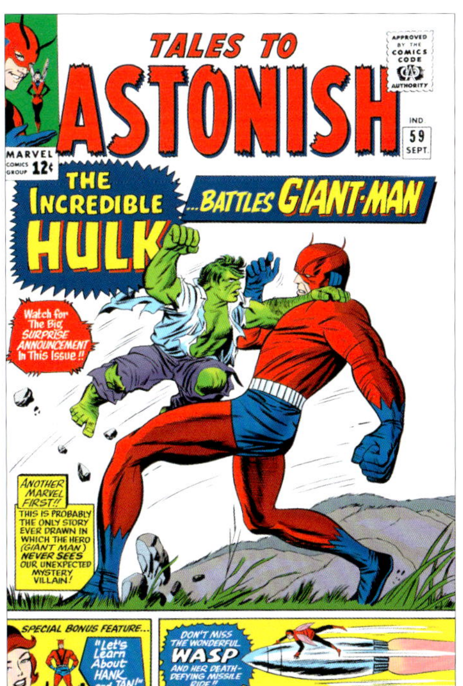

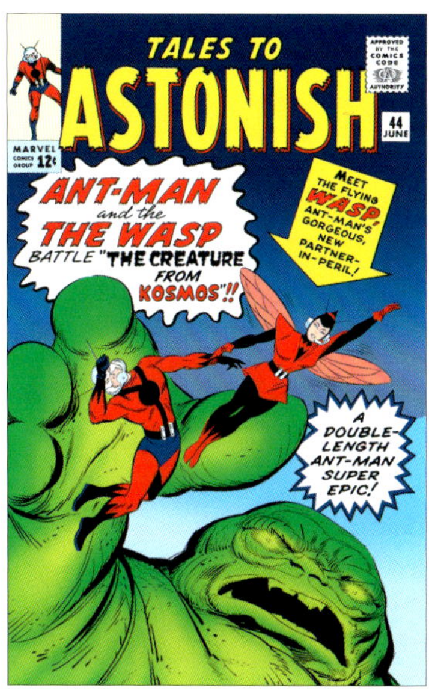

ABOVE
Tales to Astonish #44 (June 1963). Art by Jack Kirby (pencils), Don Heck (inks), Stan Goldberg (colours).

LEFT
Tales to Astonish #59 (September 1964). Art by Jack Kirby.

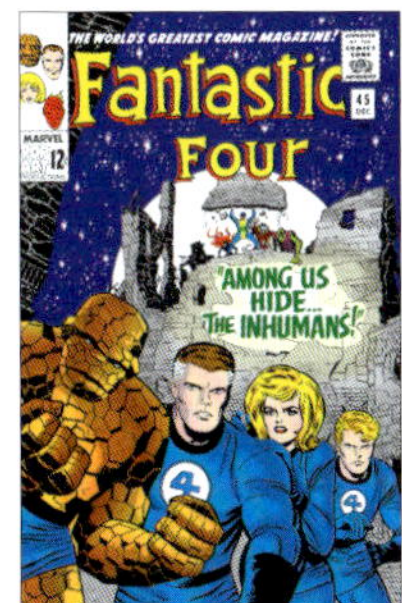

DECEMBER 1965
Month after month, Lee and Kirby continue to redefine comics and creativity with the *Fantastic Four*. Issue #45 saw the debut of the mysterious Inhumans.

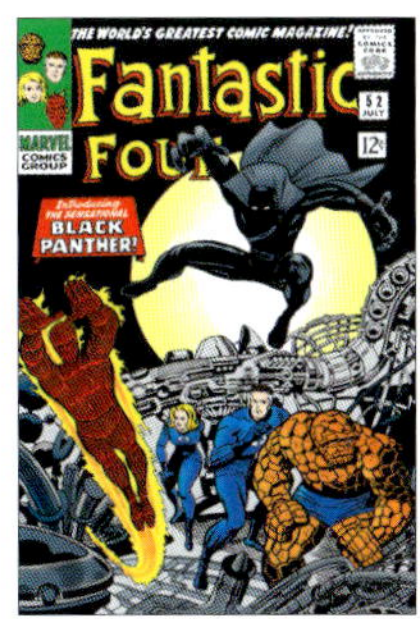

MARCH–JULY 1966
Black Panther, Marvel's first black Super Hero, makes his debut in the pages of *Fantastic Four #52*. He would eventually join the Avengers, and star in his own solo series in the 1970s.

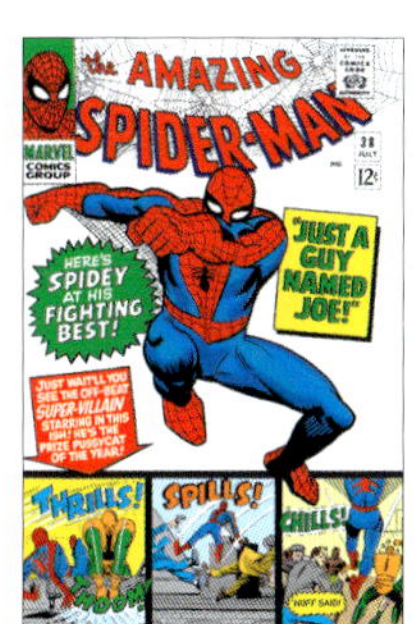

AUGUST 1966
Marvel shake-up: Steve Ditko quits after issue #38 of *The Amazing Spider-Man*. John Romita, Sr. takes the reins with issue #39, ushering in a new era of creativity.

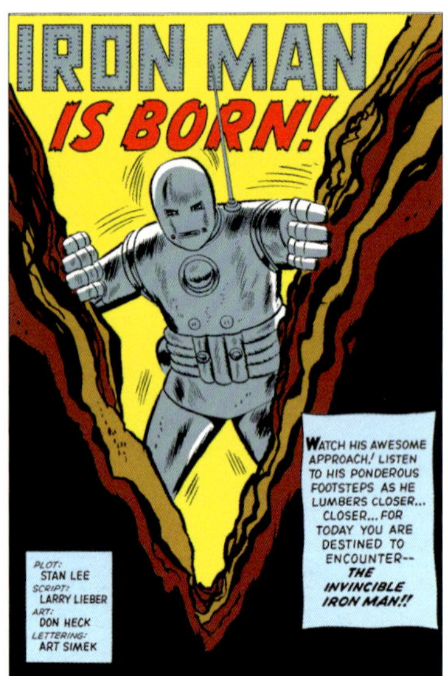

Splash page to *Tales of Suspense #39* (March 1963), the first appearance of Iron Man. Script by Larry Lieber. Art by Don Heck (pencils and inks), Stan Goldberg (colours), and Art Simek (letters).

few Super Heroes are accustomed to. For one thing, he had a habit of changing identities—from Ant-Man to Giant-Man to Goliath to the Yellowjacket. He also involuntarily created his archnemesis Ultron, his 'son' of sorts.

Ever in search of new scenarios and narrative angles, Lee and Kirby turned to the stuff of Norse legends to come up with another illustrious character, Thor. As in all of their creations, the main focus would be the human aspect. It all began in a cave in Norway, where American surgeon Don Blake comes across Thor's hammer, Mjolnir, in the guise of a walking stick. When he bangs it on a rock, Blake is transformed into the Asgardian God of Thunder Thor, son of Odin. In reality, Don Blake never existed. He was only a fictional identity created by Odin as punishment for his son's arrogance, after the wayward lad had become overly powerful and lost all restraint. Odin wiped out his memory and relegated him to an existence that wasn't anything close to the one the blond-haired, invincible god had ever known—a healing man, one who tended to the sick and injured. He learned humility—a lesson Thor would never forget.

If Thor's was the most symbolic and 'moralistic' origin in Marvel history, then Iron Man's was no less intense and involved just as much commitment. Industrialist Tony Stark suffers a life-threatening wound in Vietnam, the brutal and widely unpopular conflict that gripped America throughout the 1960s and early '70s. Tony was cut in the mould of billionaire playboy Howard Hughes—rich, intelligent, good-looking, an incurable lady's man. In the Vietnamese jungle, Stark has an all-too-close encounter with a landmine and is subsequently taken prisoner by a local warlord bent on forcing him to build weapons for the enemy. But to save himself from the shrapnel lodged dangerously close to his heart, Tony, along with fellow prisoner and Vietnamese physicist Yinsen, secretly builds a magnetic chest plate to ward off the threat.

His first somewhat primitive suit of armour gives Stark the power he needs to escape. Later on, that

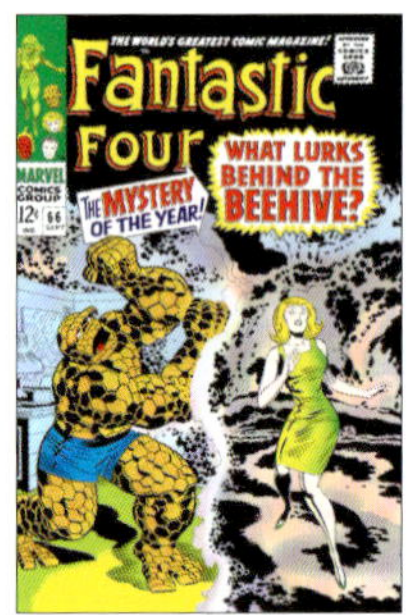

SEPTEMBER 1967
Lee and Kirby are unstoppable: for *Fantastic Four #66* they create another extraordinary Super Hero, Adam Warlock, who was originally called Him.

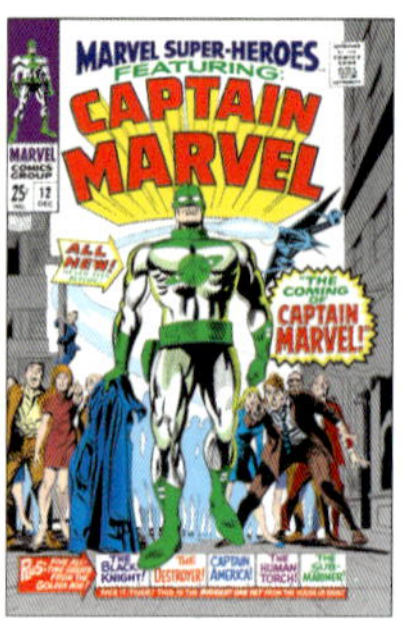

DECEMBER 1967
An unlikely hero from space appears in *Marvel Super-Heroes #12*: Captain Marvel. Created by Lee and Gene Colan, Mar-Vell was a Kree warrior, fascinated by the people of Earth.

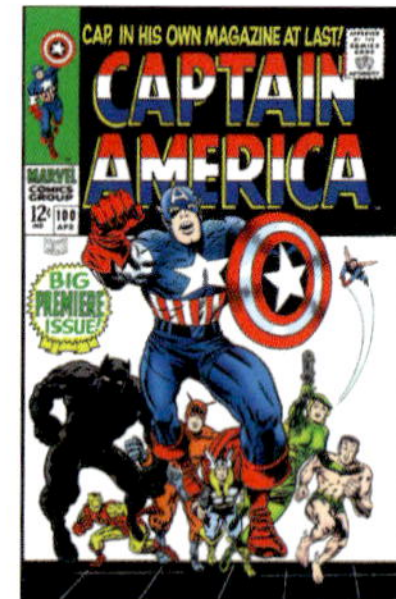

APRIL 1968
Captain America receives his own title in *Captain America #100* (April 1968), with a cover and story penciled by Jack Kirby.

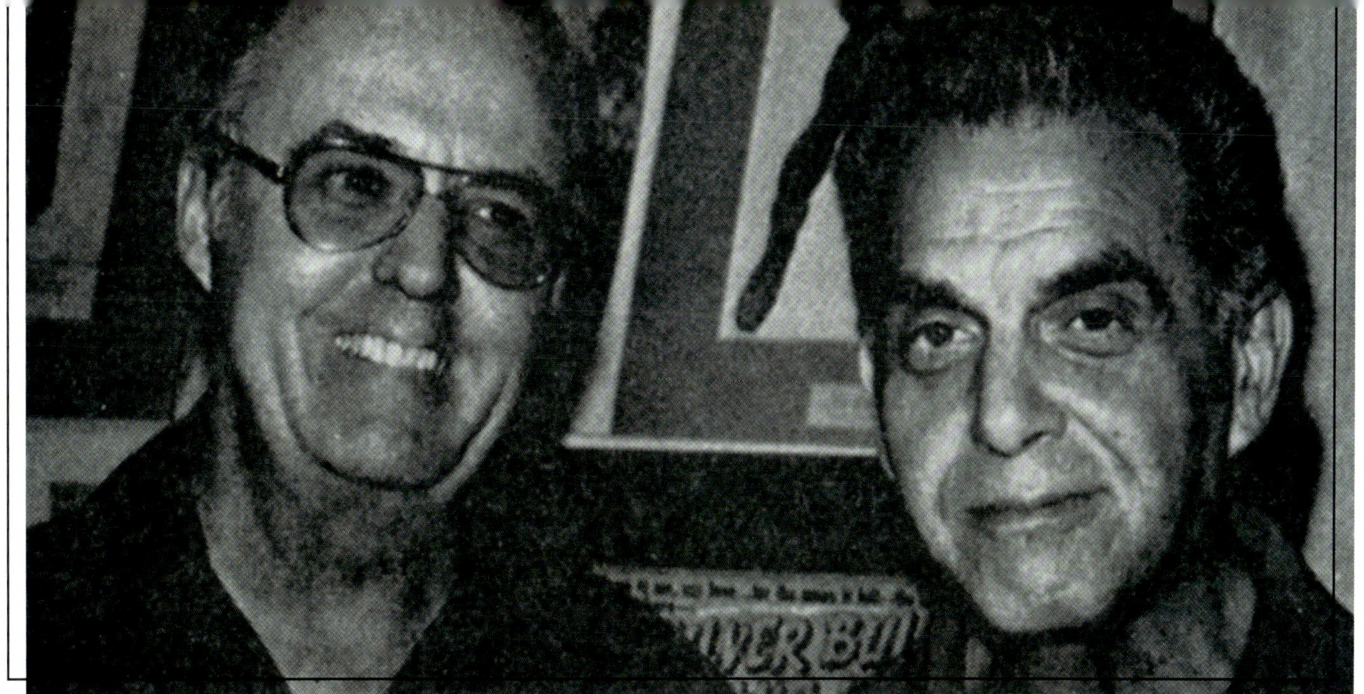

first suit would be replaced by gold, then red-and-gold models that were increasingly high-tech. The stories featuring Tony Stark focused on adult themes. His heart problems remained a constant, his own mortality looming large. He was a unique Super Hero, and lived a tormented existence. He had to be super just to stay alive.

But torment comes in many forms. Thanks to the Super-Soldier Serum, Steve Rogers—Captain America himself—survived 20 years of suspended animation to be revived in the 1960s. But he is a man out of time, a man guided by principles and passions that have more to do with the 1940s than the 1960s. He is haunted by the memory of his old sidekick, Bucky Barnes, whom he believed was killed on their last mission together, and was racked by feelings of guilt over his death. Of course, comic-book readers and movie fans know that Bucky never died, but wound up doing a stint as a secret agent for the Soviets as the Winter Soldier. He's since returned to Captain America's side, and we'll be talking more about him in the chapters to come.

Daredevil was another solitary Super Hero with a heart-rending,

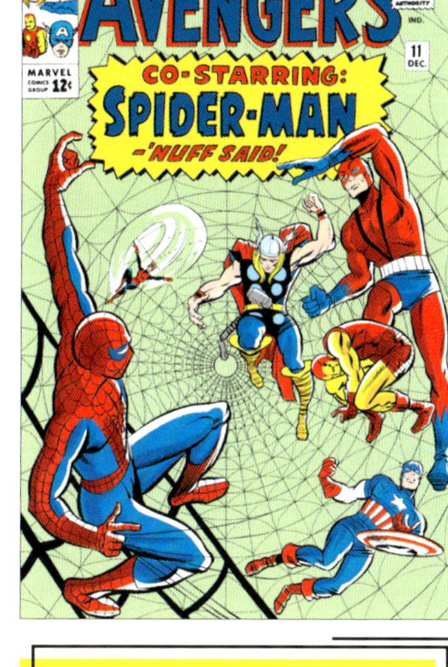

TOP
Joe Sinnott (left) and Jack Kirby, circa 1975.

BOTTOM
The Avengers meet Spider-Man (almost!) in *The Avengers #11* (December 1964). Art by Jack Kirby (pencils) and Dick Ayers (inks).

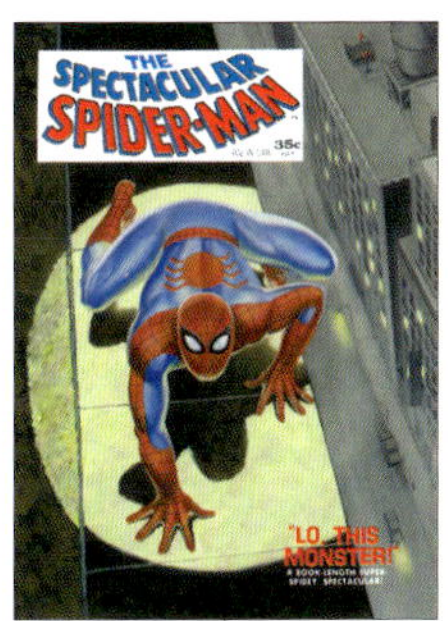

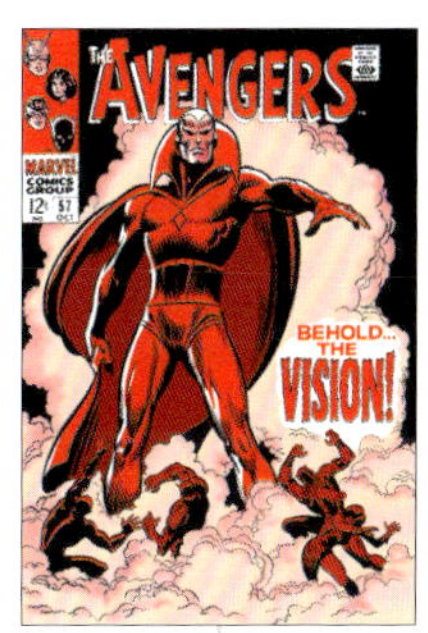

1970

JULY 1968
Lee and Romita come up with a new magazine, *The Spectacular Spider-Man*. Giant-sized and black and white, only two issues were released.

OCTOBER 1968
Two new heroes appear in the pages of *The Avengers*: the Vision, an android with emotions, and Yellowjacket (A.K.A. Hank Pym, the former Ant-Man/Giant-Man).

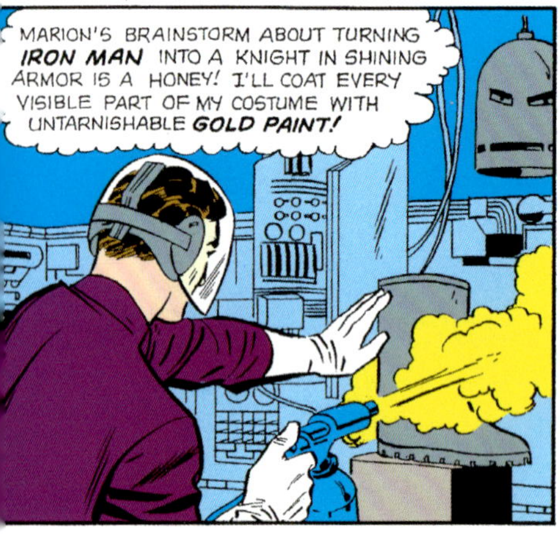

Tony Stark decides on a gold paint job for his Iron Man armour in *Tales of Suspense #40*. Script by Stan Lee and Robert Bernstein. Art by Jack Kirby (pencils), Don Heck (inks), Stan Goldberg (colours), Artie Simek (letters).

melodramatic past. Raised by his father, the hapless boxer, Battlin' Jack Murdock, Matt was blinded after he saved a blind man from an oncoming truck carrying barrels of a radioactive isotope (once again, the atomic menace). The truck crashed and spilled the toxic substance on the brave young hero's face. Though he lost his sight, Matt's other senses were amplified way beyond normal human capacity. Meanwhile, his father was murdered for not taking a dive in the ring. Out of all that wreckage, Daredevil was born. In time, the crime fighter's alter ego Matt would open a law practice with friend Franklin 'Foggy' Nelson.

While Daredevil's ultrakeen senses were the result of an accident, the X-Men would be born with their superpowers—which is to say, the genetic mutations that made them 'different'. And there lies the greatness of the new supergroup, featuring team members Cyclops, Marvel Girl, Beast, Angel, and Iceman. Mutants were a metaphor of discrimination against anyone that might be different, and proved to be a profound and dramatic excursion into teenage angst. The X-Men took their name from their mentor, Professor Charles Xavier, the world's preeminent telepath.

Among the classic characters of the Silver Age, it's impossible to forget Doctor Strange, a practitioner of mystic arts who makes his home in Manhattan's Greenwich Village. His alter ego is one Stephen Strange, formerly a haughty, cynical world-class surgeon, whose career went down the drain after his hands were severely damaged in a car crash. Broke and depressed, Strange tries his luck at a monastery in the Himalayas, where he meets up with the Ancient One, a wise man who teaches him the secrets of mysticism and changes his life forever. Steve Ditko worked with Lee to come up with this unforgettable Super Hero.

Meanwhile, by 1963 Lee and Kirby had created former World War II commando Nick Fury, now an eyepatch-wearing, cigar-smoking spy—a James Bond–type character who heads the fictional

Captain America is revived in the then-modern 1960s in *The Avengers #4* (March 1964). Script by Stan Lee. Art by Jack Kirby (pencils), George Roussos (inks), Stan Goldberg (colours), Artie Simek (letters).

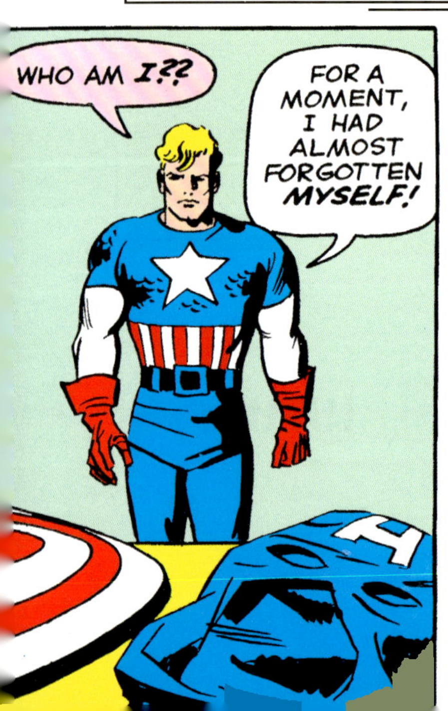

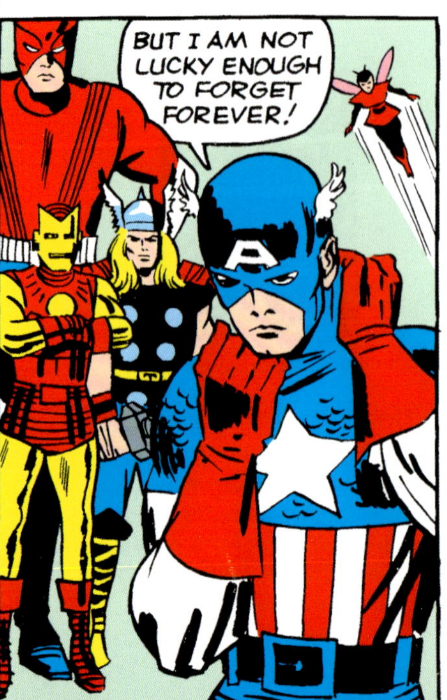

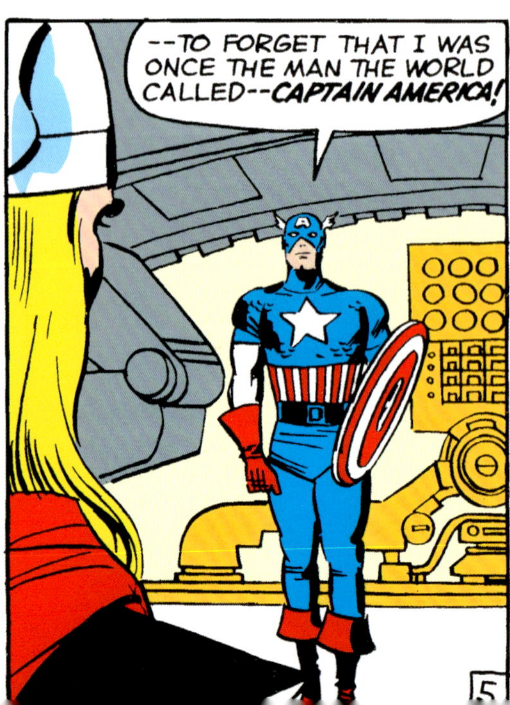

espionage organisation known as S.H.I.E.L.D. (Supreme Headquarters International Espionage Law-Enforcement Division).

Kirby's far-reaching imagination and Lee's taste for dialogue proved to be an irresistible combination. Together, they created the Black Panther, one of the bravest and most well-known Super Heroes. Black and African, his character was born during the heyday of the American civil rights movement. His alter ego T'Challa was king of Wakanda, a tiny but highly developed country in the heart of Africa, where technology was more advanced than in the western world.

Lee and Kirby continued to take chances and amaze. The Inhumans were a group of human beings who possessed bizarre super-powers and lived hidden from the rest of mankind in the Himalayan city of Attilan. Inhumans like Black Bolt, Gorgon, Karnak, Triton, and Medusa would take part in the adventures of the Fantastic Four.

Then there was the ultra-intense, ultra-tragic Silver Surfer, A.K.A. Norrin Radd, from the planet Zenn-La, who made his first appearance in *Fantastic Four #48*. He travelled through space on a silver surfboard—taking his cue from the surf craze at that time—and sacrificed himself to save his people, who were threatened by Galactus, the 'world devourer'. The Silver Surfer serves as his herald until Galactus reaches Earth, where, won over by the humanity of the planet's inhabitants, the Silver Surfer rebels against him.

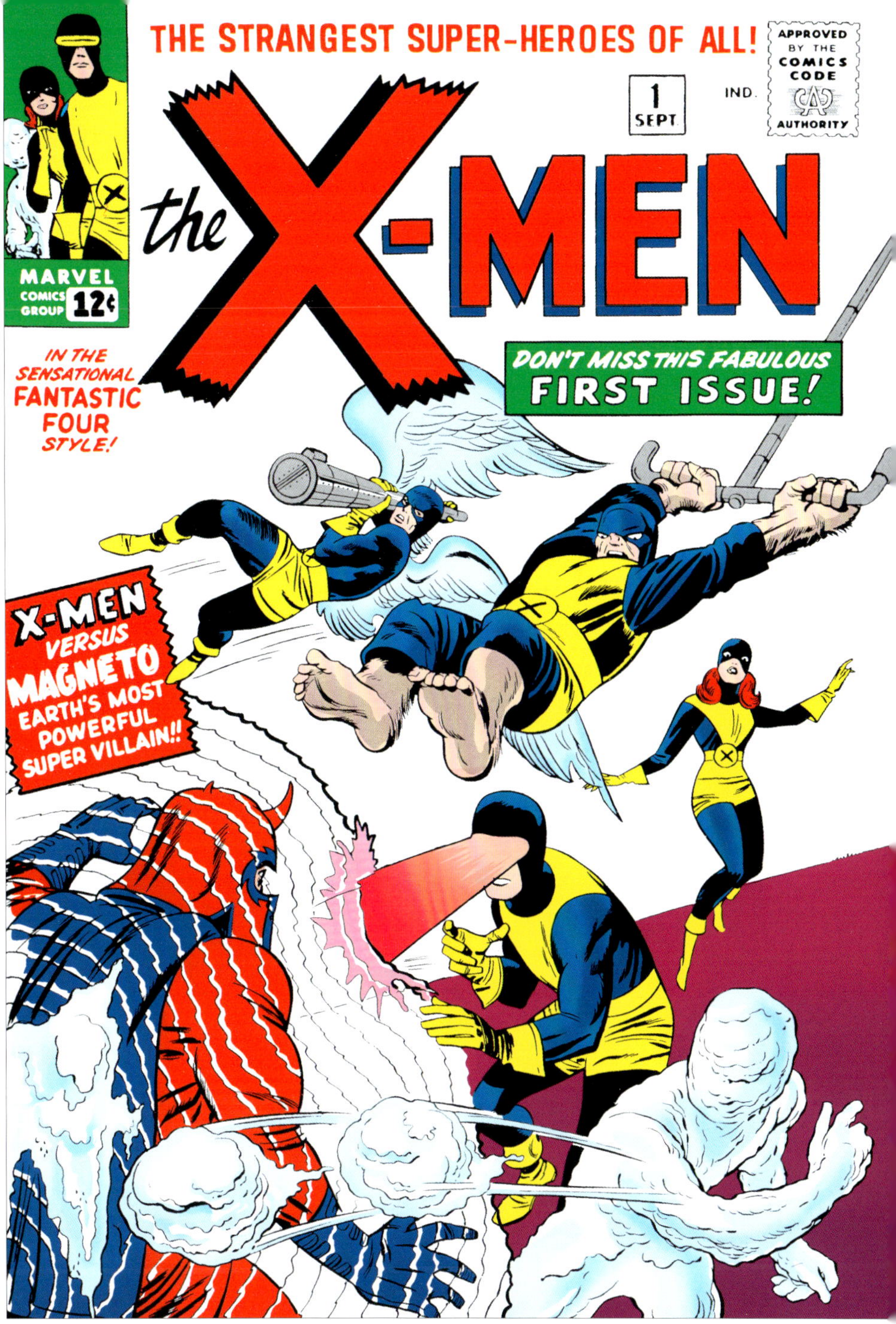

The X-Men #1 (September 1963). Art by Jack Kirby (pencils), Sol Brodsky (inks).

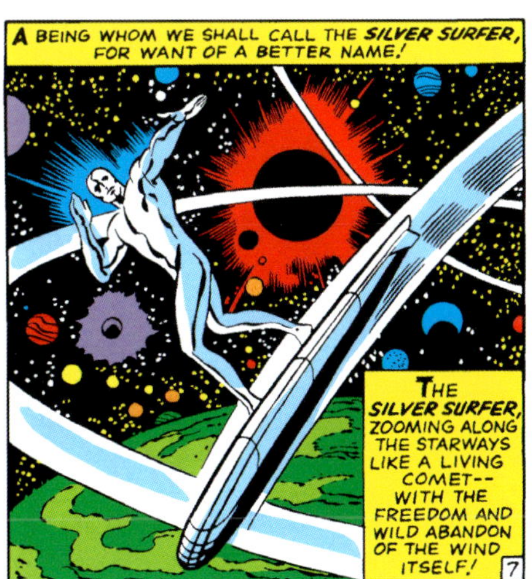

The Silver Surfer appears for the first time in *Fantastic Four #48* (March 1966). Script by Stan Lee. Art by Jack Kirby (pencils), Joe Sinnott (inks), Artie Simek (letters).

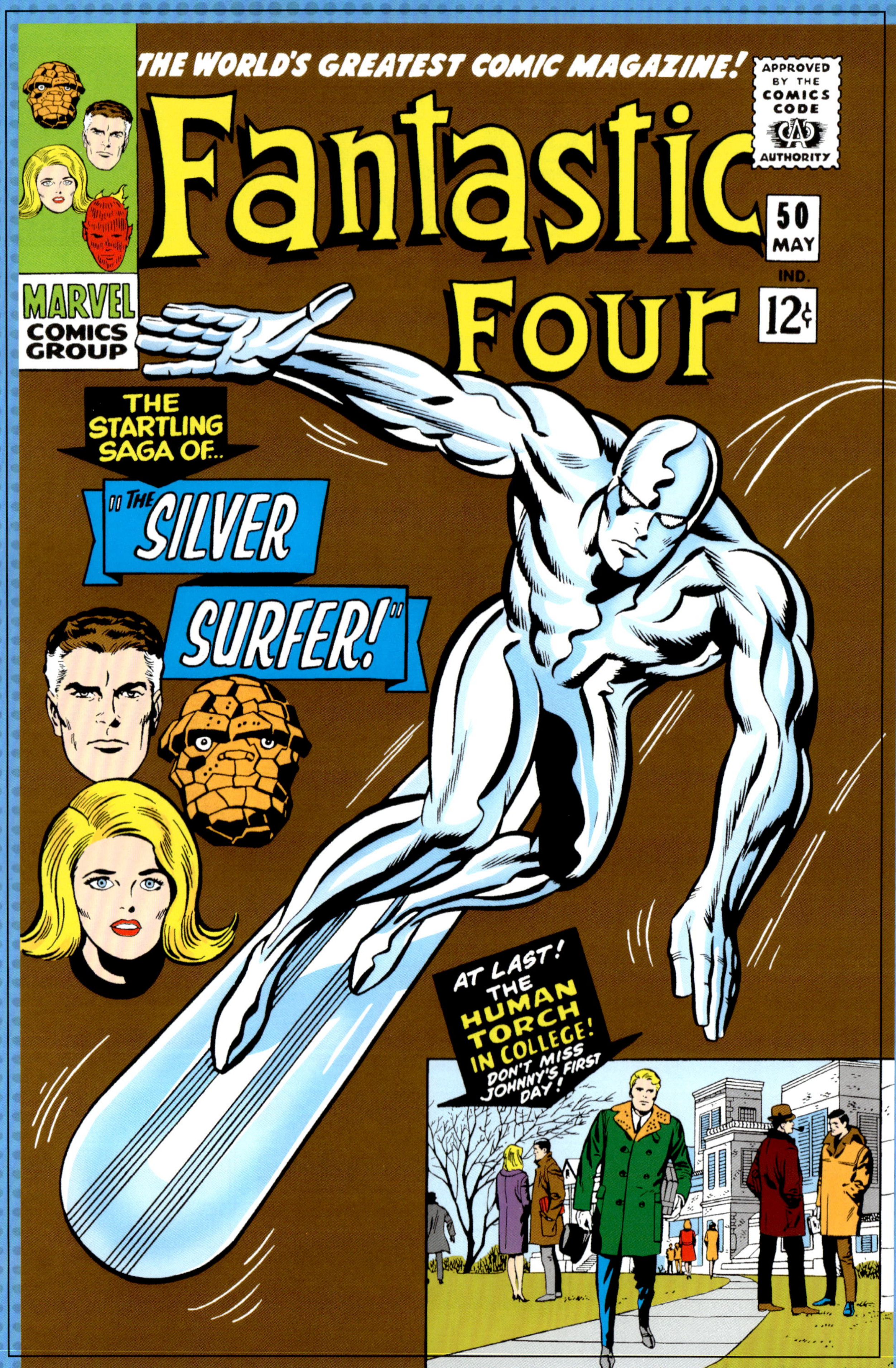
THE WORLD'S GREATEST COMIC MAGAZINE!
APPROVED BY THE COMICS CODE AUTHORITY
Fantastic Four
50 MAY
IND. 12¢
MARVEL COMICS GROUP
THE STARTLING SAGA OF...
"THE SILVER SURFER!"
AT LAST! THE HUMAN TORCH IN COLLEGE! DON'T MISS JOHNNY'S FIRST DAY!

THE MERRY MARVEL BULLPEN

With the rise of the Marvel Universe came the legend of the Marvel Bullpen—the men and women who created the stories the fans loved.

He came to symbolise Marvel Comics. The front man, the spokesman, the poster boy. He was but a teenager when he first set foot in the offices of Martin Goodman's Timely Publications, and for the rest of his life would remain a seminal figure in the world of comic books. Stan 'the Man' Lee left us in 2018, but until the end, he revelled in making cameo appearances in the live-action movies that featured characters he had co-created, to the joy of fans old and new.

The perfection of Marvel's creations lies in the fact that the writers and artists were so willing to share their art, their genius, and their amazing skills. It was one of those situations where the whole is definitely greater than the sum of its parts. There's another comparison we might make in order to underscore that idea. Founding fathers Lee and Kirby were to Marvel what John Lennon and Paul McCartney were to the Beatles. Certain chords and sounds may be the hallmarks of either John or Paul, but the final products, true works of art and beauty, can only be attributed to the both of them.

However, there is one thing we can be sure of, and that is how irreplaceable Lee was in his role as editor. He was the one who chose the pencillers and inkers, his was the last word regarding which direction stories would take when he wrote the dialogue for panels whose artwork had already been completed. Lee himself invented an approach to working together that was on the surface chaos, but in reality harnessed the ultimate creativity of the artists. This was the so-called 'Marvel Method', born out of the demands made by a particular publishing situation. Marvel started out as a small publishing outfit,

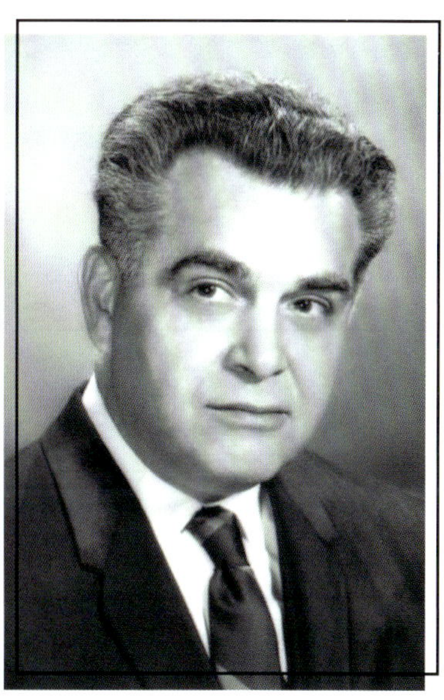

Studio photo of Jack Kirby, circa 1969-1970.

The Silver Surfer appears on the cover of *Fantastic Four #50* (May 1966). Art by Jack Kirby (pencils), Joe Sinnott (inks), and Stan Goldberg (colours).

CORNER BOXES

A few months earlier, on the already dazzling, modern covers, so dynamic and action-packed that they practically told entire stories by themselves, something new appeared in the upper left corner box. For the very first time, that little rectangle contained the faces of the Super Heroes featured in that issue. Lee attributed the concept of the corner boxes to Steve Ditko. A reader from Ohio sent congratulations for that corner box, to which letter Lee replied, "Steve was the one who came up with that, and we're grateful to him for it." For decades, these corner boxes would be associated with the covers of Marvel Comics.

with a small staff. Nearly everything was written by Lee, including the synopses—plots—for his artists. If he had relied on traditional methods, which called for full scripts, deadlines would have been missed. There would have been no Marvel Comics at all.

This, of course, was possible because Lee's artists were the best in the business, capable of writing stories as they went along. And as those stories materialised, pencillers and inkers turned into something like movie directors. Lee would write a one- or two-page plot, or, if time was of the essence, might even convey the message over the phone, or act out a story in front of the artists right there in his office.

Artists would then expand upon the original idea, adding or subtracting scenes, perhaps scribbling notes for the dialogue in the margins, as they pencilled stories of 20 or more pages. Once the artwork was finished, it would go back to Lee, who filled in the panels with dialogue like no one else could. The words he put in characters' mouths were brilliant, funny, emphatic, tragic, human, entertaining. This was the innovation that set Marvel apart. Stories were built in layers, freewheeling, one-of-a-kind masterpieces.

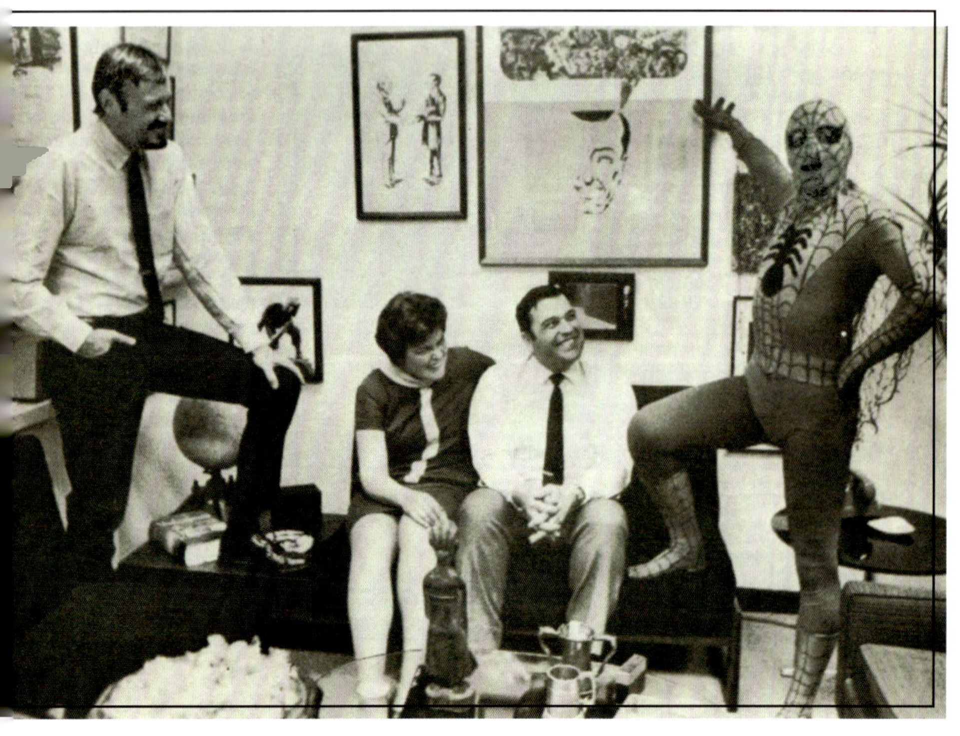

The Marvel Bullpen in the mid-1960s: (from left to right) Stan Lee, Marie Severin, John Romita, Sr., and Roy Thomas (as Spider-Man).

Lee worked as Marvel's editor in chief and main writer until 1972, when the new ownership promoted him to publisher. But in the meantime, he had hired his right-hand man, young Roy Thomas, an English teacher from Missouri—not to mention a big comics fan, well-versed in the Golden Age, with literary aspirations of his own. Thomas had come to New York to work for the Distinguished Competition, but after spending a harrowing week under Mort Weisinger, the *Superman* editor who was notoriously difficult to work with, he wrote Lee asking if they could meet. Lee wasted no time in replying. The two met, and Lee, after testing out Thomas's writing skills, offered him a job on his staff. Thomas would go on to become Lee's most in-synch collaborator, and took up Lee's work on projects involving the Fantastic Four, Spider-Man, the Avengers, and other characters.

For the first time, comic-book writers and artists had achieved

MEET THE GANG IN THE MERRY MARVEL BULLPEN!

(Our fearless answer to those who claim we're Martians!)

let's polish off the big brass . . .

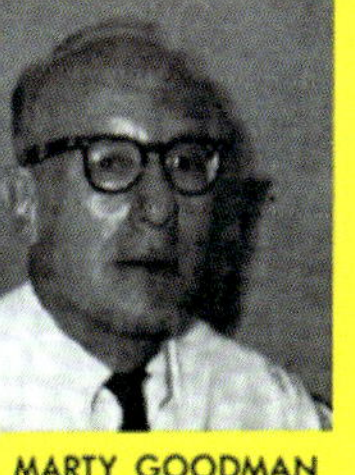

MARTY GOODMAN
Publisher
Guardian Angel

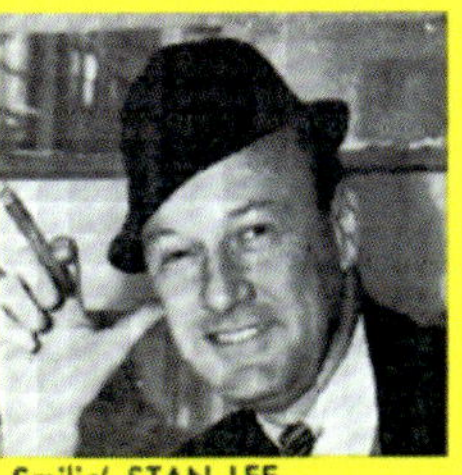

Smilin' STAN LEE
Writer/Editor
Bullpen Boss

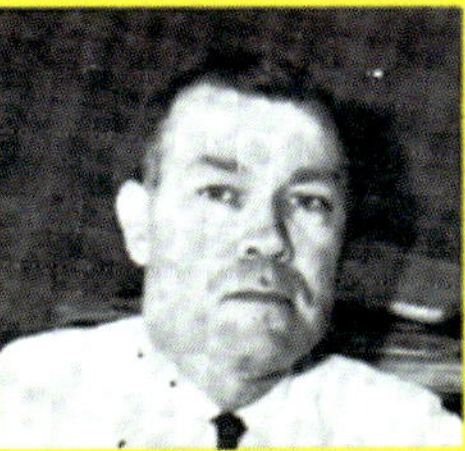

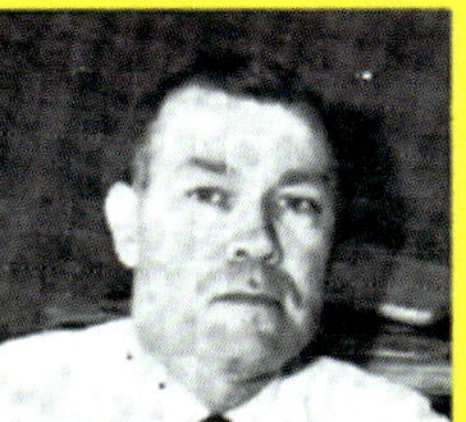

Joyful JOHNNY HAYES
Business Manager
Kibitzer de Luxe

ow, our own madcap pencil pushers and ink splatterers:
(In alphabetical order—to prevent a possible riot!)

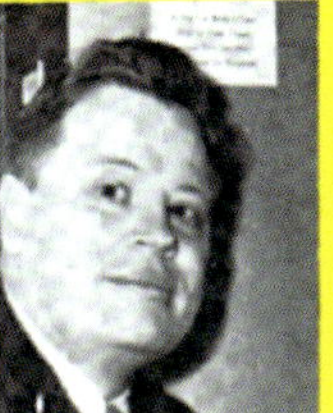

DICK AYERS

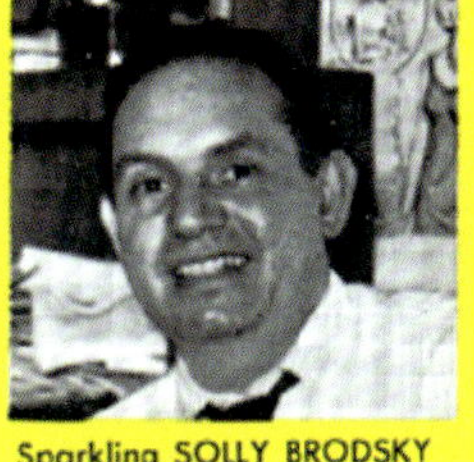

Sparkling SOLLY BRODSKY

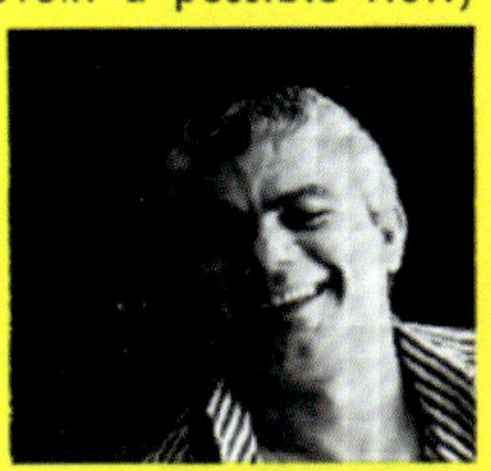

Valiant VINCE COLLETTA

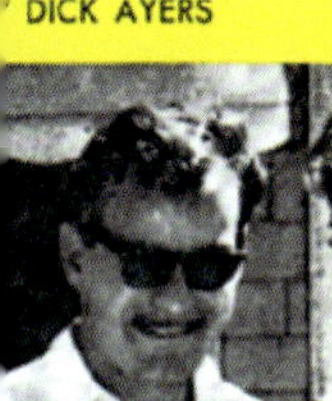

STAN G.

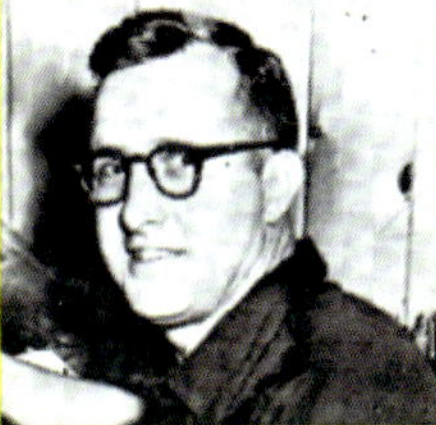

Affable AL HARTLEY

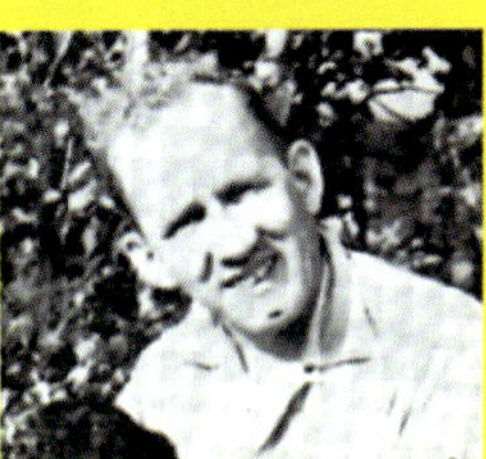

Debonaire DON HECK

Joyful JACK KELLER

Jolly ol' JACK KIRBY

Laughin' LARRY LIEBER

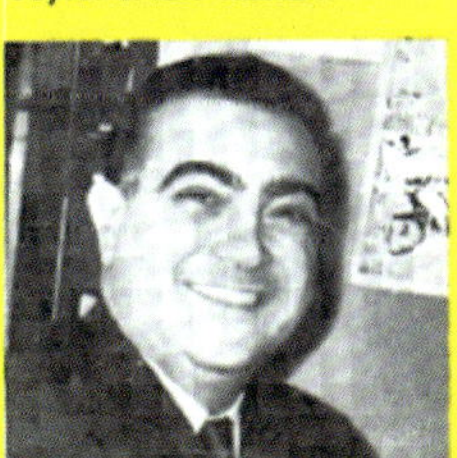

Jovial JOE ORLANDO

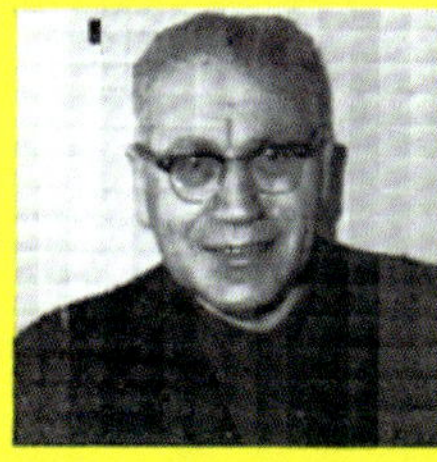

Peerless PAUL REINMAN

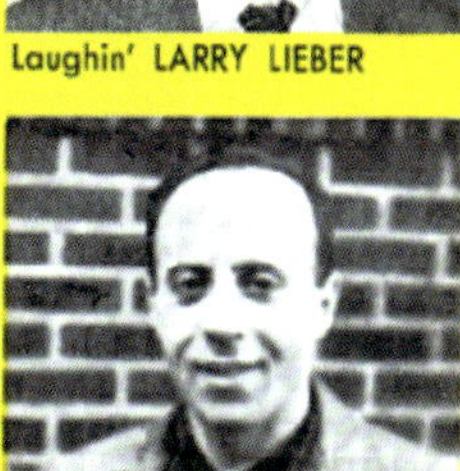

Sprightly SAM ROSEN

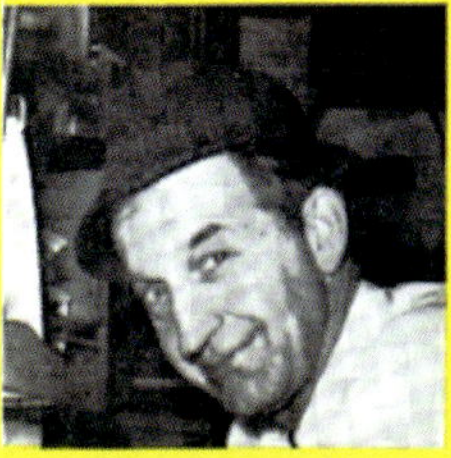

Adorable ARTIE SIMEK

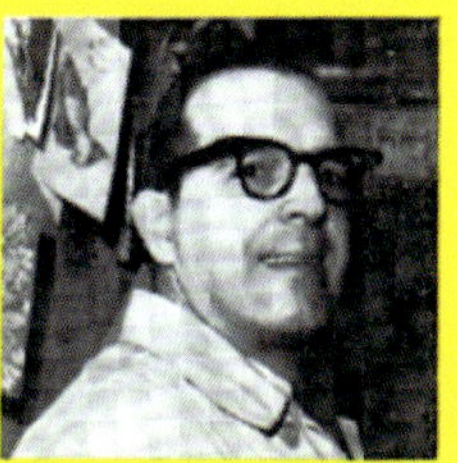

Cheerful CHIC STONE

A few of our bullpen buddies were out of town when these pix were taken—so we'll try to print their pans later on. (A sneaky way to coax you to read all our future issues!)

And now, we present our ever-lovin' glamor department . . .

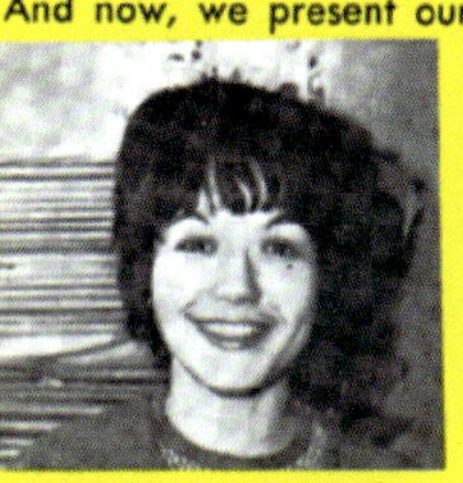

Fabulous FLO STEINBERG
Corresponding Secy.
Gal Friday

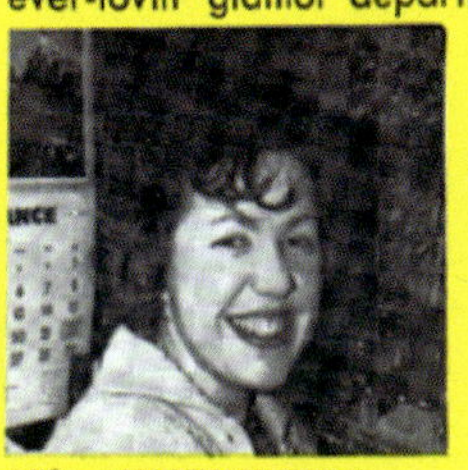

Nifty NANCY MURPHY
Subscriptions
Overseas Mailings

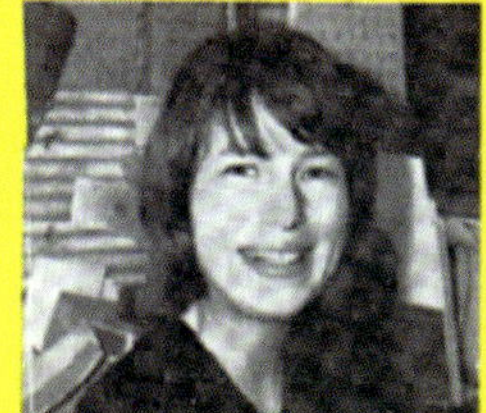

Dazzling DEBBY ACKERMAN
Campus Rep.
Student Surveys

The Marvel Bullpen from the pages of Marvel Comics.

celebrity status. Until then, their names were practically unknown to fans. In the 1950s, EC Comics had made some strides with regard to informing readers as to the artistic components involved, but Lee ushered in the concept of turning artists and authors into stars, with their names appearing on opening splash pages, oftentimes with amusing nicknames: Jack 'the King' Kirby, 'Rascally' Roy Thomas, Gene 'the Dean' Colan, 'Jazzy' John Romita, 'Sturdy' Steve Ditko, Stan 'the Man' Lee...

Jack Kirby and Steve Ditko were Marvel's big guns. Kirby was considered a model to follow, known for his cinematographic imagery and larger-than-life portrayals, an emphatic expressionism that revelled in large-size panels, muscular bodies, and kinetic lines. With his cigar, his smile, and his Lower East Side spontaneity, Kirby could very well have been one of his own characters—Ben Grimm and the Thing might be considered his comic-book counterpart. Ditko, on the other hand, was introverted, refined, a fan of Ayn Rand—the author who, to put it very succinctly, shunned nuances and viewed things pretty much in black and white. Indeed, his Spider-Man character reflects those trademarks.

At least in Spidey's first 38 stories. After which, Ditko packed up and left

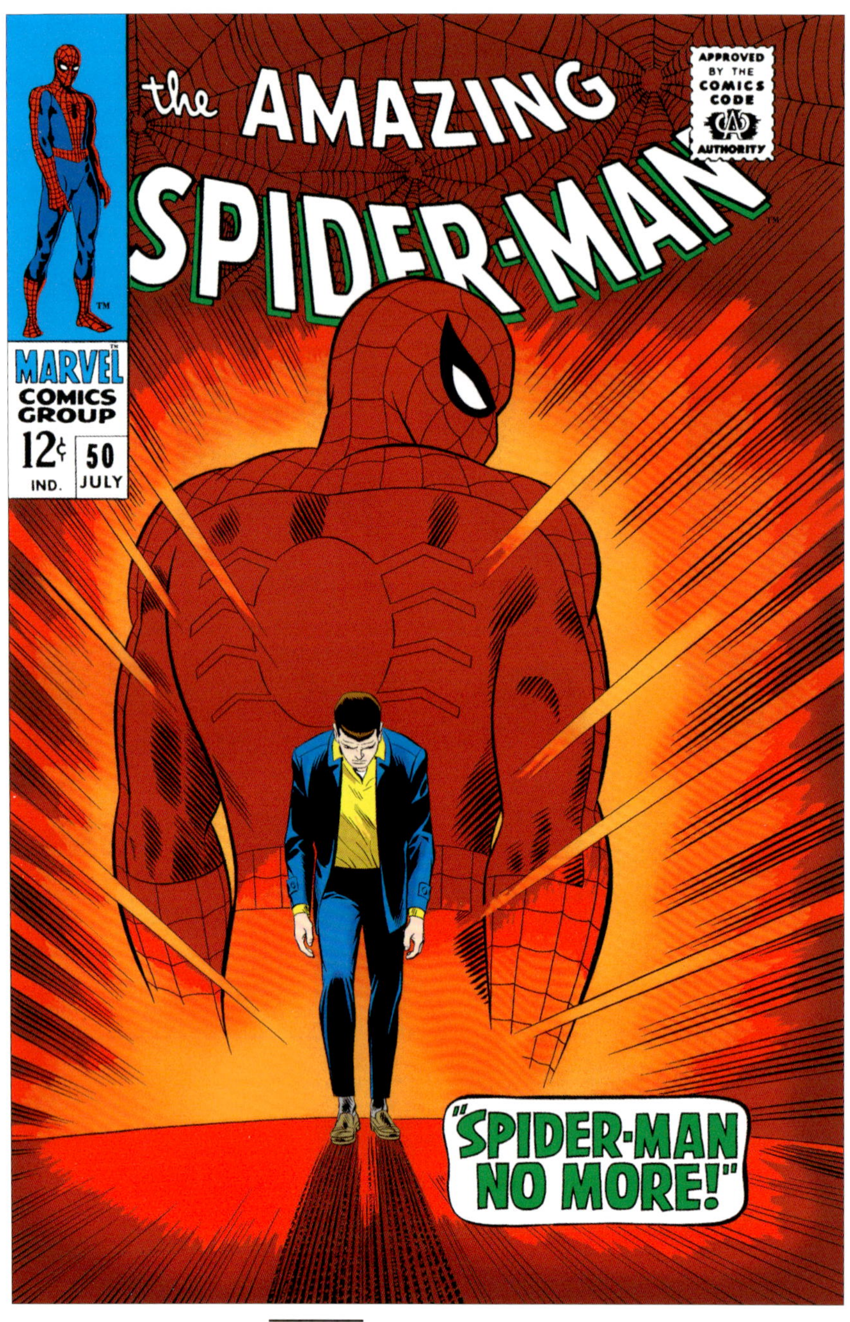

The Amazing Spider-Man #50 (July 1967). Art by John Romita, Sr. (pencils and inks), Stan Goldberg (colours).

Marvel (though he would return in the 1970s, and continued working for Marvel through the 1990s). Ditko was considered a master storyteller. His pages typically contained nine panels, three to a row, treating readers to unsurpassed readability. Ditko's departure could have spelled disaster for Marvel. Spider-Man had probably become its best-loved character—how would readers take it? Fortunately, Lee was ready for anything. He had recently hired John Romita, Sr., who had cut his teeth on romance comics and knew how to draw pretty women and magnetising men. Although Romita had begged Stan to limit his duties to inking, he was called on to pencil Daredevil—the urban-set stepping-stone to Spider-Man. Under Romita, the wall-crawler took on a more glamorous and pleasing appeal. Gone was Peter Parker's awkwardness, and Spider-Man soon became Marvel's best-selling Super Hero.

Year after year, the House of Ideas, as Marvel came to be known, edged ever closer to the sales figures achieved by the Distinguished Competition, until Marvel finally took the lead in 1972. DC was puzzled over the secret behind Marvel's success, and in vain they tried to imitate their compelling graphics and storytelling. They never realised that it was the complexity of Marvel's characters that made the difference. They weren't the kind of Super Heroes who hid behind detached alter egos to conceal their identities. Rather, they were real people who, caught up in exceptional circumstances, became Super Heroes despite themselves. The key, then, to Marvel's success was its characters and the people who told their stories.

Two of the biggest stars at this time had to have been John Buscema and Gene Colan. Buscema was a refined artist skilled in depicting anatomy. Known as the

Michelangelo of comic-book art, his mark became Marvel's mark. He and Lee eventually collaborated on the book *How to Draw Comics the Marvel Way*—written by Lee, artwork by Buscema. From Thor to the Fantastic Four to the Avengers, Buscema's touch became a hallmark of greatness. In the 1970s he'd conquer the world with his interpretation of Conan the Barbarian. His approach contrasted with the classic style of Gene Colan, the artist behind the beloved *Daredevil* series. He was known for his fleeting, ethereal touch, where shadows and movement reigned. Considering how far apart their styles were, Colan was among a select group of artists that Lee kept from basing his work on Kirby's.

Jim Steranko was yet another world-class comic-book artist at Marvel. He hailed from a rough-and-tumble background in Reading, Pennsylvania, and had spent his early days working any number of odd jobs to get by—he is even said to have earned a living as a fire eater and a magician. Steranko had a psychedelic style and preferred futuristic layouts. He was a visionary whose work on Nick Fury stories (in *Strange Tales*, and the *Nick Fury, Agent of S.H.I.E.L.D.* series) broke new ground.

Then came many more behind-the-scenes figures, such as Larry Lieber, the writer who helped create Iron Man and Thor; artist Don Heck; Joe Sinnott, the master inker who handled Kirby's Fantastic Four panels; and people like Dick Ayers, Wally Wood, Paul Reinman, Werner Roth, Herb Trimpe (his Hulk series remains a classic), and John Severin, a superbly sleek artist who had previously worked for EC, and his sister, Marie, known for her eye-catching covers and extraordinary sense of humour.

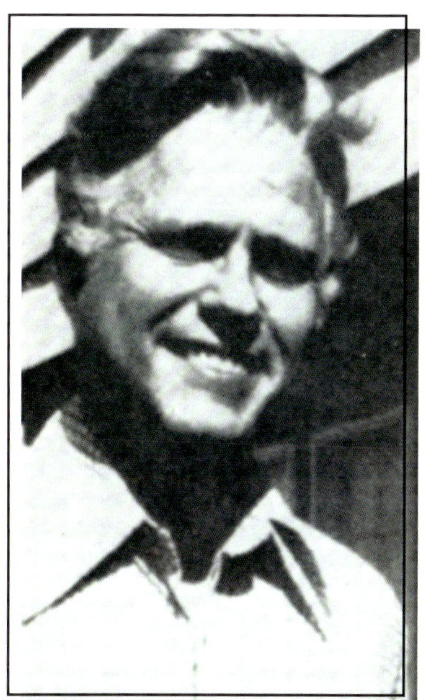

ABOVE
Artist Gene Colan.

BELOW
Featurette from *Marvel Treasury Edition #1: The Spectacular Spider-Man* (1974). Gerry Conway (writer), Marie Severin (art).

EXTRA **DAILY BUGLE** FINAL ★★★★

THE PICTURE NEWSPAPER

.1. No.1. New York, N.Y. 10017, Tuesday, June 18, 1974. WEATHER: Mostly sunny, breezy, warm

n Lee and Steve Ditko Introduce reen Goblin in Spider-Man #14

. THIS, AND THE INCREDIBLE HULK, TOO

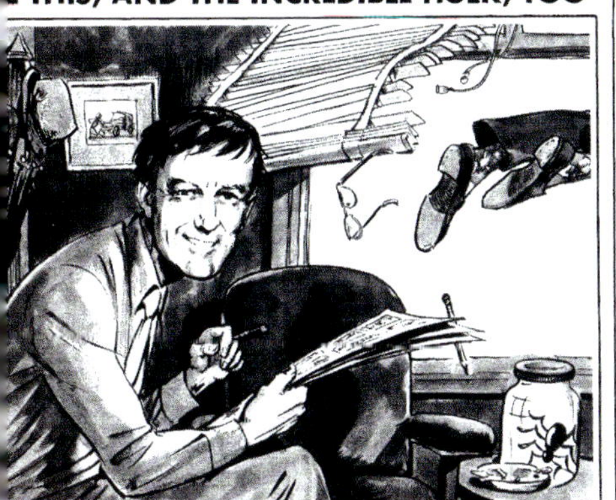

1964 photo of Stan Lee and Steve Ditko discussing the latest issue of SPIDER-MAN.

rvel Press International, June 1964. – It's universally known by now that in ing *Fantasy* #15 (August 1962), the creative team of writer/editor Stan d artist Steve Ditko introduced the masked superhero known as Spider-Man waiting world. So instantly popular was this unique super-doer – and so was Stan of Spidey's potential stardom – en though *Amazing Fantasy* #15 was be a last issue, Stan had soon managed to hen-publisher Martin Goodman into put-

witty, introspective dialogue and characterization – Steve for his somehow awkward-yet-graceful portrayal of Spidey. This time they pulled out all

JOHN ROMITA PULLS OFF ARTISTIC TOUR-DE-FORCE IN SPIDER-MAN #42

Spidey Becomes the Greatest Super-Star of All

When Steve Ditko moved on to different pastures, Stan and Marvel were fortunate in having recently obtained the talents of one of the finest superhero artists in the field – who had spent the previous decade buried thyroid-deep in romance comics at another company. This was Johnny Romita (surname: Jazzy), who had previously drawn the wall-crawler in a couple of now-classic issues of *Daredevil*, and who now was destined to become the longest-running, perhaps most important Spidey artist ever.

For, over the next year or two, under Johnny's pencil-point and Stan's typewriter, *Spider-Man* was able to surpass even the firmly-entrenched *Fantastic Four* as Marvel's (and maybe the world's) most popular superhero comic-book. John combined the characterization which he'd learned doing romance strips, his own vital interest in dynamically power-packed drawing, and some of the clearest, smoothest storytelling in the history of the medium.

Besides introducing such new super-villains as the Rhino, the Kingpin, and others, Stan and John also more fully developed the personality of *Daily Bugle* publisher J. Jonah Jameson's son, John – and, beginning with the startling, memorable final panel of issue #42 (Johnny's fourth), we finally met one of the most famous Spidey characters of all – Mary Jane Watson.

[For the full, unfettered story, see p. 38.]

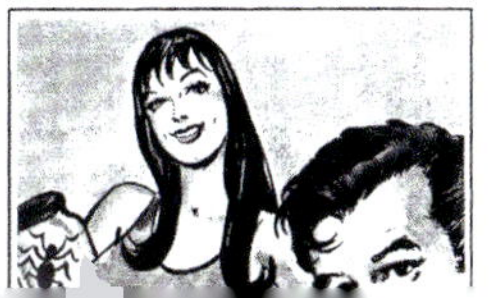

BULLPEN BRAIN-TRUST KEEPS SPIDER-MAN A FAMILY AFFAIR

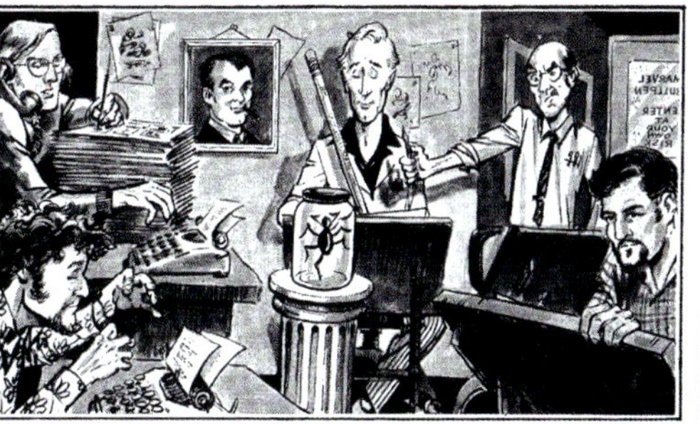

A composite photo of the hard-working heirs of the Lee-Ditko-Romita legacy.

The Torch Is Passed – But The Grandeur Goes On And On

One of the open secrets of Spidey's early success was that, unlike so many heroes, he was handled by a small select group of just three talented guys (Stan Lee, Steve Ditko, John Romita) during his formative days. Luckily, when the need arose for more Spidey stories than even the prolific team of Lee and Romita could turn out, there was a small and dedicated band which worked hard and long to keep up that integrity, that quality.

For instance, in the very early days, even fast-working Steve Ditko was occasionally unable to keep pace with the growing demand for Spider-Man epics. So Jumpin' Jack Kirby, artist of *F.F.* and *Thor*, stepped in once or twice to pencil a tale, which Steve then inked. One of their few but fabulous collaborations – in which Spidey and the F.F. meet – is re-presented *en toto*, starting on p. 32.

Several early *Spidey Annuals*, too, were penciled with loving care by *Larry Lieber*, under John R.'s

the most action-oriented superhero pencilers of all time. Beginning with issue #90 [see p. 79], he loaned his own unique storytelling style to Spidey for a time, and even now does certain special stories about our web-spinning wonder.

Eventually, when Stan's schedule simply didn't allow him to continue as Spidey's scripter, he turned over the writing reins to Roy Thomas, Marvel's then-associate editor. During his brief tenure on the strip, Roy (working closely with Gil Kane) introduced Morbius the Living Vampire, who has since graduated to his own strip, and also took Gwen, J.J.J., and crew on a long-remembered

Conway and Andru Latest Heirs To the Spider-Man Crown

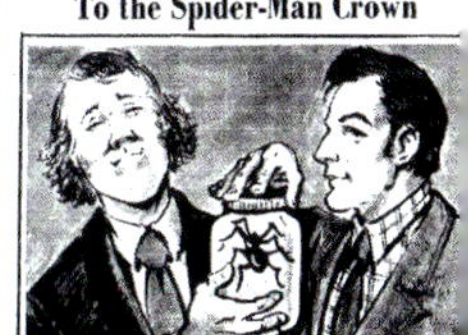

G. Conway, R. Andru, and Friend.

Writer and Artist Say They're Here To Stay

When Roy was casting about for the best possible replacement for Stan Lee as writer of Spidey capers, his first choice was Gerry Conway, and he hasn't regretted the decision for a moment since.

Gerry came into the field in his teens, and swiftly rose to become one of the most productive and talented of the lot. He now handles three of Marvel's most popular titles: *Spider-Man*, *Fantastic Four*, and *Thor*. Not bad for a guy who just turned 21, no?

Another of Roy's lucky choices as Gerry's colleague and accomplice was one Ross Andru. An artist in the field for some years, Ross has now rocketed to instant stardom as the peerless penciler of *Spider-Man*. It's well agreed by writers Gerry, Len, and Roy that Ross is one of the supreme storytellers in the field's history, and one eminently capable of filling the ink-stained shoes vacated by John Romita.

But, how many readers recall that Ross' first big break with Spidey came 'way back in 1968, several years *before* he became the wall-crawler's regular artist? [For the story *behind* this story behind-the-story, see p. 59.]

SPIDER-MAN IS A FINK! SAYS J. JONAH JAMESON

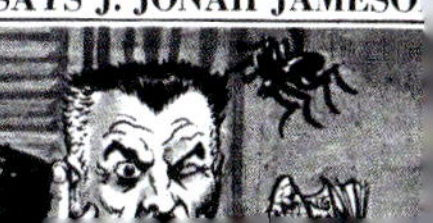

THE SPIRIT OF THE 1960S

In the Marvel Age, inspiration comes from the real world—and the real world sees a need for this new mythology.

Real-world figures (like U.S. Press Secretary Pierre Salinger in panel 1, and John F. Kennedy in panel 2) appeared in the Marvel Universe. *Journey into Mystery #96* (September 1963). Script by Stan Lee. Art by Larry Lieber (pencils, inks), Artie Simek (letters).

Marvel characters do not live in nonexistent fairy-tale worlds, but in places like the boroughs of New York City—their homes may be in Queens or in some Manhattan skyscraper. The president of the United States could very well be John F. Kennedy. Enemy number one? The Soviet Union. The Cold War is in full swing, with all its repercussions on everyday life, and the fear of an all-out war around the corner is palpable. Readers realise that the world portrayed by Marvel is the world they themselves live in; it's not life on some other planet, or set

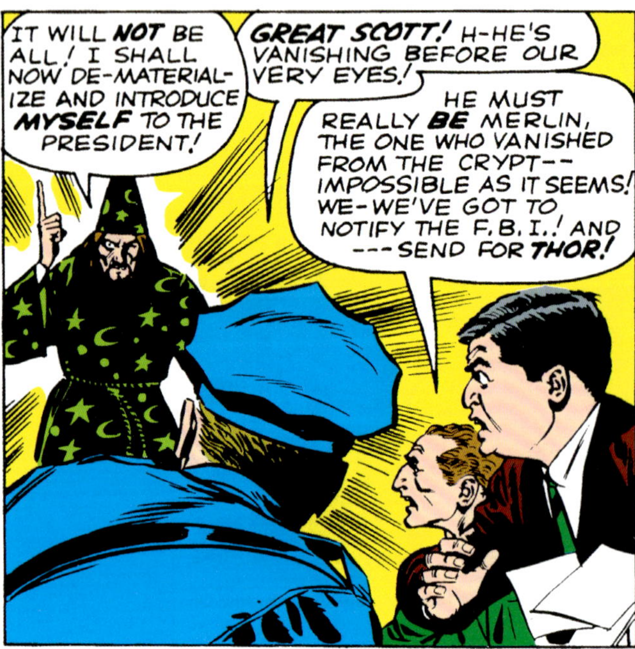

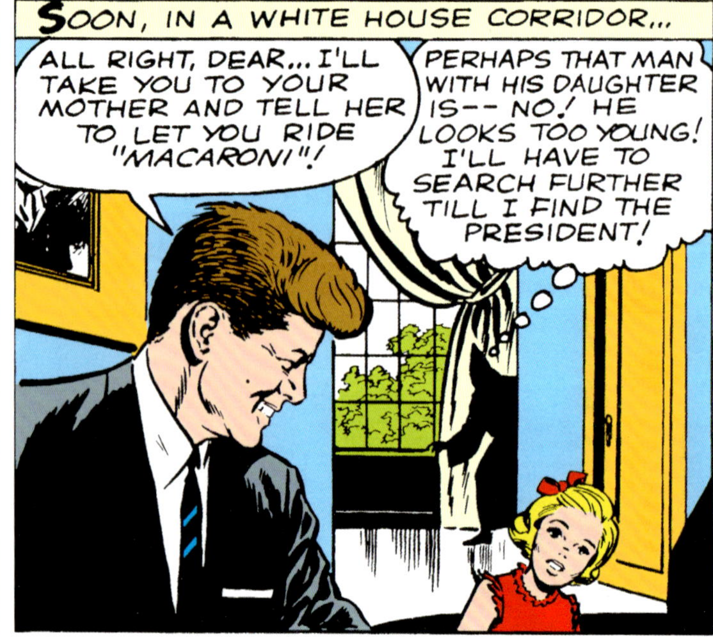

in a fictional city like Metropolis or Gotham. Marvel stories are awash in all the problems and anxiety of the times. Topping the list is the dread of a nuclear holocaust in the wake of Hiroshima and Nagasaki.

Science opens up new cans of worms every day—do the benefits outweigh the dangers? People were worried about what tomorrow would bring. Back in the 1960s, folks wondered where destiny was leading them. So did the fragile Super Heroes that Marvel created.

Those days, the vision of the future also comprised the conquest of space. President John F. Kennedy was eager to expand the space programme in 1961, so the U.S. could catch up—and surpass—the Soviet Union. That's why the Fantastic Four risked everything to get into orbit, and why the theme of space travel became a recurrent theme—beginning with John Jameson, the son of Spider-Man's foe at the *Daily Bugle*, who eventually found a rock on the moon that wound up turning him into the Man-Wolf.

If patriotism—i.e., the U.S. vs. the Soviet Union—was considered a given in some earlier stories, Marvel's position on domestic issues remained more nuanced. But Lee's liberal spirit would shape stories whose tones became more progressive and in step with modern times. Lee approved of student protests against the war in Vietnam, and was in favour of civil rights. College campuses became settings for his stories, and college kids would be among the first to recognise him as a champion for peace and equality. Marvel Comics would be considered a friendly island in touch with the changing times, driven by the wave of reformism sweeping the country. John F. Kennedy, Martin Luther King, the Black Panthers and Beat generation authors had all left their mark. Lee began getting invitations to speak at universities and conferences where he outlined Marvel's philosophy—a school of

Black Panther appears in *Fantastic Four #52* (July 1966). Art by Jack Kirby (pencils), Joe Sinnott (inks).

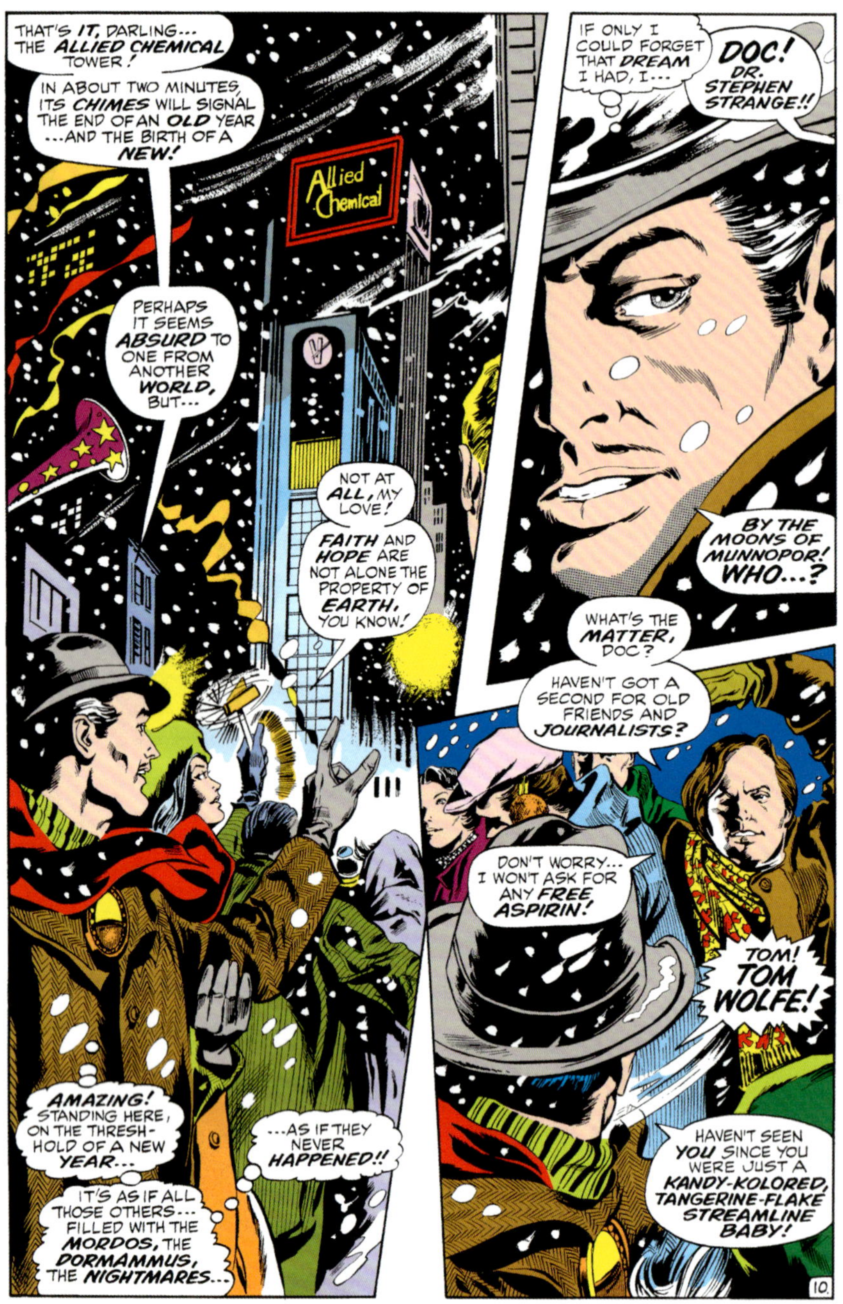

Doctor Strange meets author Tom Wolfe in *Doctor Strange #180* (May 1969). Script by Roy Thomas. Art by Gene Colan (pencils), Tom Palmer (inks), Sam Rosen (letters).

thought very much appreciated by young people and the 1960s counterculture (Doctor Strange and the Silver Surfer were considered symbols of the times). Stan Lee had become Marvel's 'public persona'.

While other publishers of comic books didn't dare touch upon issues regarding racial equality, whose few characters of colour were only included for comic relief, black characters in Marvel stories were portrayed with dignity and power. Black Panther was the first black Super Hero in comic book history, and in the 1970s was followed by Falcon, Captain America's new partner, and Luke Cage, the wrongly accused 'Hero for Hire' out of Harlem. But even in the 1960s, the House of Ideas had taken on the issue of racism with courage and foresight, introducing irresistible supporting characters like Joe 'Robbie' Robertson, city editor at the *Daily Bugle* and perhaps Peter Parker's closest friend.

Marvel's anti-war stance was even more clear-cut and resolute. The threat of Nazism was long gone, but by the 1960s new dangers had appeared, and anti-war themes began to appear in the books regularly. From the advent of the Hulk onward, anti-war themes became the watchword. People everywhere began to take note of the nonconformist, liberal tide. Even intellectuals now admitted they were Marvel fans. Author and journalist Tom Wolfe, one of the founders of 'New Journalism', was among the admirers of the Marvel style and its all-too-human, tri-dimensional characters, just like the ones that inhabit great novels.

The Italian filmmaker Federico Fellini loved the far-sightedness of the stories concocted by Lee, Kirby, and Ditko—he must have felt a certain kinship there, and one day even showed up unannounced at the Marvel offices for a surprise visit. The story Lee told about that fabled encounter, with Fellini and two other gentlemen in black suits and hats walking through the door in single file, was absolutely charming. Alain Resnais, a director from France, was another big fan and even became friends with Lee.

Lee was extremely active when it came to international P.R., and instilled a warm relationship with Marvel readers across the globe, creating an inchoate virtual community. He hit the mark when he started answering fans' letters, because young Americans couldn't wait to get serious feedback from an editor like Lee, whose tone was always upbeat and playful, and he was always glad to provide info on Marvel's writers, artists, and publishing strategy. Lee even started the Merry Marvel Marching Society, a fan club which counted thousands of members and contributed to the creation of a generation of responsible readers and collectors who would be tomorrow's critical minds.

A Marvel comic book wasn't simply read—it was analysed, commented on, and critiqued from literary and artistic perspectives. A new way of creating and appreciating comic books had been born—an exquisite blend of high and popular culture. The 1960s were drawing to a close, and Marvel had become a cultural phenomenon that was poised to conquer the world.

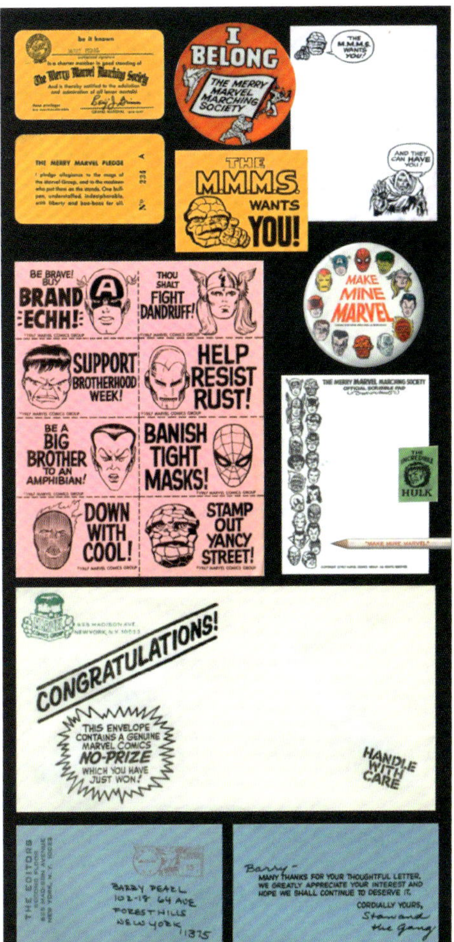

STAN'S SOAPBOX

Let's lay it right on the line. Bigotry and racism are among the deadliest social ills plaguing the world today. But, unlike a team of costumed super-villains, they can't be halted with a punch in the snoot, or a zap from a ray gun. The only way to destroy them is to expose them — to reveal them for the insidious evils they really are. The bigot is an unreasoning hater — one who hates blindly, fanatically, indiscriminately. If his hang-up is black men, he hates ALL black men. If a redhead once offended him, he hates ALL redheads. If some foreigner beat him to a job, he's down on ALL foreigners. He hates people he's never seen — people he's never known — with equal intensity — with equal venom. Now, we're not trying to say it's unreasonable for one human being to bug another. But, although anyone has the right to dislike another individual, it's totally irrational, patently insane to condemn an entire race — to despise an entire nation — to vilify an entire religion. Sooner or later, we must learn to judge each other on our own merits. Sooner or later, if man is ever to be worthy of his destiny, we must fill our hearts with tolerance. For then, and only then, will we be truly worthy of the concept that man was created in the image of God — a God who calls us ALL — His children.

Pax et Justitia,

Stan.

ABOVE
Regularly featured in each issue of Marvel Comics of the 1960s and 1970s, 'Stan's Soapbox' presented Lee's thoughts to the readers.

LEFT
The Merry Marvel Marching Society fan club kit, circa 1967.

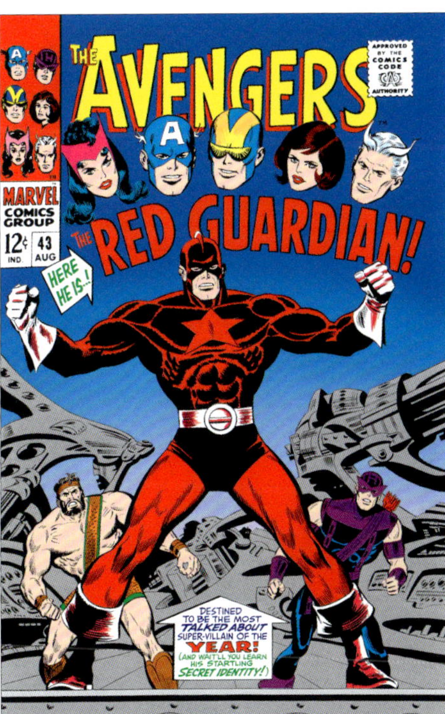

Marvel introduces a Soviet Super Hero in the form of the Red Guardian, *The Avengers #43* (August 1967). Art by John Buscema (pencils), George Bell (inks).

The 1970s

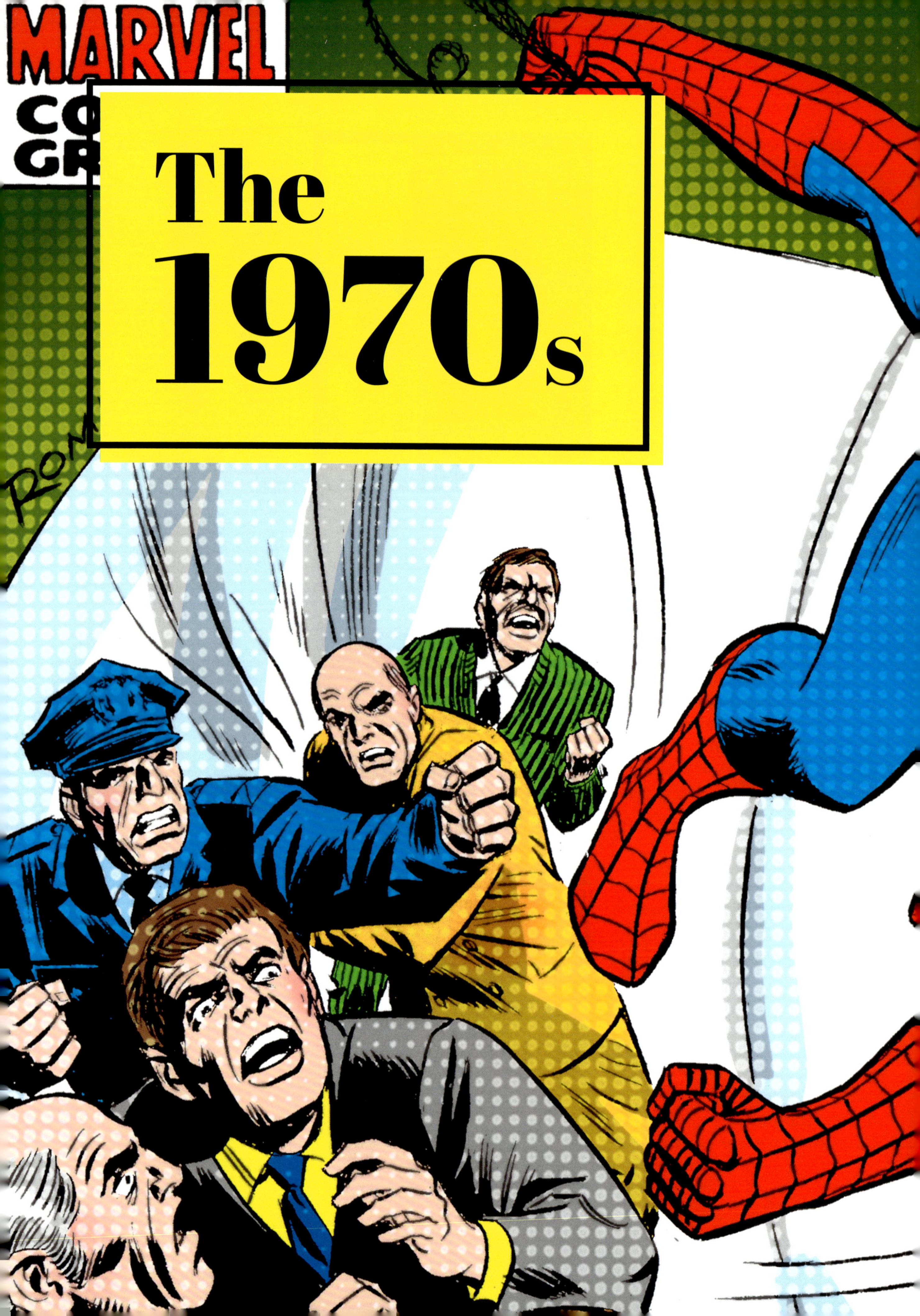

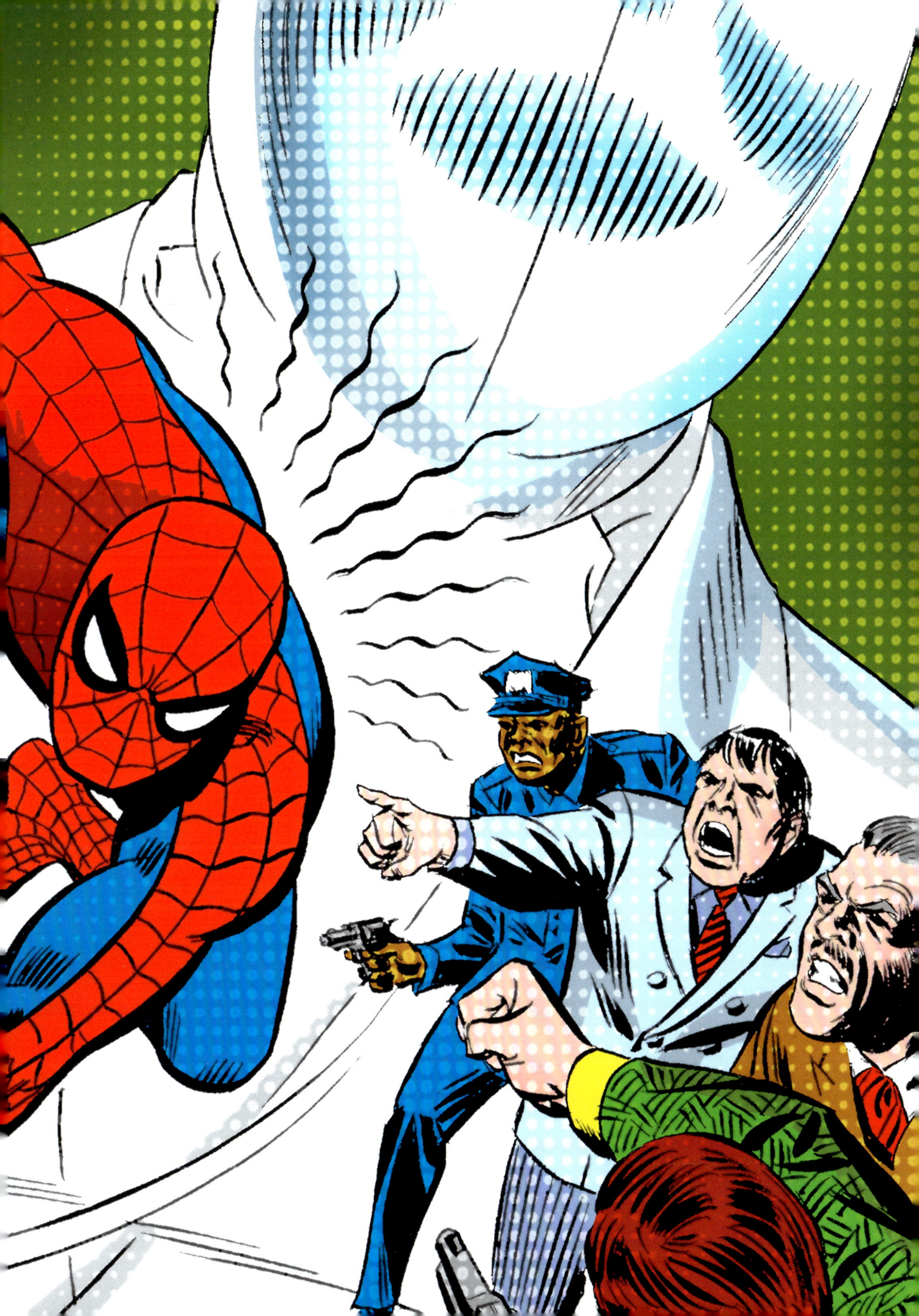

AN ERA OF IMAGINATION AND INNOVATION

'The Night Gwen Stacy Died' was the night innocence came to an end, too. It marked the passage to adulthood. Nothing would ever be the same after that Spider-Man story. Marvel had made its way into the new decade.

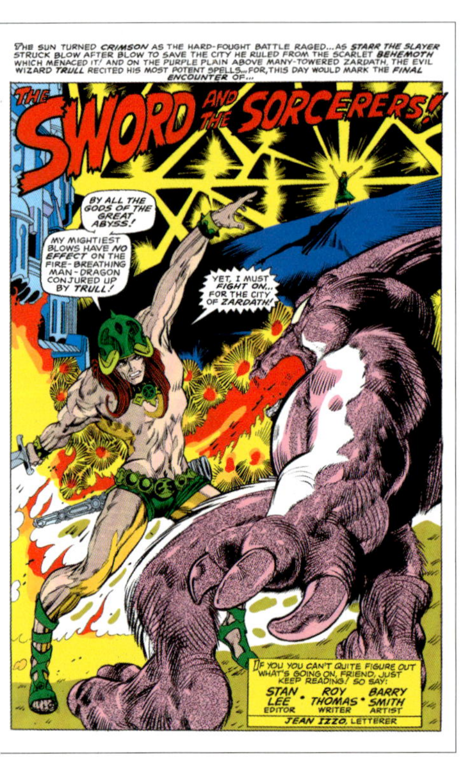

If the 1960s had been characterised by Marvel's pursuit of the Distinguished Competition—thanks to a cast of more human, three-dimensional characters, stories based on loads of melodrama and realism, artwork that was visionary and spectacular, writers that revolutionised the genre, a solid, two-way relationship with the cultural backdrop of the times, and the creation of a virtual community—the following decade witnessed a development that no one would have thought possible: Marvel outdid its rival not only in terms of quality, but in terms of sales as well. In fact, that supremacy, apart from brief, disconnected intervals along the way, is a trend that has continued to this day.

It didn't matter that Jack Kirby had quit, or that Lee, as we shall see, would do less comic-writing as the years went by. The new writers and artists had grown up reading the classic Marvel stories, and embarked upon careers in comic books not out of necessity, but because it was a future they'd always dreamed of. They had learned their lessons from the masters to perfection. The big standout among the latest generation of creators was Roy Thomas, whose publishing acumen proved matchless. A tireless reader possessed of

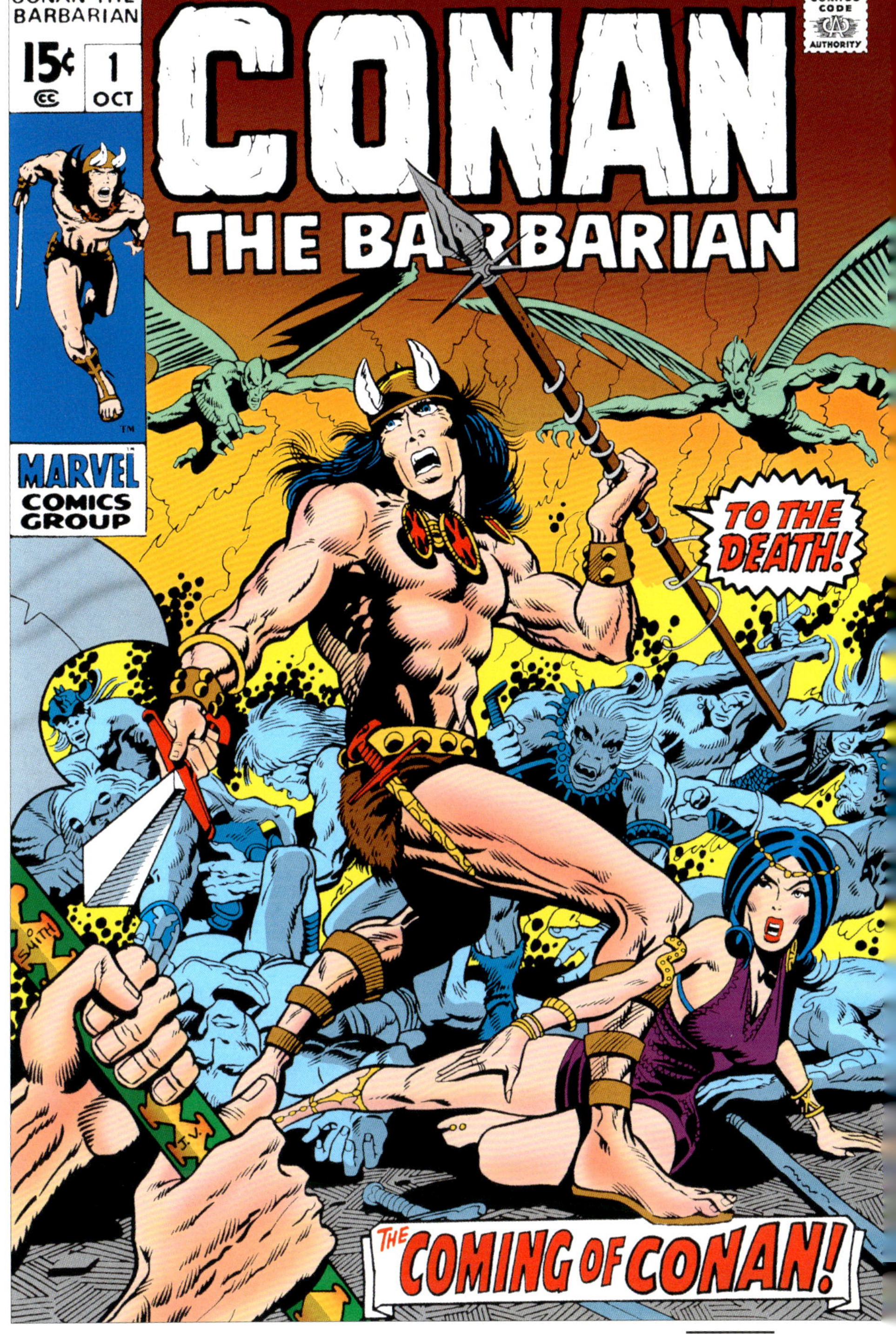

great curiosity, he was the one who suggested introducing an old pulp hero into the comic-book format—a hero who lived in some other undefinable dimension in space and time. One armed with only his brawn, his sword and his courage. A guy surrounded by women to seduce and enemies to kill.

Lee took a liking to the idea, and was especially pleased with the character's name—Thongor—which sounded just right for a comic book. But negotiations with the author, Lin Carter, got nowhere. From there, Thomas contacted Robert E. Howard's agents. Howard had been a pulp-fiction writer in the 1930s, best known as the creator of Conan the Barbarian, until he committed suicide in 1936. His novels were a gold mine of ideas and adventures that Thomas would adapt with the help of Barry Smith (later known as Barry Windsor-Smith), a young British artist who, to complicate matters, had trouble obtaining a work visa for the United States and was often forced to return to the U.K., where he lived in a London suburb. Interestingly enough, his smooth and elegant touch was just right when it came to creating the harsh, wild settings of Conan's fictional homeland Cimmeria. This marked the start of Smith's extraordinary career.

Conan turned out to be a success right off the bat, with fans and critics alike. But once the first series had run its course—22 stories in all—Smith was out and John Buscema was in. Buscema focused on bringing out Conan's physical prowess and an attitude that was violent and noble at the same time, even in black-and-white comic books where the tone was more adult-oriented. Conan would become an icon that transcended comics, and by the 1980s he had hit the silver screen, played by none other than Arnold Schwarzenegger.

ABOVE
Conan the Barbarian #1 (October 1970). Art by Barry Smith (pencils).

OPPOSITE PAGE
Roy Thomas and Barry Smith featured their proto-Conan character, Starr the Slayer, in *Chamber of Darkness #4* (April 1970). Script by Roy Thomas. Art by Barry Smith (pencils, inks), Jean Izzo (letters).

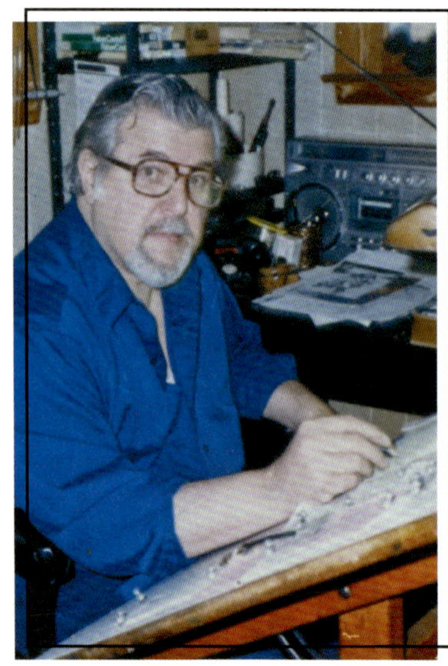

Artist John Buscema at work in his home studio.

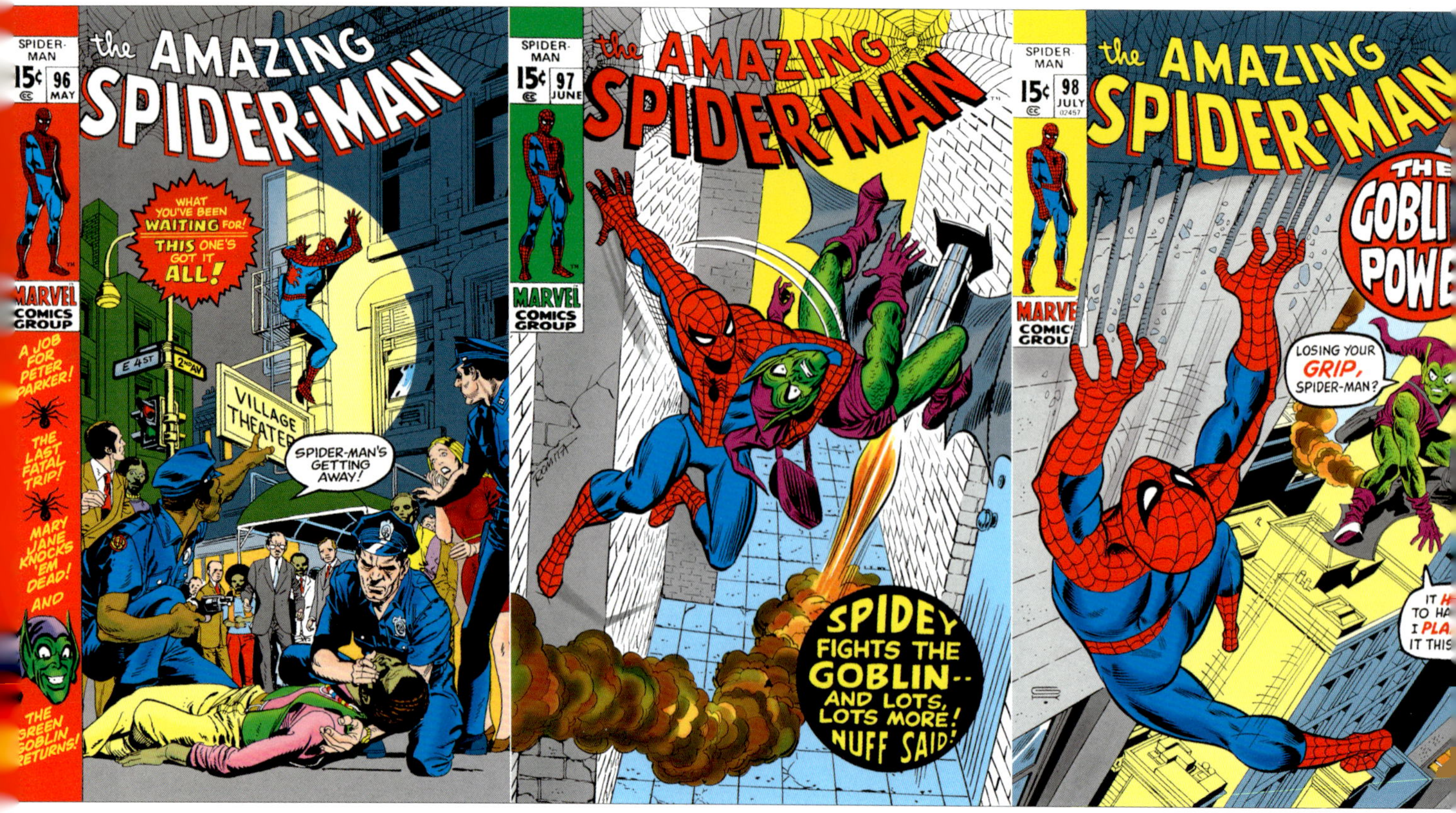

The three issues of *The Amazing Spider-Man* published without the approval of the Comics Code Authority.

While Conan was a revolution in publishing terms, an ideological development, masterminded by Lee himself, was about to send shock waves through the American comic-book industry. For the time being, the Comics Code Authority still imposed strict limits on content. With Marvel's success and its influence over the country's youth in mind, in 1971 the U.S. Department of Health, Education and Welfare asked Marvel to come up with a story that put the spotlight on the evils of drug abuse, which at that time was growing rampant. Lee seized the opportunity to script what would become a classic three-part story that appeared in *The Amazing Spider-Man* (issues #96–98). Snared by the web of addiction would be Peter Parker's best friend, Harry Osborn, the son of Norman Osborn, A.K.A. the Super Villain Green Goblin. The Comics Code Authority rejected the story because it did not meet their strict guidelines, despite its important message. Lee, however, refused to give up, and sent the trilogy to print without the Authority's seal of approval on the front cover. It turned out to be a smash hit and led to the revision of the Code.

It was no fluke, then, that by the 1970s Marvel had become America's leading publisher of comic books. Nor was it a coincidence that the business community had begun courting Marvel, a company that had practically started from nothing and was now a major focus of the mass media. In 1968 a large

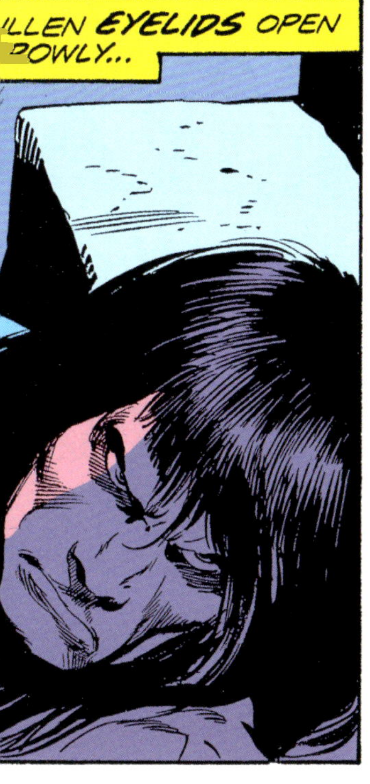

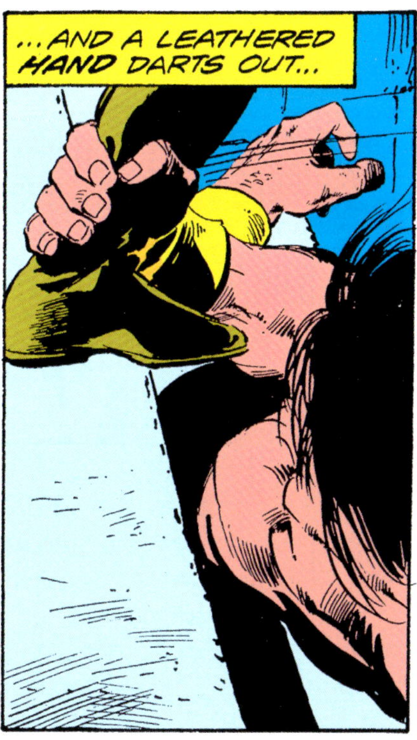

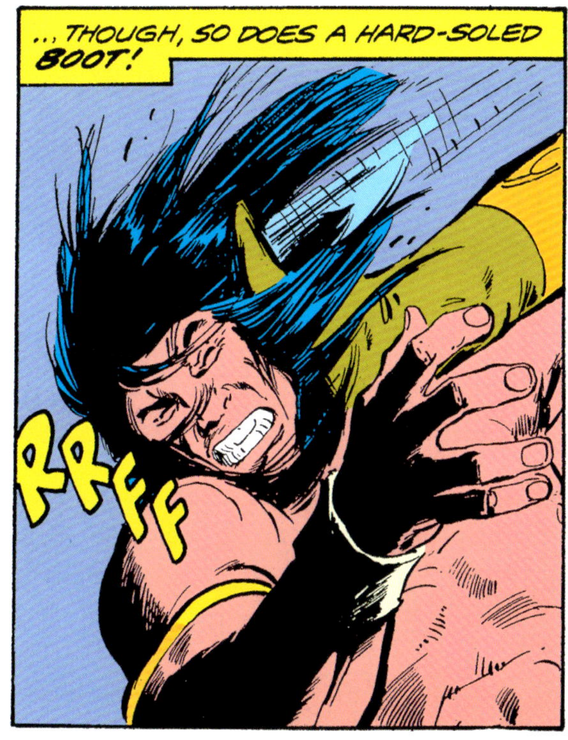

conglomerate, the Perfect Film & Chemical Corporation (which would soon become Cadence Industries), bought Marvel from Martin Goodman for about $15 million. Goodman, however, remained Marvel's de facto publisher until 1972, when he finally left. The move from being a family business to one run by a multinational corporation was not exactly painless and it didn't happen overnight. The company's structure underwent a thorough reorganisation. Lee was promoted to publisher and sent to work developing multimedia projects for television and the movies. However, the dream of Hollywood incarnations of Marvel characters would come true only with the spread of 21st-century digital culture.

Roy Thomas, Lee's right-hand man and heir to the throne, became Marvel's editor in chief—but Thomas was more interested in writing, and left that role in 1974. This turn of events marked the start of one of the most chaotic, albeit also one of the most creative, periods in Marvel history. With an increased number of monthly releases, centralised control became more and more difficult. This meant that writers of each individual series would, in practical terms, often be their own editors. The unbridled creativity of Marvel's writers, who had never experienced so much freedom, was able to generate a slew of high-power series and characters.

Meanwhile, the successors to Lee and Thomas came and went at a stunning rate, and some lasted for no more than a few days. People like Marv Wolfman, Len Wein, Gerry Conway, and Archie Goodwin

ABOVE
Panels from *Conan the Barbarian #44* (November 1974). Script by Roy Thomas. Art by John Buscema (pencils), Crusty Bunkers, Neal Adams, Dick Giordano, Larry Hama, Ralph Reese (inks), Glynis Wein (colours), John Costanza (letters).

BELOW
Writer-turned-editor in chief Roy Thomas in 1973.

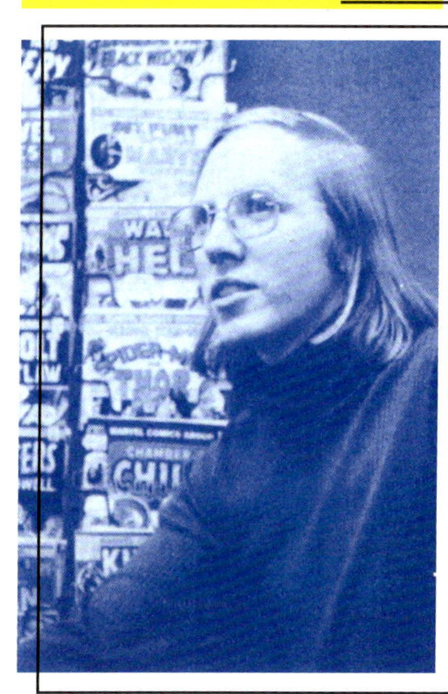

RIGHT
Roy Thomas (first panel, left) and wife Jean made a cameo appearance in the pages of *The Avengers #83* (December 1970). Script by Roy Thomas. Art by John Buscema (pencils), Tom Palmer (inks), Herb Cooper (letters).

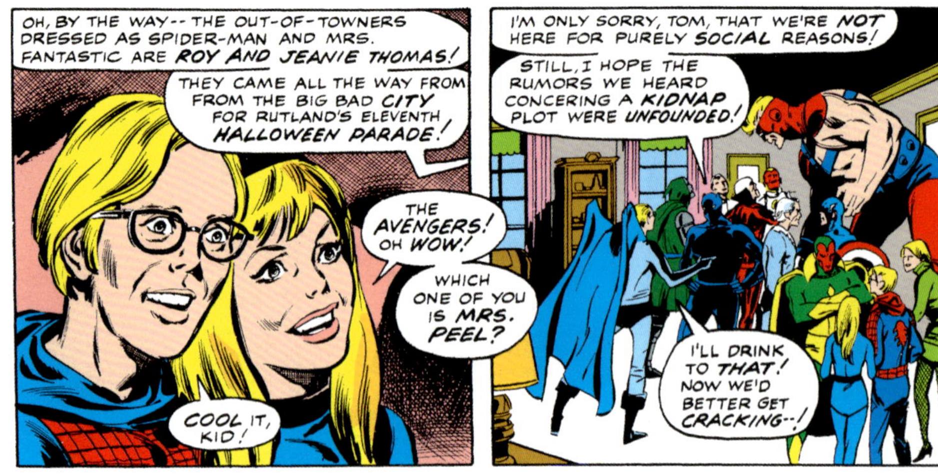

BELOW
The full-blown first appearance of Wolverine, *The Incredible Hulk #181* (November 1974). Art by Herb Trimpe (pencils), John Romita, Sr. (inks).

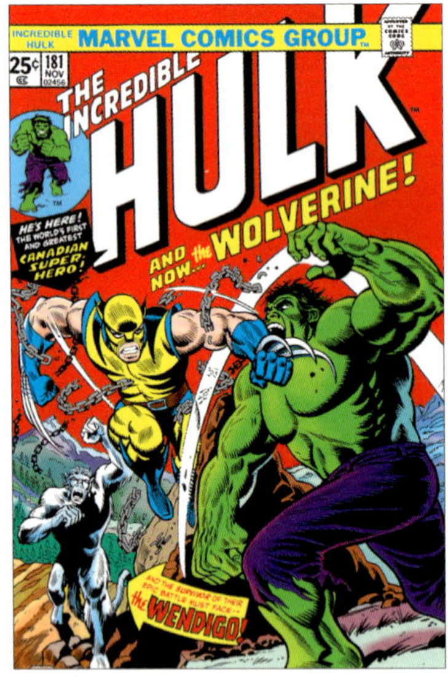

were editors in chief. It would not be until Jim Shooter came along in 1978, who was in for a nearly 10-year run as editor in chief, that things stabilised. Under his reign, series and characters would be revised and revamped, leading to classic runs such as Frank Miller's *Daredevil* and Walter Simonson's *Thor*. Marvel remained in step with the times, and American sociopolitical realities would continue to influence its creators, as seen in comic-book stories that showed increasing commitment to and relevance regarding the issues at hand.

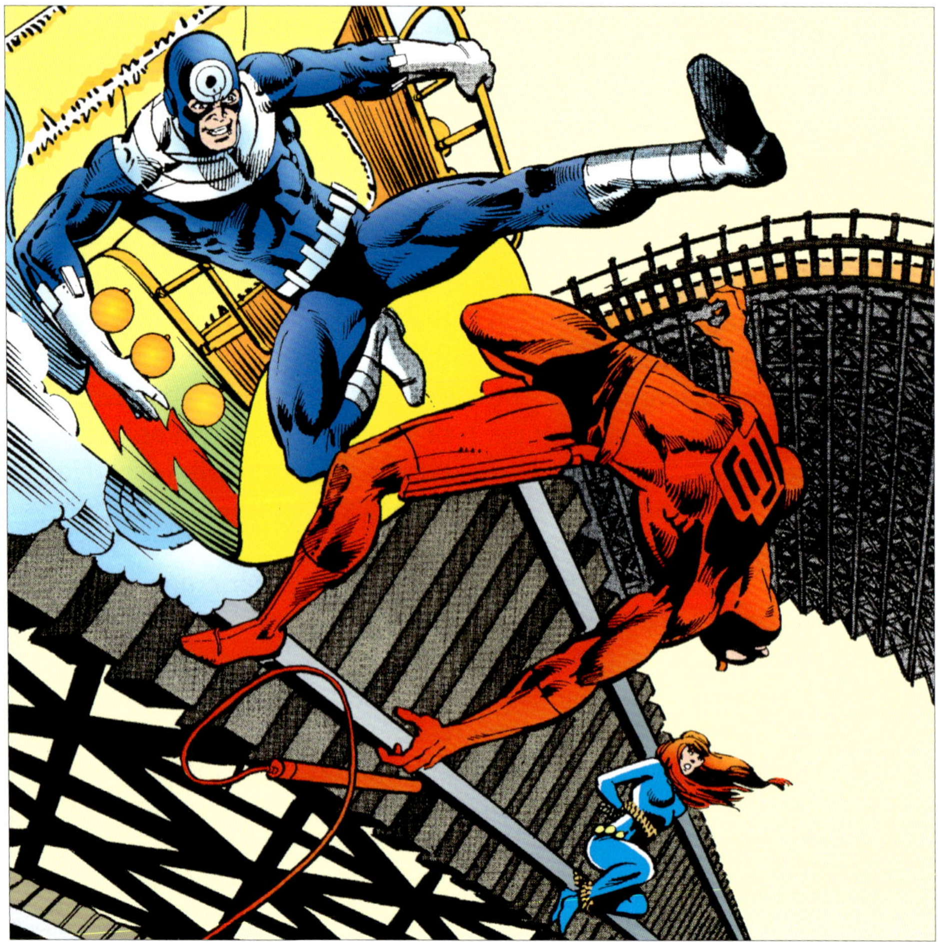

Daredevil #161 (November 1979). Art by Frank Miller and Klaus Janson.

MARVEL'S MIGHTY MUTANT REVOLUTION

A series that went from running reprints catapults to the top of the charts with the introduction of some offbeat, amazing mutants.

In terms of comic-book thrills and spills, arguably the high point of the '70s came with the 1973 release of the story 'The Night Gwen Stacy Died' in *The Amazing Spider-Man* (#121). In it, Spider-Man tries to rescue Peter Parker's girlfriend Gwen Stacy after she has been abducted by the Green Goblin—who, of course, knows the identity of his adversary's alter ego. In the ensuing battle, the Green Goblin hurls Gwen from the Brooklyn Bridge. But Spider-Man is the one who actually causes Gwen's death; her neck snapping as Spidey uses his webbing to try to stop her fall. A moving story indeed, with dialogue and characters that flaunted all-new heights in realism, which literally jettisoned readers—many of whom must have considered the blonde bombshell their girlfriend—into mourning. Some even mailed death threats to writer Gerry Conway for having sent Gwen to an early grave. In truth, having her die was a group decision approved by Lee—the idea was to kill off an important supporting character in order to shake things up. At first, it looked like Aunt May would be the victim. But then Romita suggested Gwen...

From an artistic perspective, there may have been one story that could compete with the greatness of thal chapter in the annals of Spider-Man. It involved the revival of the X-Men, whose

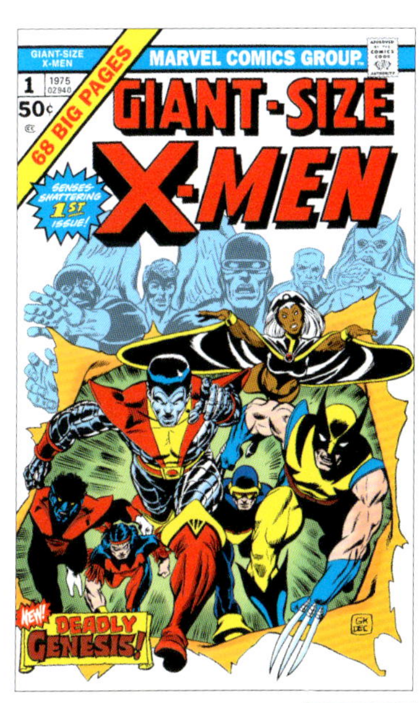

Giant-Size X-Men #1 (May 1975). Art by Gil Kane (pencils) and Dave Cockrum (inks).

STAR WARS

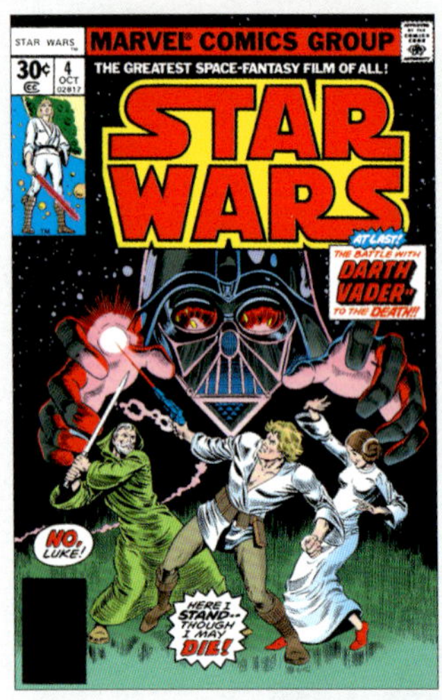

One of Marvel's biggest hits in the 1970s was the comic-book version of *Star Wars*. Oddly enough, it was Lucasfilm that approached Marvel about making a deal, but at first Stan Lee turned them down. Roy Thomas, however, convinced him to change his mind. The first *Star Wars* comic book, written by Thomas and featuring artwork by Howard Chaykin, hit newsstands in March 1977, before the release of the movie, and sold millions of copies.

series had stopped publishing new stories, before starting up again with *Giant-Size X-Men #1*. Marvel's new ownership wanted a new supergroup made up of characters from different countries in order to broaden its sales base. In 1975 writer Len Wein and artist Dave Cockrum revived two of the original X-Men, Cyclops and Marvel Girl, along with Professor X, and teamed them up with a crew of young mutants in the Marvel milestone *Giant-Size X-Men #1*. That marked the start of an epic series that ran through the 1980s and went on to become Marvel Comics' biggest commercial success.

Such an accomplishment was mostly thanks to the writer Chris Claremont, who replaced Wein, whose duties as editor in chief took up most of his time. British-born Claremont might be described as an author with a penchant for soap-opera-style comic book stories. He would be later joined by artist/writer John Byrne to create some of the greatest moments in X-Men history.

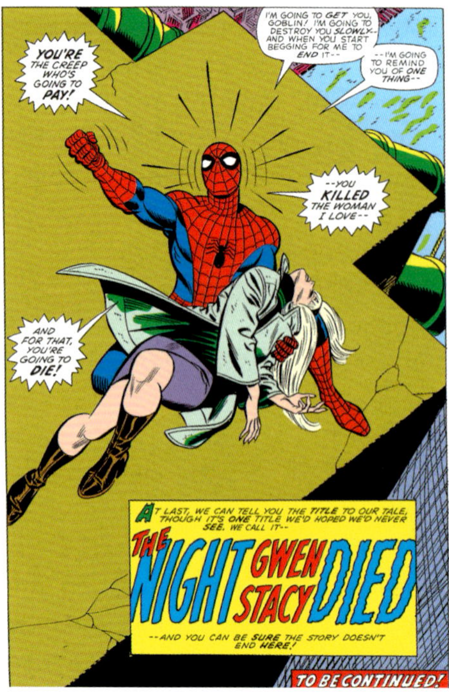

The last page of *The Amazing Spider-Man #121* (June 1973), featuring the death of Gwen Stacy. Script by Gerry Conway. Art by Gil Kane (pencils), John Romita, Sr. and Tony Mortellaro (inks), Dave Hunt (colours), Artie Simek (letters).

The new team of mutants also happened to include Wolverine, the Canadian Super Hero with retractable claws who would soon have the honour of being the most famous among the second generation of Marvel characters. Wolverine had made his debut in 1974, in *The Incredible Hulk #180–181*. Based on an initial suggestion by Roy Thomas, Wolverine was designed by John Romita, Sr., and brought fully to life by writer Len Wein and artist Herb Trimpe.

Readers were immediately mesmerised by this muscle-bound maniac in yellow and black, but no one ever imagined he'd become a superstar the world over. One of the reasons must have been the decades-long secrecy regarding his origins—he had been kidnapped and forced to undergo experiments involving Adamantium implants that reinforced his bones and claws, and gave him regenerative powers, otherwise known as the healing factor, which for all practical purposes made him immortal.

The pencils and inks for page 32 of *The Incredible Hulk #180* (October 1974), marking the first appearance of Wolverine. Script by Len Wein. Art by Herb Trimpe (pencils), Jack Abel (inks), Christie Scheele (colours), Artie Simek (letters).

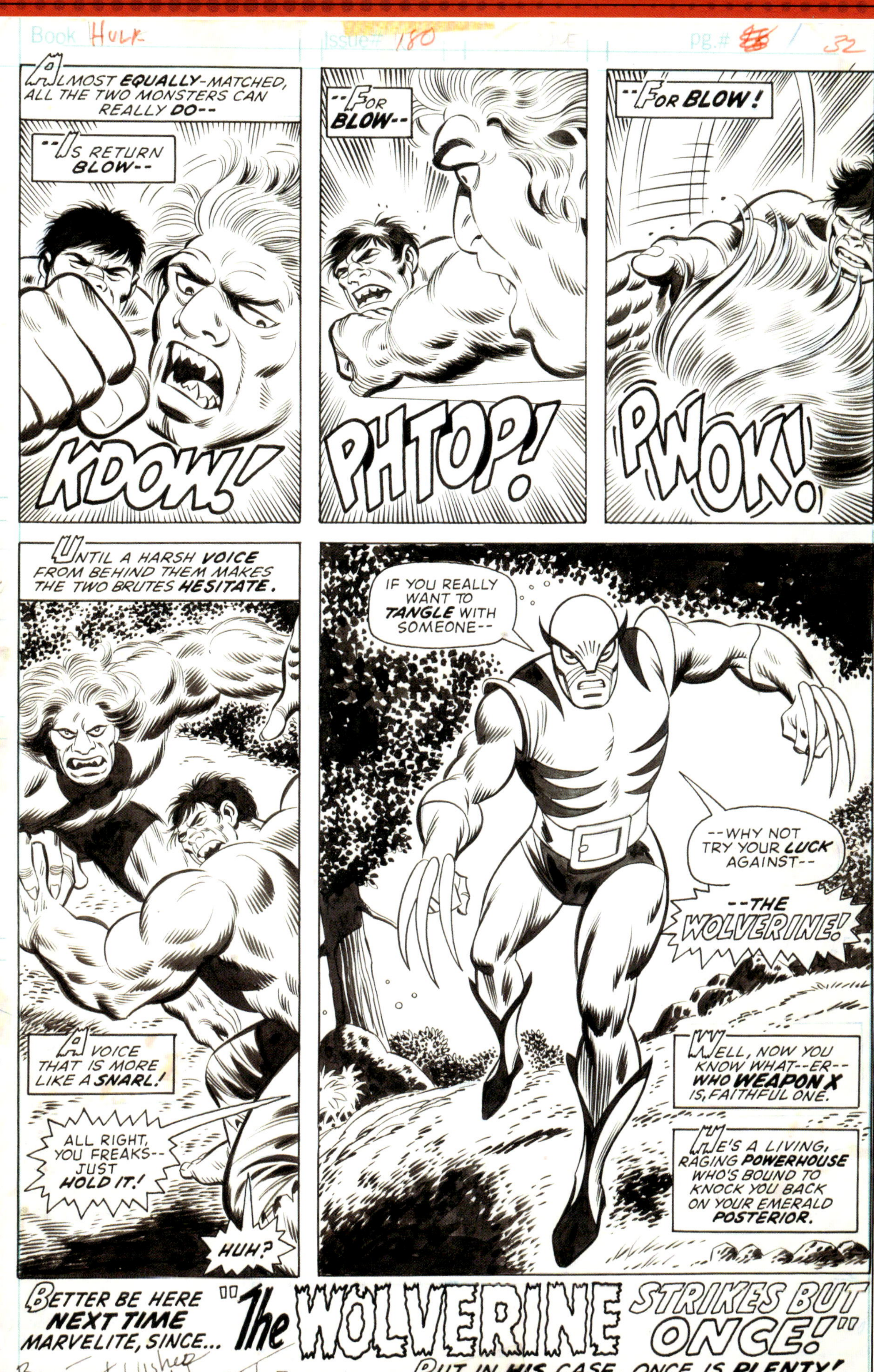
Book HULK
Issue # 180
pg. # 32
ALMOST EQUALLY-MATCHED, ALL THE TWO MONSTERS CAN REALLY DO--
--IS RETURN BLOW--
KDOW!
--FOR BLOW--
PHTOP!
--FOR BLOW!
PWOK!
UNTIL A HARSH VOICE FROM BEHIND THEM MAKES THE TWO BRUTES HESITATE.
A VOICE THAT IS MORE LIKE A SNARL!
ALL RIGHT, YOU FREAKS-- JUST HOLD IT!
HUH?
IF YOU REALLY WANT TO TANGLE WITH SOMEONE--
--WHY NOT TRY YOUR LUCK AGAINST--
--THE WOLVERINE!
WELL, NOW YOU KNOW WHAT--ER-- WHO WEAPON X IS, FAITHFUL ONE.
HE'S A LIVING, RAGING POWERHOUSE WHO'S BOUND TO KNOCK YOU BACK ON YOUR EMERALD POSTERIOR.
BETTER BE HERE NEXT TIME MARVELITE, SINCE... "The WOLVERINE STRIKES BUT ONCE!" BUT IN HIS CASE, ONCE IS PLENTY!

COSMIC ADVENTURES AND HORRIBLE HORRORS

The Comics Code relaxes its restrictions, as Marvel returns to the horror fold. Meanwhile, new talent takes the Super Heroes into the depths of space—and beyond.

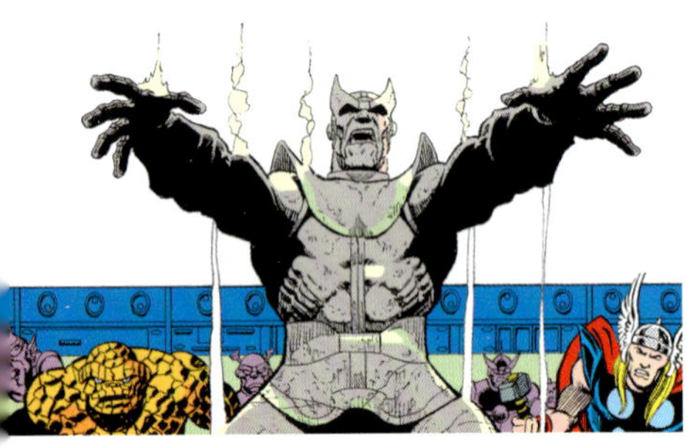

Thanos is turned to stone in the pages of *Marvel Two-In-One Annual* #2 (December 1977). Art by Jim Starlin (pencils), Joe Rubinstein (inks), Petra Goldberg (colours).

Lee's 'rebellion' against the Comics Code Authority helped usher in a new era for comic-book genres like horror and suspense. As of 1971, publishing stories featuring zombies, werewolves, vampires, and bloodbaths no longer breached CCA regulations. Marvel took advantage of this development to launch a new line of comic books in colour and in black and white, which to this day retain their cult following. The best-known and best-selling was

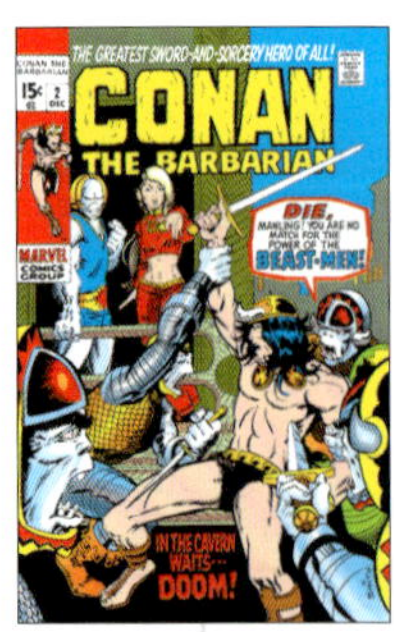

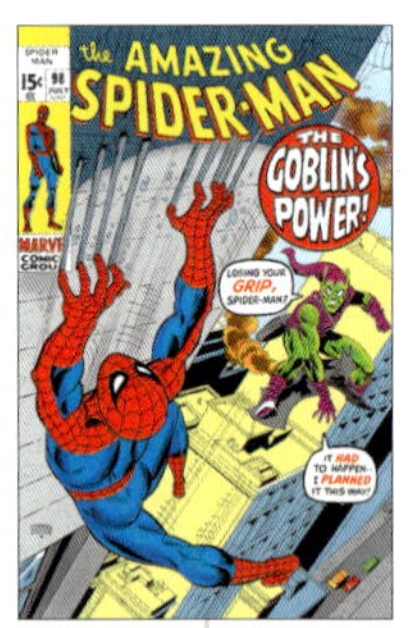

1970

AUTUMN 1970
The decade opens with the successful *Conan the Barbarian*, Marvel's adaptation of Robert E. Howard's pulp hero, by writer Roy Thomas and artist Barry Smith.

MAY–JULY 1971
The U.S. Department of Health, Education, and Welfare asks Stan Lee to publish a story about drug abuse—which appears in *The Amazing Spider-Man* without the approval of the Comics Code.

probably *The Tomb of Dracula* series. Writer Marv Wolfman, penciller Gene Colan, and inker Tom Palmer worked together to come up with their own original, up-to-date version of Bram Stoker's creation, whose facial features were based on the actor Jack Palance's physiognomy. The series racked up some 70 issues and introduced successful new characters like Blade, who starred in his own three-film franchise, launched in the 1990s.

Dracula wasn't the only new Marvel Super Hero that struck fear in the hearts of fans and foes alike. Other scary creations included Werewolf by Night, afflicted by the curse of lycanthropy, which in his family went back many a generation; Ghost Rider, a biker who sold his soul in a futile attempt to save his girlfriend's father; Brother Voodoo; Frankenstein's Monster, another spectacular literary classic redux; Morbius, the Living Vampire, A.K.A. Dr. Michael Morbius, who made his debut in *The Amazing Spider-Man #101* as an incurable blood-drinker afflicted by leukaemia; Man-Wolf, A.K.A. the astronaut John Jameson, son of the ornery publisher of the *Daily Bugle*, who was transformed by the Godstone he found on the moon; and the Son of Satan, A.K.A. Daimon Hellstrom, who waged war against the forces of evil for humanity's sake. Just to name a few.

The space-based Super Heroes were yet another avenue that spelled success for Marvel. It all began with Jim Starlin's revamped version of Captain Marvel, a Lee-Colan creation from the 1960s. Starlin was a young writer fascinated by the counterculture and alternative themes. His Captain Marvel—a Kree warrior who fought for the survival of mankind, who donned a sleek red and yellow costume featuring an eight-pointed star on his chest, and was not immune to tragedy—was another Marvel highpoint of the 1970s.

Starlin also revised Warlock, a character originally created by

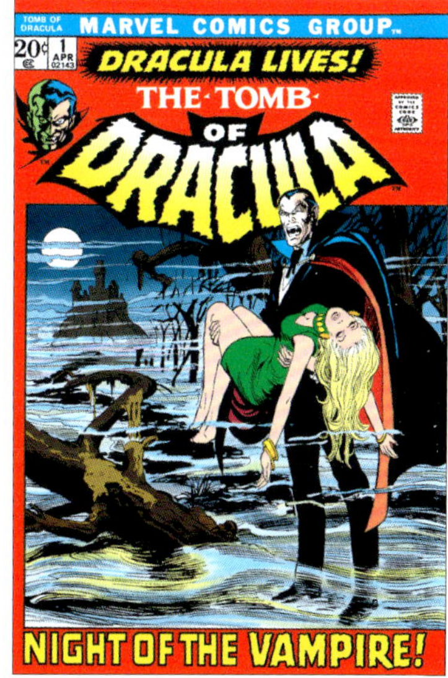

The Tomb of Dracula #1 (April 1972). Art by Neal Adams.

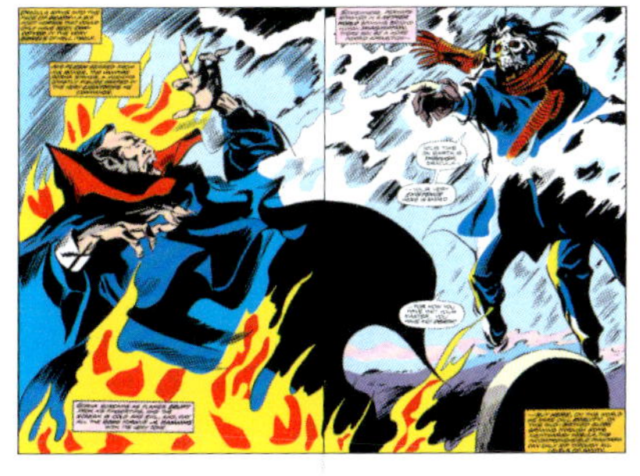

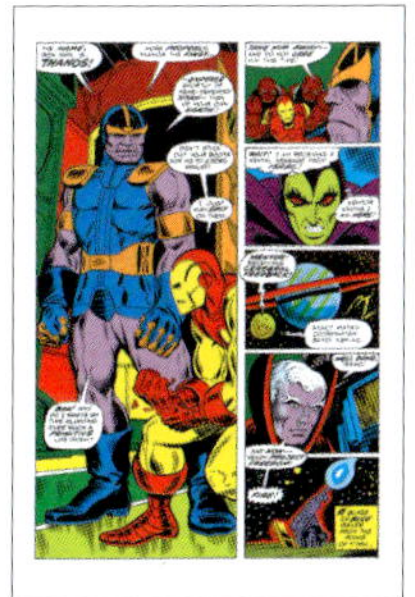

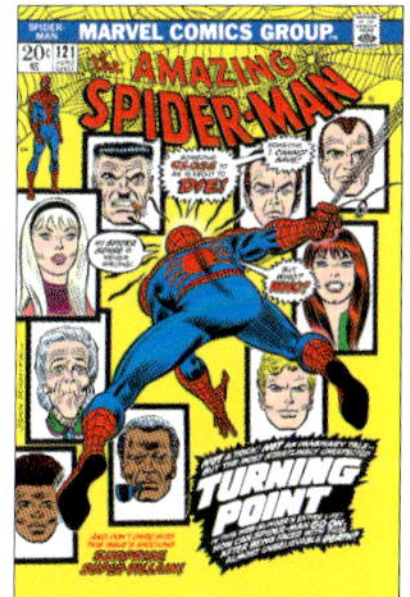

1972–1973
The latest trends are horror and the martial arts. Marvel responds with *The Tomb of Dracula* in April 1972, and *Shang-Chi, Master of Kung Fu*, in December 1973.

FEBRUARY 1973
Thanos, created by Jim Starlin, makes his first appearance in the pages of *The Invincible Iron Man #55* (February 1973).

JUNE 1973
Marvel rocks fandom in the pages of *The Amazing Spider-Man #121* with the death of Gwen Stacy at the hands of the Green Goblin.

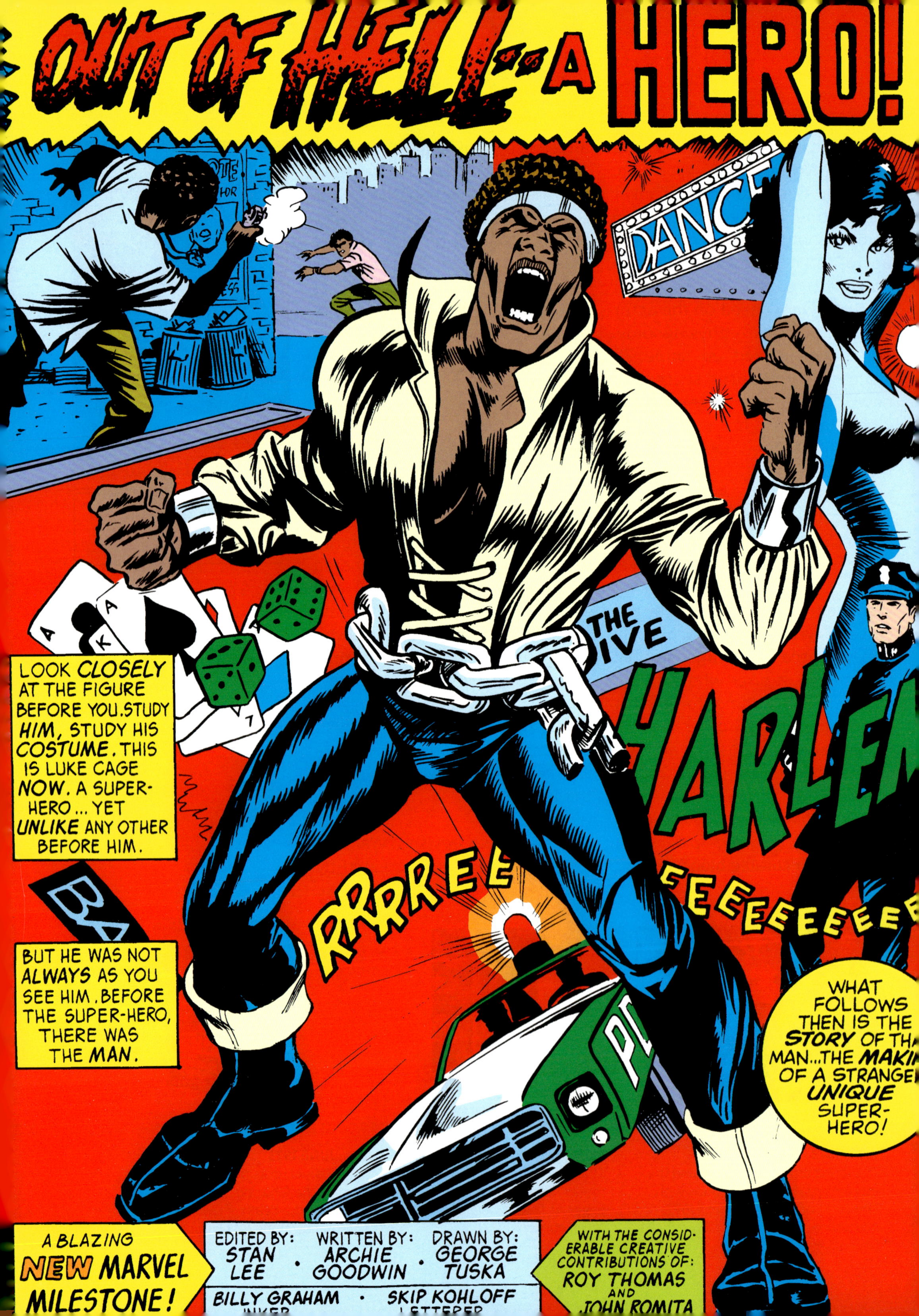
OUT OF HELL--A HERO!
LOOK CLOSELY AT THE FIGURE BEFORE YOU. STUDY HIM, STUDY HIS COSTUME. THIS IS LUKE CAGE NOW. A SUPER-HERO ... YET UNLIKE ANY OTHER BEFORE HIM.
BUT HE WAS NOT ALWAYS AS YOU SEE HIM. BEFORE THE SUPER-HERO, THERE WAS THE MAN.
RRRREEEEEEEEEEEE
WHAT FOLLOWS THEN IS THE STORY OF TH MAN...THE MAKI OF A STRANGE UNIQUE SUPER-HERO!
A BLAZING NEW MARVEL MILESTONE!
EDITED BY: STAN LEE · WRITTEN BY: ARCHIE GOODWIN · DRAWN BY: GEORGE TUSKA
BILLY GRAHAM · SKIP KOHLOFF
WITH THE CONSIDERABLE CREATIVE CONTRIBUTIONS OF: ROY THOMAS AND JOHN ROMITA

Lee and Kirby, and later developed for a series by Thomas and Kane. Starlin transformed him into an enigmatic, almost lysergic hero from outer space, and a sacrificial one at that. Last but not least, Starlin introduced Thanos, the most feared of all Super Villains in the Marvel Universe. His appearances at this time would lead to the limited series *Infinity Gauntlet*.

The 1970s also played host to the martial arts and blaxploitation—two incredibly fascinating subgenres—and, of course, Marvel couldn't help but join the bandwagon. New arrivals on the scene included Shang-Chi, Master of Kung Fu (1973), rebel son of the lethal Fu Manchu. Created by Steve Englehart and Jim Starlin, Shang-Chi owes his status as Marvel mainstay largely to the long run by writer Doug Moench and artist Paul Gulacy. Also introduced were the Sons of the Tiger (1974); and the big performer Iron Fist (1974), whose martial arts skills were enhanced by the powers of K'un-L'un, the ancient mystical city of the Orient where young heir-to-a-fortune Danny Rand attains the power of the Iron Fist after the deaths of his parents.

At the same time, hero for hire Luke Cage opens an office in Times Square. A black ex-con who did time in prison after being framed, Cage got his super-powers while in the pen, courtesy of a cellular regeneration experiment gone haywire. A.K.A. Power Man, he was the latest Super Hero of colour to hit the spotlight, after Black Panther and the Falcon, and the very first with his own comic-book series.

Giant-Size Master of Kung Fu #1 (September 1974). Art by Ron Wilson (pencils), Mike Esposito (inks).

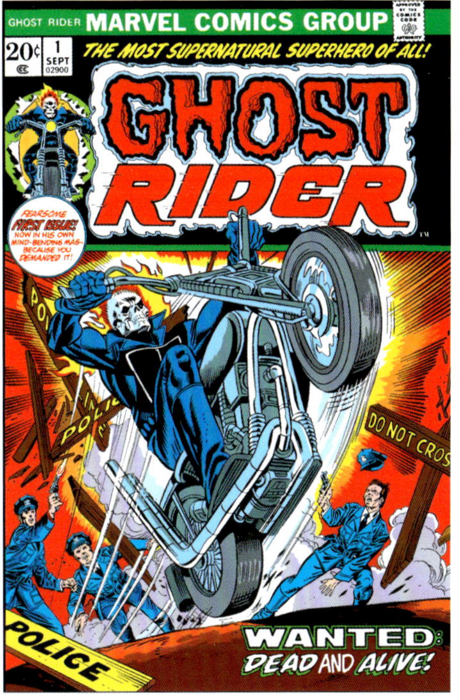

LEFT
Ghost Rider #1 (September 1973). Art by Gil Kane (pencils) and Joe Sinnott (inks).

OPPOSITE PAGE
Splash page from *Luke Cage, Hero for Hire #1* (June 1972). Script by Archie Goodwin. Art by George Tuska (pencils), Billy Graham (inks), Skip Kohloff (letters).

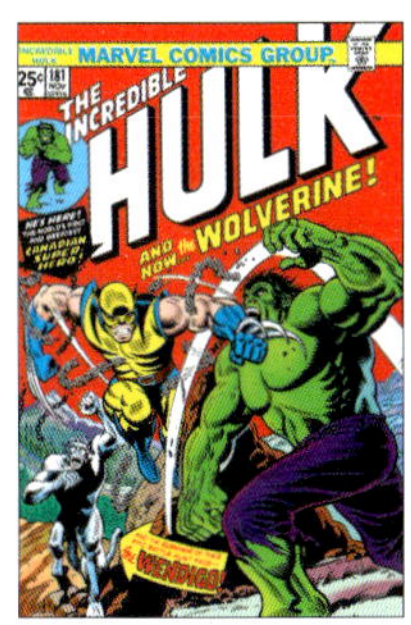

AUTUMN 1974
Conan is followed by another seminal Marvel character of the 1970s, Wolverine, who made his first appearance in *The Incredible Hulk #180–181*.

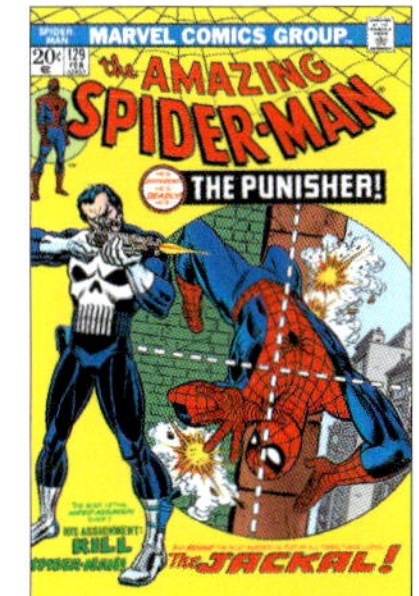

WINTER 1974
Inspired by turbulent times and such films as *Death Wish* starring Charles Bronson, the Punisher, a Vietnam-vet-turned-vigilante, debuts in *The Amazing Spider-Man #129*.

JULY 1975
Giant-Size X-Men #1 ushers in an all-new era with the debut of a team of international mutants. The series would grow in popularity throughout the 1970s.

ALL THE MAN'S MEN

As Stan Lee moves Marvel into the media spotlight, new faces come aboard to guide the comics to new heights.

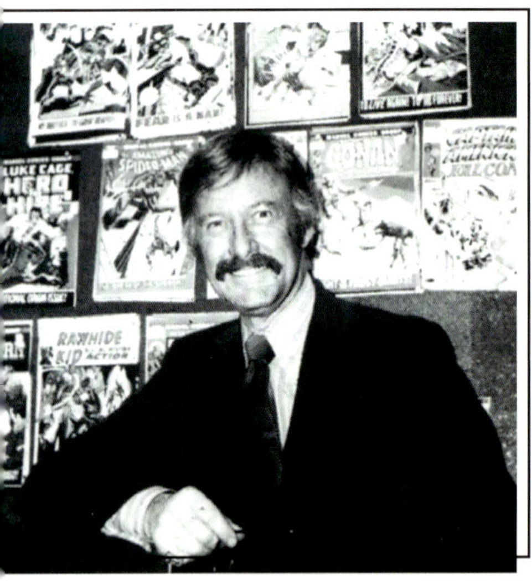

Stan Lee in the Marvel offices, with the latest comic book offerings behind him.

As Lee became more and more involved in projects outside the realm of publishing, his attention was moved away from comics. His work with Kirby on *The Fantastic Four* series came to an end with issue #114; *The Amazing Spider-Man* wound up in the hands of Thomas and Conway. Meanwhile up-and-coming writers and artists breathed new life into a host of other well-known characters. Come to think of it, Lee's true heir may have been Conway. He'd joined Marvel as a young man and soon got the nod to write for Spider-Man. It seemed the perfect choice—at the tender age of 19 he could definitely relate to the issues that roiled the wall-crawler and his peers. Conway brought out the soap-opera aspect of the series starring Lee and Ditko's most famous creation, giving the world a Spider-Man in step with the times, surrounded by a slew of revamped supporting characters.

While Starlin focused on outer space scenarios, and Trimpe carried on with anti-militarist sentiment in the Hulk's realm, Sal Buscema, John's younger brother, stepped onto the scene. Sal was a true craftsman of comic book art, an artist so talented he could draw any Marvel character you happened to pull out of the

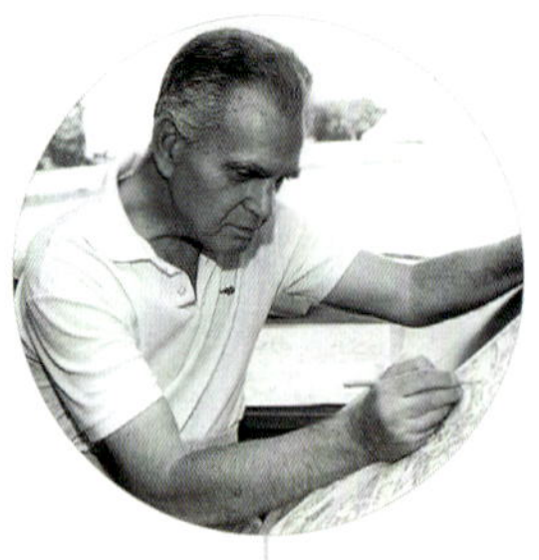

1975

Jack 'the King' Kirby is back at Marvel after a five-year absence. He would create new hits like the Eternals, and tell new adventures of Captain America and Black Panther.

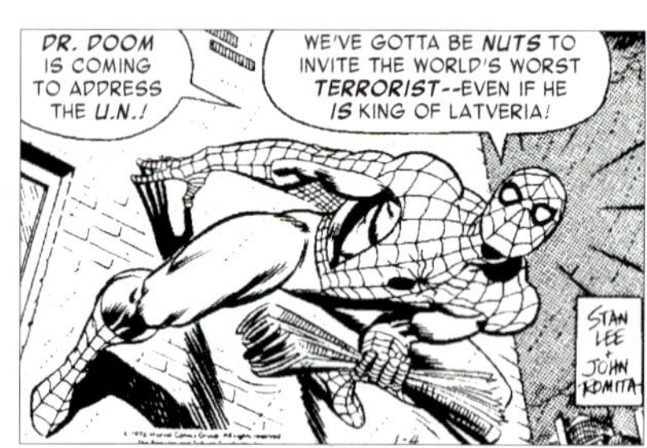

JANUARY 1977

3 January 1977, sees the launch of the syndicated *Spider-Man* comic strip by Stan Lee and John Romita, Sr.

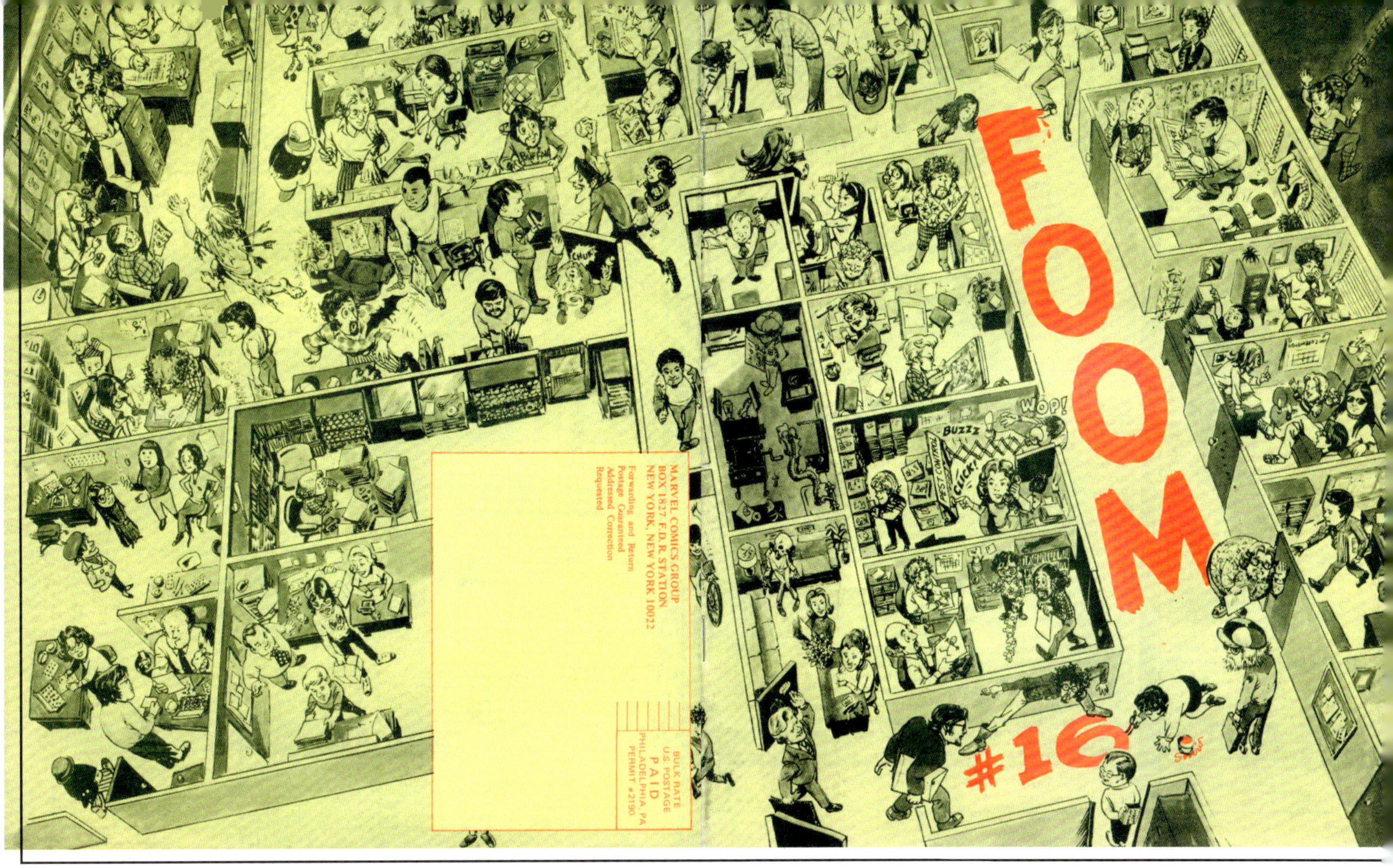

A map of the mighty Marvel bullpen from the pages of *FOOM #16*. Art by Marie Severin.

hat—at the drop of a hat. He and a handful of others were the go-to guys when editors needed to make up for lost time and get their panels to print. Sal Buscema and Bob Brown pencilled one of Marvel's first crossover events, *The Avengers vs. The Defenders*, the latter comprising a 'non-team' of characters we might call anarchic outsiders that included Doctor Strange, Namor, the Silver Surfer, the Hulk, and Valkyrie, who would take on the classic Avengers line-up led by Thor and Captain America.

British-born writer and artist John Byrne definitely left his mark on the history of Marvel Comics. Before teaming up with Claremont on the *X-Men* series, he helped develop characters like Iron Fist and Star-Lord, and in the 1980s worked on memorable runs featuring the Fantastic Four

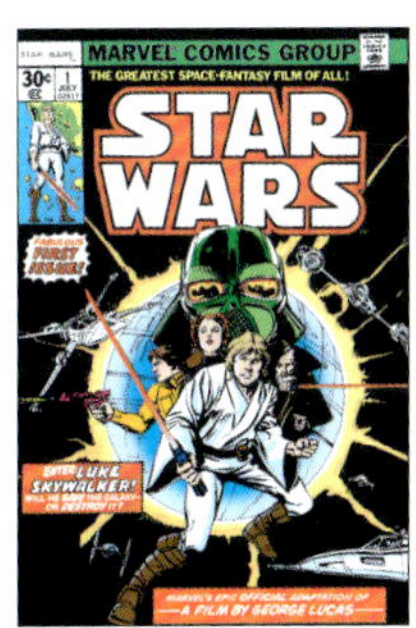

SPRING 1977
Lucasfilm approaches Marvel, pitching a comic-book version of the soon-to-be released film *Star Wars*. Thomas convinces a reluctant Lee to agree. The series is an immediate success.

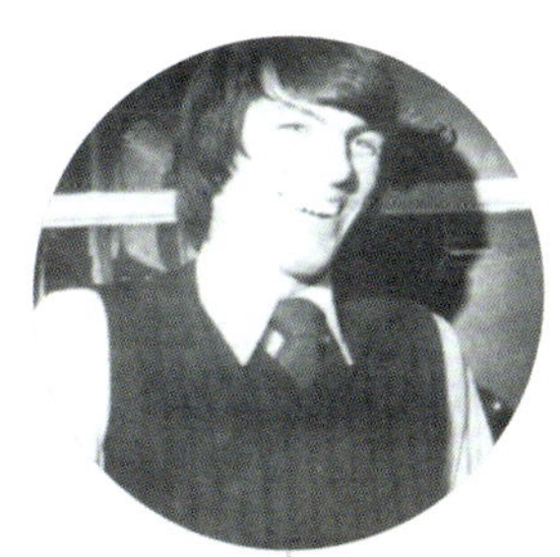

1978
Following Lee's promotion to publisher, several individuals held the title editor in chief. In 1978, Jim Shooter was named to the position, where he would remain until 1987.

1980

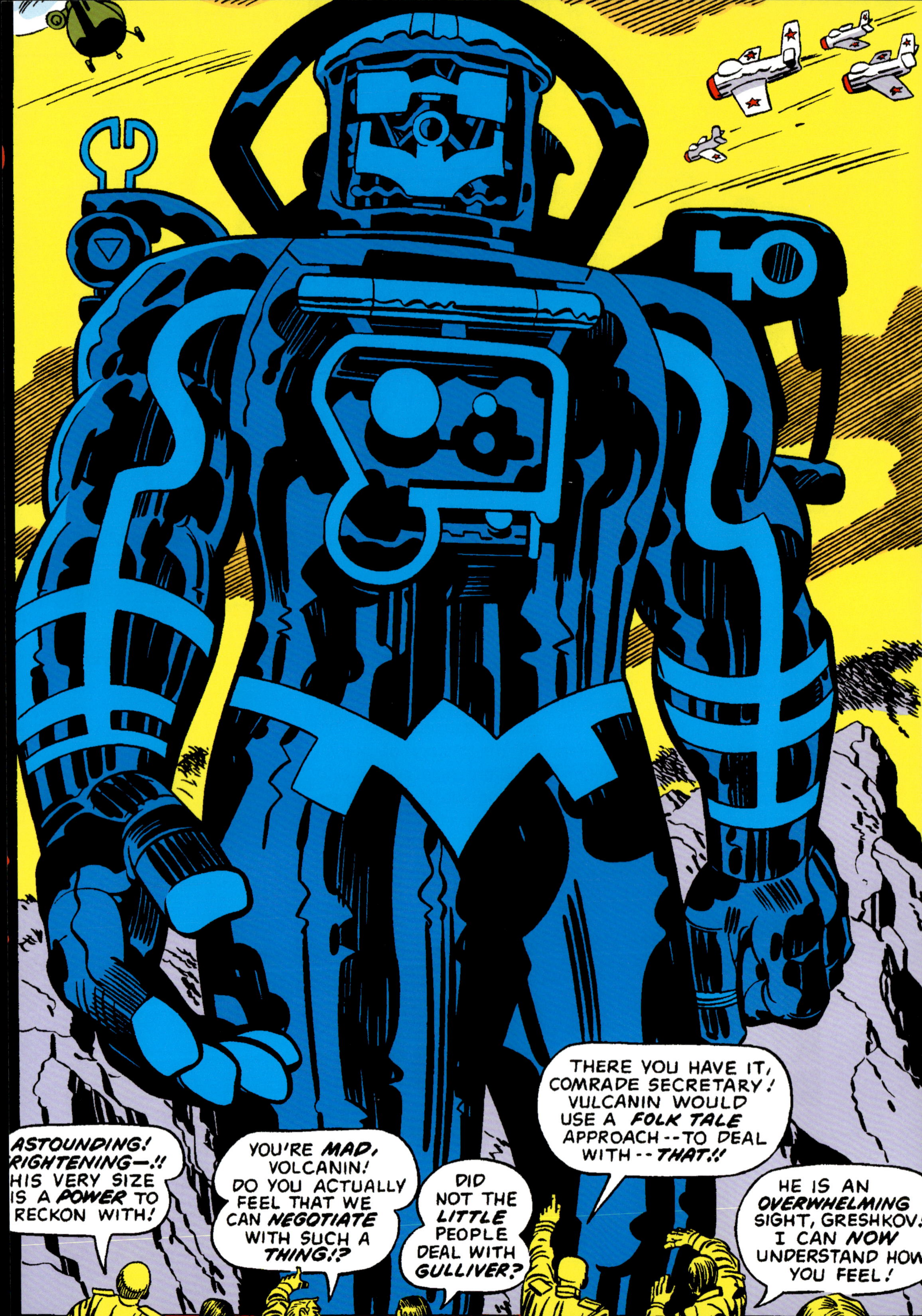

ASTOUNDING! RIGHTENING—!! HIS VERY SIZE IS A POWER TO RECKON WITH!
YOU'RE MAD, VOLCANIN! DO YOU ACTUALLY FEEL THAT WE CAN NEGOTIATE WITH SUCH A THING!?
DID NOT THE LITTLE PEOPLE DEAL WITH GULLIVER?
THERE YOU HAVE IT, COMRADE SECRETARY! VULCANIN WOULD USE A FOLK TALE APPROACH--TO DEAL WITH--THAT!!
HE IS AN OVERWHELMING SIGHT, GRESHKOV. I CAN NOW UNDERSTAND HOW YOU FEEL!

and Captain America. But in all probability, at that time the main man on the scene was Frank Miller, a young visionary embarking on what would be an extraordinary career as comic-book artist. Enthralled by inner-city settings and noir fiction, in the late '70s he reinvented Daredevil, transforming him into a dark, tormented hero, a character imbued with strong religious connotations.

Shock waves: Jack 'the King' Kirby left the Distinguished Competition in 1975 and made his way back to Marvel, where no one had forgotten him. He was given absolute artistic freedom and set about writing, drawing, and editing his own work. His unbounded imagination gave us the saga *The Eternals*, featuring off-shoots of humanity who received their powers from genetic experiments conducted by the intergalactic Celestials and wound up siding with Marvel's pantheon of Super Heroes. Kirby also recouped two classic characters, Captain America and Black Panther, to write and draw them in their very own series. Also worth remembering are Kirby's Devil Dinosaur, Machine Man and his extraordinary comic book adaptation of Stanley Kubrick's *2001: A Space Odyssey*.

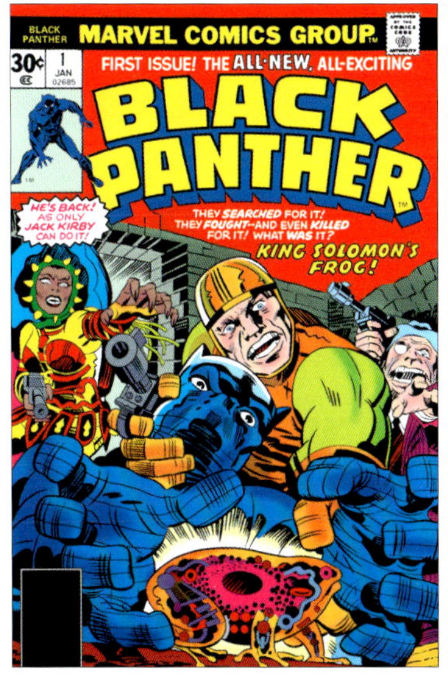

Black Panther #1 (January 1977). Art by Jack Kirby (pencils), John Verpoorten (inks).

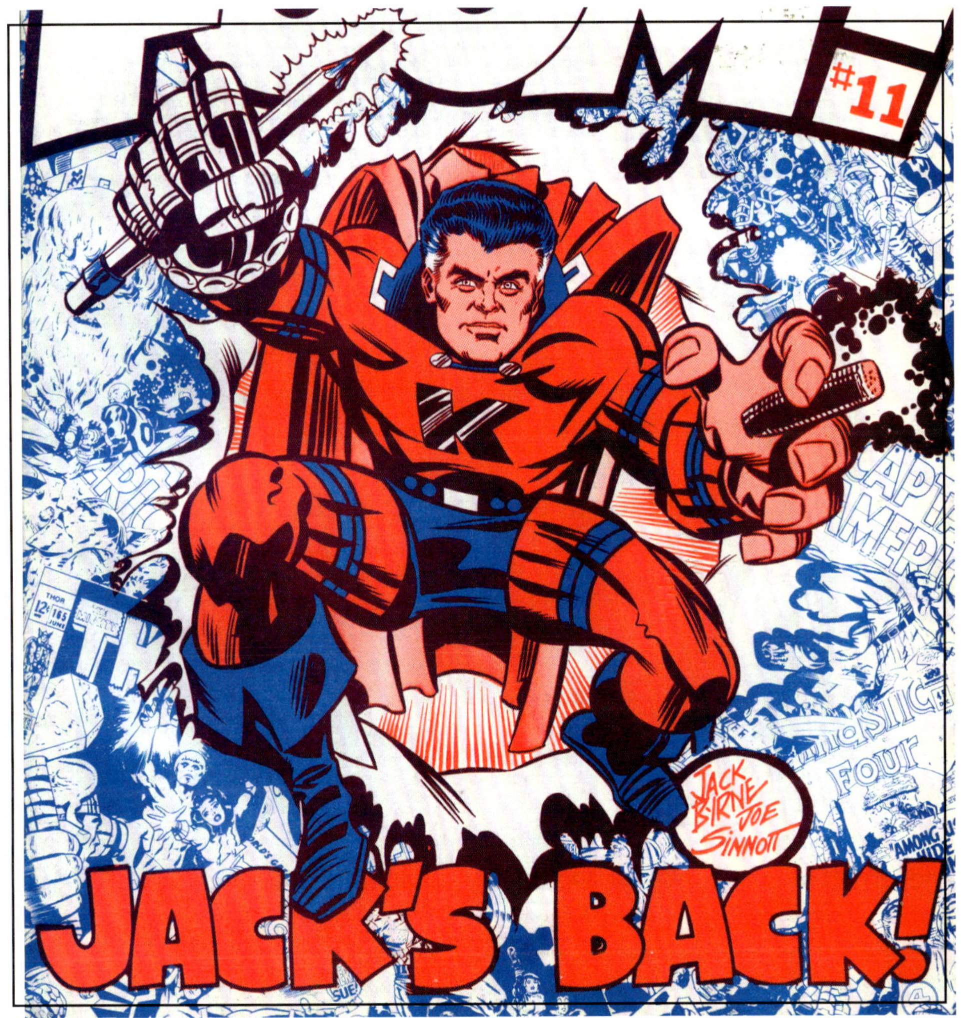

LEFT
The return of Jack Kirby to the Marvel fold is announced in *FOOM #11* (art by John Byrne and Joe Sinnott).

OPPOSITE
The U.S.S.R. attacks the Celestial Nezarr in *The Eternals #11* (May 1977). Script by Jack Kirby. Art by Jack Kirby (pencils), Mike Royer (inks, letters), Glynis Wein (colours).

FROM STREET CRIME TO WATERGATE

The 1970s prove to be turbulent in all aspects, and Marvel reflects the changing times with gritty realism and stories pulled from the headlines.

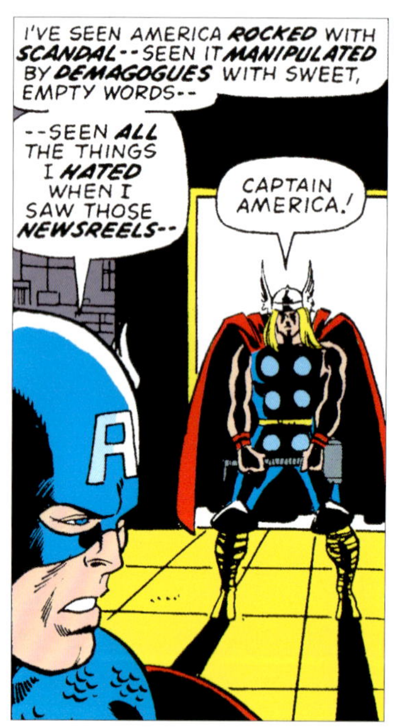

Captain America contemplates his future in *Captain America* #176 (August 1974). Script by Steve Englehart. Art by Sal Buscema (pencils), Vince Colletta (inks), Linda Lessmann (colours), Artie Simek (letters).

In the 1940s, Marvel Super Heroes fought against the Nazis. The 1950s and '60s saw them commie-bashing their way through the Cold War, and dealing with threats of nuclear war and the latest developments that science had to offer, not to mention post-1968 student protests and antiwar sentiment. But the 1970s ushered in a host of new problems for the average American. Political identity came under fire when the president himself turned out to be a crook and was forced to resign.

Another young, politically aware Marvel writer, Steve Englehart, was the genius behind the Secret Empire, about a government plot involving high-ranking officials in the ultimate power grab. Incredibly enough, the conspiracy is led by the President of the United States himself—although we only catch a glimpse of his silhouette—who in the end winds up committing suicide. It was a powerful story that dissected the political reality of the times, in the same way the Punisher provided a critique on a social level.

Life was tough on America's big city streets. Crime rates spiked, daily life was torn upside down by robberies, rapes, and murders. The police, like the citizens they were sworn to protect, appeared helpless. At the movies, people's longing for vigilante justice found expression in the 1974 classic *Death Wish*, starring Charles Bronson, which spawned four sequels. It portrayed an architect-turned-vigilante following the murder of his wife and the rape of his daughter, a man who took justice into his own hands after losing all faith in the authorities.

Marvel came out with its own version of a do-it-yourself

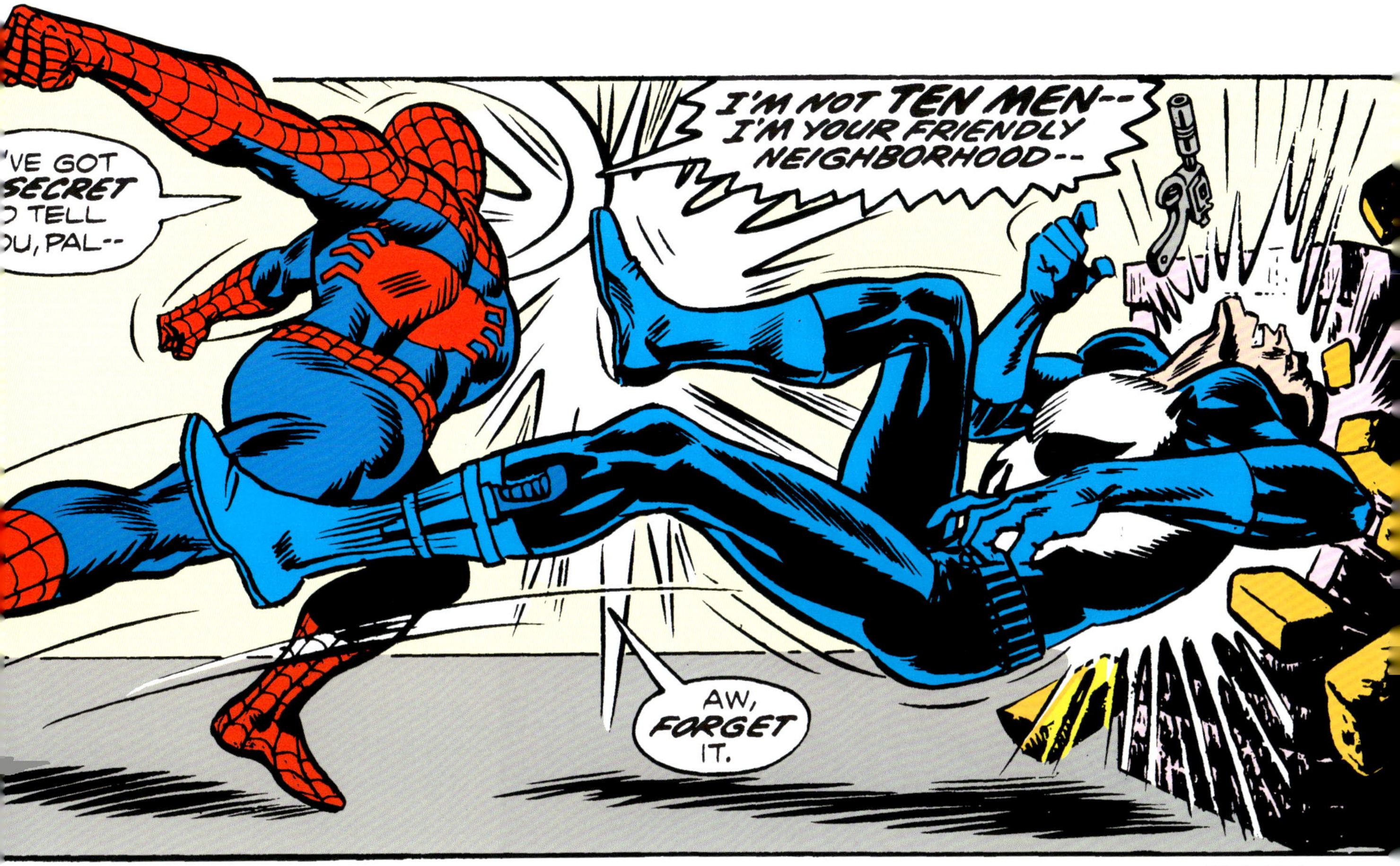

crime-stopper that same year: the Punisher, a new character created by Conway, Romita, and Ross Andru, who debuted in *The Amazing Spider-Man #129*.

Frank Castle was a Vietnam vet whose wife and two small children were killed after they had by chance witnessed a mob killing in Central Park. Vowing revenge, Frank Castle dons a black costume emblazoned with a skull across the front, and becomes the Punisher. He takes to the streets, a one-man war machine targeting criminals of every sort.

The character is still popular today, and like Iron Fist and Luke Cage, has starred in his own series on Netflix (2017-2019). Whether right or wrong, he treats audiences to an expression of commonly felt sentiments. Anti-heroes like the Punisher would give us a taste of things to come in a decade that promised to be grim and gritty, the perfect backdrop for what would be a revisionist overhaul of our favourite Super Heroes.

The time had come for Marvel characters to branch out, and the company's top brass had their sights set on TV and the movies. The new owners put Stan Lee in charge of the mission, and he began travelling back and forth to Los Angeles to promote various projects.

Not an easy task at the time, since technology back then was

ABOVE
The wall-crawler takes out the Punisher in *The Amazing Spider-Man #129* (February 1974). Script by Gerry Conway. Art by Ross Andru (pencils), Frank Giacoia and Dave Hunt (colours), John Costanza (letters).

BELOW
Writer Gerry Conway.

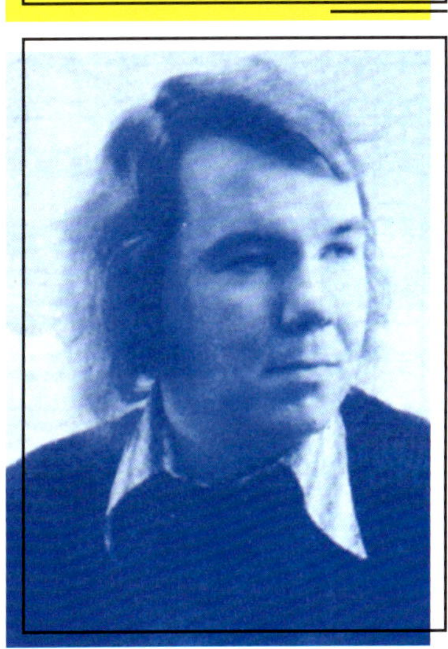

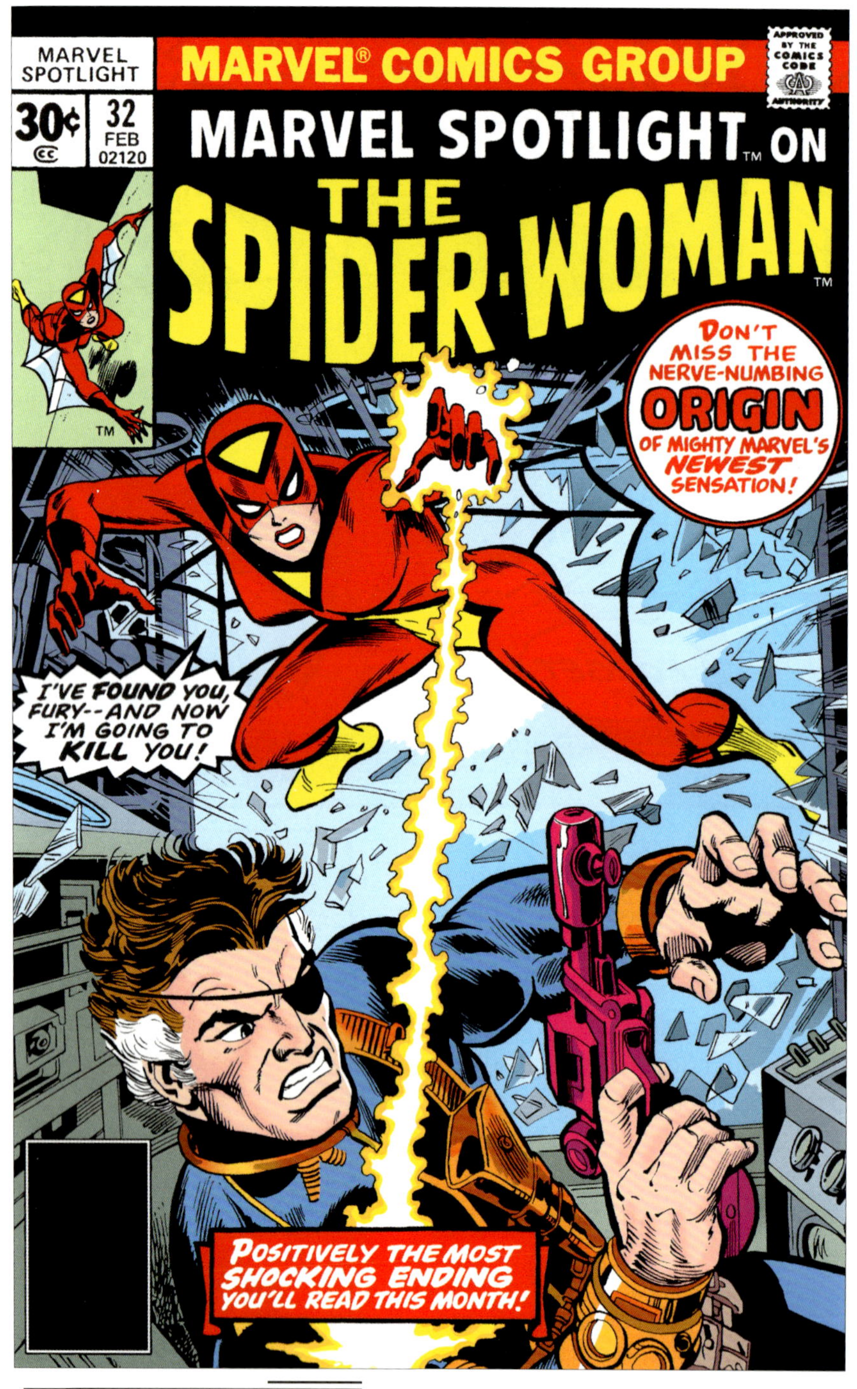

The first appearance of Spider-Woman from *Marvel Spotlight* #32 (February 1977). Art by Gil Kane (pencils), Dick Giordano and John Romita, Sr. (inks).

hard put to recreate incredible comic-book effects for film.

The first step would be cartoons. In 1966, the first ever Marvel cartoon series, *Marvel Super Heroes*, appeared, followed in 1967 by *Spider-Man* and *Fantastic Four*. In 1978 NBC came out with a *Fantastic Four* cartoon series, featuring Herbie the robot in place of the Human Torch. The following year, ABC ran a weekly cartoon series featuring one of the new Super Heroes from the 1970s, Spider-Woman, which was created by Archie Goodwin and Marie Severin.

As for live-action on television and in the movies, things were somewhat more complicated. Spider-Man would be the character to focus on first. In 1977, CBS produced the TV series *The Amazing Spider-Man*, which was limited to just 13 episodes before it was cancelled (1977–79).

The same network also came out with a TV movie, while some of the TV series episodes were pieced together and released as full-length motion pictures for distribution outside the United States. The series starred a fairly credible Nicholas Hammond as Peter Parker, but supporting characters were different from the ones comic-book readers were accustomed to. Among fans, the series eventually achieved cult status.

The live-action TV series *The Incredible Hulk* (1977–82) proved to be of much higher production value, and achieved much greater success. It starred Bill Bixby as Dr. David Banner and body builder Lou Ferrigno as the Hulk, and featured the theme song, dripping with emotion, 'The Lonely Man' by

Joe Harnell. Banner grappled with his curse for 80 episodes, plus three made-for-TV movies.

While feature films for theatre distribution were still beyond Marvel's reach, more TV movies were made. The best known of these was *Captain America* (1979), only loosely based on the comic-book Super Hero. It featured a motorcycle-riding Cap who got his superpowers from a steroid called F.L.A.G., short for 'full latent ability gain'. Another was *Doctor Strange* (1978), which placed a psychiatrist in the lead role and veered significantly from the comic-book version. It was produced by CBS as a pilot for a TV series that would never see the light of day.

22

MOVIE

SPIDER-MAN

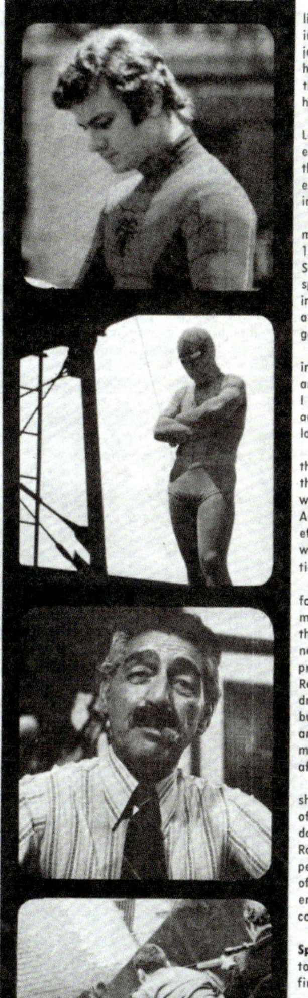

A little while ago, we heard that there was a Marvel movie in the works, so we made a few inquiries. Our search led us to Bruce Cardozo and his fellow classmates at NYU, all of whom had gathered together to produce a live-action Spider-Man movie as a film project. We asked Bruce to tell us how the web-spinner's cinema escapade got started and what's being done. His reply follows—and represents yet another milestone in the madcap Marvel Age! ●

Since I first started reading Spider-Man in the early sixties, I knew the character was cinematic and would probably make a blockbuster film. I always wondered if the film would be made and who would make it. I tried some experiments in 8mm, but I soon realized that to do the film correctly it would take a gargantuan budget and a very carefully chosen cast.

As I grew older, I produced superhero and fantasy films which were exhibited in film festivals, and won a couple of awards. An important thing I strived for was believability. Even if the idea was totally outrageous, the audience could believe in the situation because of the way it was portrayed. I was very disappointed in the superhero adaptations of the sixties because they, like every super-hero on film produced in the last decade, lacked any kind of depth. Even in the Marvel cartoon series, every element of realism and credibility, which is a key factor in Marvel Comics, was totally lost. Film producers (both live action and animation) could not believe in the characters the way a comic fan does, and this failure shows up in the finished project.

When I entered college, the idea of a live action Spider-Man movie still lingered in my mind. I thought of how I would do justice to the character, unlike the superhero adaptations of the sixties. I wanted the audience to feel as though the comic had come to life.

In October 1972, I wrote a letter to Stan Lee explaining the project. I received a very enthusiastic letter of approval providing the film was limited to non-commercial exhibition (because of commercial licensing commitments Marvel had at the time).

Next, I presented the idea to my experimental film class, proposing a half hour, 16mm, color, sound, semi-professional Spider-Man movie. When I outlined the special effects the class felt that it was impossible, but my instructor, Peter Glushanok, was very interested and gave me the go-ahead.

The first term was spent almost entirely in pre-production. I was a perfectionist, and I spoke with hundreds of people before I decided on the cast alone. I wanted the audience to say to themselves, "he or she looks and acts exactly like the characters."

Daphne Stevens and Marilyn Hecht made the costumes, Richard Eberhardt designed the graphics, such as the spider-signal, (as well as playing Spider-Man in costume) and Art Schweitzer created the unusual lighting effects featured throughout the film. I worked on the scenario, production direction and the special effects.

We built an entire section of a building for Spider-Man to climb. We used traveling matte shots to make Spider-Man swing through Times Square at night with all the neon signs flashing in the background to produce breath-taking and dazzling visuals. Rather than using a phony looking backdrop when Spider-Man climbs up and down buildings, we matted in colorful sunsets and backgrounds, and utilized travelling mattes in a scene where Kraven sends lions after Spider-Man in the final conflict.

The second term was hectic with more shooting and editing by Julie Tanser. As of this August 1, the film was about 3/4 done. On that date; we gave Stan Lee, Roy Thomas and other members of the bullpen, a preview of some of the key scenes of the film. They were very impressed and enthusiastic about the results and encouraged us to finish the project.

The screenplay is adapted primarily from **Spider-Man** 15 with various scenes added to update the story concerning Kraven's first arrival in America.

Our casting has gotten considerable applause—Jameson, as played by Andrew Pastorio, and Parker, played by Joe Ellison, have been described as "dead ringers" for the characters.

We hope in the future to have the film distributed in some form, and perhaps, with the support of FOOM members across the country, we might find a solution to the situation.

Bruce Cardozo

Feelin' Foomy – Dave Farr

Foom on a Hot Tin Roof – Ray Bonnice

FOOM #4 (Winter 1973) took a look at a New York University student film based on Spider-Man.

MEGO

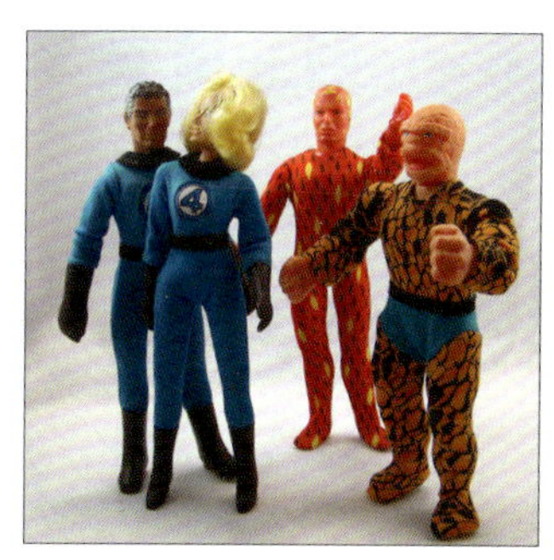

With an ever-growing impact on popular culture in America and throughout the world, in the 1970s Marvel began a highly successful merchandising campaign. Its most famous characters soon appeared on an array of objects and clothing, and kids played with action figures that were destined to become collectors' items. In 1971 Mego, the leading manufacturer of action figures in those days, purchased the rights to make and market models based on Marvel characters. First off the assembly line were miniature versions of Spider-Man and the Hulk—toys that would become best-sellers worldwide.

The 1980s

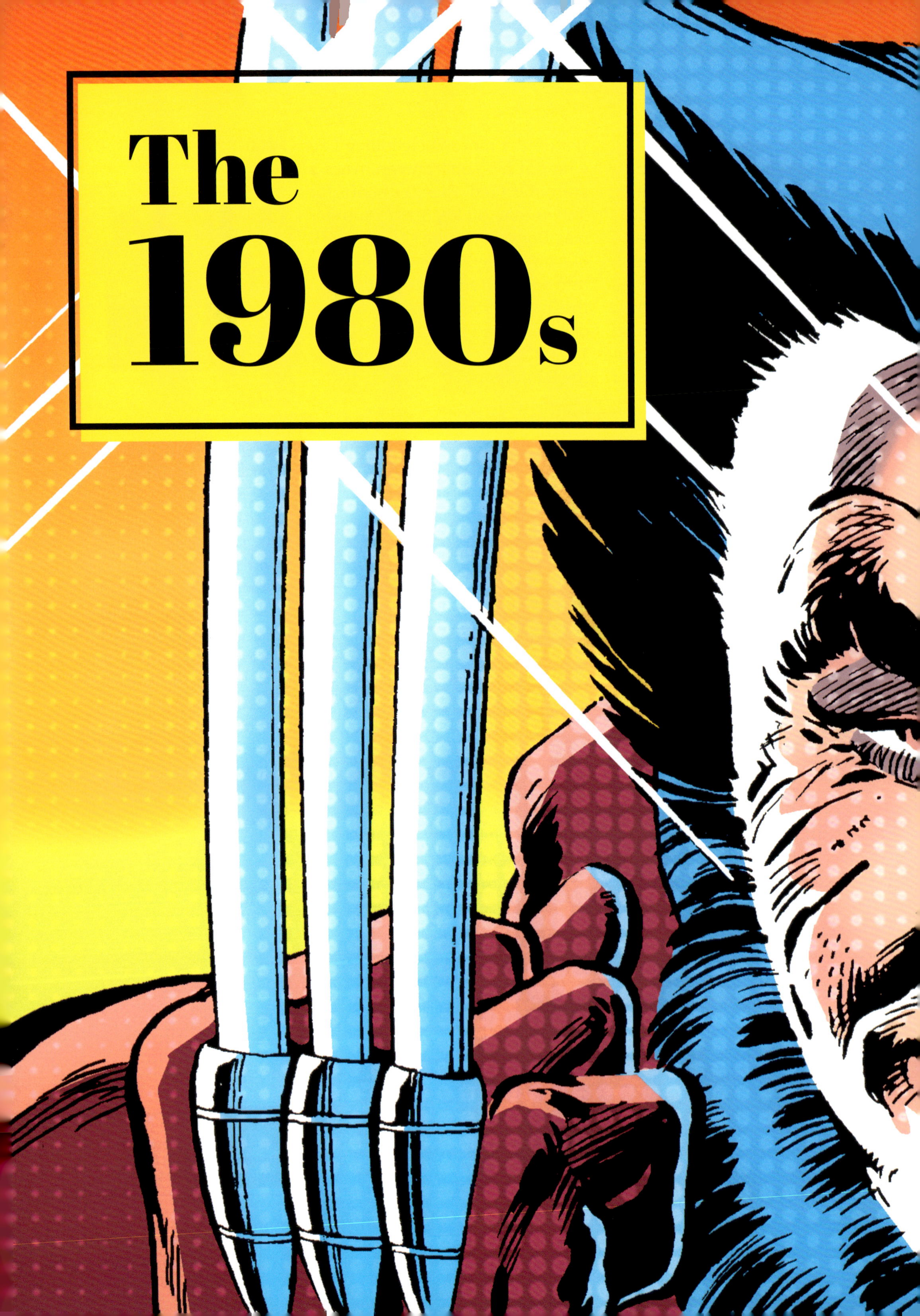

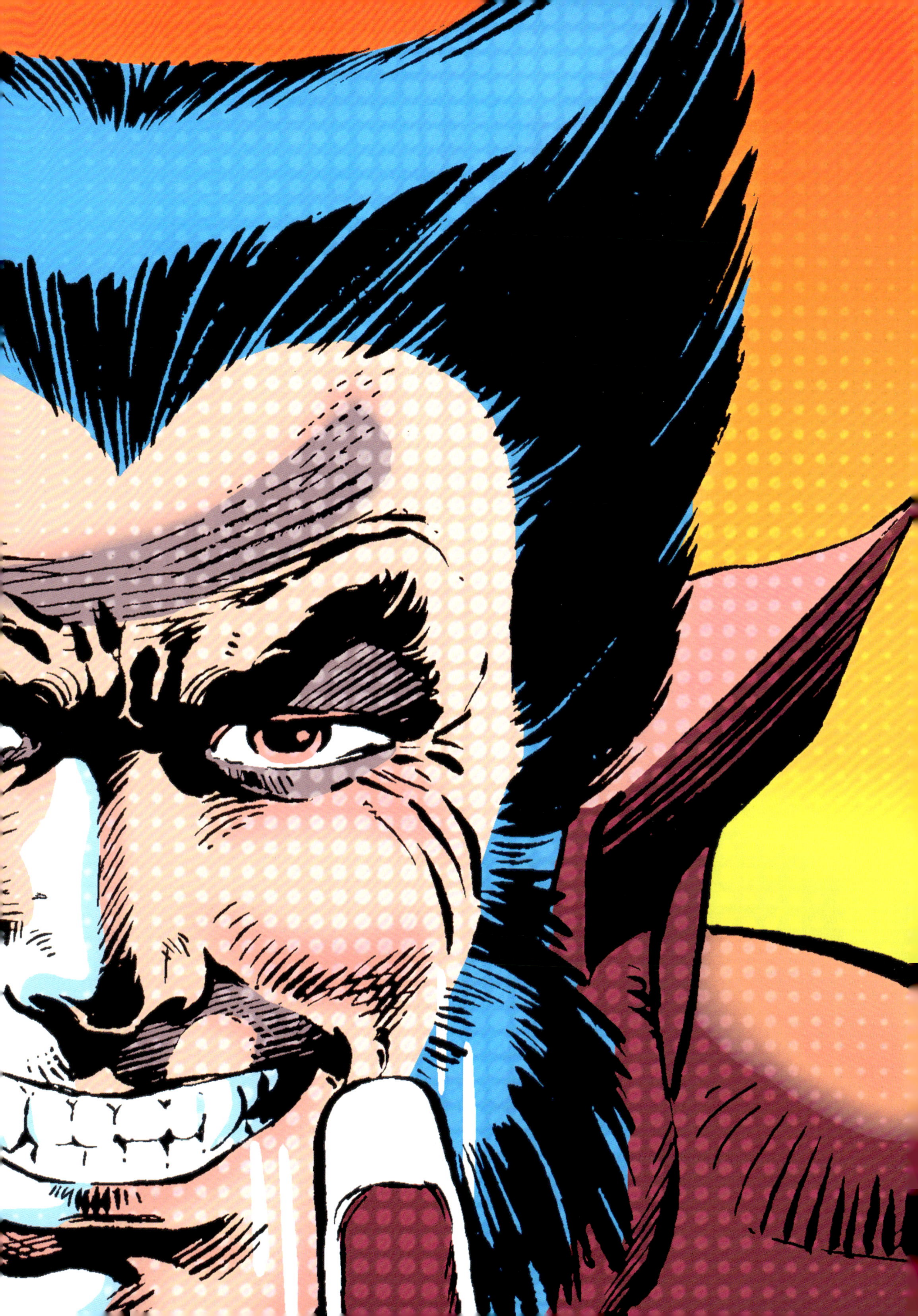

SECRET WARS AND NEW WORLDS

In the 1980s, Marvel celebrated the 25th anniversary of the Marvel Universe—but they refused to rest on their creative laurels.

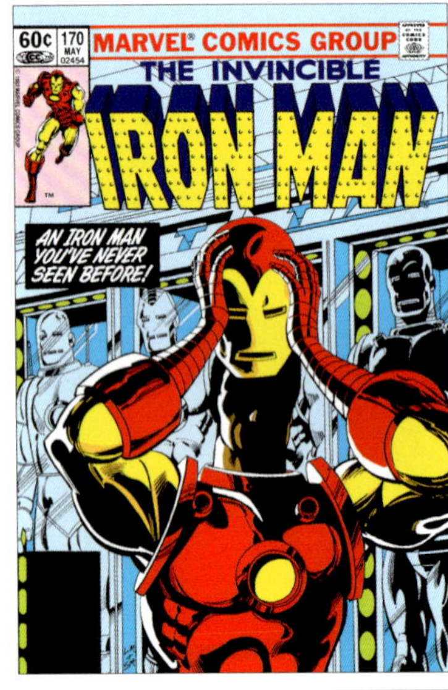

TOP
The Invincible Iron Man #170 (May 1983). Art by Luke McDonnell (pencils), Steve Mitchell (inks), Bob Sharen (colours).

OPPOSITE PAGE
The Amazing Spider-Man #252 (May 1984). Art by Ron Frenz (pencils), Klaus Janson (inks), Glynis Wein (colours).

The 1980s were all about innovation at Marvel, in terms of experimentation, quality, and new characters, approaches, and trends that would set the stage for future developments. A significant portion of the editorial decisions, including the key takes on the narrative end, would be guided by editor in chief Jim Shooter. Meanwhile, things began to change industry-wide. With the gradual disappearance of old sales channels and the rise of comic-book shops and direct market sales, publishers set out to create projects that exclusively targeted specialty venues. It was a winning bet. The first issue of *Dazzler*, which featured a heroine that had originally been created for a cross-media project that never took off, sold 428,000 copies.

What drove commercial success were the publishing events, to the point where they began appearing annually. Event comics became the big sellers, bringing together the pantheon of Marvel characters in releases like *Contest of Champions*, which was the first limited series that appeared in this format, and others featuring tie-ins, like *Secret Wars* and *Secret Wars II*. The decade also saw the comics pushing into uncharted territory. It saw the first time that someone took the place of an iconic hero under the mask. Make that... under the *helmet*.

In 1983's *Iron Man #170*, James Rhodes, Tony Stark's trusted pilot and friend, took Iron Man's place when the inventor endured a debilitating personal crisis. In *Captain America #333* (1987), Cap himself assumed the new identity of the Captain and found himself on a collision course with the U.S. government and a violent super-patriot John Walker, who became the 'new' Captain America.

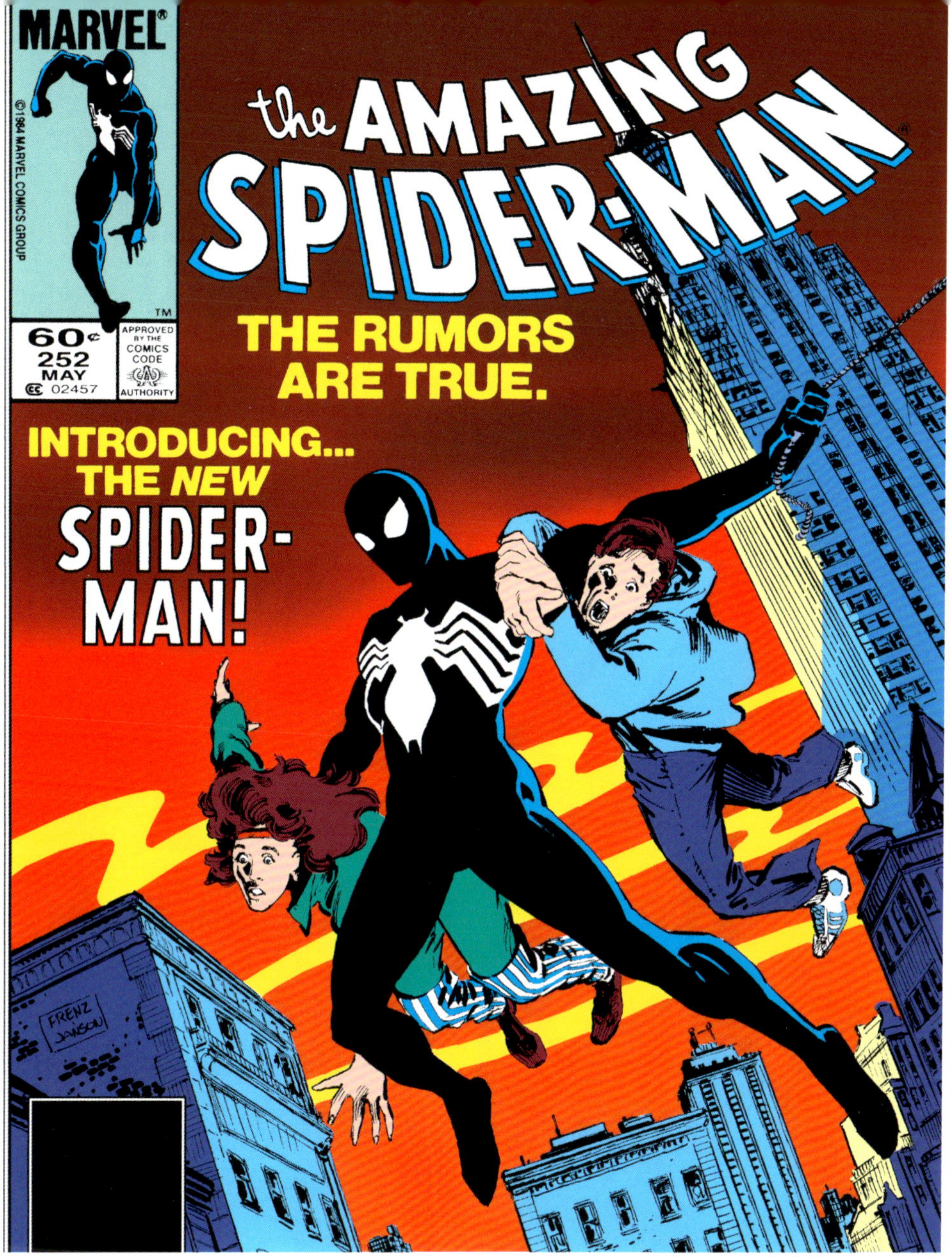

Then there was Thor, who, in the climax of the cycle scripted and drawn by Walt Simonson, and under a spell cast by the Goddess of Death Hela, wound up sporting new heavy armour. The sequence of stories was so innovative that at one point the God of Thunder relinquished his hammer to the horse-like alien Beta Ray Bill!

Spider-Man, too, would change his look in *The Amazing Spider-Man #252* and *Secret Wars #7*, and don a black costume for four years. In the late 1980s, Hulk became grey again and took on the clever Joe Fixit identity. The Avengers' latest lineup change saw the creation of the West Coast branch, led by Hawkeye.

Many of these new developments were masterminded by Shooter, who, once the idea of doing away with the main heroes altogether was scrapped, launched the imprint New Universe, featuring a cast of all-new characters. But the series that bore more changes than any other starred a group of mutants known as the Uncanny X-Men. Even after Shooter left in 1987 and Tom DeFalco became editor in chief, the Uncanny X-Men's popularity continued to soar.

EPIC STORIES

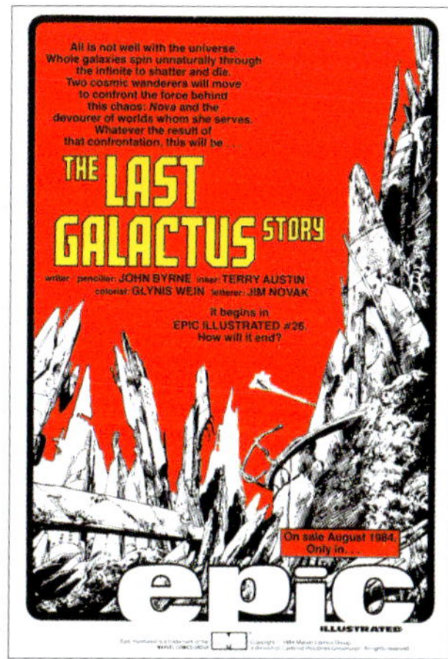

Inspired by magazines like *Heavy Metal*, Marvel launched *Epic Illustrated* in 1980, aiming for an older audience. *Epic* occasionally presented adventure stories featuring Marvel Super Heroes. But it was more focused on stories that spanned a wide array of different genres, often by mainstream comic-book writers and artists making their Marvel debuts, as well as talent from the independent press and the U.K. Cover paintings were created by the likes of Frank Frazetta, Richard Corben, and the Hildebrandt brothers, and the whole shebang was overseen by Archie Goodwin, a highly esteemed editor. *Epic Illustrated* would pave the way for an entire line of products brimming with masterpieces.

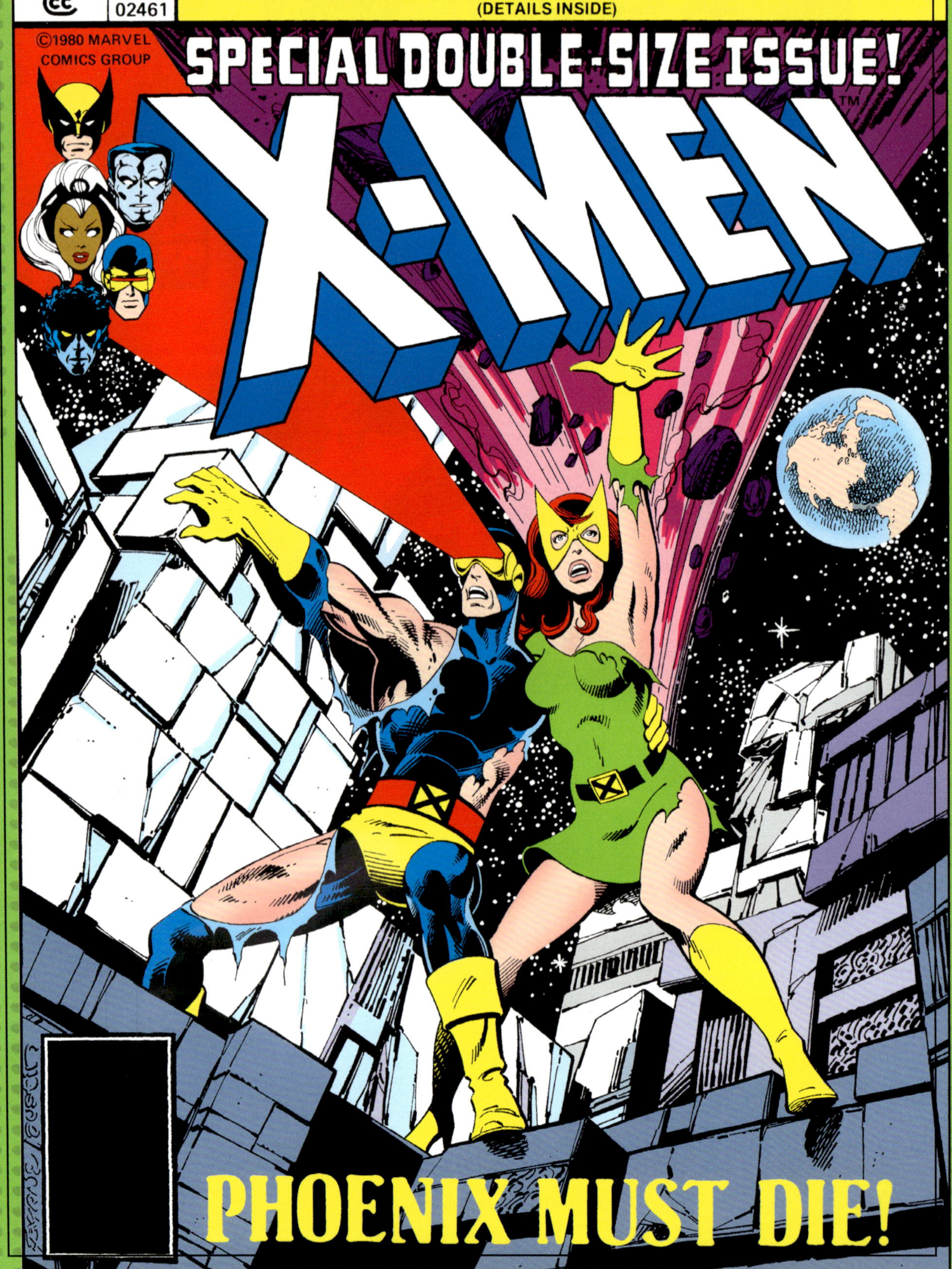
MARVEL® COMICS GROUP
75¢
CC
137
SEPT
02461
THIS MARVEL® COMIC COULD BE WORTH $2500 TO YOU!
(DETAILS INSIDE)
©1980 MARVEL COMICS GROUP
SPECIAL DOUBLE-SIZE ISSUE!
X-MEN™
PHOENIX MUST DIE!

MUTANTS, NINJAS, AND BIG EVENTS

The 1980s saw the rise of the X-Men, Daredevil, and the Punisher, as Marvel embraced the changing tastes of its audience.

In *The Uncanny X-Men #137* (cover-dated September 1980) writer Chris Claremont and artist John Byrne, who often worked as a team, brought a long cycle, begun in 1976, to an end. Jean Grey, the former Marvel Girl who had assumed the powerful Phoenix identity under the watch of artist Dave Cockrum, was corrupted by an ambitious Super Villain, the mutant Mastermind, and became a force of evil. Power-crazed Dark Phoenix unleashed death and destruction on a rampage among the galaxies.

In a touching moment of lucidity, she ended her life in the arms of her beloved Cyclops on a desolate lunar landscape. Such a finale had a strong narrative and editorial impact—having the former heroine die was a big step for the creators, and for Shooter in particular.

A year later, Claremont and Byrne would go their separate ways, but not before creating another momentous saga: 'Days of Future Past.' After that, the title was illustrated by artists like Paul Smith, known for his humanising touch, and the explosively talented John Romita, Jr. 'Jazzy John's' son was one of his generation's most highly skilled and versatile artists (he also lent his prowess to artwork for *The Amazing Spider-Man* and, over the course of the '80s, *Iron Man* and *Daredevil*).

But even if Byrne had left the series to pursue other projects, throughout the years he spent working alongside Claremont, the

OPPOSITE PAGE
The Uncanny X-Men #137 (September 1980).
Art by John Byrne (pencils), Terry Austin (inks), Glynis Wein (colours).

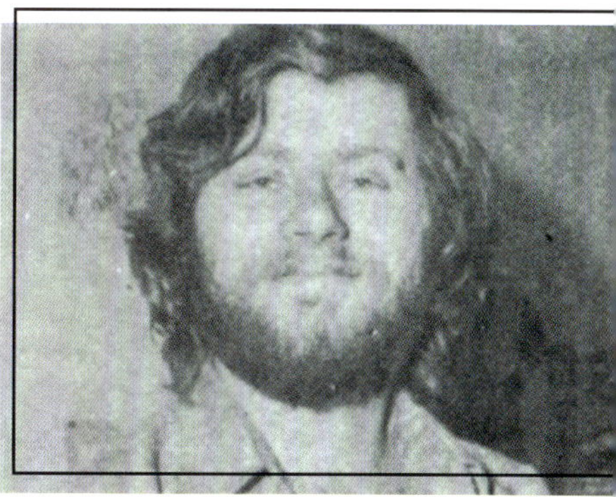

Writer Chris Claremont.

"As Dave [Cockrum] and I honed our craft, as individuals and a team, so did the characters make their initially halting and occasionally clumsy steps into becoming a team, and ultimately a family... the characters had only just met then, as opposed to having been together for longer than many readers' and some creators' lifetimes. There was the marvel of discovery to every aspect of the book."

—Chris Claremont

URBAN VIGILANTE

On the streets of New York, another Marvel Super Hero would rise to popularity in the 1980s: the Punisher. Vigilante Frank Castle made his debut in *The Amazing Spider-Man #129* in 1974, and in the years that followed was relegated to bit parts. Marine veteran Castle had declared his own personal war on crime after his family was gunned down in a hail of crossfire in an exchange between rival mob factions. For years, the writer Steven Grant had tried proposing to Marvel a limited series based on the character. He finally got the green light for the project when artist Mike Zeck, riding the success of *Secret Wars*, signed on. The 1986 limited series *The Punisher* became an iconic hit and spawned more comics starring Castle in the years to come. In 1987, the ongoing series *The Punisher* made its debut, which ran all the way to 1995 and issue #104. Fans were also treated to *The Punisher War Journal* (80 issues, 1988–1995), *The Punisher War Zone* (41 issues, 1992–1995), and a slew of specials and graphic novels.

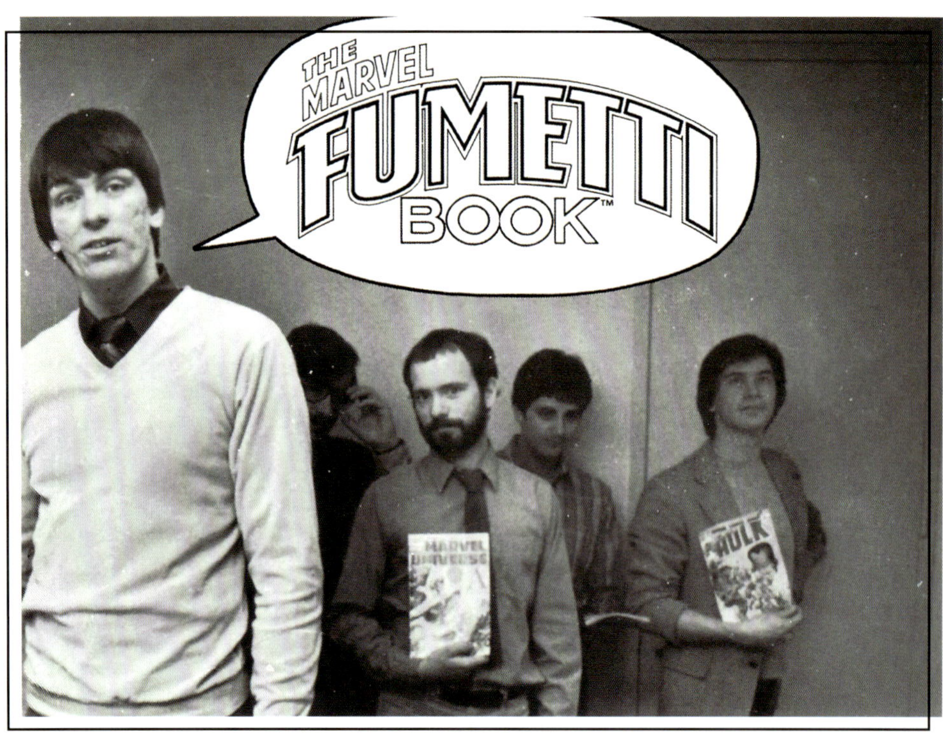

two had laid the foundations for future decades of success for the X-Men, including the basis for film plots to come. And when a series is that successful, it's sure to spawn its share of spin-offs.

The first was *The New Mutants*. While everyone thought the X-Men were dead, Professor Xavier brought together a new team of teenage mutants from around the world to complete their training. The series debuted in 1983, and eventually racked up a hundred issues, with plenty of changes in squad line-ups, leadership, and the artists and writers who created them. At one point, Professor X himself was replaced by his longtime nemesis, the reformed Magneto. One of the best-known cycles saw Claremont using the visionary artwork of

1980

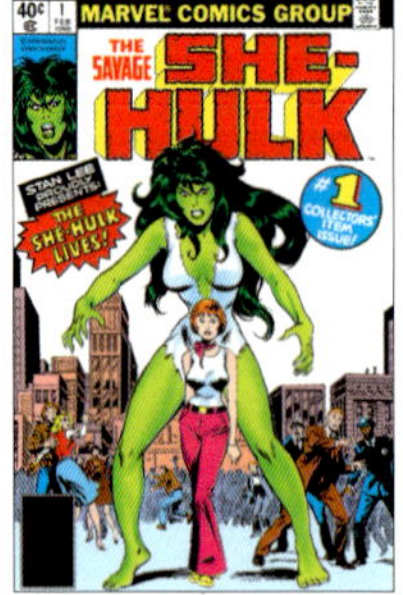

FEBRUARY 1980
Jen 'She-Hulk' Walters, a Stan Lee and John Buscema creation, makes her debut in *The Savage She-Hulk #1*.

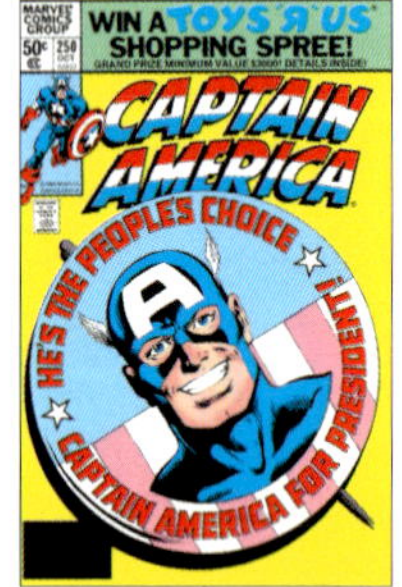

OCTOBER 1980
Cap for President! In *Captain America #250*, by Roger Stern and John Byrne, Steve is asked to run for the country's highest office, but refuses.

Bill Sienkiewicz, which helped shift the series in a direction that incorporated horror atmospheres.

Another mutant spin-off marking the reunion of the original X-Men formation appeared in 1986. In *The Avengers* and the *Fantastic Four*, readers learned that Jean Grey was, in fact, still alive. In truth, she had never really died, in that the Phoenix Force had made a duplicate of her—it was this version who had turned into Dark Phoenix, and who made the ultimate sacrifice.

Meanwhile, the real Jean was joined by her old teammates: Beast, Angel, Iceman, and, of course, Cyclops. The *X-Factor* series would soon come into its own thanks to the work of the husband-and-wife team of Walter and Louise Simonson—she wrote, he drew—who created, among other characters, the Super Villain Apocalypse.

In 1988, Chris Claremont and John Buscema introduced Logan's own personal series entitled *Wolverine*, which grew out of earlier adventures in a solo limited series of the same name created by Claremont and Frank Miller in 1982.

In the years that followed, Logan would reappear in the anthology *Marvel Comics Presents*. In 1989 Claremont also teamed up with British writer and artist Alan Davis to launch a series set in the U.K., *Excalibur*, featuring X-Men characters alongside local Super Heroes like Captain Britain.

Meanwhile, a young writer who had debuted as an inker was poised to make his mark on comic-book history when he turned his sights on a series that had been lagging in terms of sales. Frank Miller had honed his skills on *Marvel Team-Up* and a couple of issues of *The Spectacular Spider-Man* guest-starring Daredevil.

Not long thereafter, Miller was assigned to *Daredevil* beginning with issue #158 (cover-dated May 1979), where he initially worked with writer Roger McKenzie. Ten issues later, Miller took over writing duties

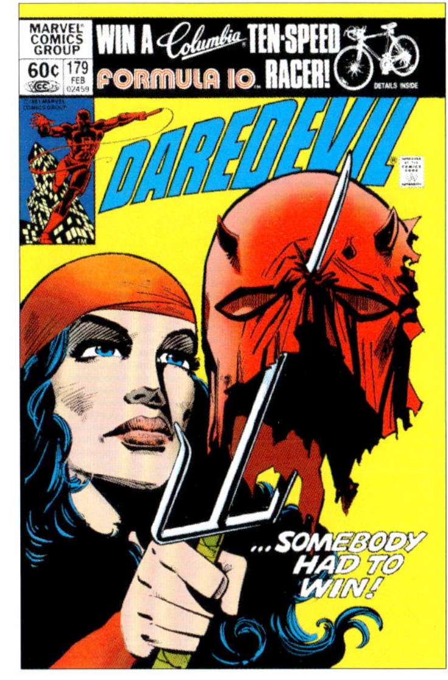

ABOVE
Daredevil #179 (February 1982). Art by Frank Miller (pencils) and Klaus Janson (colours).

OPPOSITE PAGE
Detail from *The Marvel Fumetti Book* (April 1984), a humorous behind-the-scenes look at Marvel featuring photo comics. From left to right: Jim Shooter, Tom DeFalco, Mark Gruenwald, Ralph Macchio, Carl Potts.

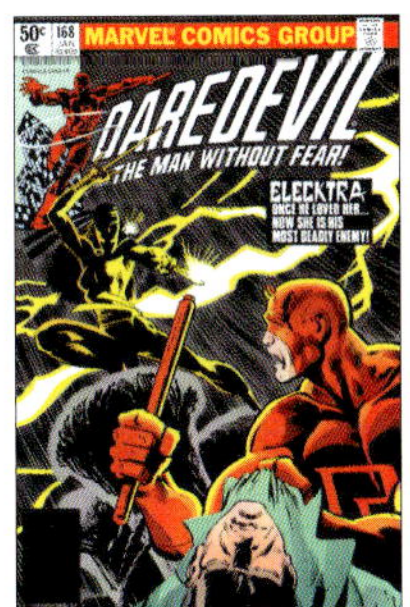

JANUARY 1981
Elektra makes her debut in *Daredevil #168*.

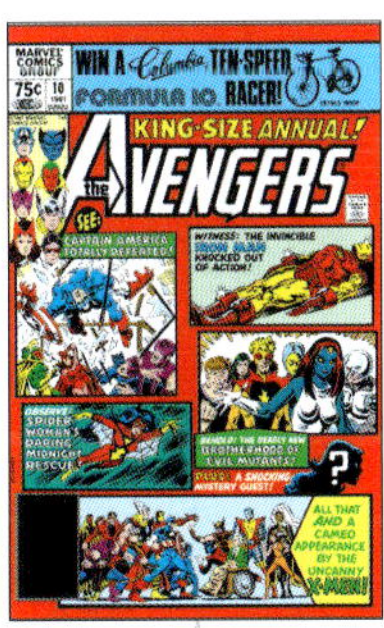

DECEMBER 1981
The Avengers Annual #10 features the first-ever appearance by Rogue, as a member of the Brotherhood of Evil Mutants.

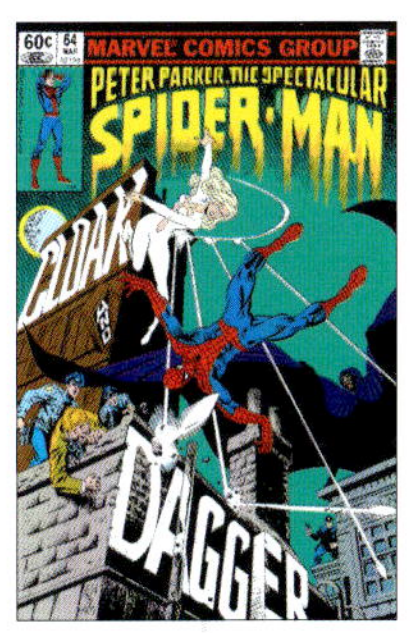

MARCH 1982
Vigilantes Cloak and Dagger make their debut in *The Spectacular Spider-Man #64*.

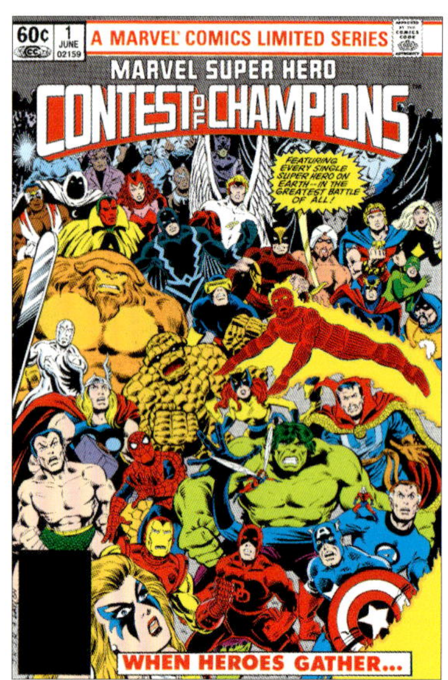

Marvel Super Hero Contest of Champions #1 (June 1982). Art by John Romita, Jr. (pencils) and Bob Layton (inks).

and began to develop the darker atmospheres that had already been a hallmark of his artwork. He was responsible for introducing characters like the sensei Stick and Elektra, a tormented ninja and Matt Murdock's former girlfriend; he also redefined supporting characters like crime boss Wilson 'Kingpin' Fisk, the lethal assassin Bullseye, and investigative journalist Ben Urich.

Over the course of a handful of issues, with the help of inker Klaus Janson, Miller would lay the foundation for Daredevil's most celebrated and imitated incarnation. The high point of Miller's first run on *Daredevil* was the death of Elektra in issue #181 (cover-dated April 1982).

Three years after leaving the series, Miller resumed writing for *Daredevil* in issue #227, in what was to be the start of yet another earth-shattering cycle: 'Born Again.' In this saga, illustrated by David Mazzucchelli, who was heavily influenced by Miller's dark themes, Matt's old flame and secretary Karen Page revealed Daredevil's secret identity to Kingpin. Thus began the fall and redemption/rise of Matt Murdock.

Meanwhile, event comics featuring expanded casts of Super Heroes fulfilled every reader's question, "I wonder what would happen if X met Y and they fought Z?" The first of its kind, *Contest of Champions*, had originally been slated for publication as a limited series to be released in conjunction with the start of the 1980 Summer Olympics in Moscow. But the U.S. boycott following the Soviet invasion of Afghanistan led Marvel to delay the release and revise the project. As a result, it wasn't until 1982 that *Contest of Champions* reached fans.

The three issues recount a cosmic game played by two powerful Super Villains who use Super Heroes from all over the world as pawns. A couple of years down the road, Marvel raised the stakes when it released *Marvel Super Heroes Secret Wars*, a series written by Jim Shooter, with

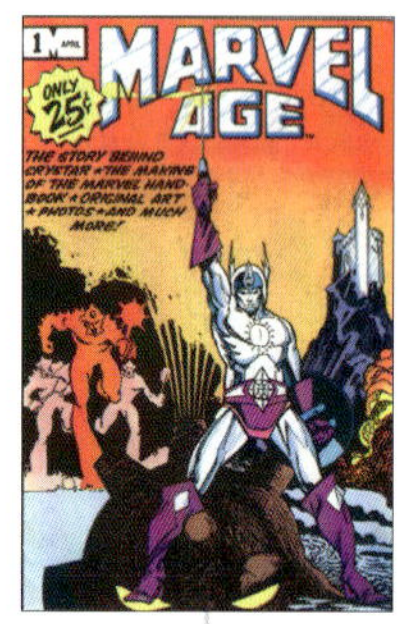

MARCH 1983
The first issue of *Marvel Age*, a long-running magazine featuring news and previews, hits the stores.

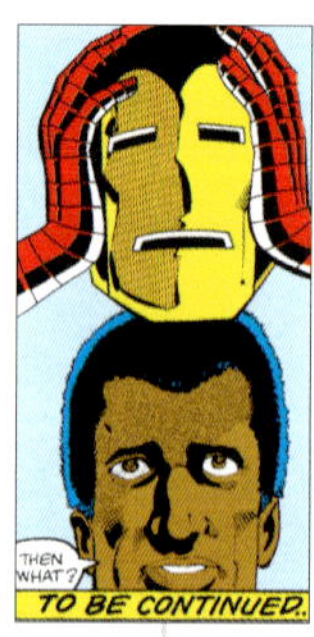

APRIL 1983
African-American Marines pilot James Rhodes dons the Iron Man armour.

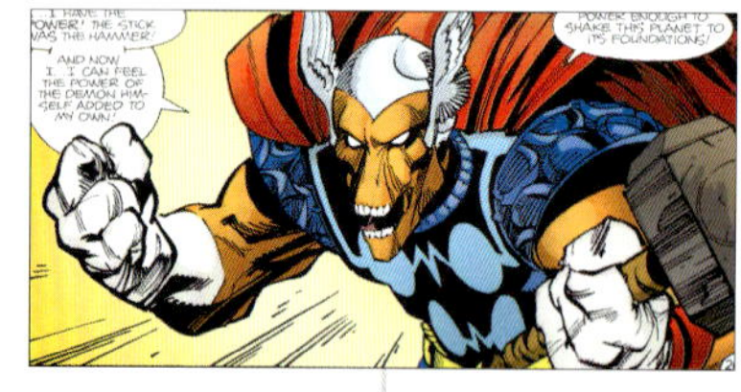

NOVEMBER 1983
Alien Beta-Ray Bill wields Thor's hammer for the first time.

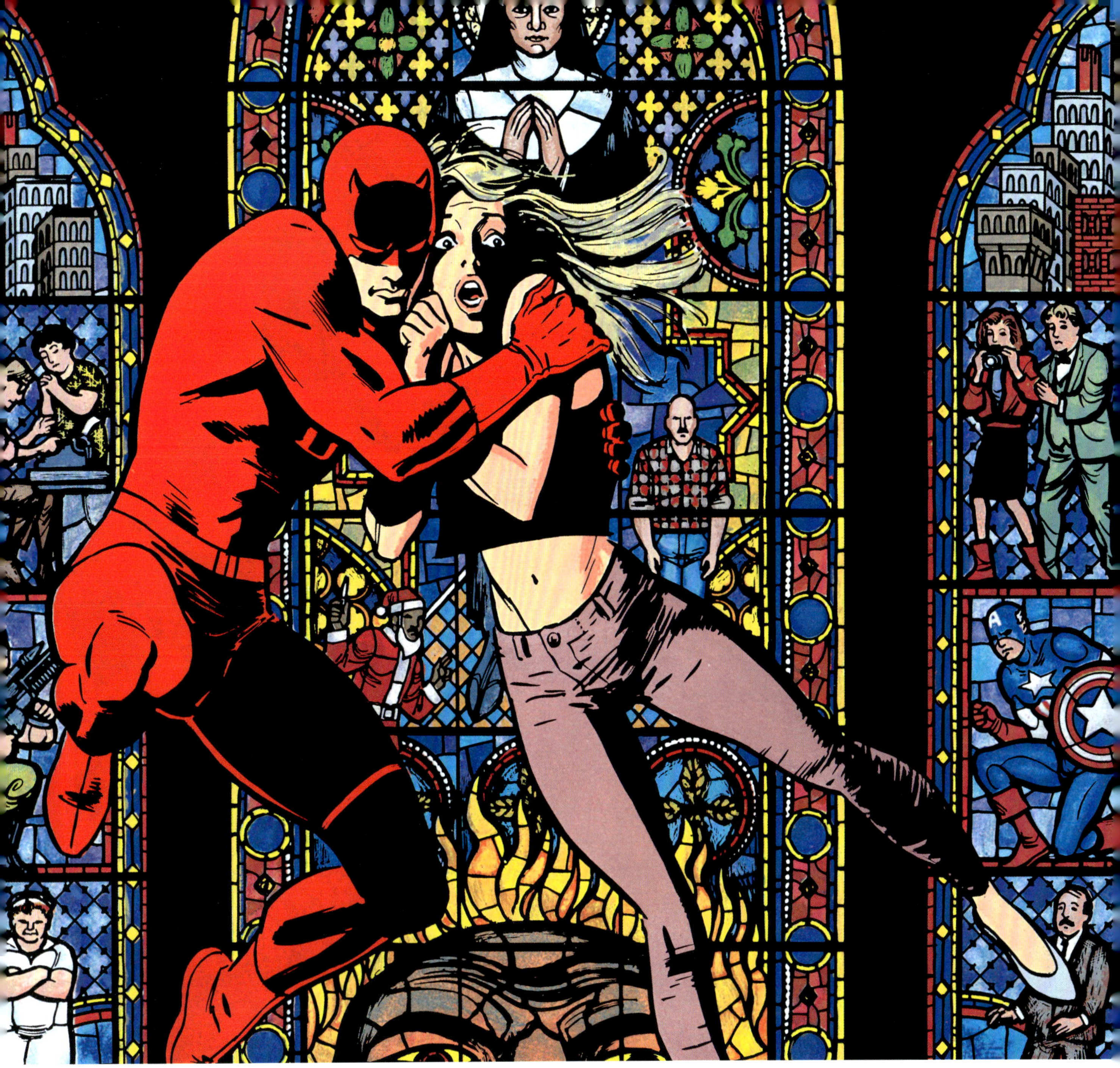

Cover detail from *Daredevil: Born Again* (1987), collecting the 'Born Again' storyline from *Daredevil* #227–231. Cover by David Mazzucchelli.

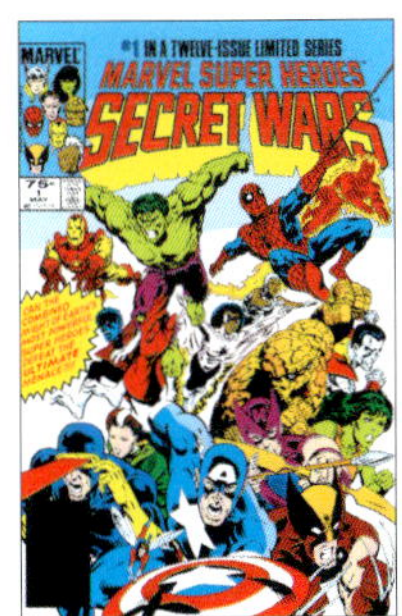

MAY 1984
Marvel Super Heroes Secret Wars #1 goes on sale.

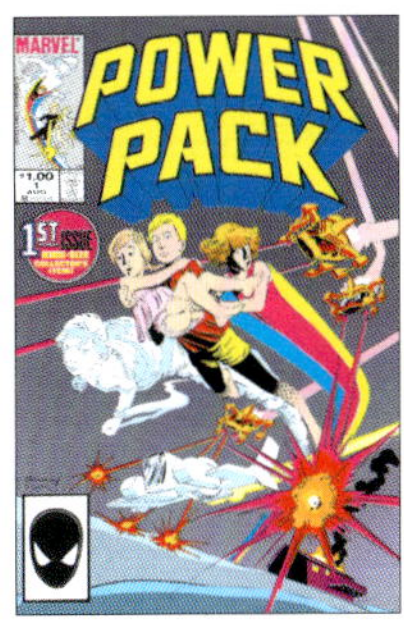

AUGUST 1984
Writer Louise Simonson and artist June Brigman launch *Power Pack*, featuring a team of kid heroes.

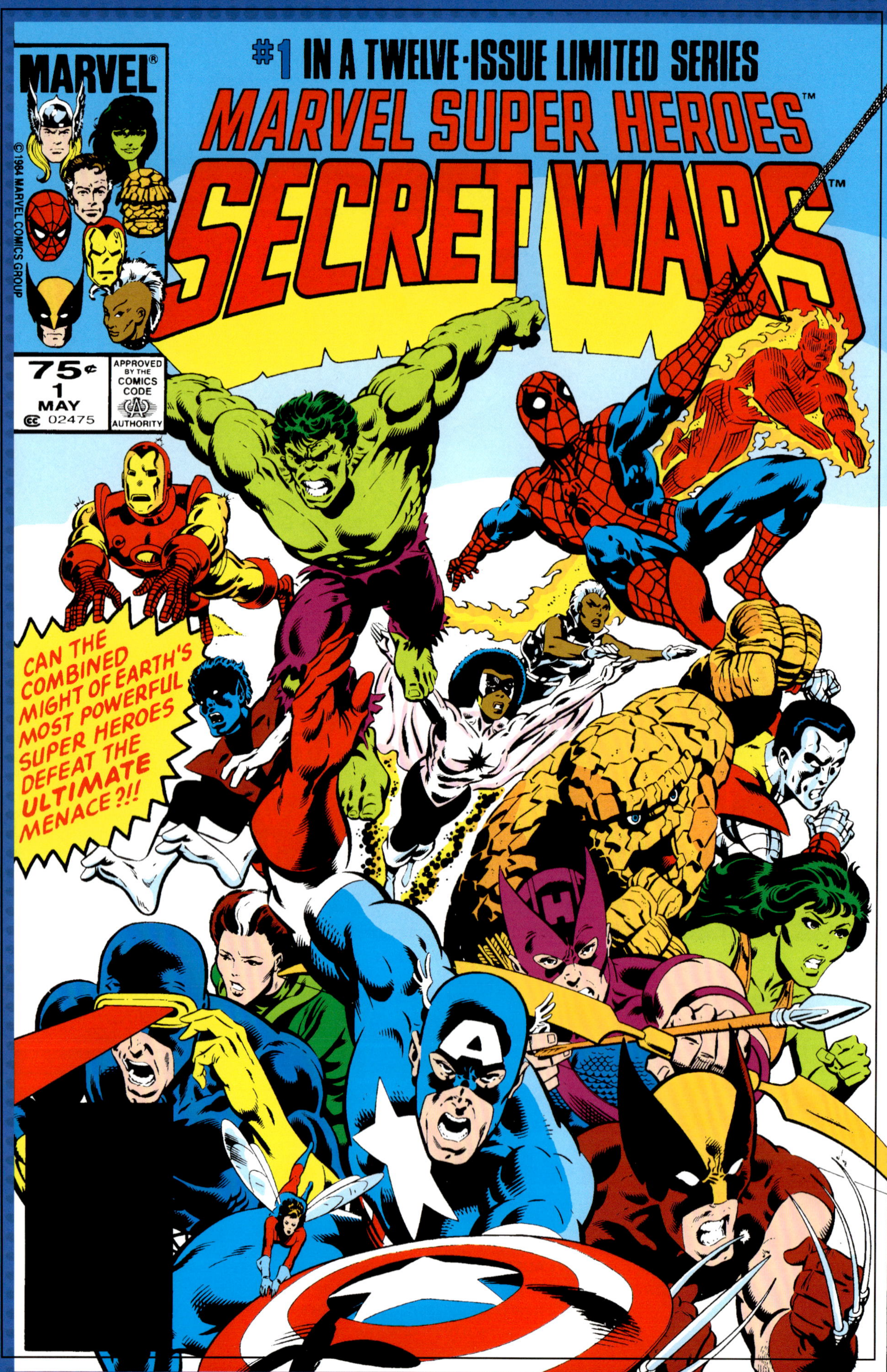

MARVEL
#1 IN A TWELVE-ISSUE LIMITED SERIES
MARVEL SUPER HEROES™
SECRET WARS™
© 1984 MARVEL COMICS GROUP
75¢
1
MAY
02475
APPROVED BY THE COMICS CODE AUTHORITY
CAN THE COMBINED MIGHT OF EARTH'S MOST POWERFUL SUPER HEROES DEFEAT THE ULTIMATE MENACE ?!!

artwork by Mike Zeck. The 12-issue limited series featured all-time favourite Super Heroes and their most formidable Super Villains, locked in a fight to the finish staged by the almost omnipotent Beyonder on Battleworld, a planet he created in a far-off galaxy.

The project tied in with a successful toy line from Mattel. *Marvel Super Heroes Secret Wars* was such a big hit that the impact on the Marvel Universe was astounding. It wasn't long before work began on a sequel. Among the developments it sparked a brand-new costume for Spidey, a new line-up for the Fantastic Four, and the debut of the second Spider-Woman. A year later, Shooter wrote the scripts for *Secret Wars II*, whose plot wound up branching out to various monthly series.

OPPOSITE PAGE
Marvel Super Heroes Secret Wars #1 (May 1984).
Art by Mike Zeck (pencils).

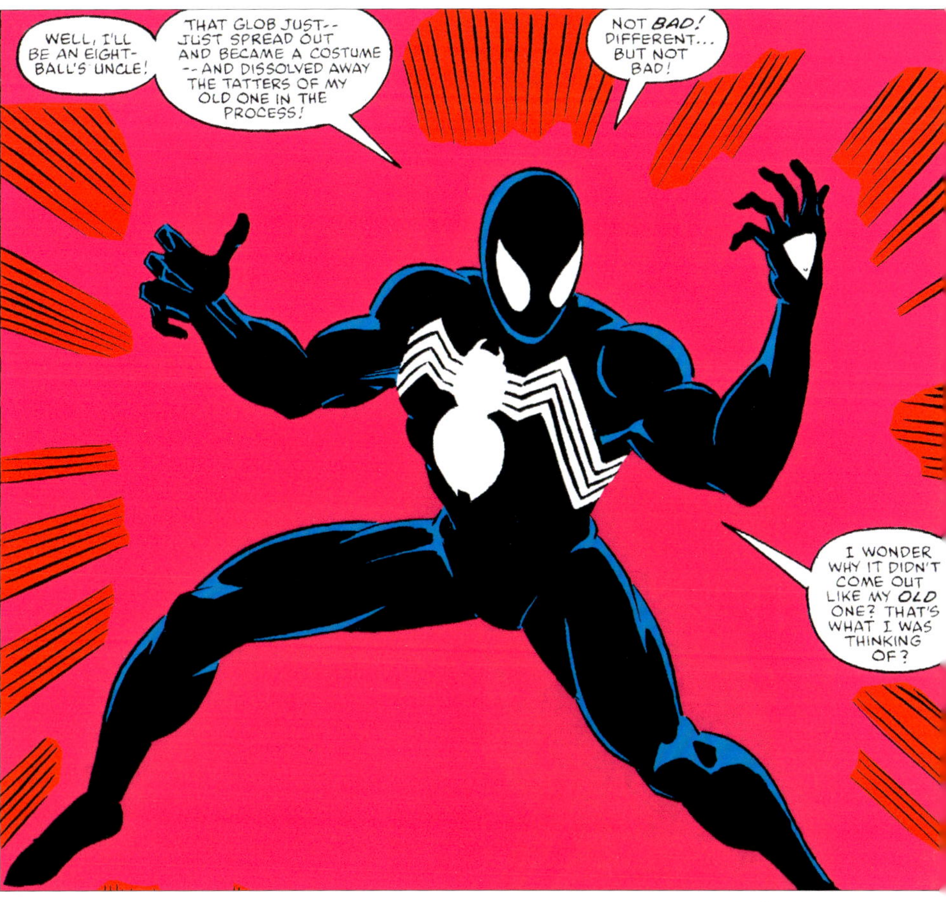

Spider-Man tries on his new costume for the first time in *Marvel Super Heroes Secret Wars #8* (December 1984). Script by Jim Shooter. Art by Mike Zeck (pencils), John Beatty, Jack Abel, Mike Esposito (inks), Christie Scheele (colours).

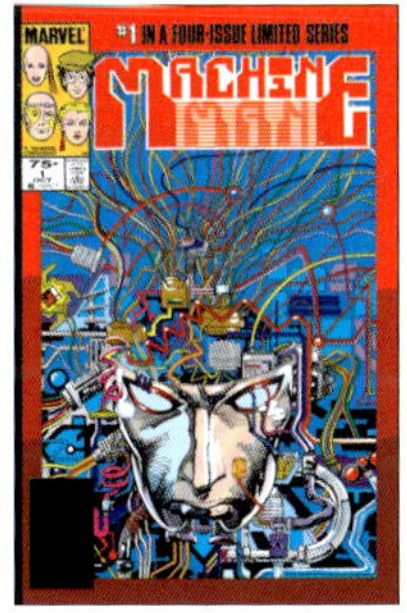

OCTOBER 1984
Barry Windsor-Smith illustrates the limited series starring Machine Man, the Super Hero created by Jack Kirby for the comic-book adaptation of *2001: A Space Odyssey*.

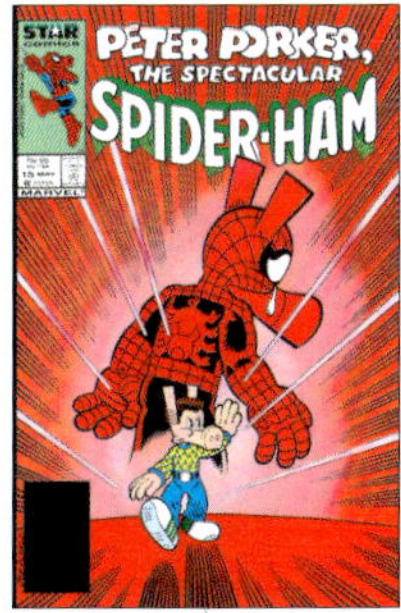

MAY 1985
The series *Peter Porker, the Spectacular Spider-Ham*, a Spider-Man parody, makes its debut under the newly born imprint for children Star Comics.

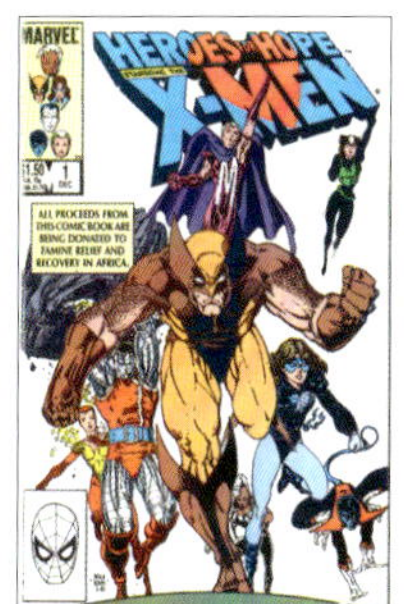

DECEMBER 1985
Marvel launches *Heroes for Hope*: Starring the X-Men, the comic book was designed to promote awaress of famine in Africa. Proceeds went to relief efforts.

MARVEL-OUS WOMEN

The 1980s saw the rise of heroes like Captain Marvel, She-Hulk, Elektra, and others who would change the face of the Marvel Universe.

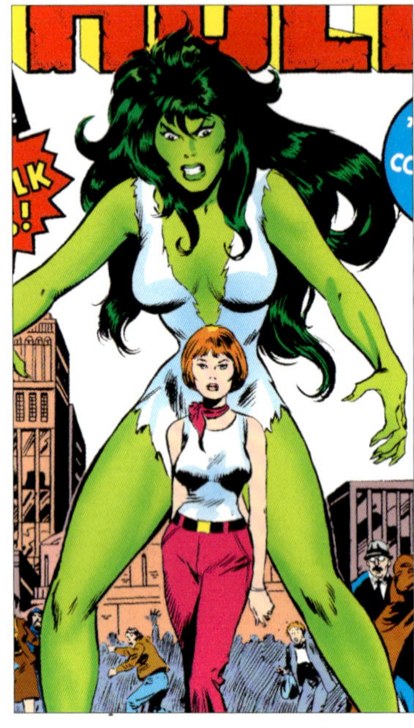

Cover detail from *The Savage She-Hulk #1* (February 1980). Art by John Buscema.

The 1980s saw the rise of a new wave of female characters. When the Kree hero Mar-Vell was struck down by cancer (in the first Marvel Graphic Novel, Jim Starlin's *The Death of Captain Marvel*), the code name was inherited by a new heroine, Monica Rambeau. The new Captain Marvel made her debut in 1982 in *The Amazing Spider-Man Annual #16*. She would soon join the Avengers, and eventually became the team's leader.

Then there was She-Hulk, who got her super-powers through a blood transfusion from her cousin, Bruce Banner. She first appeared in *The Savage She-Hulk #1* (1980), a series launched by Stan Lee and John Buscema. Thanks to John Byrne, who had her take the Thing's place in the Fantastic Four, She-Hulk became more than just her cousin's female counterpart.

During Byrne's acclaimed tenure at the helm of *The Fantastic Four* (#232–293), he turned Susan Richards into an even more three-dimensional character, a far cry from the damsel in distress she'd been at the start. New arrival Elektra, despite her death in

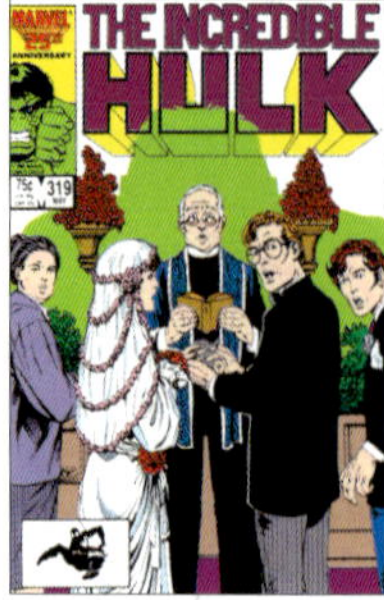

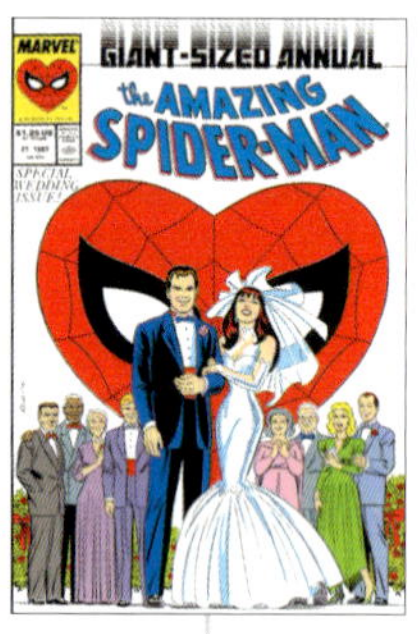

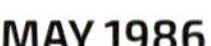

MAY 1986
Bruce Banner and Betty Ross are married in *The Incredible Hulk #319*.

1987
Peter Parker and Mary Jane Watson tie the knot in *The Amazing Spider-Man Annual #21*.

Daredevil, was a big hit with fans. She would soon be brought back to life and featured in memorable sagas and graphic novels, some of which were written by Frank Miller—like the limited series *Elektra: Assassin* (illustrated by Bill Sienkiewicz) and the 1990 graphic novel *Elektra Lives Again* (which was also illustrated by Miller).

Meanwhile, in *The Uncanny X-Men*, Chris Claremont was painstakingly developing the cast of female supporting characters, which included Rogue, who went from Super Villain to Super Hero; Storm, in search of redemption after temporarily losing her powers; teenager Kitty Pryde, who cut her teeth on the battlefield; and Carol Danvers, the former Ms. Marvel who morphed into the powerful Binary in *The Uncanny X-Men*.

The 1980s also ushered in some big changes for Spider-Man. There was his fiery relationship with reformed thief Black Cat; the death of his ally, N.Y.P.D. captain Jean DeWolff; and, most notably, his marriage to Mary Jane Watson.

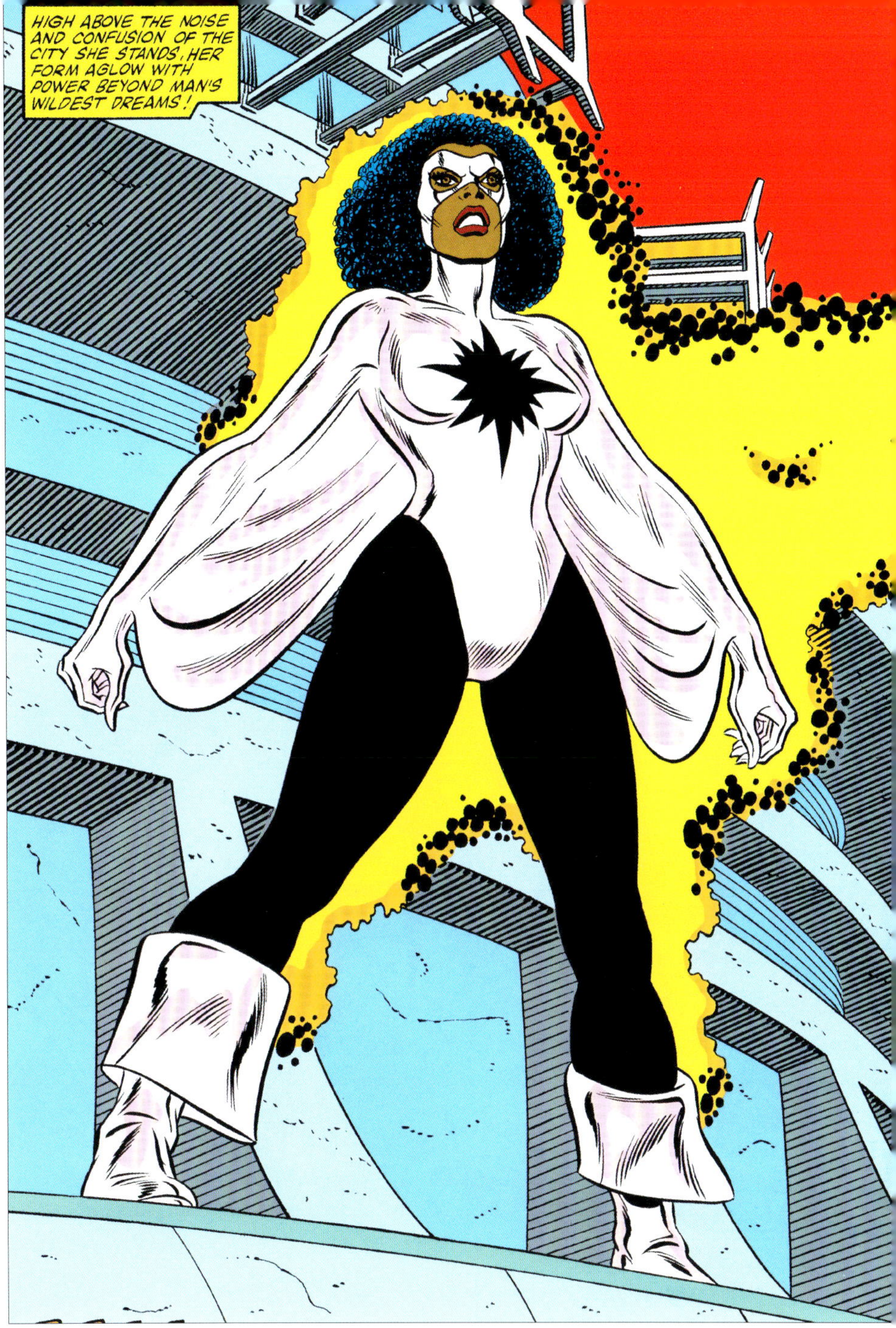

Monica Rambeau makes her appearance as Captain Marvel from *The Amazing Spider-Man Annual #16* (October 1982). Script by Roger Stern. Art by John Romita, Jr. (pencils), John Romita, Sr. (inks), Stan Goldberg (colours), Jim Novak (letters).

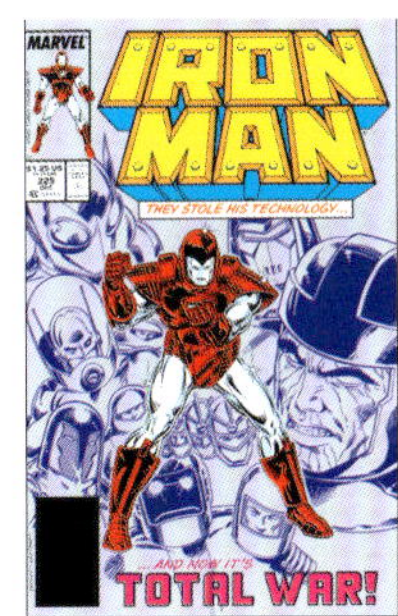

DECEMBER 1987
The high-power saga 'Armor Wars' gets underway in *Iron Man #225*.

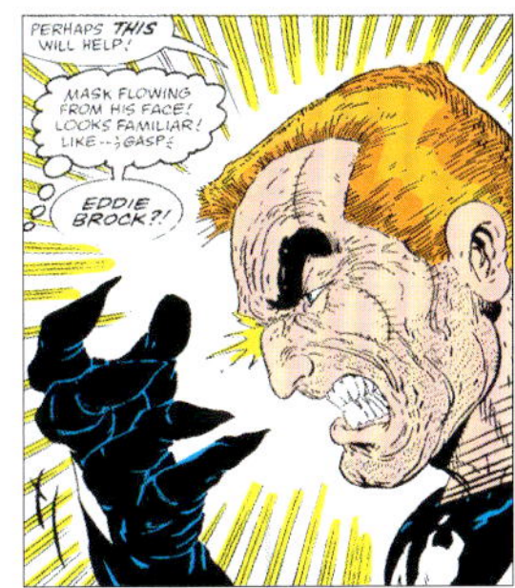

MARCH 1988
Venom reveals himself to his nemesis Spider-Man in *The Amazing Spider-Man #300* by David Michelinie and Todd McFarlane.

IN A CLASS OF THEIR OWN

As the 1980s roared on, new artists arrived on the scene to take Marvel to even greater heights.

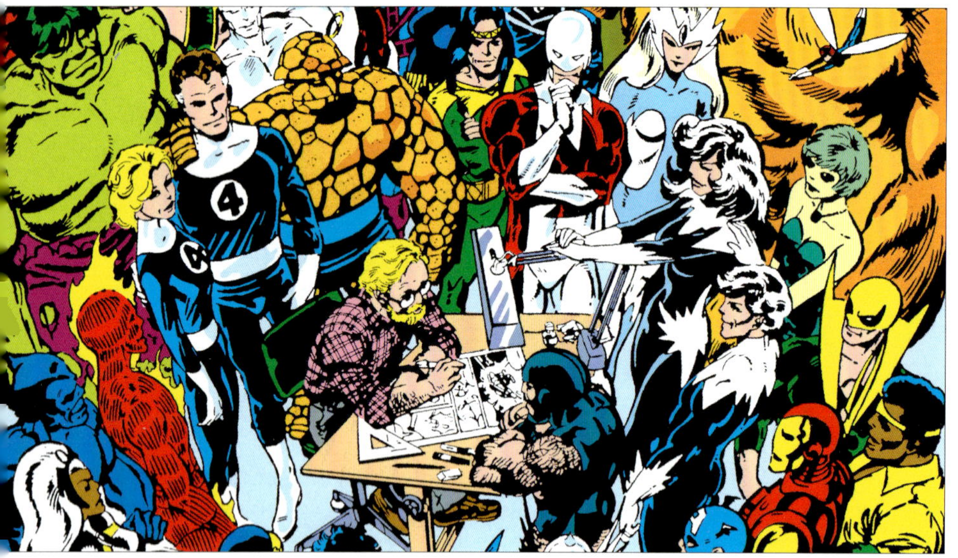

Artist John Byrne with some heroic friends. Art by John Byrne.

Frank Miller. John Byrne. Chris Claremont. Walt Simonson. Jim Lee. Rob Liefeld. Todd McFarlane. Mike Mignola. Arthur Adams. Peter David. An impressive array of talents who shaped the world of Marvel in the 1980s (and '90s). In a decade that proved crucial in the evolution of the medium, the Marvel talent roster was home to a bevy of masters of their crafts, par excellence. There was Byrne, who, following the success of *The Uncanny X-Men*, was known as the King Midas of Comics.

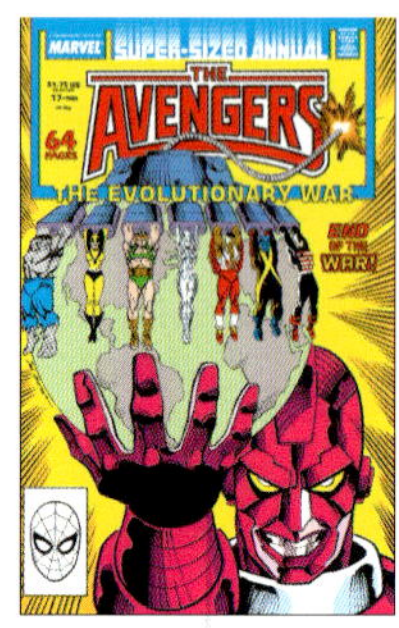

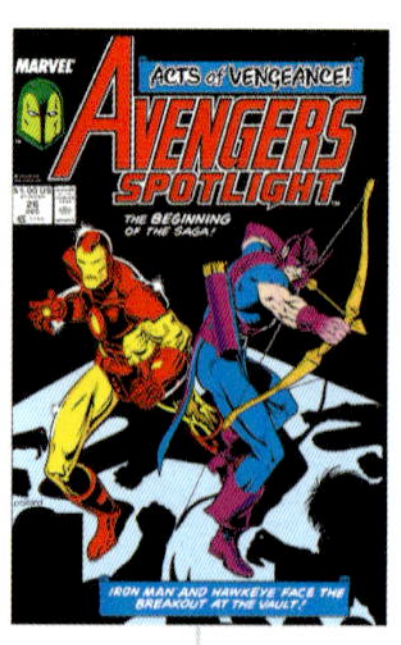

1990

AUGUST 1988
'The Evolutionary War' is the first of a new generation of crossover stories in annuals, linking various Marvel series together.

DECEMBER 1989
'Acts of Vengeance', an event that incorporated various series, featured Super Villains exchanging foes.

In those years, artists with a penchant for the classics consolidated their careers—people like Barry Windsor-Smith, who was the man behind some of the best-loved X-stories, and Bob Layton, who drew the definitive version of Iron Man, as well as several of that character's most important sagas. The masters of the '60s and '70s made way for their most worthy heirs, including the aforementioned John Romita, Jr., who in his younger days incorporated much of his father's style, but went on to develop his own unique synthesis; and Bill Sienkiewicz, who experimented with oil painting, collages, and other unorthodox techniques.

Another revamping of Daredevil got underway in the late '80s thanks to writer Ann Nocenti, who, working with Romita, Jr., explored themes like environmental protection, religion, and women's rights through the mutant psychopath Typhoid Mary. Not lacking were writers and artists who exploited their in-depth knowledge of Marvel continuity to come up with memorable stories. Among them, Mark Gruenwald surely stood out. He created the young new Super Hero Quasar, and also penned long cycles for Captain America and Squadron Supreme, featuring a revisionist interpretation of the Avengers' old foes.

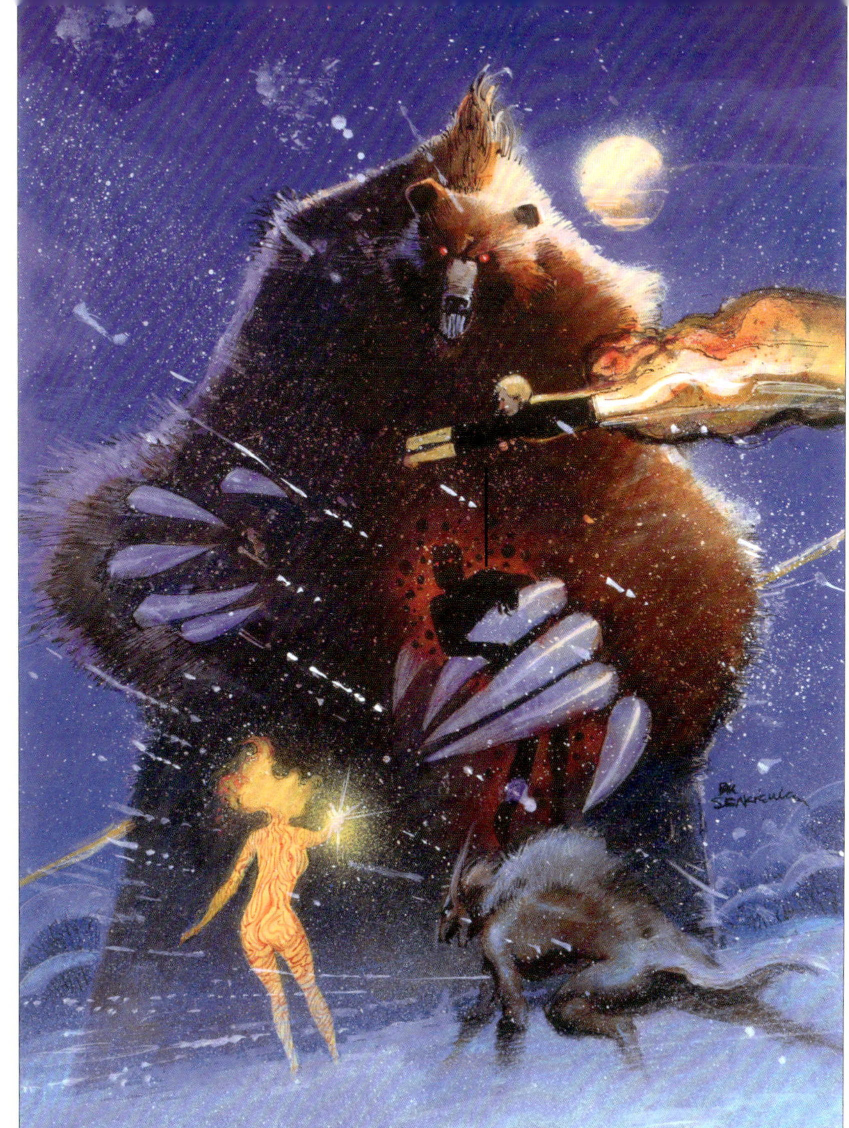

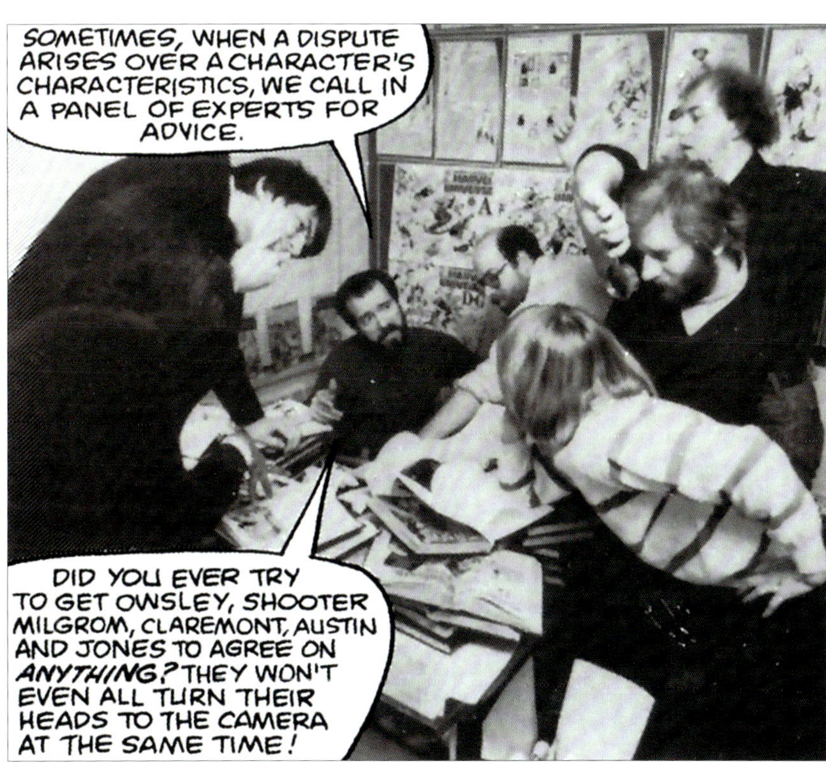

TOP
Artist Bill Sienkiewicz's *New Mutants #19* cover art (September 1984).

BOTTOM
Detail from *The Marvel Fumetti Book*.

MIGHTY MEDIA ON THE MOVE

Marvel continued to make a mark in popular culture, as it became a staple of one of the most beloved celebrations in the U.S.

The popularity of Marvel characters continued to grow year after year. In part, this was due to their ever-expanding presence on TV. Newly founded, Hollywood-based Marvel Productions produced a pair of cartoon series destined to become classics. In 1981 the company simultaneously debuted *Spider-Man and His Amazing Friends* (which teamed Spidey up with Iceman and a new heroine, the flaming mutant Firestar) as well as the syndicated *Spider-Man*. They were joined in 1982 by *The Incredible Hulk*, which Stan Lee himself narrated. Meanwhile, two of the most unlikely candidates from the Marvel pantheon would appear in live-action movies: *Howard the Duck* (1986, directed by Willard Huyck) and *The Punisher*, starring Dolph Lundgren (1989, directed by Mark Goldblatt).

The Incredible Hulk live-action series returned to the airwaves,

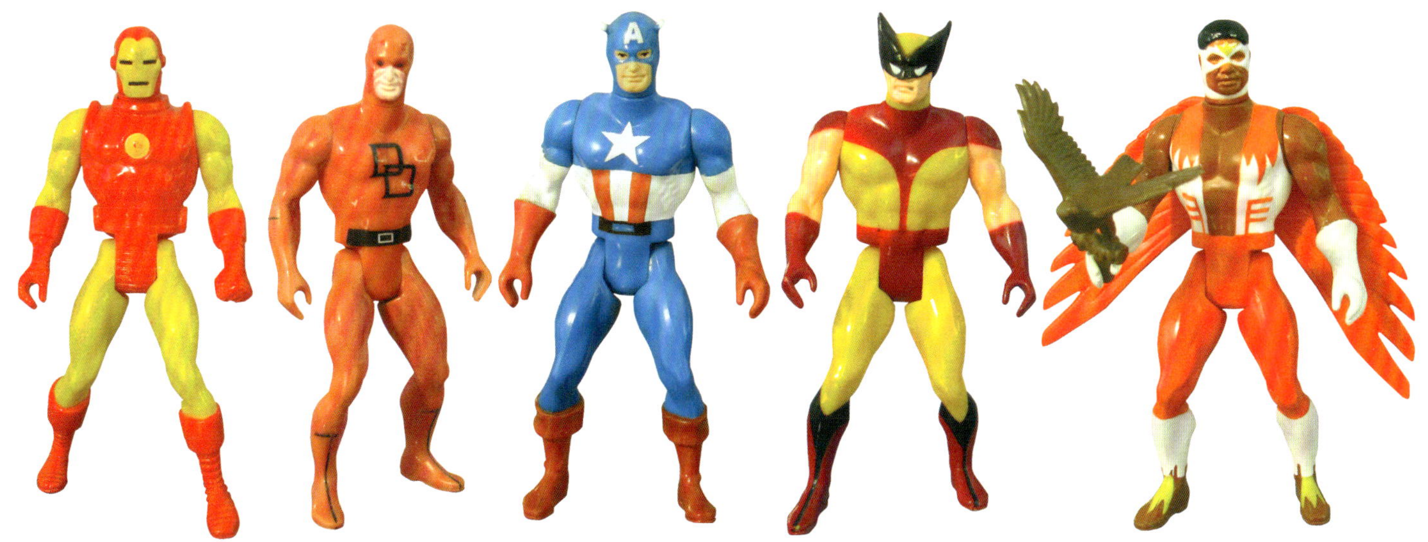

spawning three made-for-TV movies: *The Incredible Hulk Returns* (1988), *The Trial of The Incredible Hulk* (1989) and *The Death of The Incredible Hulk* (1990). The first of these featured an appearance by a very loosely interpreted version of Thor, while Daredevil showed up in the latter—in the hopes that Matt Murdock's alter ego might get a TV series of his own if the movie proved successful enough.

If year in, year out comics stories gradually alluded to the end of the Cold War with the phasing out of once-frequent Soviet villains, wounds from the Vietnam War took a long time healing. Marvel explored that theme in *The 'Nam*, a war series based on the memories of writer Doug Murray and editor Larry Hama. Some characters featured in Super Hero series were still haunted by their experiences at the front, like Flash Thompson, an old acquaintance of Peter Parker's, and Daredevil's disturbed foe Nuke, another Frank Miller brainchild.

Meanwhile, children were playing with action figures from Mattel's *Marvel Super Heroes Secret Wars* collection, which took its cue from the comic-book series created by Shooter and Zeck. G.I. Joe and the Transformers characters took the opposite route, beginning their lives as toy lines by Hasbro, with Marvel helping to develop the storylines and publishing two long-running comics series.

But it was Spider-Man who helped elevate Marvel to pop-culture immortality. To celebrate his and Mary Jane's wedding in 1987's *The Amazing Spider-Man Annual #21*, Marvel arranged a wedding ceremony at Shea Stadium in Queens, New York, where Peter Parker grew up. Prior to the Mets-Pirates game, with Stan Lee himself officiating, two actors dressed as Spidey and his beloved exchanged vows before a crowd of 45,000.

Later that year, a giant Spider-Man balloon made its debut in the Macy's Thanksgiving Day Parade—at long last, the web-slinger really was soaring amid the skyscrapers of New York!

ABOVE
Mattel's 1984 *Marvel Super Heroes Secret Wars* action figures.

OPPOSITE PAGE
The executives of Marvel Productions, Ltd. From left to right: Lee Gunther, David DePatie, Jim Galton, and Stan Lee.

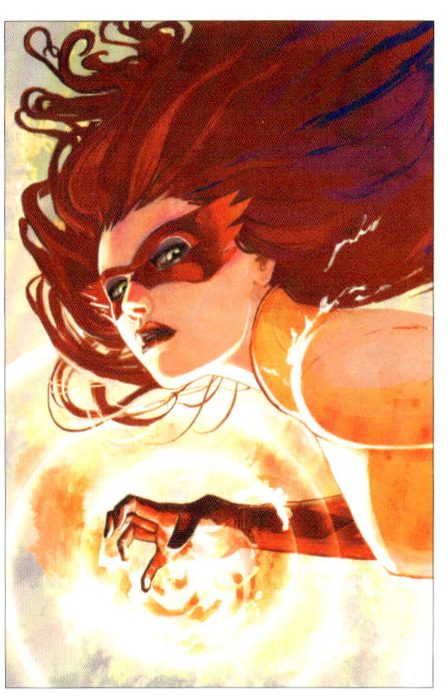

Flaming mutant Firestar (here in a later rendition by artist Stephanie Hans for the cover of *Firestar #1*, April 2010) was created expressly for the animated series *Spider-Man and His Amazing Friends*, in 1981.

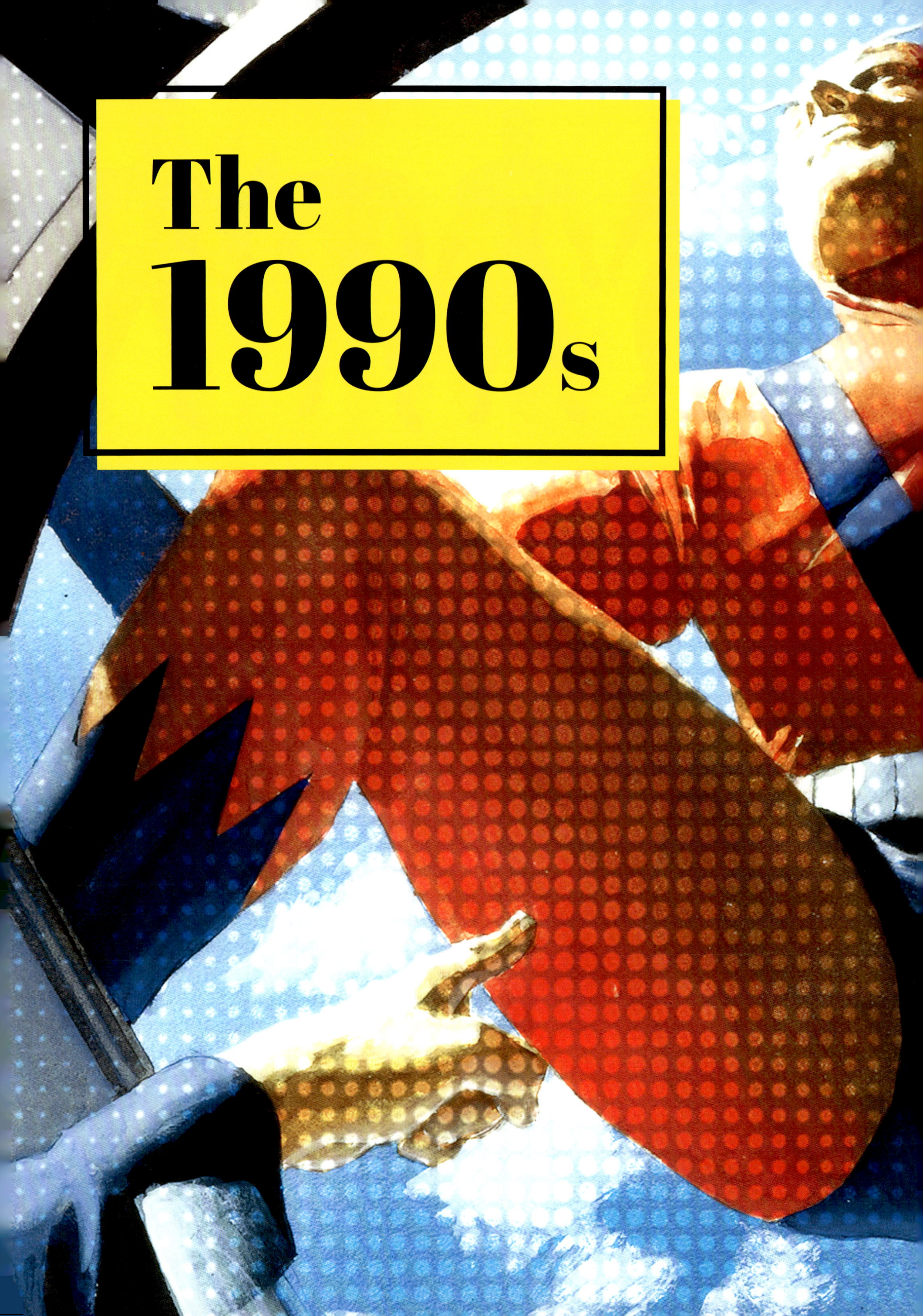
The
1990s

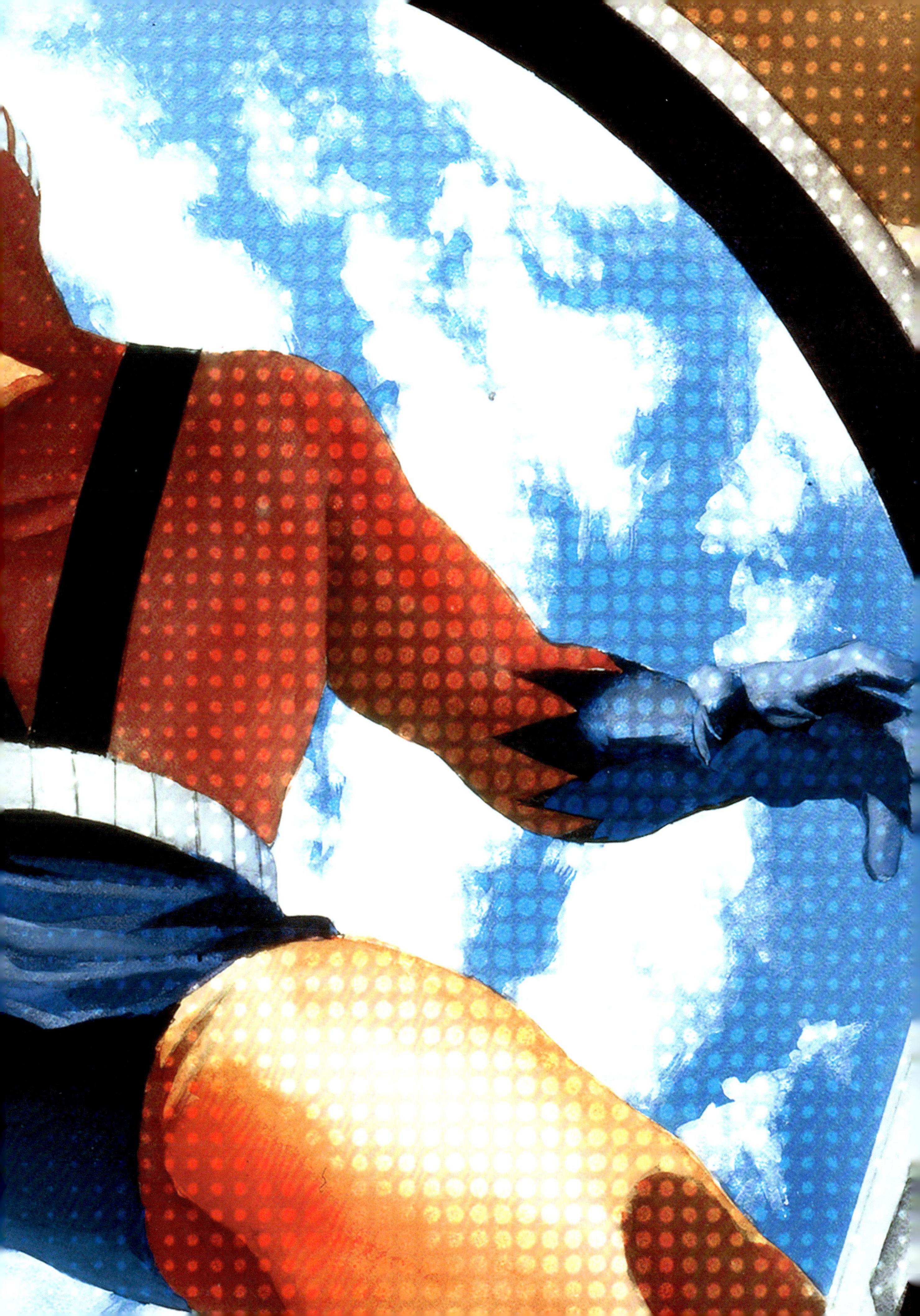

A GIANT STEP FORWARD

Spider-Man #1 (1 August 1990): 2 million copies sold. _X-Force #1_ (1 August 1991): 4 million copies. _X-Men #1_ (1 October 1991): eight million copies. For Marvel the '90s rolled in with dizzying numbers.

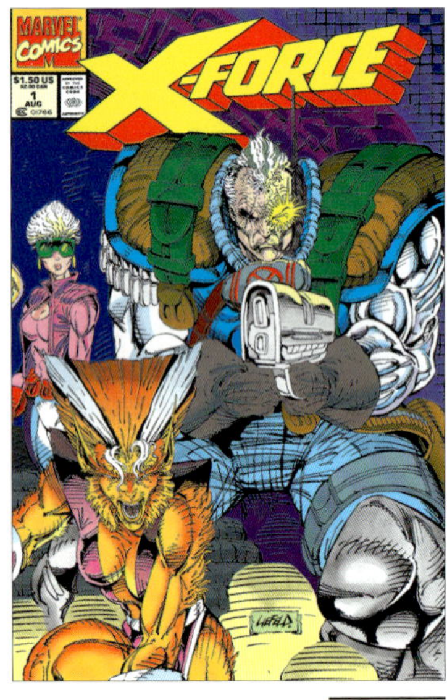

Cable takes the reins of a new X-team in *X-Force #1* (August 1991). Art by Rob Liefeld.

Behind such extraordinary figures lay a series of unique coincidences. While they certainly had to do with the spirit of the times, there was also a wave of variant covers featuring incredible effects—many of which were interlocking—and fans who worshipped the new worldwide stars, the writers and artists behind the comics, and the spread of comic-book stores and wholesale purchases by speculators. Of course, not every comic was a big hit, but sales were up even for series that had been less fortunate, and spin-offs and limited series events with connecting plots—the crossovers that had already been so successfully tried in the 1980s—came rolling off the presses in great quantities.

The British imprint Marvel U.K. also introduced a host of new characters and series, which would later show up on the American market. The House of Ideas had begun giving room to young writers and artists with fresh ideas. Todd McFarlane, who had won the hearts of fans with his run in *The Amazing Spider-Man*, was given carte blanche for 'his own' Spider-Man series.

Rob Liefeld, who did the artwork for the last issues of *New Mutants* to be written by Louise Simonson, and also contributed to the plots, transformed the team of young heroes into a hard-fighting posse, X-Force. And Jim Lee, who for a while had been doing the artwork for the famed series *The Uncanny X-Men*, with stories by Chris Claremont, would soon be heading the newly born *X-Men*, when 'X-Chris' stepped down as the main mutant writer, his job since 1975. Super Heroes got fiercer and more weaponised; their looks mirrored the styles of

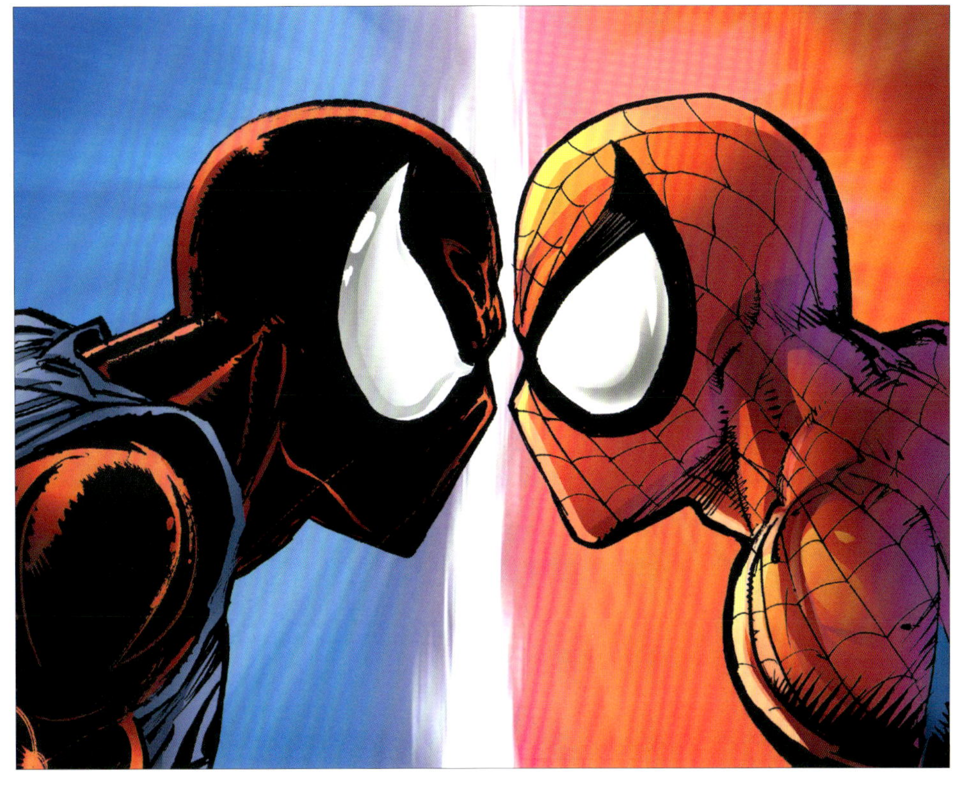

Cover detail for *Spider-Man: Clone Saga Omnibus Volume 2* (November 2017). Art by Sal Buscema (pencils), Bill Sienkiewicz (inks).

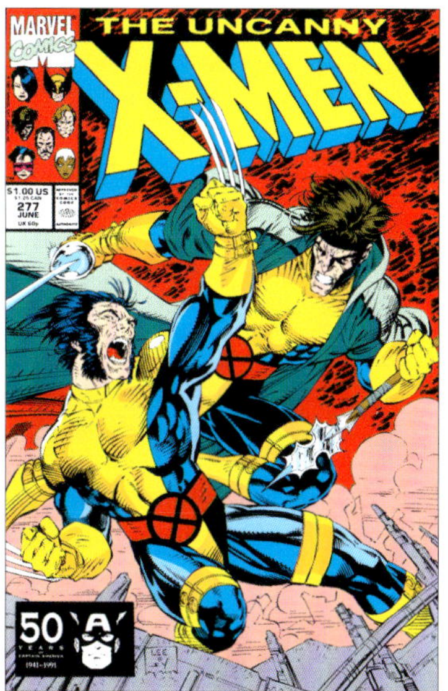

The Uncanny X-Men #277 (June 1991). Art by Jim Lee and Scott Williams.

the moment. Artists who used bold, vigorous lines replaced people with more classical approaches. Some series featured extended narratives that would go on for years, like the 'Clone Saga' in various Spider-Man publications.

Of course, success wasn't just the result of the comics themselves and their creators, or the work of speculators. The world of comics had begun attracting audiences that feasted on new opportunities to get to know all those magnificent characters. Such as the first successful arcade video games featuring Marvel Super Heroes, and Saturday mornings with one of Marvel's most successful cartoons ever, *X-Men: The Animated Series*, which ran from 1992 to 1997. The characters' looks were taken right from the then-current looks of their comic-book counterparts.

Growing commercial success meant that the company had to grow too. Marvel was no longer the tiny 'Bullpen', as the staff was referred to in the 1960s, but a company listed on the stock exchange.

The move by new president Ron Perelman, who had bought Marvel from New World two years earlier, was officially announced to investors when an actor in a Spider-Man costume was featured in the opening ceremony at the New York Stock Exchange, alongside a smiling Stan Lee. But this wasn't the place where the seeds for a bright future would be planted. It wouldn't be long before Marvel characters caught the attention of that other temple of American power, Hollywood.

In those years, Marvel was publishing so many comics releases

A promotional image for the *X-Men* animated series that premiered on 31 October 1992.

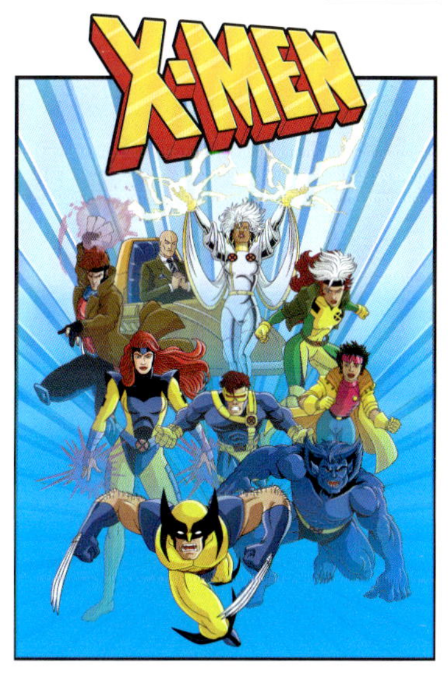

2099

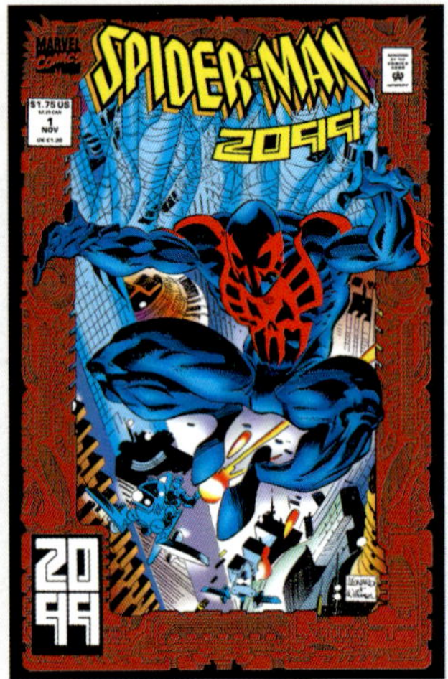

What would Marvel Super Heroes look like 100 years into the future? Who would be wearing the Spider-Man outfit? Would there be anyone left to fight for Xavier's dream? Would the Hulk still be around? Initially, Stan Lee and John Byrne were supposed to answer those questions in what would have been the special one-shot event entitled *The Marvel World of Tomorrow*, announced by Lee in one of the 1990 Stan's Soapbox columns. Over the next few years, however, the project underwent significant changes and was eventually transformed into the Marvel 2099 imprint. It kicked off in November 1992 with *Spider-Man 2099*. After the release of the other series in the hopper—*Punisher 2099*, *Doom 2099*, and *Ravage 2099* (written by Stan Lee)—more were added. They included *X-Men 2099* and *Ghost Rider 2099*, featuring the artwork of Chris Bachalo and Ashley Wood.

that in order to manage them, editor in chief Tom DeFalco broke them down into 'families': Mutants, Heroes, Urban Heroes, Spider-Family, Cosmics. When Tom left the position in 1994, for a brief time the coordinators of the various families were basically the ones running the show at Marvel. The choice to fill the gap left by DeFalco fell upon Bob Harras, the editor who had led the X-Men to stratospheric heights of popularity. A good portion of that success had certainly come thanks to creators McFarlane,

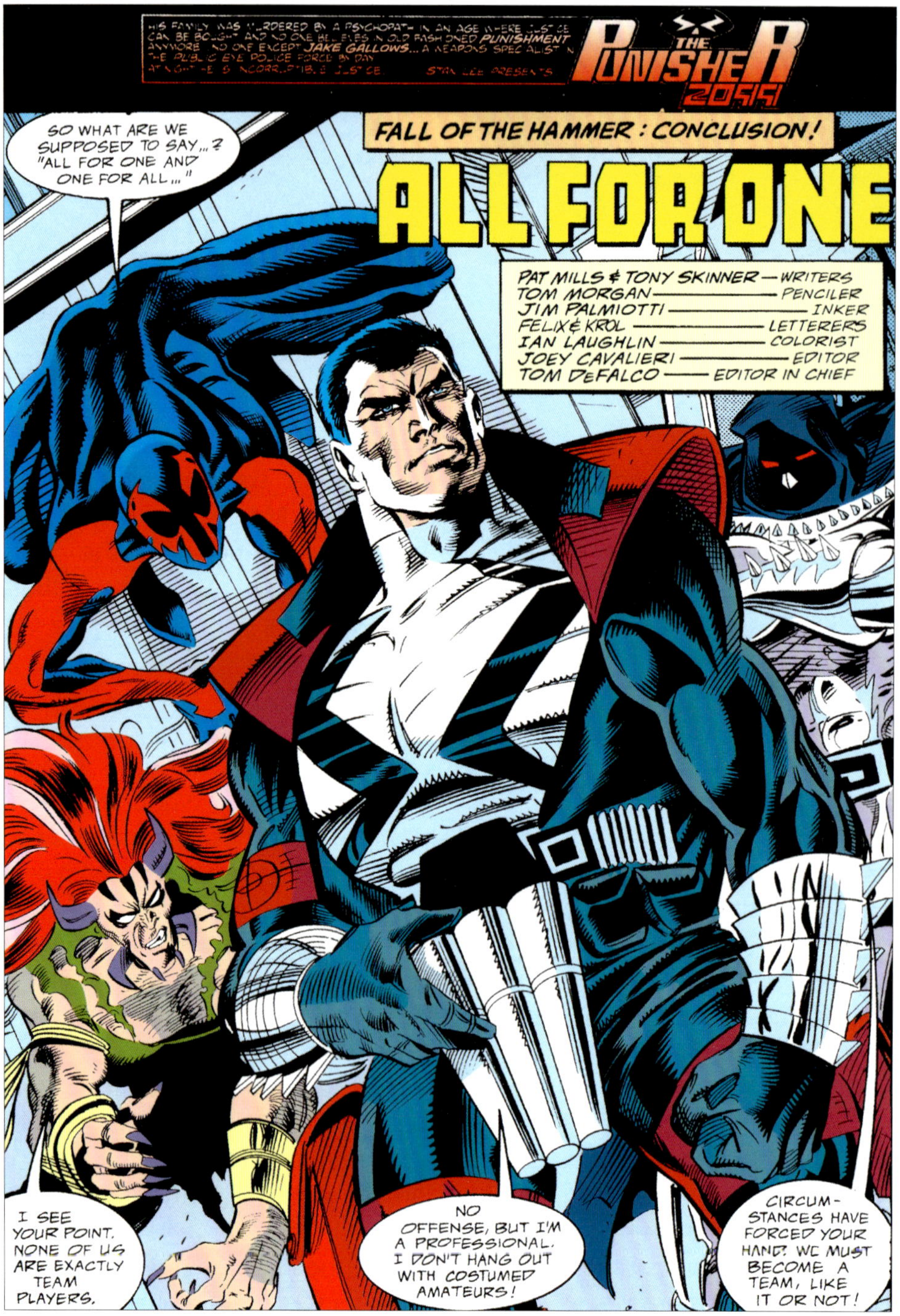

Lee, and Liefeld. Aware of their own potential strength on the market, they left Marvel in 1992 to seek new inroads. The three of them, along with other young, well-respected contemporary creators—Jim Valentino, Erik Larsen, and Marc Silvestri—soon founded Image Comics. But in 1996 Lee and Liefeld returned to Marvel when it was decided to launch new series based on classics like the Avengers, the Fantastic Four, Captain America, and Iron Man.

The Heroes Reborn project gave creators total artistic freedom—which meant resorting to a simple ploy. *Onslaught*, the saga that reunited the greatest Marvel Super Heroes, wound up stuck in a parallel dimension with the Avengers and the Fantastic Four—a narrative twist that allowed Lee and Liefeld to redevelop those characters from scratch. They were thus able to update their origins to meet modern demands, without having to worry about the burden of decades of continuity.

Marvel continued to trust their writers and artists with characters old and new, giving them free rein to develop the Super Heroes and Super Villains in new ways. It was fitting, then, that one of these artists—Joe Quesada—would go on to be named editor in chief of Marvel Comics as the new century dawned. Known for his expressive, personal style, Quesada would lead Marvel into the 2000s, leaving his mark as the company's longest-reigning editor in chief since Stan Lee himself.

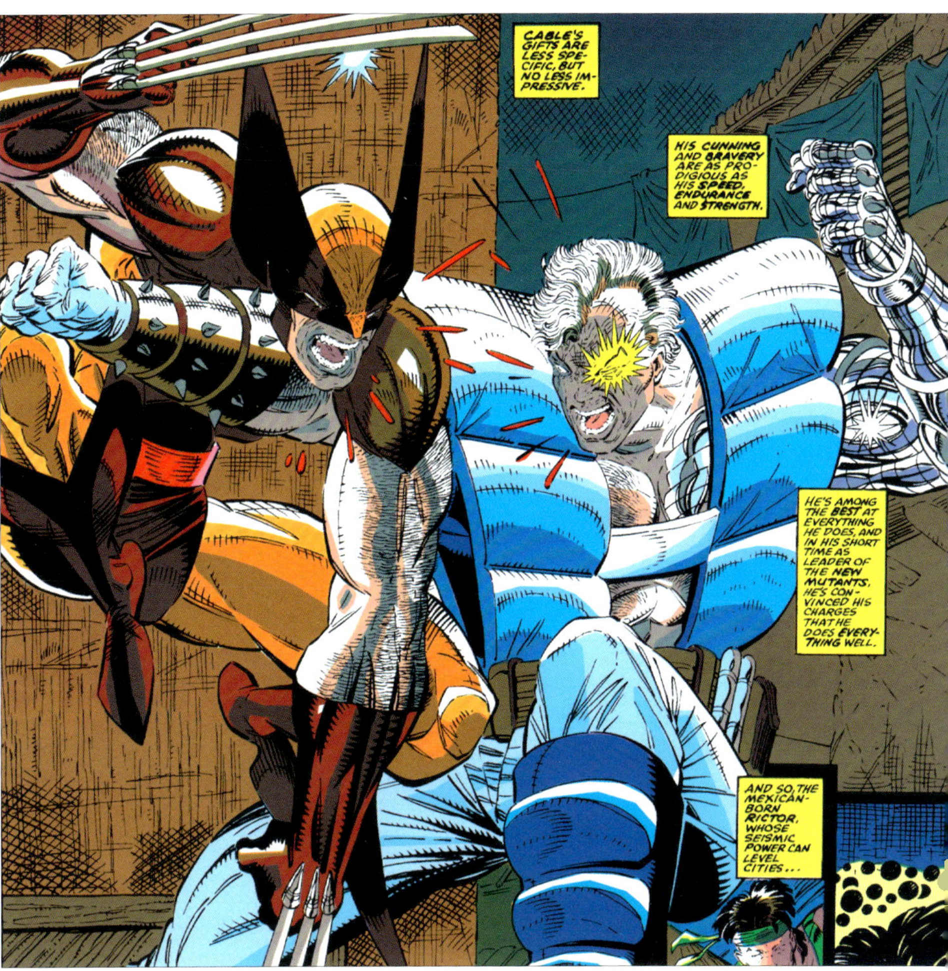

ABOVE
Wolverine battles Cable in *The New Mutants #94* (October 1990). Art by Rob Liefeld (pencils), Hilary Barta (inks), Brad Vancata (colours).

OPPOSITE PAGE
The future Punisher, from *Punisher 2099 #13* (February 1994). Script by Pat Mills and Tony Skinner. Art by Tom Morgan (pencils), Jimmy Palmiotti (inks), Ian Laughlin (colours), Phil Felix and Loretta Krol (letters).

X-Men: Onslaught #1 (August 1996). Art by Adam Kubert.

INFINITE BATTLES

The X-Men and Spider-Man unveil epic story lines, as Elektra returns, and the Marvel Universe makes some big changes.

The hologram cover for *X-Factor #92* (July 1993). Art by Joe Quesada and Al Milgrom.

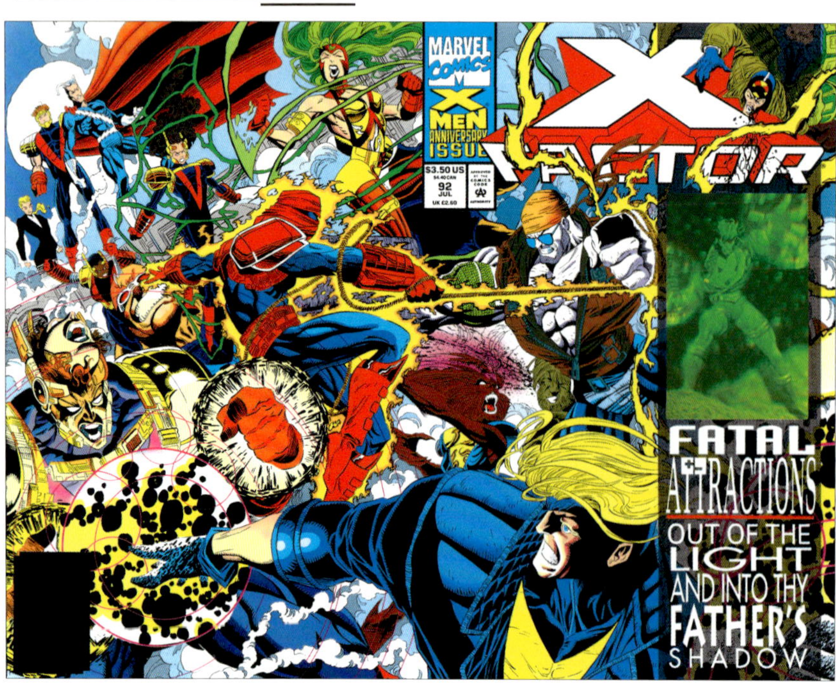

In the 1990s everything was spectacular and hyperbolic: the weapons characters wielded, their bulky armour, the spikes on their epaulets, their costumes, poses and proportions. Along with their brightly coloured spandex suits, Super Heroes often sported leather jackets, long overcoats, and various details and accessories like pockets and belts, a likely nod to street fashion of the period. Each and every panel had to be breathtaking, and sagas tended to be very long, containing numerous crossovers.

Events like 'The Crossing' (Avengers), 'X-Cutioner's Song' and 'Fatal Attractions' (X-Men) and 'Maximum Carnage' (the Spider-Man 'family') promised to change the status quo of Super Heroes over the course of many chapters and countless plot twists. Tony Stark was replaced by a teenage version of himself; the X-Men had to deal with the appearance of the Legacy Virus, which infected only mutants; Wolverine lost his Adamantium skeleton, revealing his bony claws; Spider-Man found an ally in Venom and a new enemy in Venom's offspring, Carnage. But none of these events was comparable to the 'Clone Saga', which for four years ruled the roost, outselling all other Spider-Man comics.

Taking its cue from a series of stories first published in 1975, in which Jackal created a Peter Parker clone, the creators brought back Peter's clone and led us to believe that the adventures over the past 19 years starring Peter Parker had actually involved his clone! The real Peter now called himself Ben Reilly, and assumed the identity of Scarlet Spider, fighting side by side with Spider-Man.

At one point, he even took his place, wearing a new costume designed by Mark Bagley. When Peter temporarily chose to retire from the Super Hero life, he left Reilly with the responsibility of being Spider-Man. After numerous adventures featuring the new Spidey, the truth was finally revealed in *The Amazing Spider-Man #418* (cover-dated December 1996): Ben was the clone, Peter was the original.

This sensational story, written by Howard Mackie and illustrated by John Romita, Jr., also saw Norman Osborn, the first Green Goblin, back from the dead. Upon his return, Norman sets out to become Spider-Man's worst enemy out of the many aspiring Goblins who in the past tried to take his place. For his part, Venom would star in a string of limited series releases, and along the way became one of Marvel's best-loved characters.

The early 1990s output, however, was not limited to long-running series and sagas, Super Heroes toting giant guns, and grim, gloomy tales. Amid so many products of this kind, one can't help but recall that in those years Marvel published some truly immortal gems. For instance, in 1991 Frank Miller returned to 'his' Elektra and wrote and illustrated the graphic novel *Elektra Lives Again*. That same year the acclaimed artist Barry Windsor-Smith wrote and illustrated the story 'Weapon X', unveiling a crucial moment in Wolverine's past, which was published in the anthology series *Marvel Comics Presents* and soon followed by

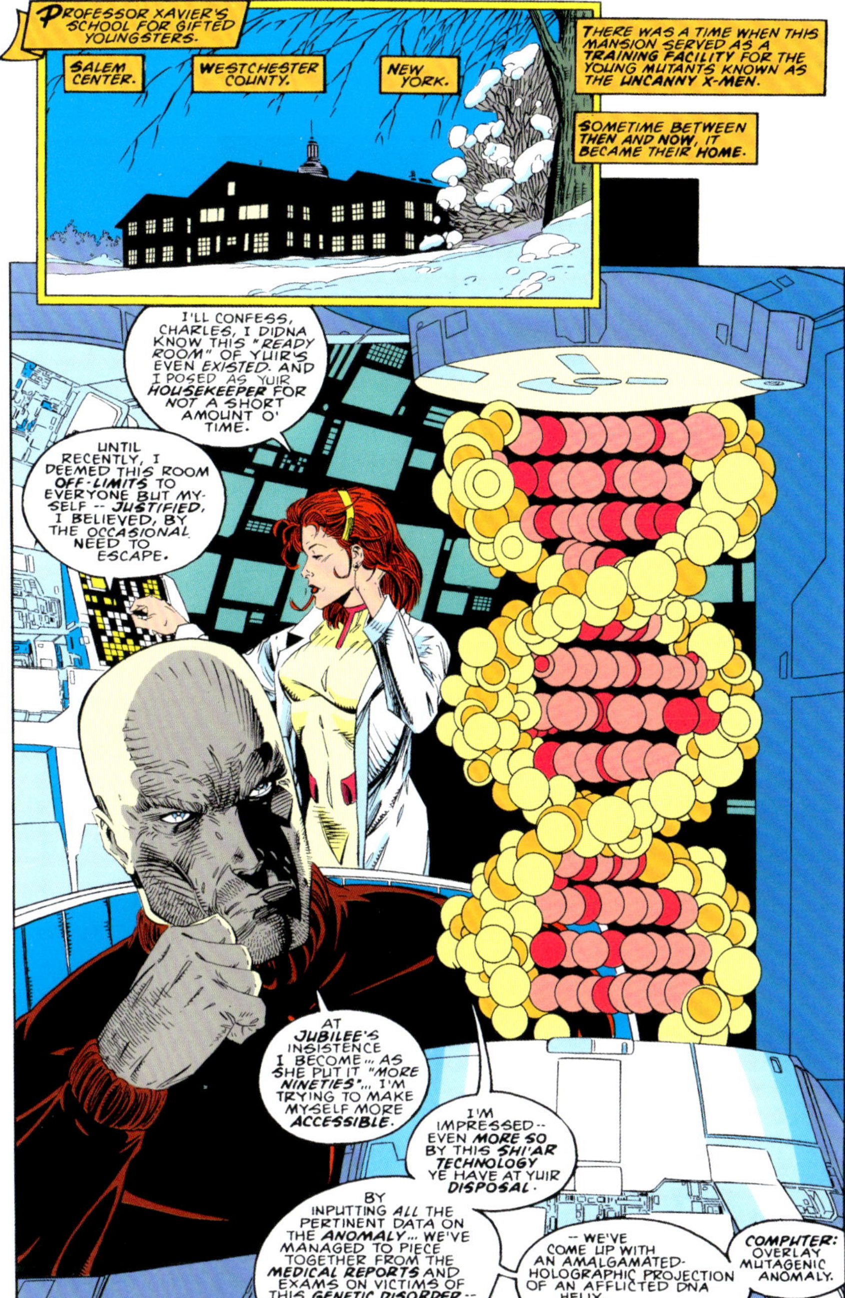

Professor X and Dr. Moira MacTaggert analyse the Legacy Virus. *The Uncanny X-Men #300* (May 1993). Script by Scott Lobdell. Art by Brandon Peterson (pencils), Dan Green, Dan Panosian, Al Milgrom (inks), Steve Buccellato, Glynis Oliver (colours), Chris Eliopoulos (letters).

THE INFINITY SAGA

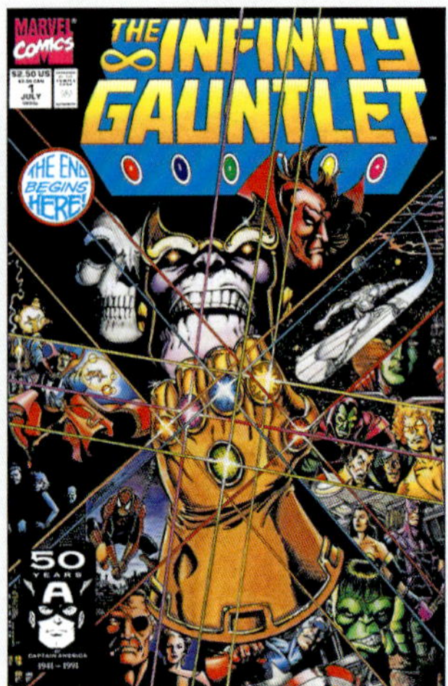

After bringing his creation Thanos back to the pages of the monthly *Silver Surfer* title and in the limited series *The Thanos Quest*, Jim Starlin, now in the role of writer, teamed up with artists George Pérez and Ron Lim on a limited series that was a huge success. In *The Infinity Gauntlet*, Thanos places all six Infinity Gems on his gauntlet, and with a snap of his fingers wipes out half the life in the universe. *The Infinity Gauntlet* proved such a hit that it immediately spawned two sequels, *Infinity War* (1992) and *Infinity Crusade* (1993), both by the team of Starlin and Lim. The *Infinity* saga is known for its wide-ranging cast.

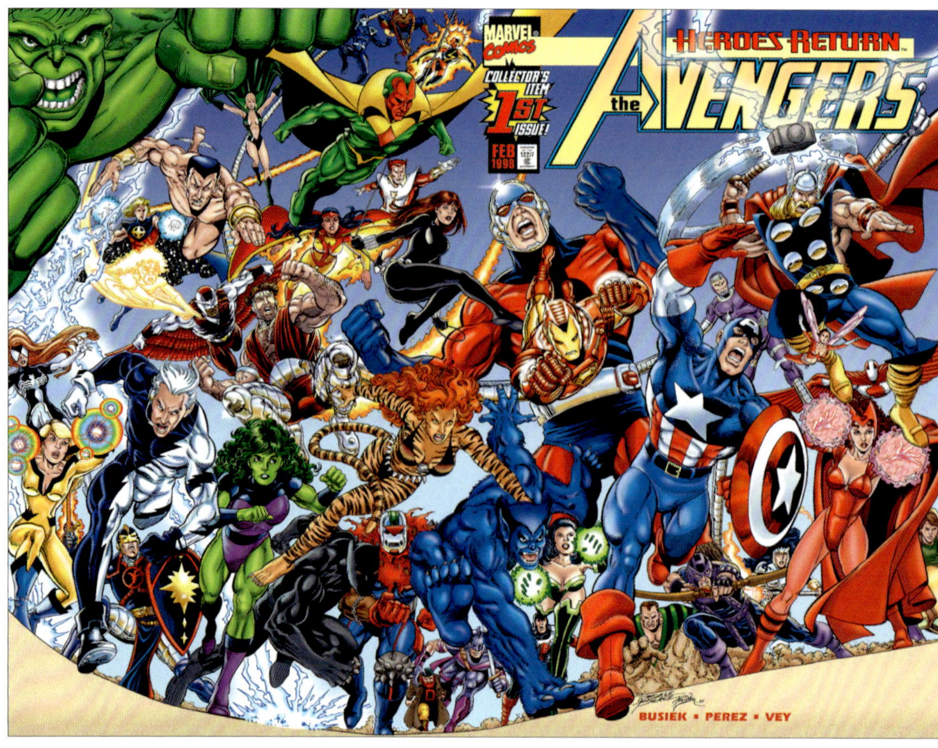

the trade paperback collection.

Miller came back to *Daredevil* in 1993, giving readers a glimpse of Matt Murdock's earliest experiences as a vigilante. Qualitatively, one of the high points of those years, and perhaps in the entire history of Marvel, was the four-issue series *Marvels*, released in a prestige format. Written by Kurt Busiek, an expert on Marvel continuity, and painted in its entirety in a hyper-realistic style by Alex Ross, it told the story of the Marvel Universe's early years from the point of view of the man on the street, news photographer Phil Sheldon. *Marvels* was a critical and commercial success and generated a slew of imitations and spin-offs.

1990

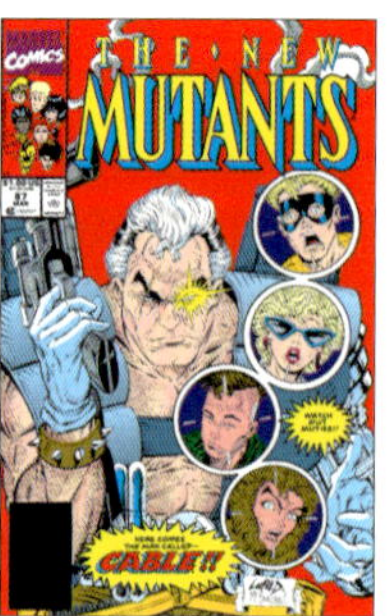

MARCH 1990
A future star of the '90s makes his debut in *The New Mutants #87*: Cable.

APRIL 1990
Namor is back in a new series, written and illustrated by John Byrne, who has made his return to Marvel in 1989.

In 1999 Alex Ross made his return to Marvel, this time as writer and cover artist. With another writer, Jim Krueger, and artist John Paul Leon alongside, he laid the groundwork for the big 12-issue saga entitled *Earth X*, which debuted in 1999. This time around, readers got to check out what the Marvel Universe might end up looking like in the future, as told by a cold, distant observer, the android Machine Man.

In the second half of the 1990s, after *Heroes Reborn* came *Heroes Return*. These crossovers starring the Avengers were created by people who did not gravitate toward current trends, but were more firmly entrenched in classic styles. They included Busiek and Pérez, who did extensive work on *The Avengers*, acclaimed by critics and readers alike, while *Captain America* featured stories written by Mark Waid and illustrated by Ron Garney that reached new qualitative heights. But some of the supporting characters still had a hard time catching the attention of the critics and fans. Frank Miller's legacy still weighed on *Daredevil*.

Other characters, like the Inhumans, had potential that for years went untapped. Taking its cue somewhat from the approach used for *Heroes Reborn*, Marvel brought in 'outsiders' to develop those characters—in this case, Joe Quesada and Jimmy Palmiotti from Event Comics, both of whom had worked for Marvel in the past, as penciller and inker respectively. This time, however, the stories would not be set in a bubble-like parallel universe, but integrated within the regular continuity. The imprint would be called Marvel Knights. Fans and specialised periodicals mainly focused their attention on *Daredevil*. The imprint made its debut with the release of *Daredevil #1*, cover-dated November 1998, featuring artwork by Quesada, and written by Kevin Smith, a successful independent film director and comics fan.

Smith and Quesada's eight-part 'Guardian Devil' story, which relied on updated versions of Miller-type atmospheres, was the first Marvel Knights hit, followed by the political fantasy series *The Inhumans*, written by Paul Jenkins, with artwork

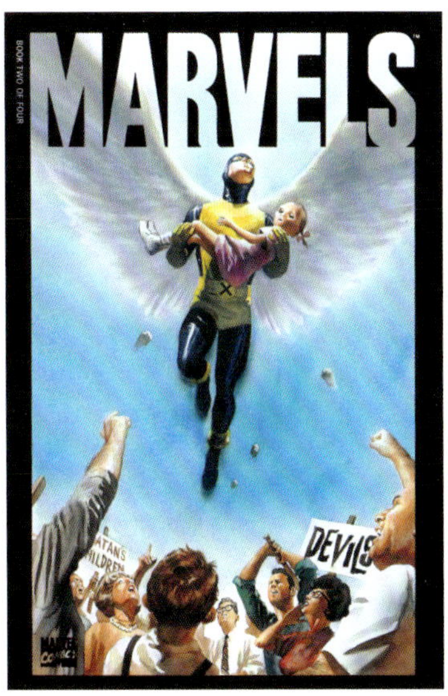

ABOVE
Marvels #2 (February 1994). Art by Alex Ross.

OPPOSITE PAGE
Earth's mightiest heroes return to the Marvel Universe in *The Avengers #1* (February 1998). Art by George Pérez (pencils), Tom Smith (colours).

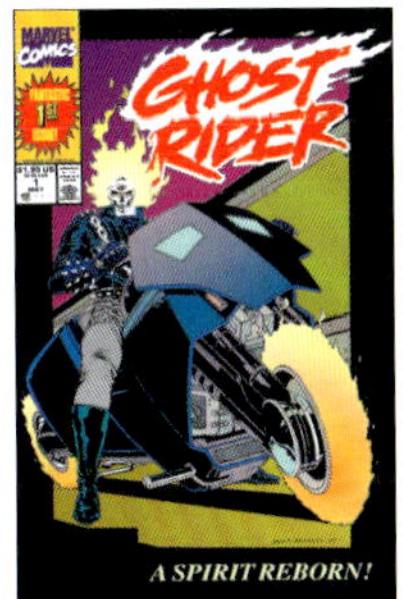

MAY 1990
A new Spirit of Vengeance appears in *Ghost Rider #1*: Danny Ketch takes the place of Johnny Blaze.

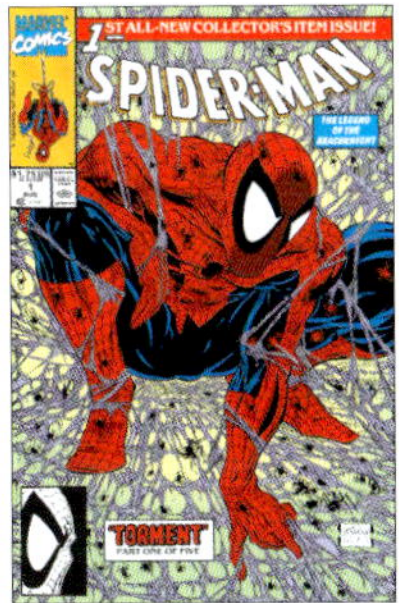

AUGUST 1990
Spider-Man #1 hits the stores—and what a hit it was! Written and illustrated by Todd McFarlane.

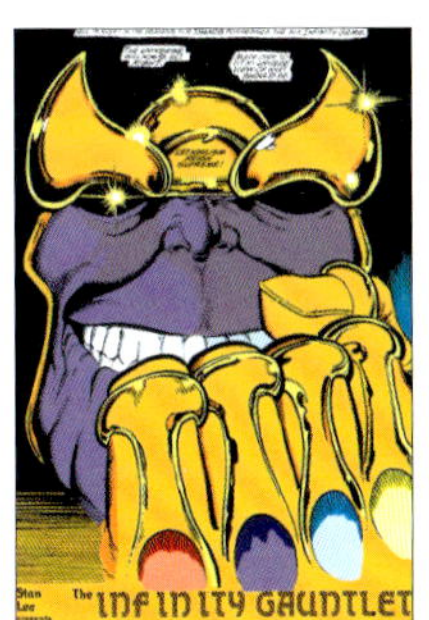

JULY 1991
The Infinity Gauntlet and *X-Force* make their respective debuts.

by Jae Lee; the brilliant ongoing series *Black Panther*; and new limited series for characters such as Black Widow and the Punisher. *The Punisher* series was designed to last only four issues, and featured the involvement of famed horror penciller Bernie Wrightson. A few years later, Frank Castle would return as the protagonist in a new Marvel Knights series, that shifted over to the new MAX imprint. It wasn't long before the imprint became synonymous with high-quality 'adult' themes.

Title panel from *Daredevil Vol. 2, #1* (November 1998). Script by Kevin Smith. Art by Joe Quesada (pencils), Jimmy Palmiotti (inks), Dan Kemp (colours), Liz Agraphiotis (letters).

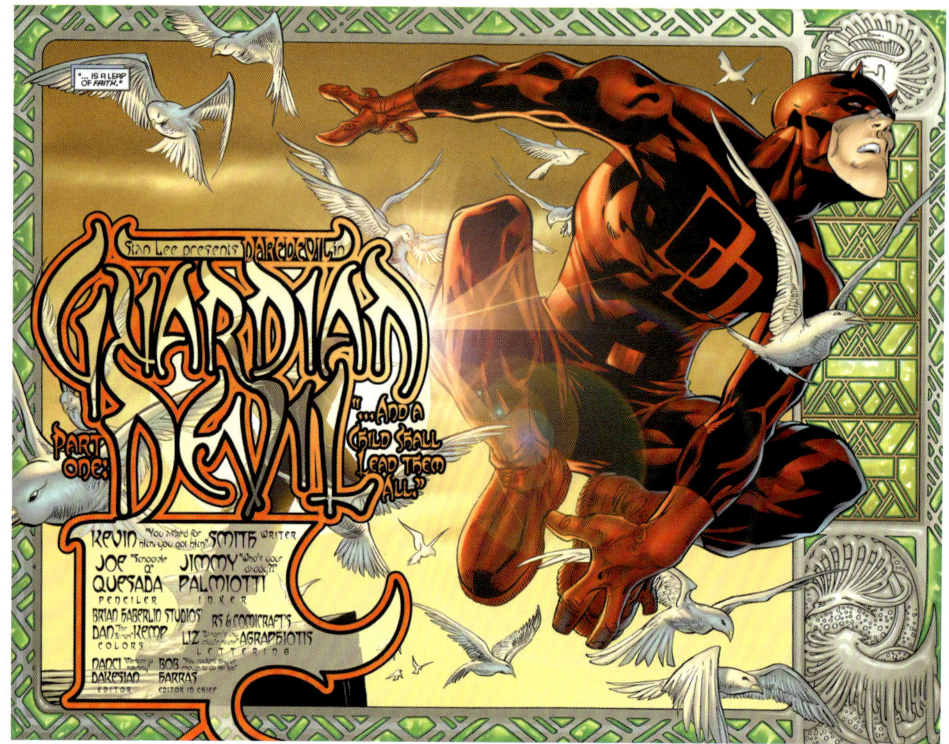

THE AGE OF APOCALYPSE

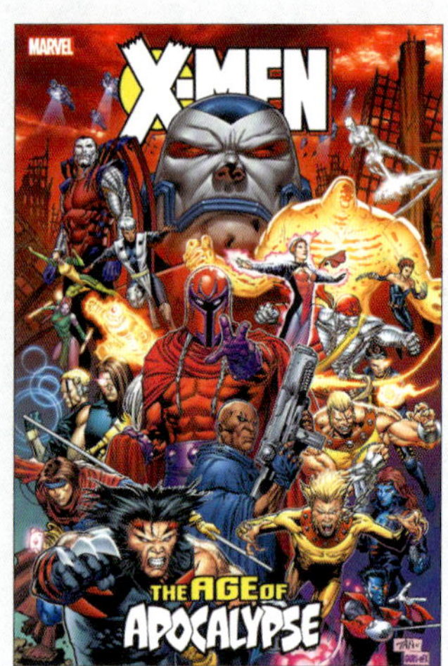

In 1995–96, the entire X-Men cast starred in one of the most ambitious comic-book cross-over events ever. Xavier's son Legion travelled back in time, seeking to murder a young Magneto so that his father's dream might prosper. But instead he mistakenly wound up killing Xavier himself, thereby altering the timeline. Thus Magneto brought together the X-Men, although they were not able to keep the immortal mutant Apocalypse from conquering half the world. It was risky business—the many series connected to the X-Men were shut down and replaced for four months by limited series with similar titles. The saga, which concluded with an inevitable return to normalcy, was a commercial success.

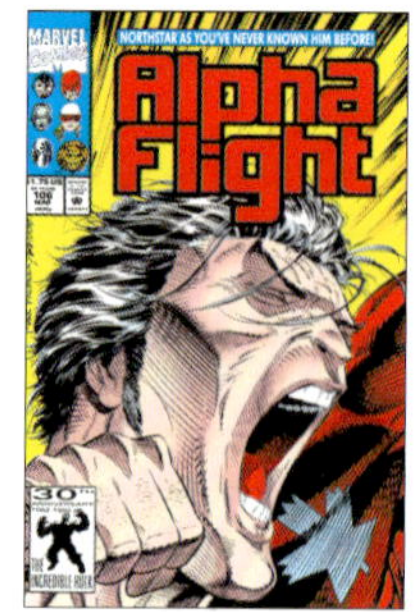

MARCH 1992
In *Alpha Flight #106* Northstar comes out soon after adopting a baby with AIDS. He is a Canadian Super Hero and Marvel's first openly gay character.

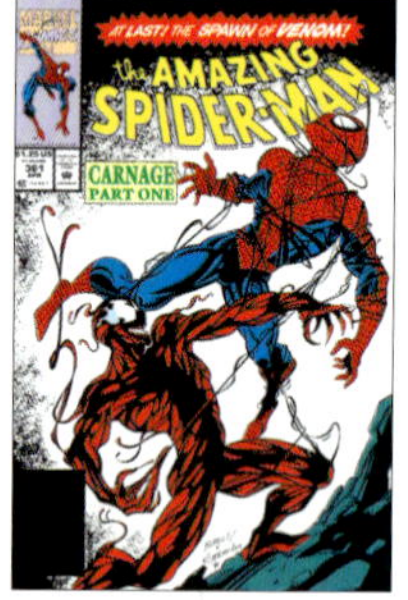

APRIL 1992
The Amazing Spider-Man #361 marks the first appearance of one of Spidey's deadliest enemies (and a favourite of fans): Carnage!

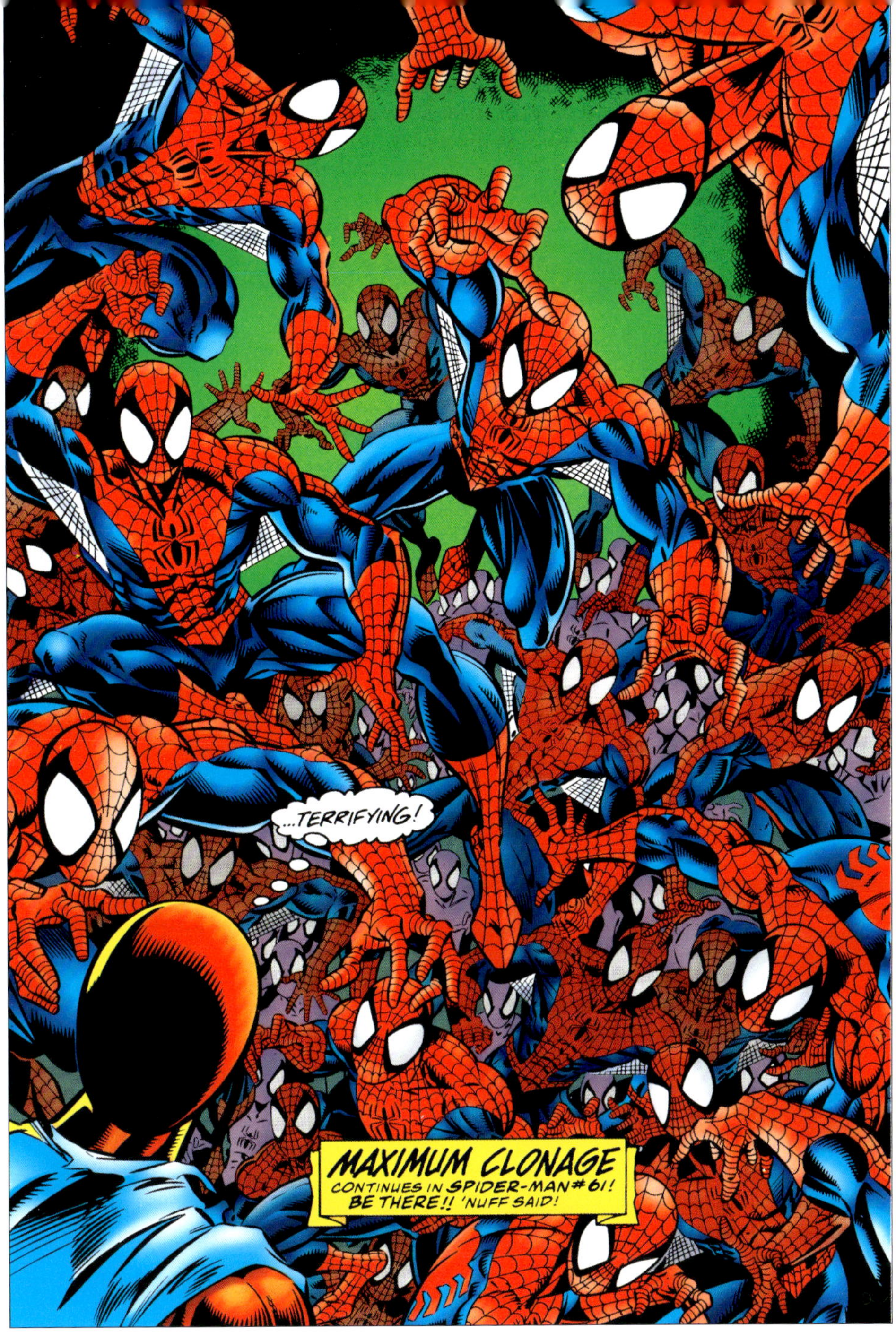

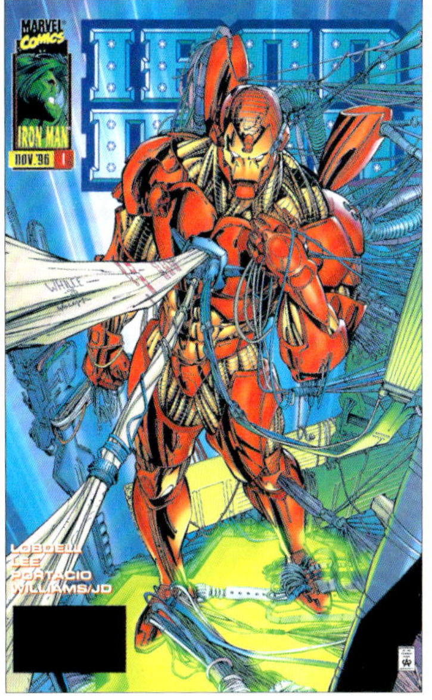

Iron Man Vol. 2, #1 (dated November 1996, released September 18, 1996). Art by Whilce Portacio and Scott Williams.

The 'Clone Saga' from *The Amazing Spider-Man #404* (August 1995). Script by J. M. DeMatteis and Todd DeZago. Art by Mark Bagley (pencils), Larry Mahlstedt, Randy Emberlin, Josef Rubinstein (inks), Bob Sharen (colours), Bill Oakley (letters).

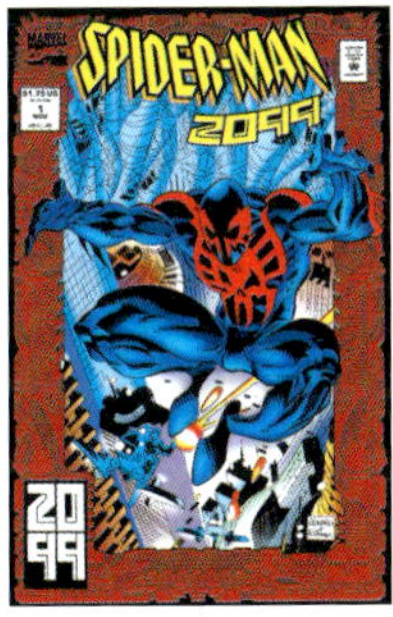

NOVEMBER 1992
Marvel *2099*'s first release: *Spider-Man 2099*.

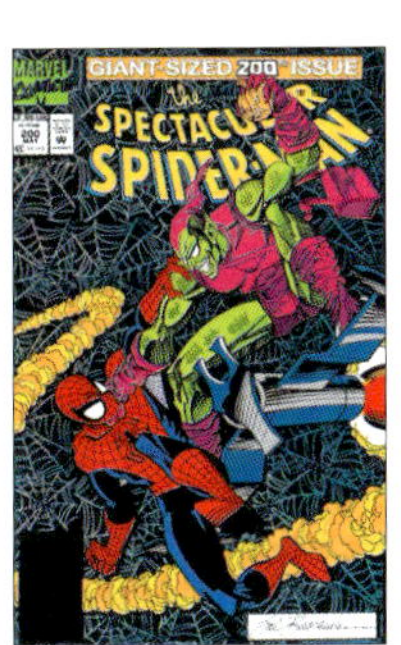

MAY 1993
In *The Spectacular Spider-Man #200*, a touching story by J. M. DeMatteis and Sal Buscema, Harry Osborn dies.

THE OLD AND THE NEW

A wave of innovative concepts crests as Marvel reinvents classic characters and introduces new creations.

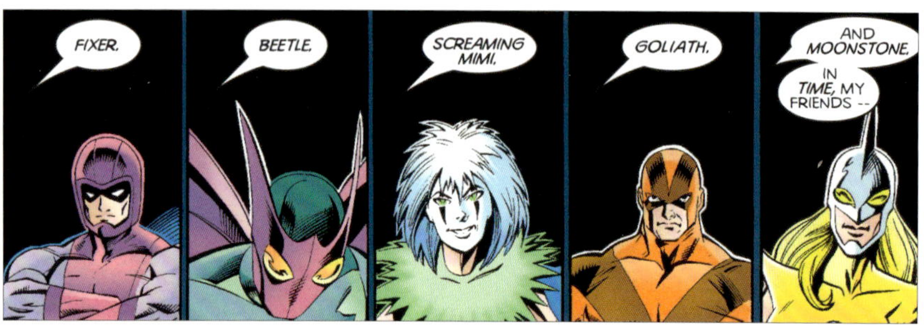

ABOVE
The team is gathered in *Thunderbolts #1*. Script by Kurt Busiek. Art by Mark Bagley (pencils), Vince Russell (inks), Joe Rosas (colours), Comicraft, Dave Lanphear, Oscar Gongorra (letters).

OPPOSITE PAGE
The cover to *Thunderbolts #1* (dated April 1997, released 19 February 1997). Art by Mark Bagley.

It must be said that the 1990s were steeped in a wealth of ideas. Besides giving fresh starts to characters from the past, the emergence of new writers and artists brought about the invention of all-new original concepts. Among them was Darkhawk, a violent, armour-clad crime-fighter who made his debut in March 1991, and the even more successful Deadpool, one of the many characters created by the explosive Rob Liefeld in stories that transitioned from the end of *The New Mutants* to the first issues of *X-Force*.

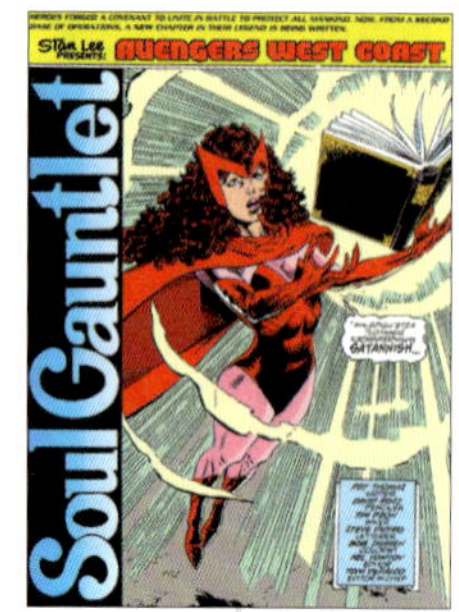

NOVEMBER 1993
Mockingbird dies in *West Coast Avengers #100*. Two issues later, the series shuts down. The team returned with a new name and a new attitude in *Force Works*.

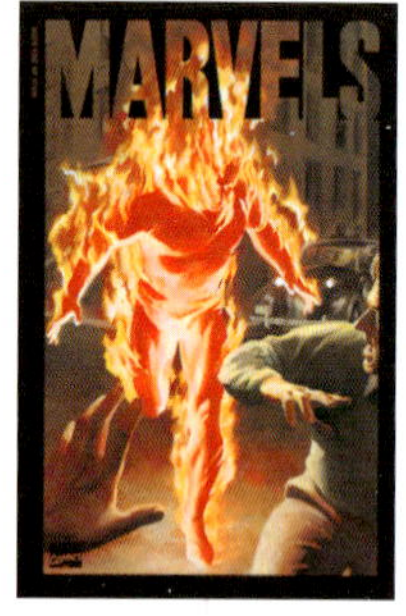

JANUARY 1994
Marvels #1 is released. The series depicts the Marvel Universe as seen through the eyes of everyday people, notably *Daily Bugle* photographer Phil Sheldon.

He was born a villain, and fans immediately picked up on him. In 1993 Deadpool went from supporting to main character in his first limited series, written by Fabian Nicieza, with illustrations by Joe Madureira, whose style came to symbolise 1990s comic book art, with influences from Japanese comics and video games. Other limited series followed for Deadpool, as did special appearances, until the launch of his first of many ongoing series in 1997.

The 1990s also saw the consolidation of Wolverine's fame, and at one time his presence on a comic-book cover guaranteed commercial success. In addition to his own ongoing series, the mutant called Logan guest-starred in countless annuals and one-shots. His attitude symbolised the Super Hero of the 1990s. The success of *X-Men: The Animated Series* also contributed to Wolverine's visibility and stature among the general public, on a par with iconic characters from the past like Spider-Man and Captain America.

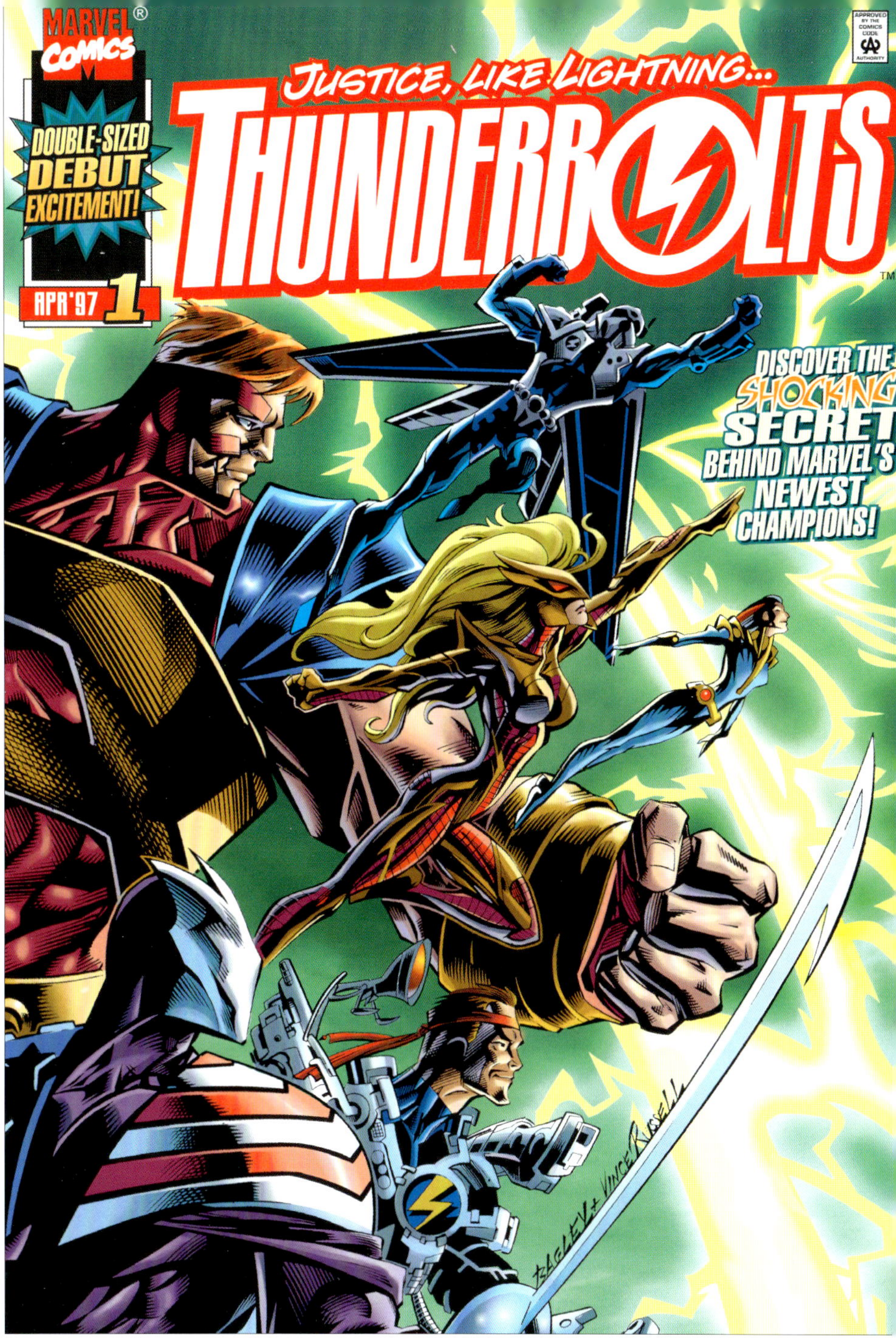

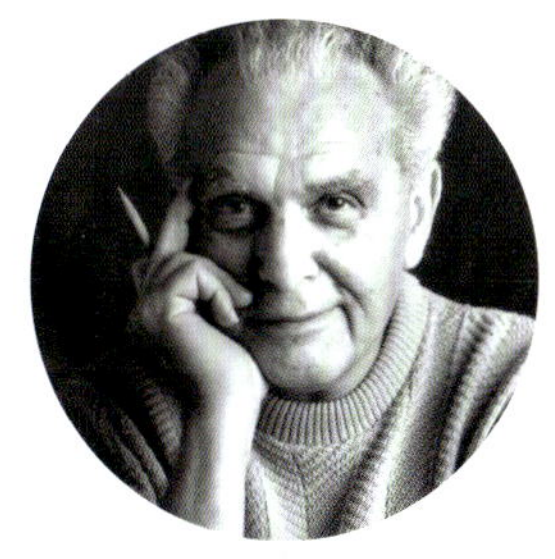

FEBRUARY 1994
On 6 February 1994, Jack Kirby, one of the founding fathers of the Marvel Universe, dies at his home in California.

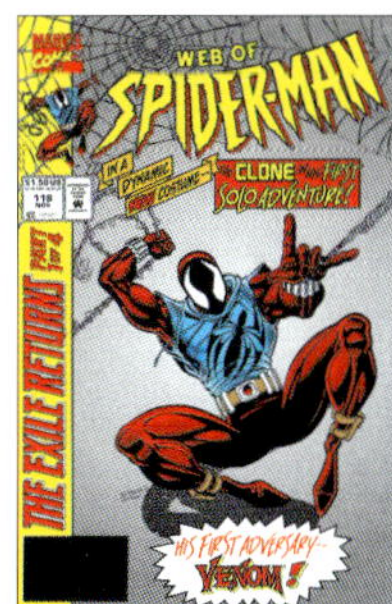

NOVEMBER 1994
Peter Parker's clone, Ben Reilly, becomes Scarlet Spider in *Web of Spider-Man #118*.

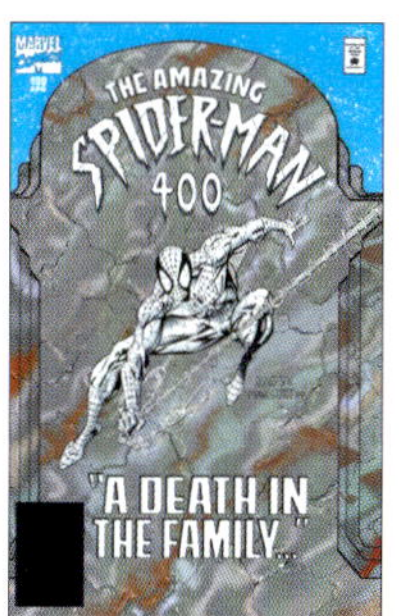

APRIL 1995
The death of Aunt May was the focal point of *The Amazing Spider-Man #400*. Years later, readers learned this 'Aunt May' was a fake, and that the real May was still alive.

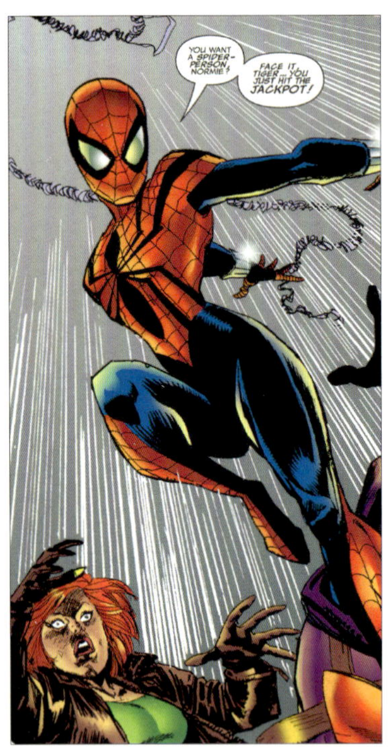

The sensational Spider-Girl as she appeared in *What If?* #105 (February 1998). Script by Tom Defalco. Art by Ron Frenz (pencils), Matt Webb (colours), Chris Eliopoulos (letters).

Deadpool makes his first appearance on the cover of *The New Mutants* #98 (February 1991). Art by Rob Liefeld.

Among the new series with links to the past, one of the biggest surprises proved to be the *Thunderbolts*. Kurt Busiek and Mark Bagley created the series that was launched to coincide with *Heroes Reborn*, so that while the most famous Super Heroes were busy in another universe, a new crew of crime-fighters would be protecting the Earth! But beneath the Thunderbolts' masks lurked the Masters of Evil, part of a complex plan orchestrated by Baron Zemo, Captain America's old foe. The series ran until 2003, and along the way many Thunderbolts actually did decide to become Super Heroes. Then there was Spider-Girl, introduced in one of the last issues of *What If?*, the series dedicated to Marvel Super Heroes involved in purely hypothetical situations.

A few years earlier, Peter Parker and Mary Jane had had a daughter, who was kidnapped shortly after she was born and was never heard from again. But what would have happened had she grown up with her parents and discovered that she too possessed spider-powers? Dated February 1998, issue #105 of *What If?* answered that question and spawned the *Spider-Girl* series, featuring young May Parker donning 'uncle' Ben Reilly's costume. Other new series would also be set in an alternative future known as MC2, which was decidedly less gloomy than life in 2099, although none achieved the success of *Spider-Girl*.

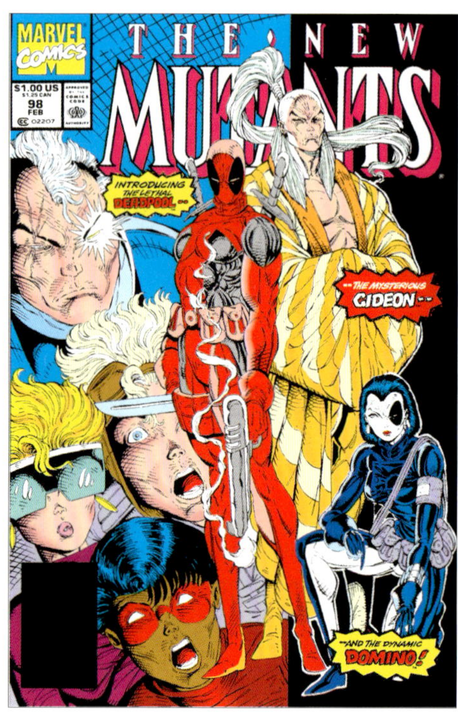

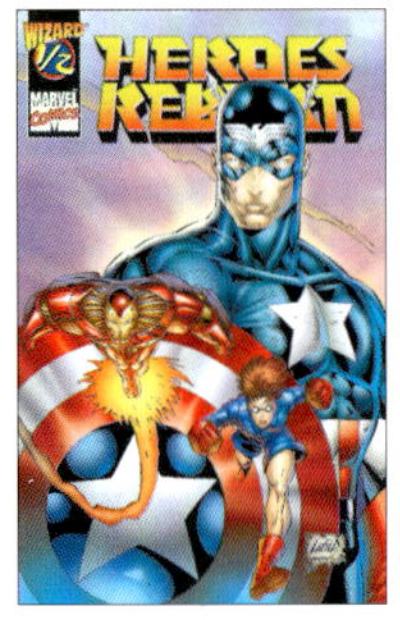

OCTOBER 1996
The 'Onslaught Saga' comes to an end. It opened the doors to *Heroes Reborn*.

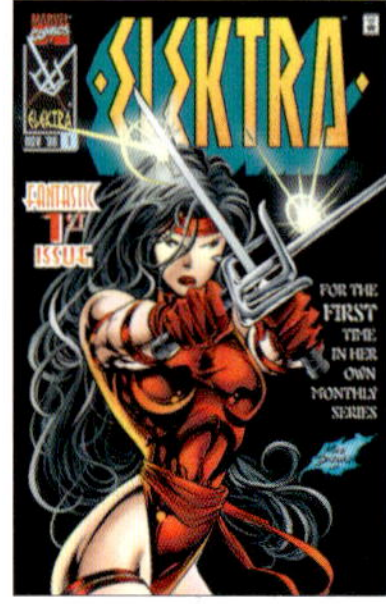

NOVEMBER 1996
Elektra is back, starring in her own series.

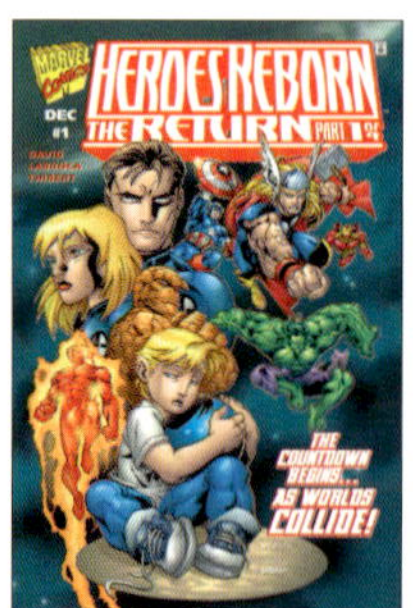

DECEMBER 1996
The Fantastic Four, the Avengers, and the Hulk all make a comeback in *Heroes Reborn: The Return*—in their original settings.

YOUNG MASTERS

A new wave of artists and writers from all areas of creative endeavour teams with Marvel to guide the Super Heroes into a new century.

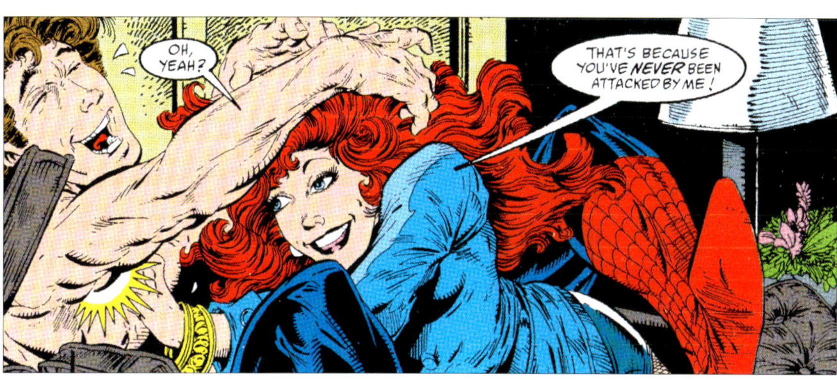

A panel from *Spider-Man #1* (August 1990). Script and art by Todd McFarlane.

As we mentioned, by the time the 1980s were drawing to a close, some comic-book creators were already working their way into fans' hearts. They were mostly artists associated with Marvel's most celebrated Super Heroes, and this contributed to their commercial success. For example, after gaining notoriety for his grotesque, innovative style in *The Incredible Hulk*, Todd McFarlane made his way to *The Amazing Spider-Man*, where he redefined the main character's look. Now Spider-Man was capable of incredible moves, pushing the limits of physics and anatomy in spectacular, never-before-attempted shots. The eyes of his mask were larger and more expressive. Even his webbing had changed—it was no longer

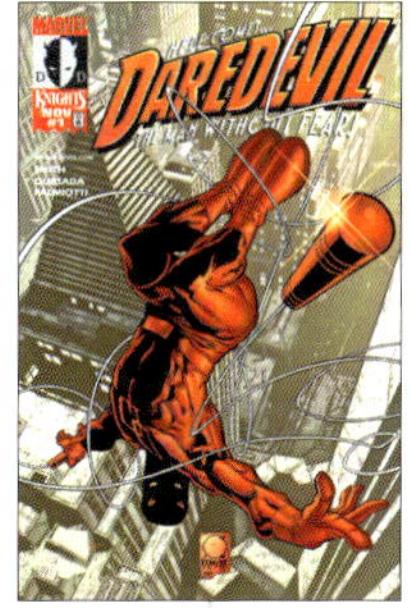

NOVEMBER 1997
The Marvel Knights imprint debuts with *Daredevil #1*, by Kevin Smith and Joe Quesada.

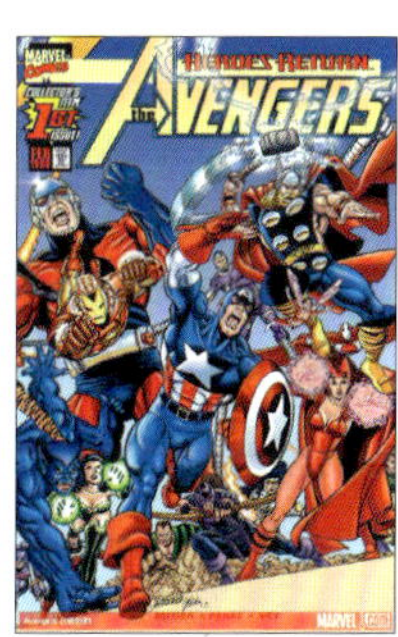

JANUARY 1998
The Avengers and the Fantastic Four return from the pocket dimension of *Heroes Reborn*. Four new series are launched, such as *Avengers* by Kurt Busiek and George Pérez.

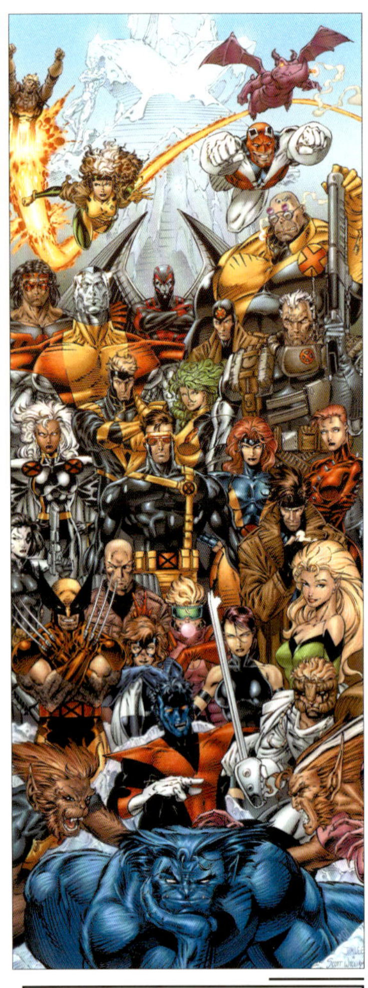

Remastered X-Men Forever Door Poster by Jim Lee (June 2009).

a set of straight lines, but spaghetti-like as it flowed from his web-shooters.

The revamped version was so successful that McFarlane was put to work on the series entitled simply *Spider-Man*, where he would also be involved in scripting stories. Something similar happened with the main artists working on the mutants at that time, Rob Liefeld and Jim Lee.

Liefeld transformed *New Mutants* into *X-Force*, introducing violent, musclebound and sexy characters into the cast. Among them were the highly successful mercenary Domino, and Cable, cyborg warrior of the future, who made an even bigger splash.

Jim Lee's *X-Men* was a staggering commercial hit. At first stories and dialogue were by Chris Claremont, but following his departure, Lee began cranking out subjects, and John Byrne, an old acquaintance of X-fans, was brought in to help with the dialogue. Other creators that were hailed by critics and fans in the early 1990s included Erik Larsen, who took over for McFarlane on *The Amazing Spider-Man*, and Marc Silvestri (cofounder of Image Comics, no coincidence there), who started out on *X-Men* and moved on to *Wolverine*.

Other artists received as much attention during the '90s, and those who did were almost all involved with best-sellers tied into the X-Men, like the Kubert brothers, Adam and Andy, sons of the legendary Joe Kubert, and Joe Madureira, as we have already seen. Others, like John Romita, Jr., and Mark Bagley, were able to combine quality and quantity, and were among the most reliable comic-book artists in the business. By the late 1990s, when artist adulation had tapered off, it was Joe Quesada who won his way into fans' hearts. Marvel readers remembered his short but powerful *X-Factor* cycle, which was written by Peter David.

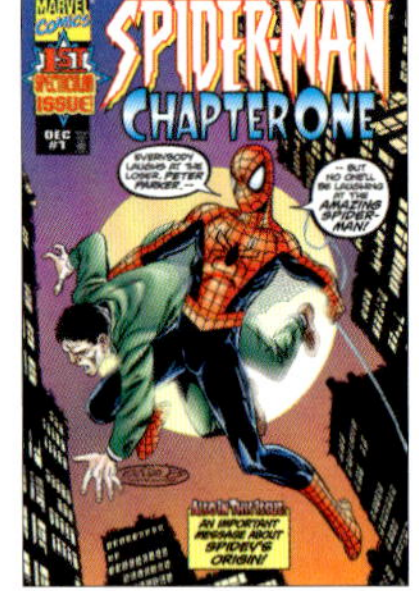

DECEMBER 1998
John Byrne is back at Marvel to write and draw *Spider-Man: Chapter One*, a limited series that retells Spidey's beginnings.

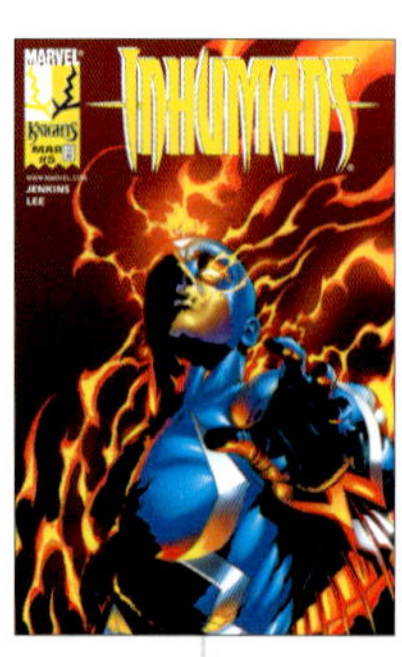

JUNE 1999
Seen for the first time in *Inhumans #5*, a new Black Widow, Yelena Belova, fights with Natasha Romanov in the mini-series *Black Widow*.

2000

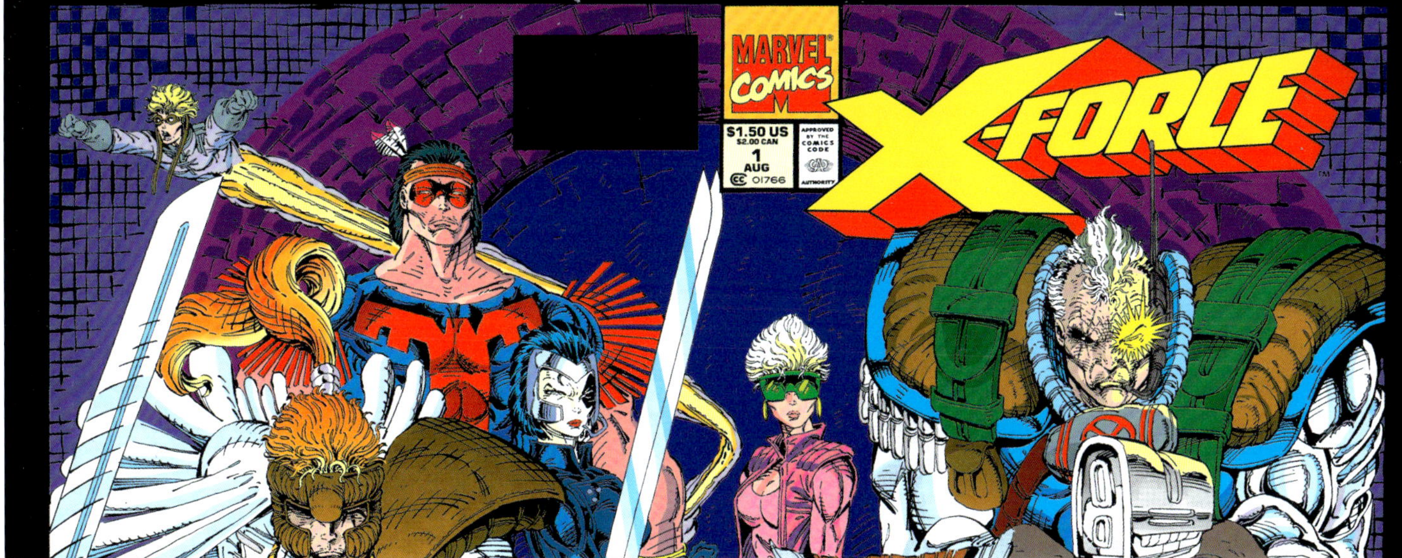

In *Daredevil*, which was part of the Marvel Knights imprint overseen by Quesada himself, he proved to be a versatile and mature illustrator, filling panels with details without compromising when it came to characters' spectacular feats and acting. Such success was also thanks to Kevin Smith, who wrote one of the best-loved and best-told stories featuring Matt Murdock, 'Guardian Devil'. As Joe Quesada wrote years later, "While there have been some guys from Hollywood who came in and did good work, nobody came in with the cachet and cred a guy like Kevin had. Kevin's jumping into the pool resonated throughout the Hollywood community and made a lot of Hollywood creators and writers who had thought about comics realise, 'You know, I could do that, too'." In recognition of the huge success of the Marvel Knights imprint, Quesada would soon be handsomely rewarded by Marvel...

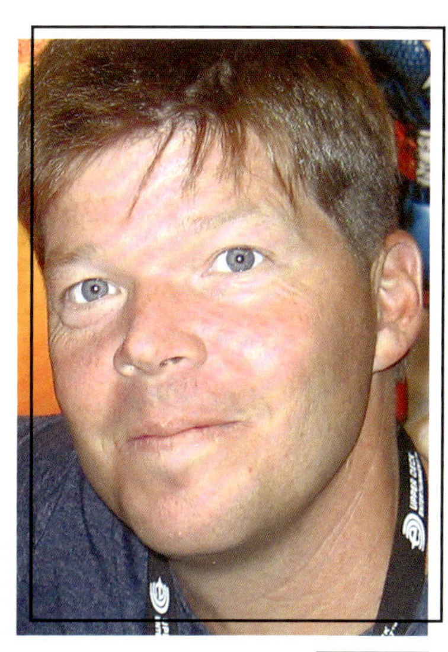

TOP
X-Force #50 (January 1996). Cover and art by Rob Liefeld.

ABOVE
Artist Rob Liefeld.

Promotional piece for the 20th anniversary of *Marvel Knights* (2018) by Joe Quesada.

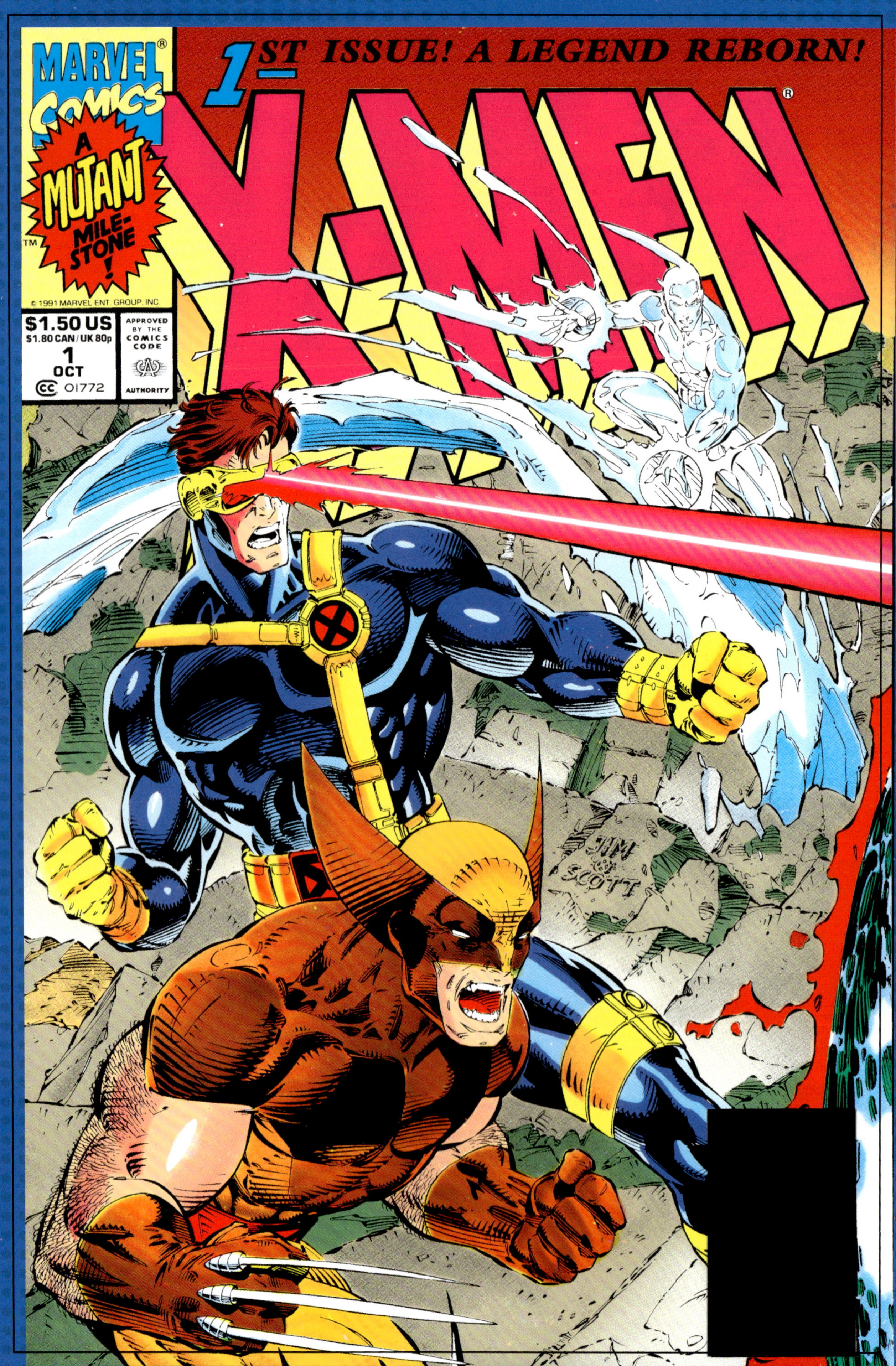

MARVEL COMICS
1ST ISSUE! A LEGEND REBORN!
X-MEN
A MUTANT MILE-STONE!
© 1991 MARVEL ENT. GROUP, INC.
$1.50 US
$1.80 CAN / UK 80p
1
OCT
01772
APPROVED BY THE COMICS CODE AUTHORITY
JIM SCOTT

A NEW MILLENNIUM AWAITS

As the dawn of a new century looms, Marvel experiments and tackles the issues of the day in a way that only Marvel could.

The Cold War was over. The Berlin Wall had fallen. The threat of a nuclear war seemed to have subsided. Yet fear remained... fear sparked and stoked by invisible, microscopic threats, like viruses. Peter David and Gary Frank brought AIDS, a hot topic throughout the '90s, to the pages of comic books. Jim Wilson, nephew of the Falcon and sidekick to the Hulk in the 1970s, contracted the HIV virus and died in *The Incredible Hulk #420* (cover-dated August 1994) with the Jade Giant at his bedside. Even if at that time the Hulk possessed Bruce Banner's intelligence, he was helpless before his terminally ill friend.

The era of the speculators, who would buy up copies of comic books in bulk and sell them to collectors for a profit, was coming to an end. This was the start of a new and different chapter, which would be more focused on TV and the movies, and characters that loomed ever larger in the collective consciousness, in part due to the impact of cartoons and merchandising. In particular,

OPPOSITE PAGE
X-Men #1 (October 1991). Art by Jim Lee.

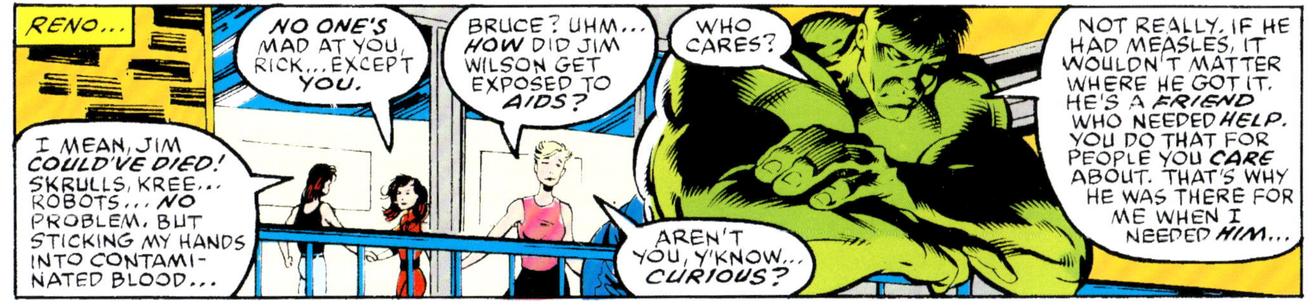

Bruce Banner learns his friend Jim Wilson has HIV in *The Incredible Hulk #388* (December 1991). Script by Peter David. Art by Dale Keown (pencils), Mark Farmer (inks), Glynis Oliver (colours), Joe Rosen (letters).

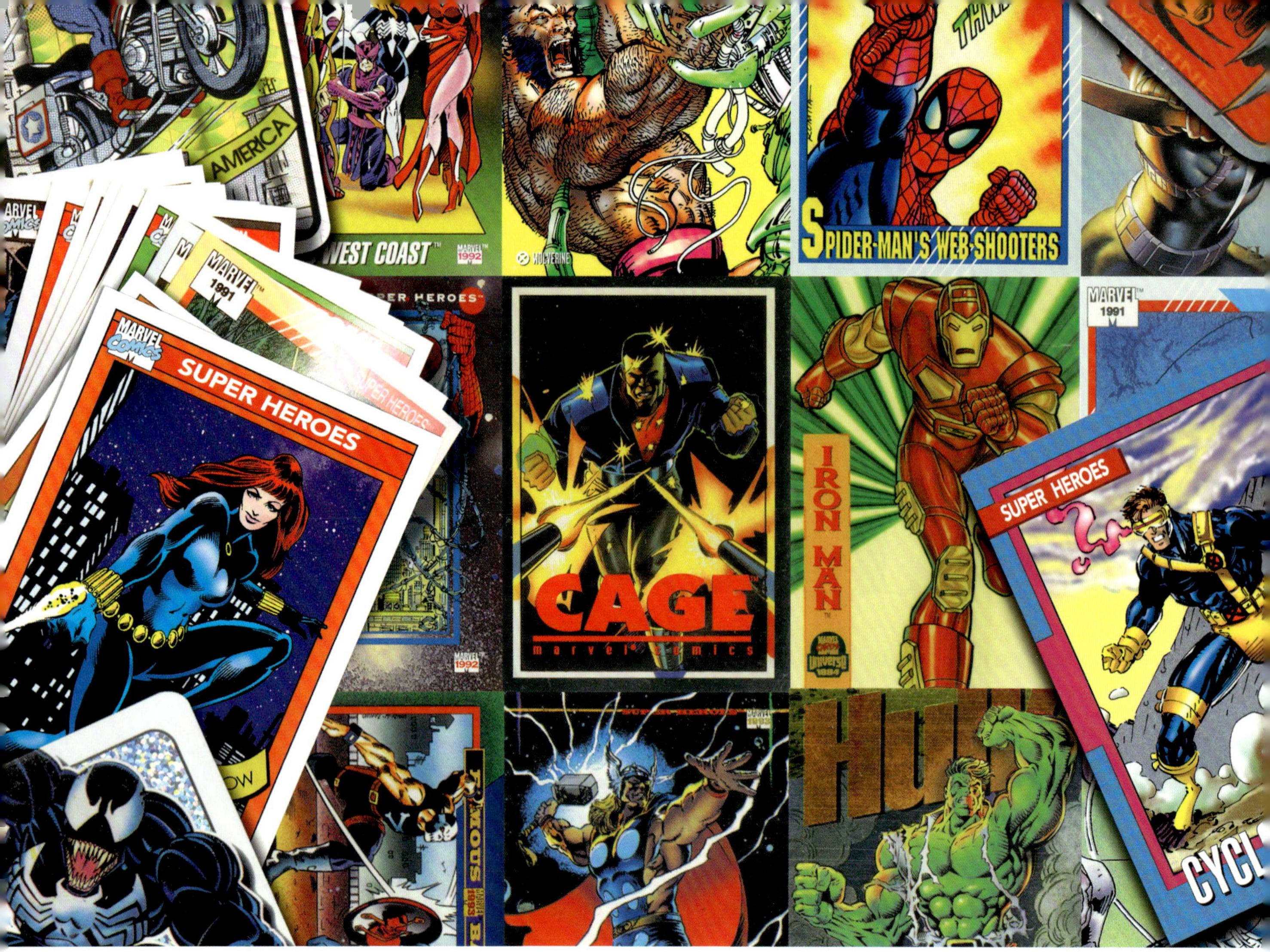

ABOVE
An assortment of Marvel trading cards from the early 1990s.

BELOW
Stan Lee's Skybox trading card by John Romita, Sr.

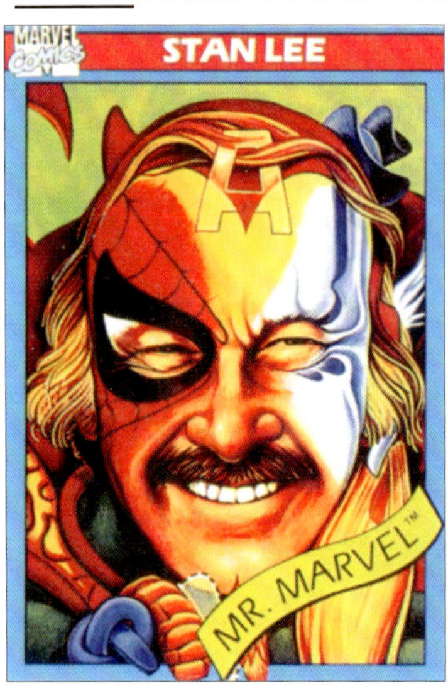

trading cards became so popular that Marvel acquired one of the leading card manufacturers, the Fleer Corporation, to produce custom-designed collections that were often based on current comic book events. Cards contained replicas of special effects used on covers at that time—metallic, relief, holographic, and 3D effects were used. Collectors gobbled them up, and artists were glad to have further opportunities to illustrate the characters that had made them famous.

As for cartoons, after the incredible success of *X-Men: The Animated Series* (the longest Marvel cartoon series on record, with 80 episodes), the 1990s saw the return of Spider-Man. The 65 episodes of the *Spider-Man* cartoon series (1994–1998) weighed in on stories old and new, including the arrival of Venom. Each episode was introduced by the blistering guitar of Aerosmith's Joe Perry, who wrote an all-new theme for the web-slinger.

As arcade video games evolved, and later with the advent of the first consoles, games featuring Marvel Super Heroes became more complex too. They appeared on all the big platforms, from Sega to Nintendo, and took inspiration from comic-book events like 'Maximum Carnage'. The eponymous side-scrolling beat 'em up video game by Capcom gave players the chance

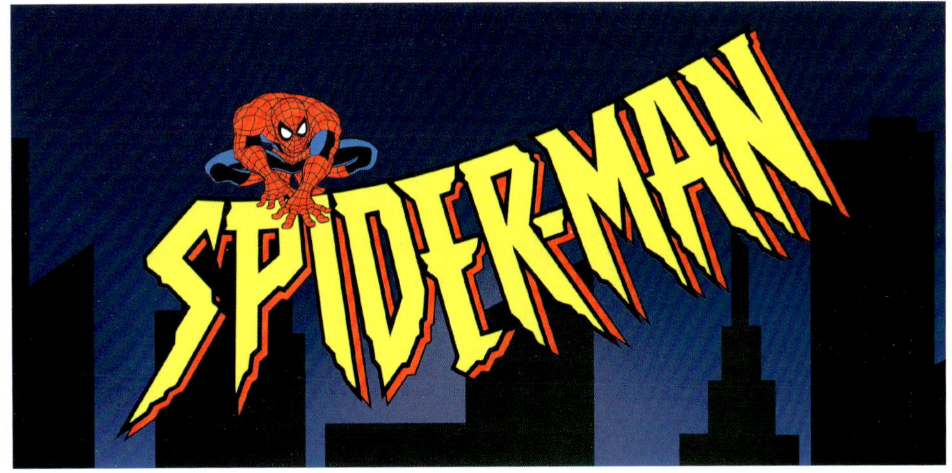

The logo from the 1990s *Spider-Man* animated series.

to play in the roles of Spider-Man, the X-Men, and even the Punisher. Besides playing with action figures, kids could now manoeuvre their favourite Super Heroes with joysticks—first in arcades, later at home. Not all Marvel video games would be hits, although some did achieve cult status. Like *Marvel Super Heroes vs. Street Fighter*, a crossover fighting game with graphics that recalled the modern design seen in comic books at that time. It was followed by more games in which Marvel Super Heroes took on various Capcom characters.

Marvel proved a popular video-game brand throughout the 1990s.

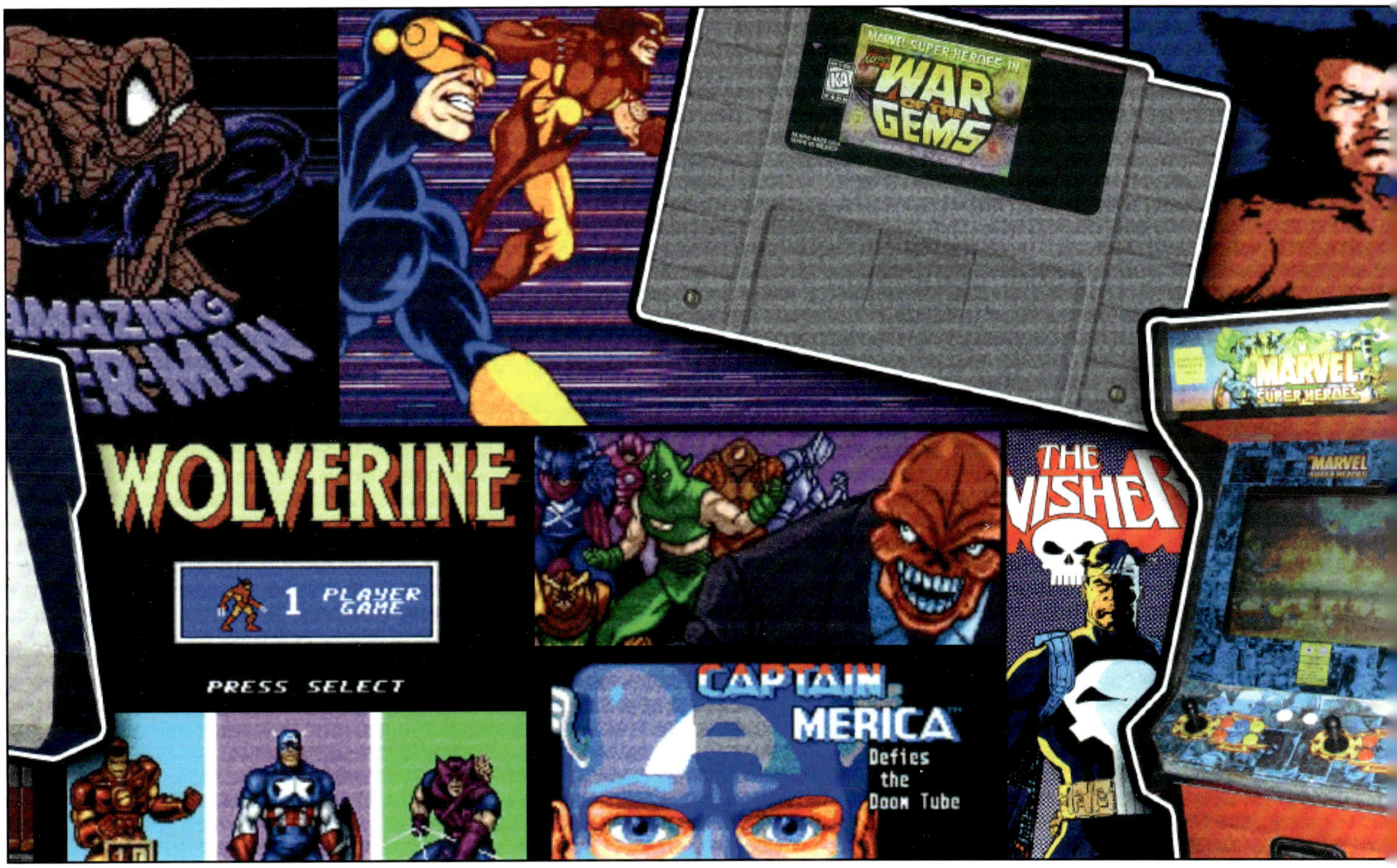

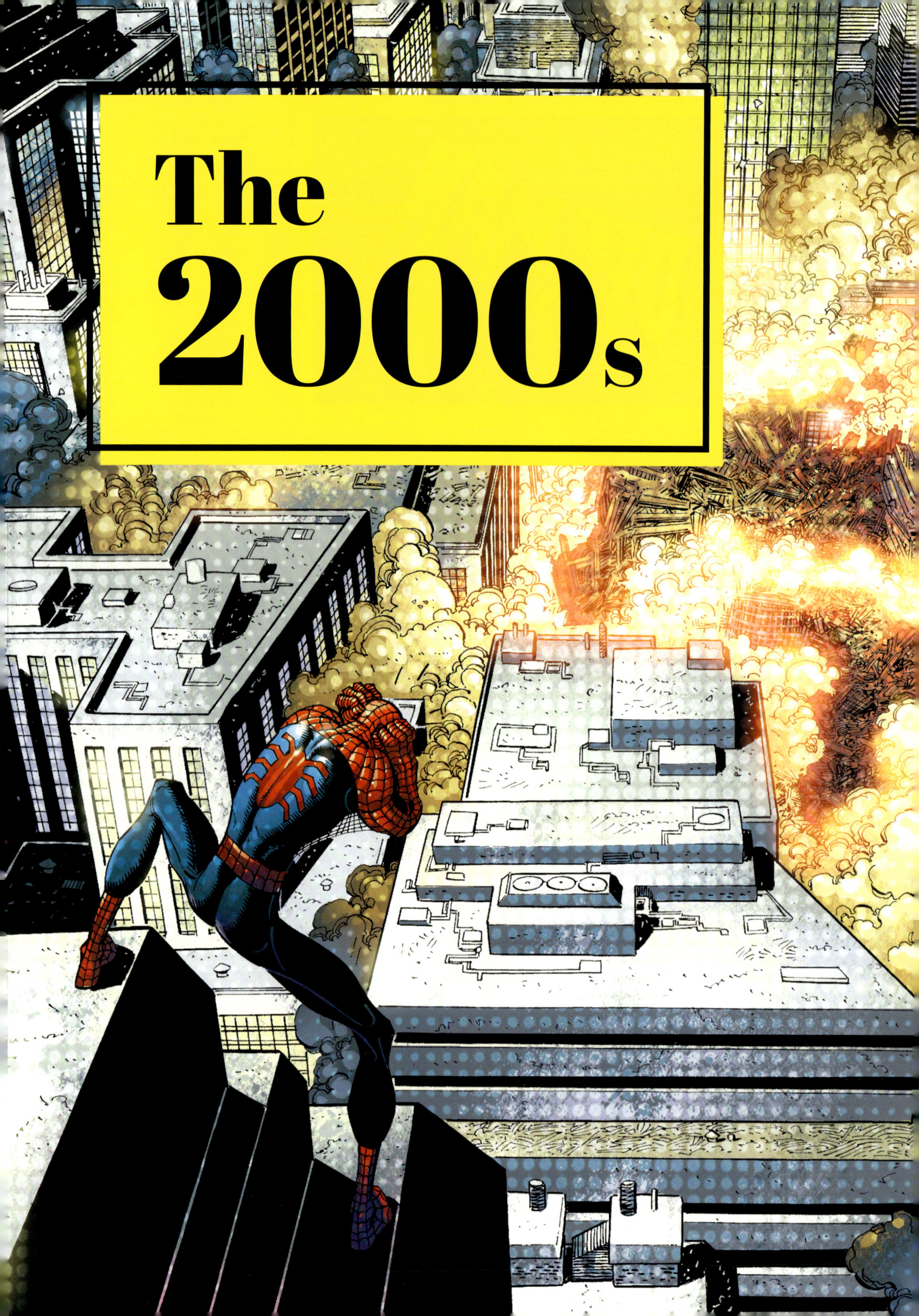

The 2000s

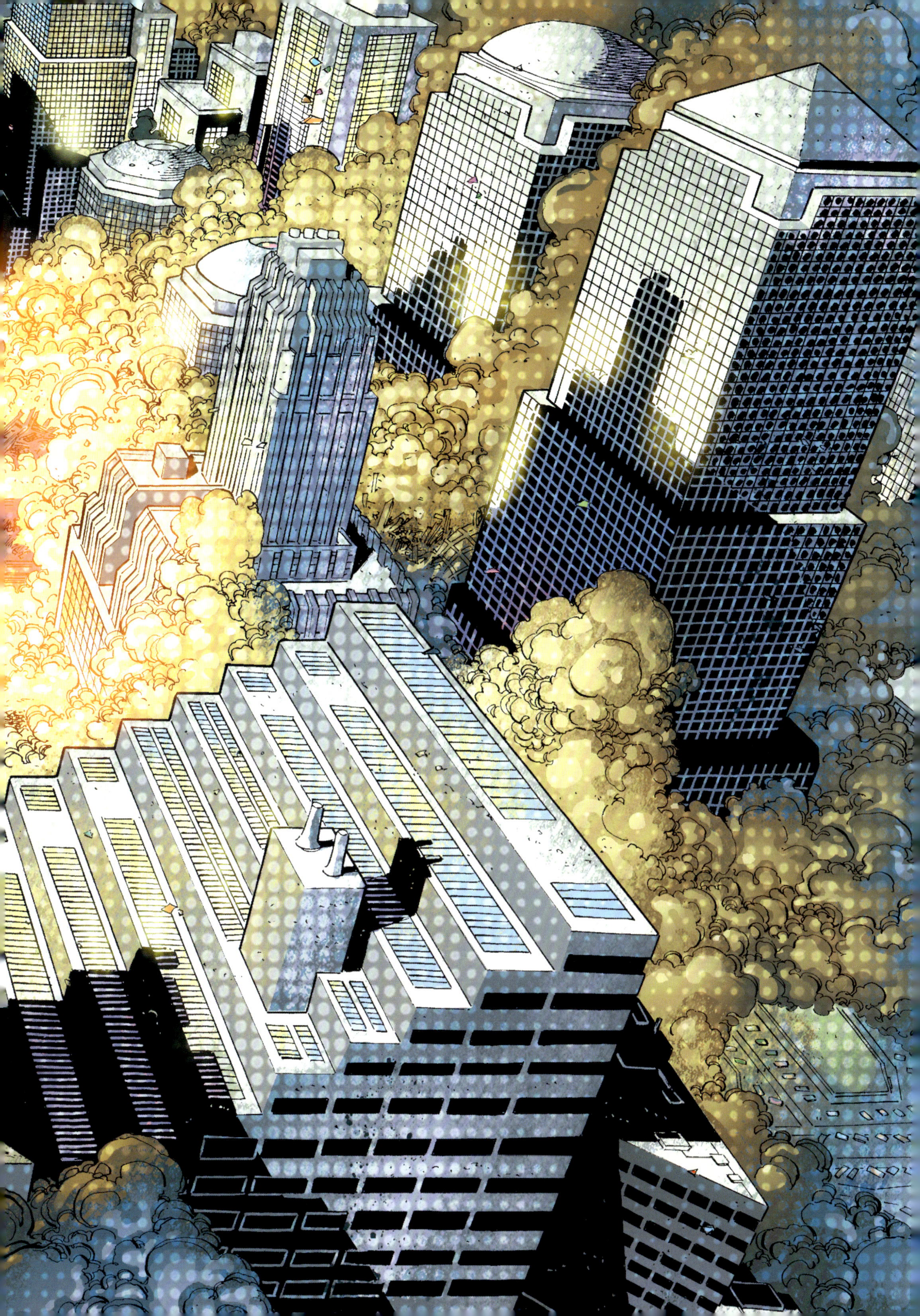

OUT OF THE DARKNESS

As Marvel entered a new millennium, there would be new challenges and obstacles to overcome—and new success as well.

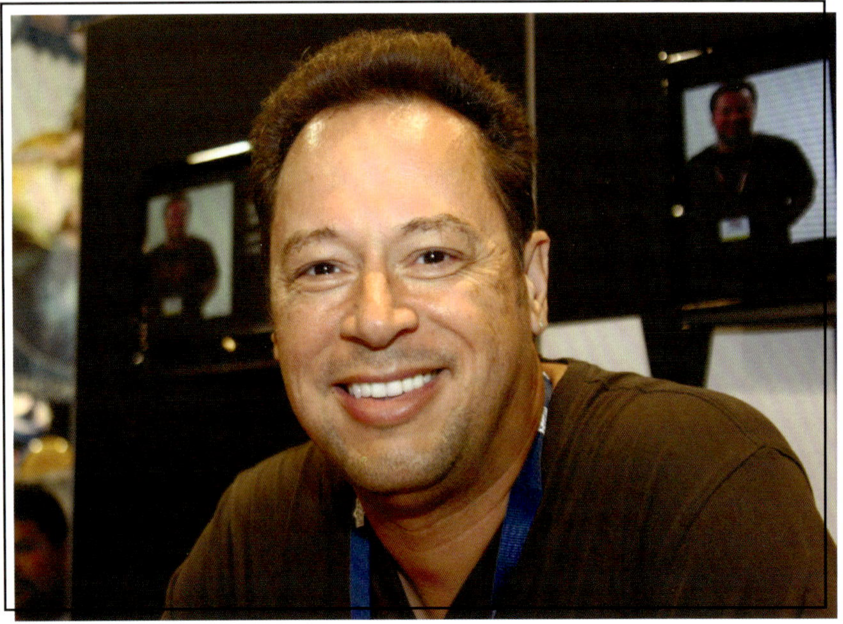

Joe Quesada, Marvel's Editor in Chief from 2000 to 2011.

Who knows, once fear of the Millennium Bug had abated, whether anyone at the dawning of 2000s would have expected this to be a crucial decade for Marvel? Hot off his success with Marvel Knights, the imprint he headed, in August 2000 Joe Quesada was appointed editor in chief. 'Joe Q' definitely played a part in making those stories among the most ground-breaking, revolutionary and adult-oriented in Marvel history. Readers had their first taste in April 2000, with the arrival of one of the biggest names in the business, Garth Ennis, who wrote *The Punisher*.

2000

APRIL 2000
The Marvel Knights imprint begins its longtime series *The Punisher*, written by iconoclast Garth Ennis.

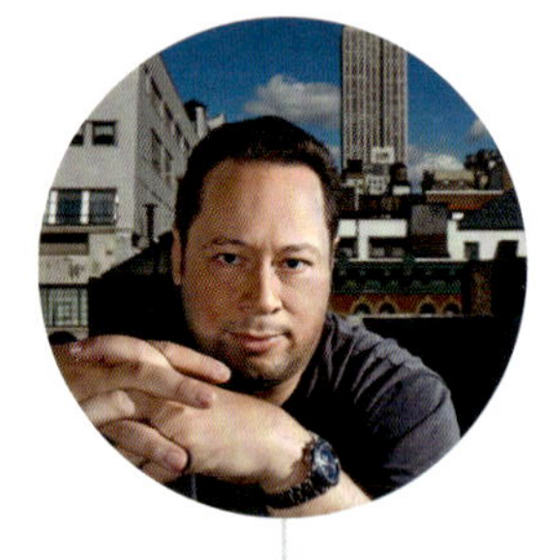

AUGUST 2000
Joe Quesada replaces Bob Harras as editor in chief. Bill Jemas is named president.

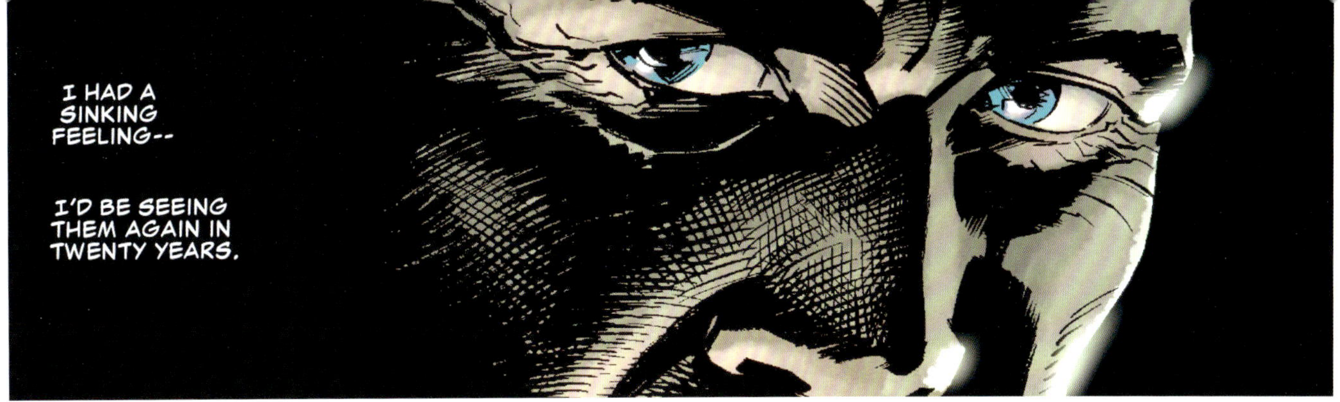

The new Marvel Knights series dedicated to the vigilante turned out to be one of Marvel's most innovative and provocative productions of all time, also thanks to the artwork of Steve Dillon, one of Ennis's long time partners.

With the promotion of Quesada and the arrival of a new president, Bill Jemas, who was very much involved in editorial decision-making, the recipe that had worked for Marvel Knights would be applied to the entire series. Writers from indie comics were called in, like Brian Michael Bendis, or from the competition, like Mark Millar and Grant Morrison, who's been active since the 1980s. Following the example of Kevin Smith, the 2000s saw more writers from Hollywood as well, such as Bob Gale (who wrote *Back to the Future*), Joss Whedon, idolised by fans for his *Buffy the Vampire Slayer*, and—most notably—J. Michael Straczynski, who at that time was riding high thanks to his sci-fi TV series *Babylon 5*. Throughout the 2000s these and other writers would relaunch history-making series featuring characters like the Avengers and Thor, consolidating sales, and winning back readers.

To reach out to new fans, however, it would be necessary to leave behind decades of continuity, just as Jim Shooter had done with the New Universe 20 years earlier. At the same time, characters that had long since made their way into the collective consciousness would have to remain recognisable, true to the classic series of the past. The Ultimate imprint was born. It wouldn't be long before even old fans were won over too. It was a parallel world where Spider-Man, the X-Men, the Fantastic Four and the Avengers (here called the

ABOVE
Panel from *The Punisher #44* (March 2007). Script by Garth Ennis. Art by Lan Medina (pencils), Bill Reinhold (inks), Raul Trevino (colours), Randy Gentile (letters).

BELOW
Marvel Knights #1 (dated July 2000, released 31 May 2000). Art by Joe Quesada, Danny Miki, and Dave Kemp.

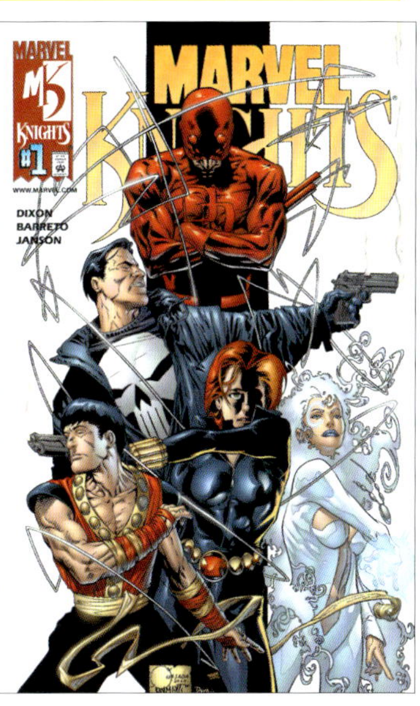

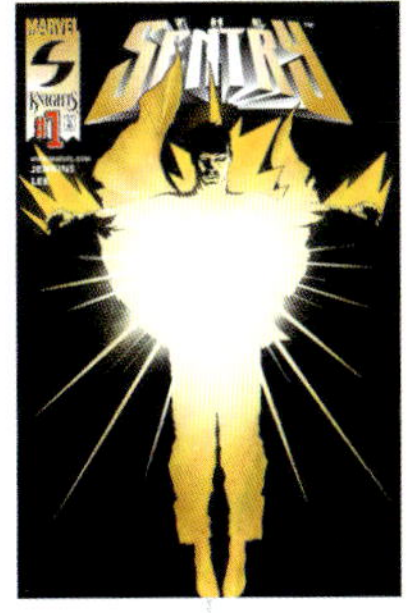

SEPTEMBER 2000
The debut of a new 'old' Super Hero, Sentry: Created by Paul Jenkins and Jae Lee, the comic was released as if it was a lost work from the 1960s.

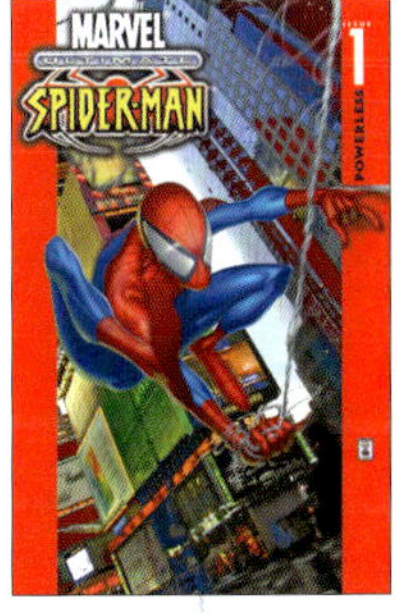

OCTOBER 2000
The Ultimate imprint is born with *Ultimate Spider-Man #1*, by Brian Bendis and Mark Bagley.

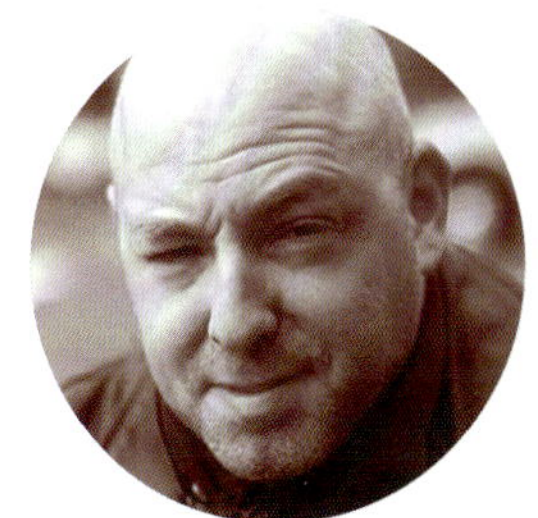

MAY 2001
Brian Michael Bendis begins writing for *Daredevil*. His stint runs four years and is much acclaimed.

NEW X-MEN

The X-Men made their comeback in the 2000s thanks to Grant Morrison and Frank Quitely, who reinvented the characters in a lengthy run which, on the one hand paid tribute to classics by Claremont in terms of themes (space travel, a dystopic future, romantic intrigue), and on the other was brimming with modern solutions. They began with the look—spandex costumes were replaced by biker wear, like the gear seen in Bryan Singer's films. In 2004 Joss Whedon would take over as writer for *The Astonishing X-Men*. He brought back classic costumes, while maintaining an up-to-date spectacular style —and we have John Cassaday to thank for the artwork.

Ultimates) took their first steps. They were written by the latest arrivals, and illustrated by Marvel superstars like Mark Bagley, Bryan Hitch, and Andy and Adam Kubert.

But no one had foreseen an event that would send comics creators for a loop, upend all certainty, and set the stage for story themes for the next ten years and beyond. The attack that destroyed the Twin Towers on September 11, 2001 sent shockwaves around the

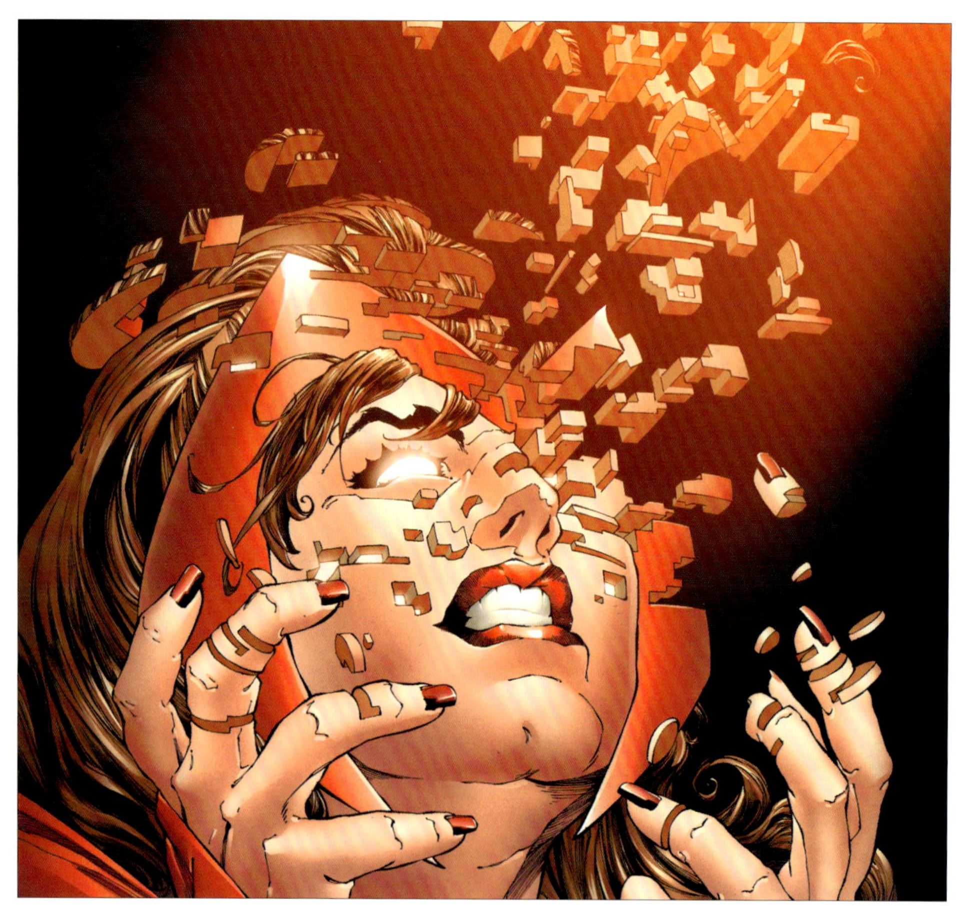

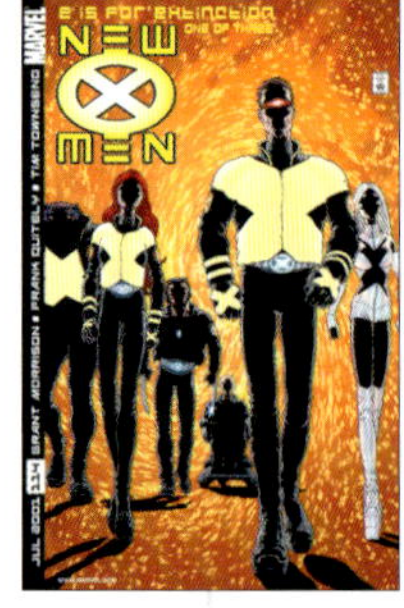

JULY 2001
Grant Morrison and Frank Quitely reinvent the mutants for the new millennium in *New X-Men #114* (following the old X-Men chronology).

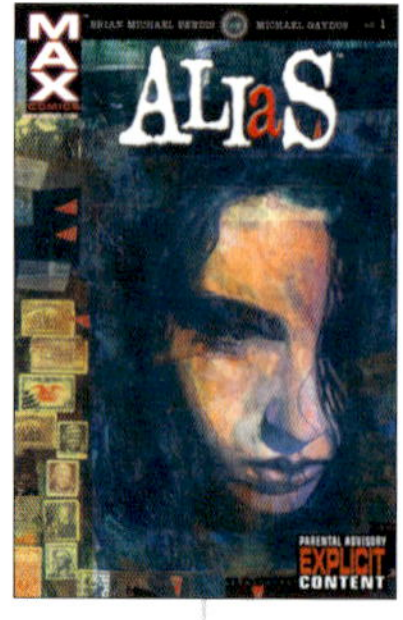

NOVEMBER 2001
The MAX imprint is born with the release of *Alias*, the new hit written by Bendis.

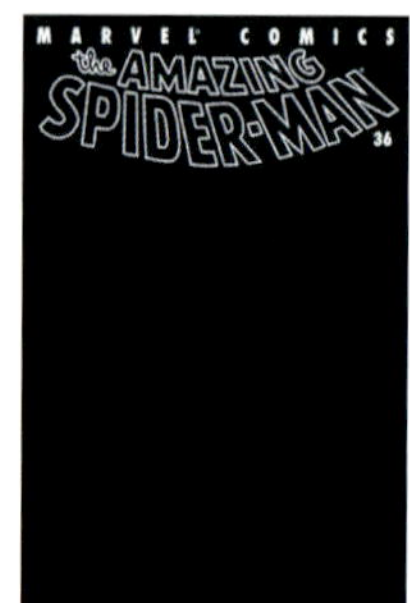

DECEMBER 2001
J. Michael Straczynski and John Romita, Jr., dedicate *The Amazing Spider-Man #36* to the 9/11 attacks.

world. The sound of the crashes and explosions echoed through the offices at Marvel, at that time on 40th Street in Manhattan, not far from Ground Zero.

Marvel people lost friends and relatives. But there was no time to despair. It was time to rise again. Just like Marvel Super Heroes, who had won so many battles in New York. Marvel went immediately to work on tributes to victims and heroes like firemen, police officers, doctors, and rescue workers. Just five weeks after the attacks the 64-page *Heroes* was released, featuring artwork by a host of world-famous artists. The first print run of 100,000 sold out in two days, hundreds of thousands of more copies came rolling off the presses, all the proceeds going to the Twin Towers Fund.

Another charitable initiative, the anthology *A Moment of Silence*, released the following February, was a collection of stories featuring fire fighters, cops, and everyday people. Apart from these two special editions, there was also a truly special issue of *The Amazing Spider-Man*, beginning with its all-black cover. Issue #36 of the new series was written by Straczynski and illustrated by Romita, Jr., and showed New York's own Spidey at Ground Zero aiding in the rescue effort just after the attacks.

His desperation is evident, even Dr. Doom and Magneto are aghast at the tragedy. Just as in real life, Super Heroes couldn't keep disaster from occurring, but as Spider-Man himself said in that story, "We could not see it coming. We could not be here before it happened. We could not stop it. But we are here now. You cannot see us for the dust, but we are here. You cannot hear us for the cries, but we are here."

The echo of 9/11 would continue to resonate in Marvel stories for years to come, recalling the creation of Marvel's New Universe—that imaginary world, even if inhabited by Super Heroes wearing costumes and by frightful villains, "is the world outside your window."

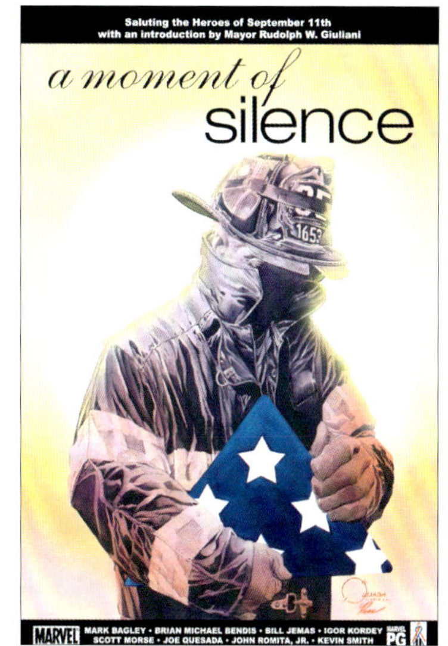

ABOVE
Saluting the heroes of September 11. *A Moment of Silence #1* (February 2002). Art by Joe Quesada, Alex Ross, Gene Ha, Shadi Petosky.

OPPOSITE PAGE
Variant cover for *House of M #1* (June 2005). Art by Joe Quesada.

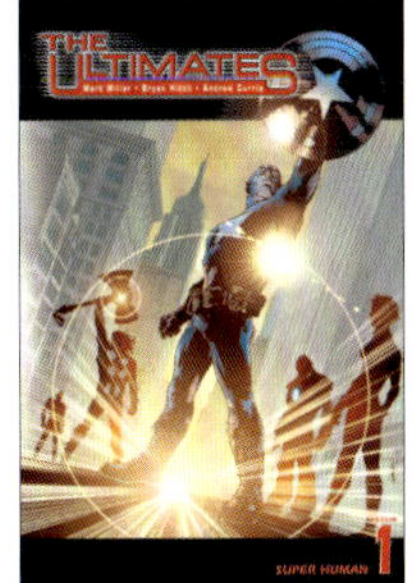

MARCH 2002
Following *The Ultimate Spider-Man* and *The Ultimate X-Men*, *The Ultimates* is released.

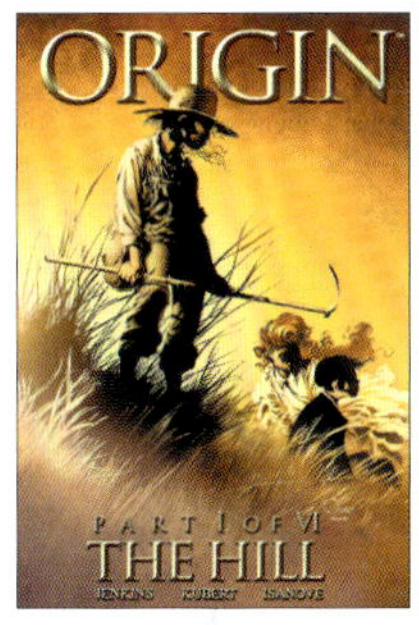

APRIL 2002
With the conclusion of the limited series *Origin*, Wolverine's early years are revealed, along with other incredible details.

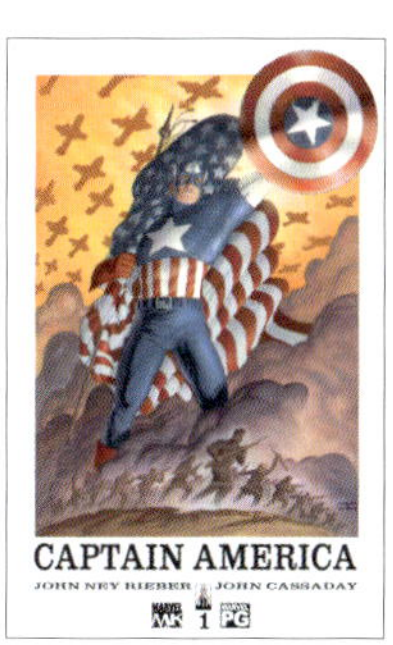

JUNE 2002
Captain America deals with the consequences of 9/11 in a new series by John Ney Rieber and John Cassaday, battling it out with Islamic terrorists.

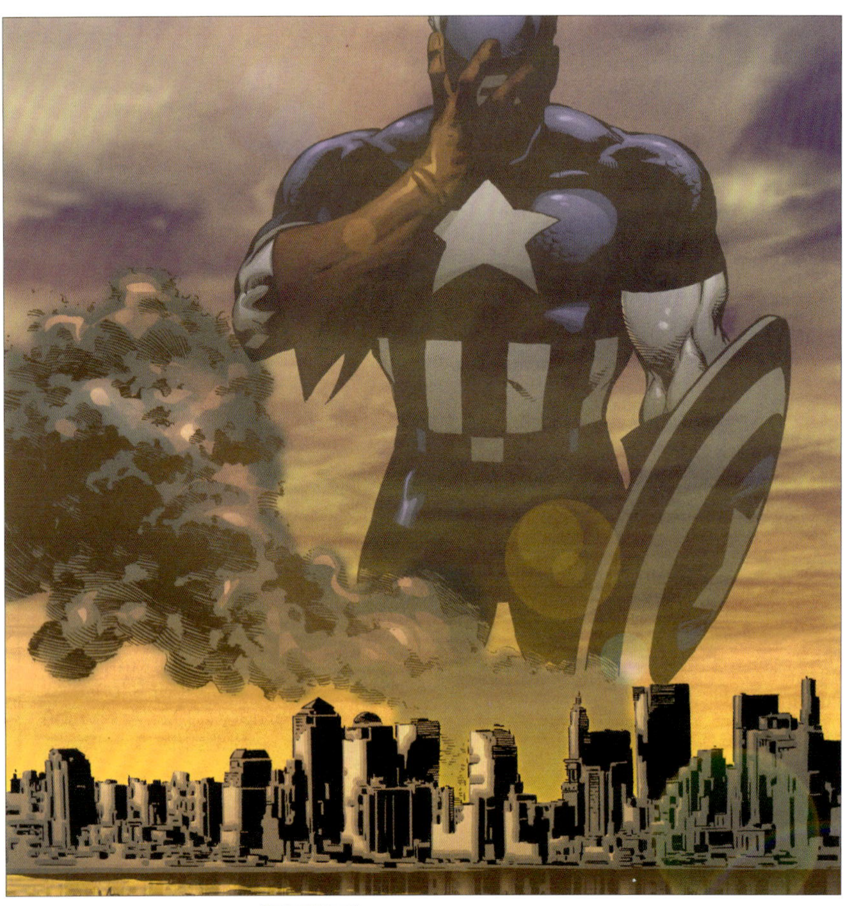

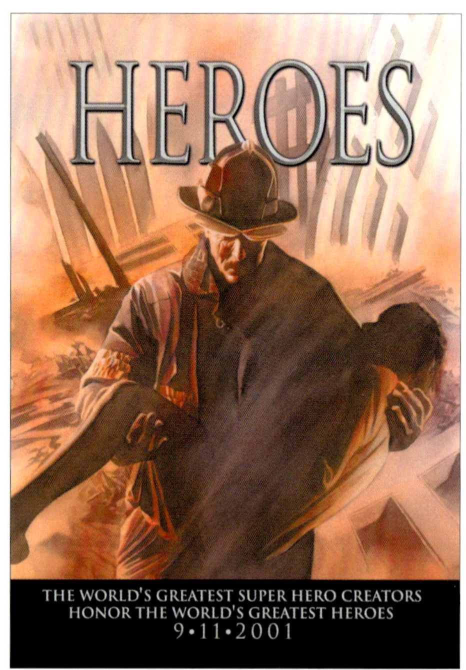

OPPOSITE PAGE
Spider-Man surveys the aftermath of 9/11, *The Amazing Spider-Man #36* (December 2001). Script by J. Michael Straczynski. Art by John Romita, Jr. (pencils), Scott Hanna (inks), Avalon Studios/Dan Kemp (colours), Richard Starkings, Wes Abbott (letters).

ABOVE
Mike Deodato, Jr. illustration of Captain America in the aftermath of the 9/11 attacks from *Heroes* (2001).

ABOVE RIGHT
Marvel's *Heroes* (2001). Art by Alex Ross.

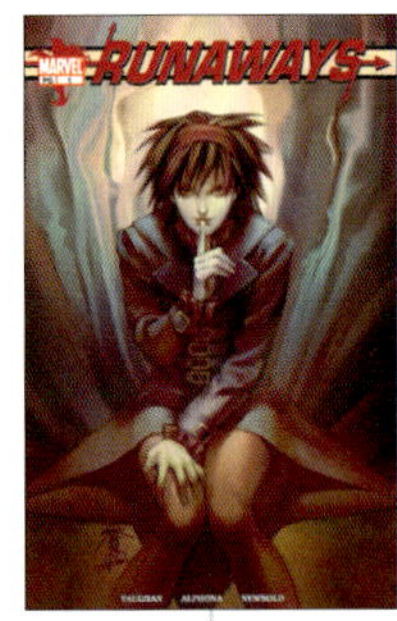

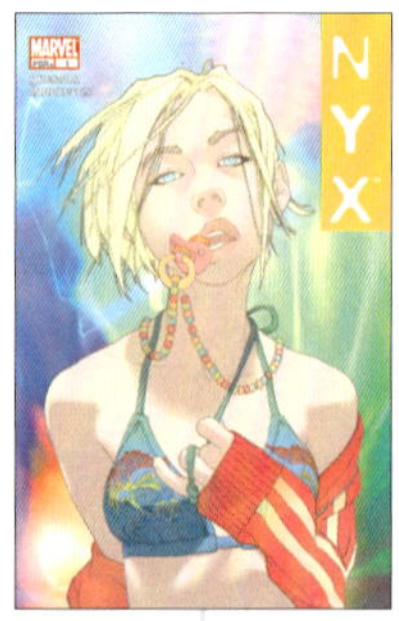

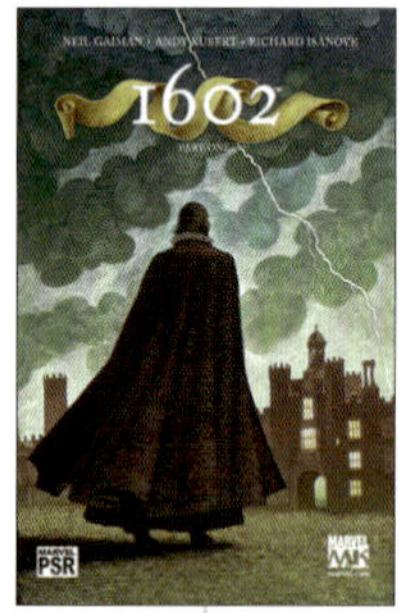

JULY 2003
The arrival of a group of new young Super Heroes, the *Runaways*. The series went on to achieve cult status.

NOVEMBER 2003
Laura Kinney (A.K.A. X-23) appears in *NYX #1*. She is a Wolverine clone who made her debut in the cartoon *X-Men: Evolution*, aired from 2000 to 2003.

NOVEMBER 2003
Also in November, Neil Gaiman's monumental *1602* is released—a reworking of the Marvel Universe set in the past.

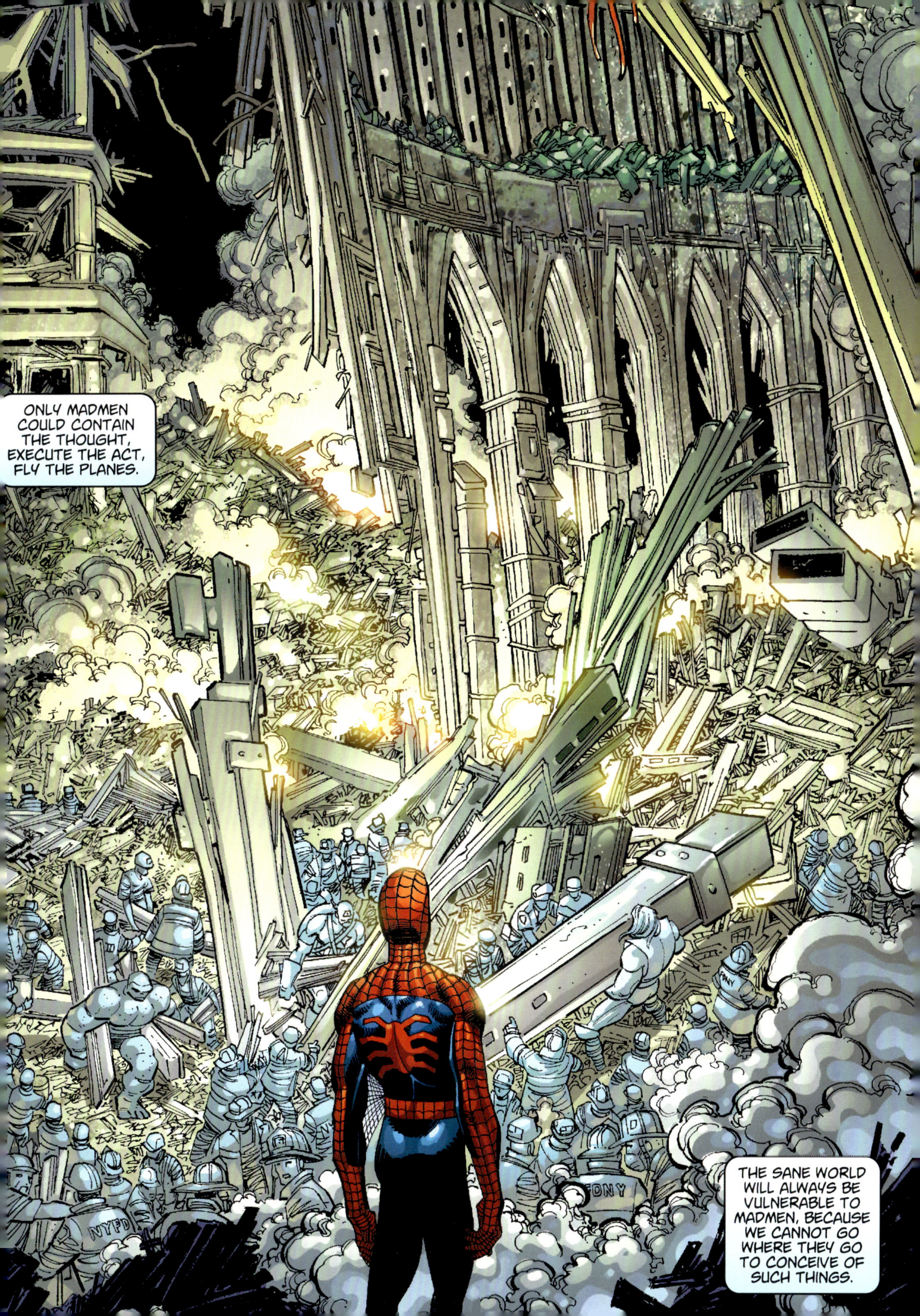
ONLY MADMEN COULD CONTAIN THE THOUGHT, EXECUTE THE ACT, FLY THE PLANES.
THE SANE WORLD WILL ALWAYS BE VULNERABLE TO MADMEN, BECAUSE WE CANNOT GO WHERE THEY GO TO CONCEIVE OF SUCH THINGS.
NYPD
FDNY
FDNY

NOIR AND FOUR-COLOUR PRINT

Marvel experiments with new genres, and reinvents the Super Hero with its outstanding *Ultimates*.

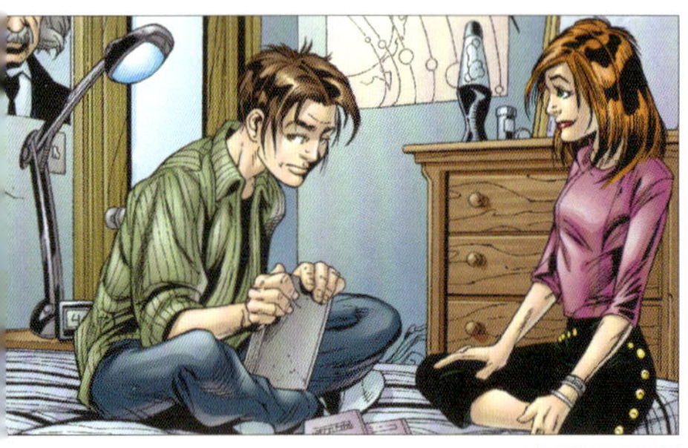

Panel from *Ultimate Spider-Man #13* (November 2001). Art by Mark Bagley (pencils), Art Thibert (inks), JC (colours), Albert Deschesne (letters).

When Brian Michael Bendis offered his services to Marvel, Quesada and Jemas knew that he was an excellent writer. He had already done great Hollywood-esque noir and combined hard-boiled fiction with fantasy in a series for Image Comics, *Sam and Twitch*. Taking him on as a writer was a natural choice. If anything was out of the ordinary, it was the series that started off his tenure at Marvel, *Ultimate Spider-Man*.

It reinvented Peter Parker for the new millennium, providing a contemporary take on his roots. We are treated to high schooler Peter's antics as he meets Mary Jane Watson and becomes a Super Hero fighting off villains the likes of Dr. Octopus and the Green Goblin. These stories, however, had a fresh, modern taste and rhythm, and at the same time were connected to the past thanks to illustrations by Mark Bagley, the

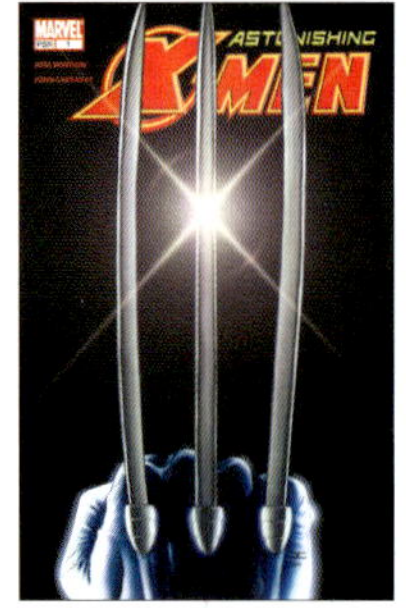

JULY 2004
Ever-popular Joss Whedon takes the reins of *Astonishing X-Men*, illustrated by John Cassaday.

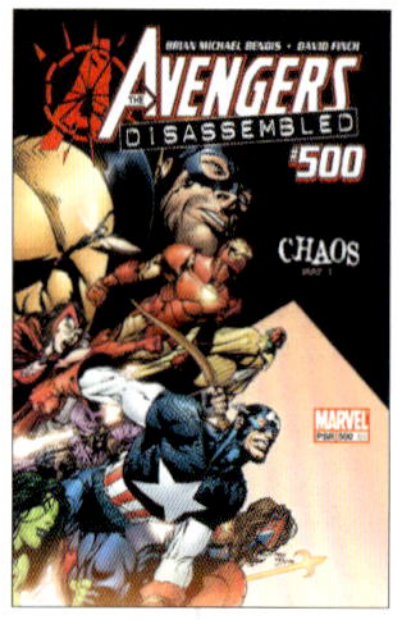

SEPTEMBER 2004
Brian Michael Bendis writes the Avengers' most devastating saga, 'Avengers Disassembled'. It would pave the way for the January 2005 release of *New Avengers*.

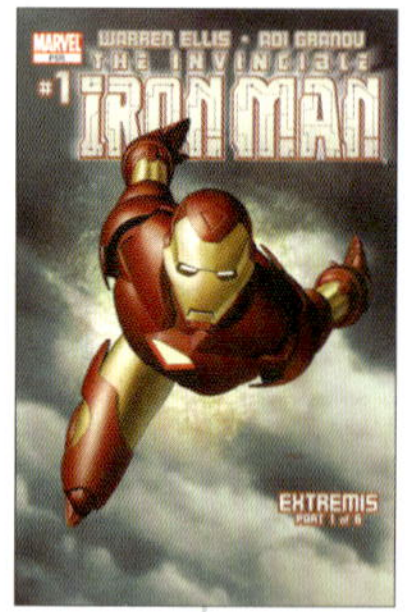

JANUARY 2005
In the saga 'Extremis', writer Warren Ellis and artist Adi Granov redefine Iron Man's look for the 21st century.

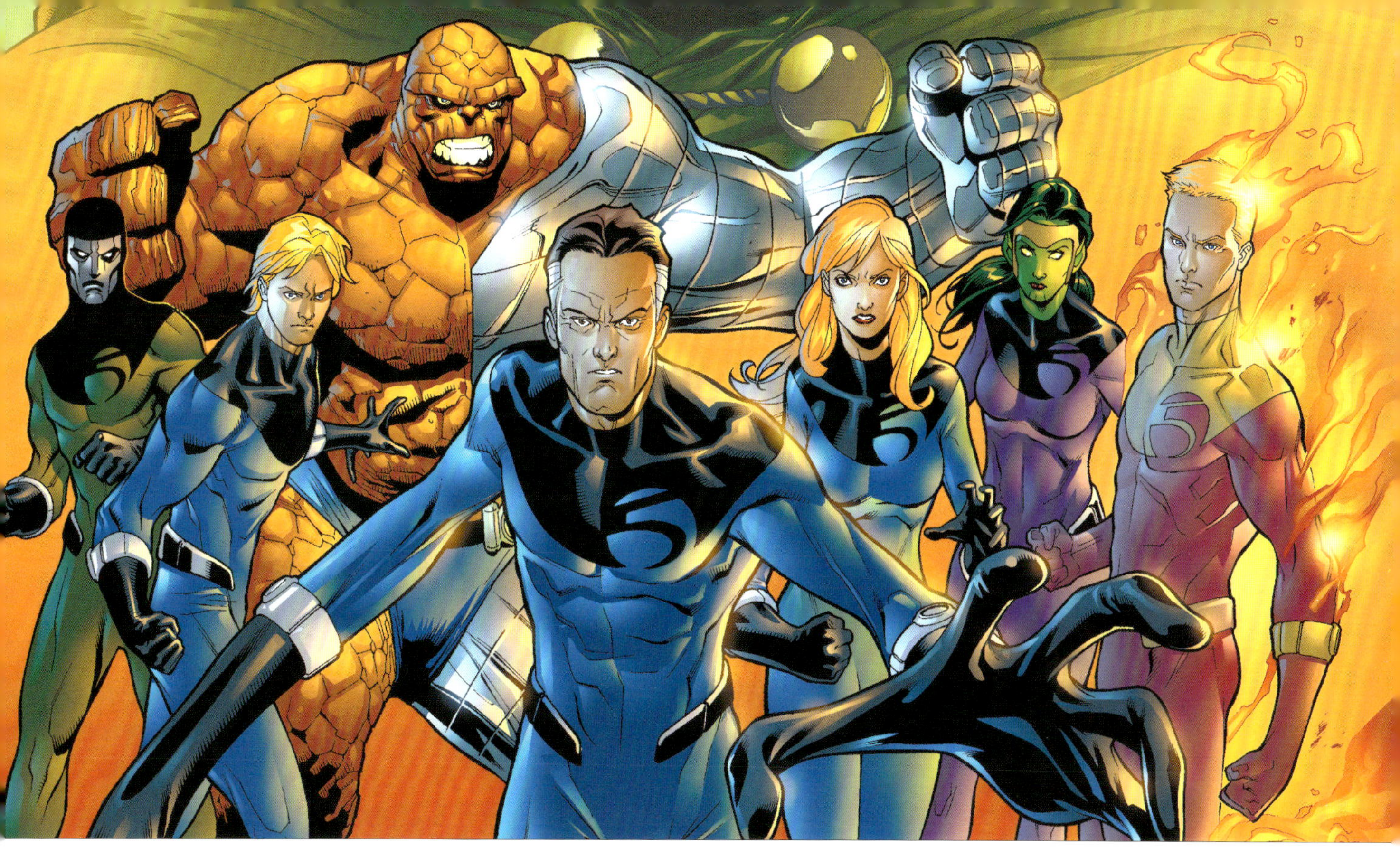

Cover detail from *Fantastic Five #1* (September 2007). Art by Clayton Henry.

benchmark artist who had drawn Spidey in the 1990s. Bendis and Bagley helmed the series for 111 issues, surpassing Lee and Kirby's record with *The Fantastic Four* for consecutive issues by the same pair of creators. Stuart Immonen would replace Bagley, and it wasn't long before he became one of Marvel's top artists, while Bendis worked on the Ultimate imprint until it was shut down in 2016. A few months after the *Ultimate Spider-Man*, came the debut of *Ultimate X-Men*, written by Mark Millar, from Scotland, illustrated by brothers Andy and Adam Kubert, who were already favourites of X-fans everywhere. Their younger and morally ambiguous counterparts were a hit too.

In 2002 Millar came out with *The Ultimates*, this universe's counterpart to the Avengers.

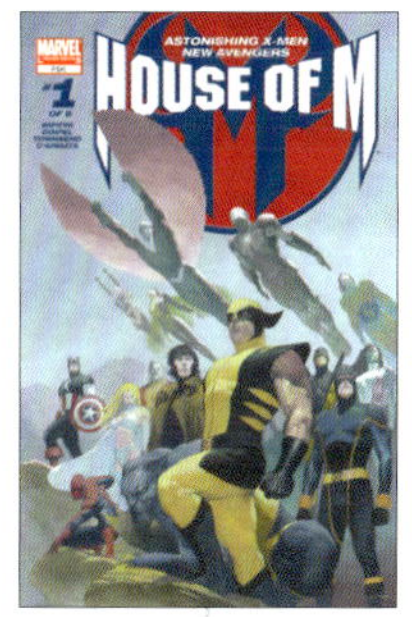

AUGUST 2005
The crossover *House of M* reunites the X-Men and the Avengers. It would relaunch the career of Carol Danvers, who would go on to become Captain Marvel.

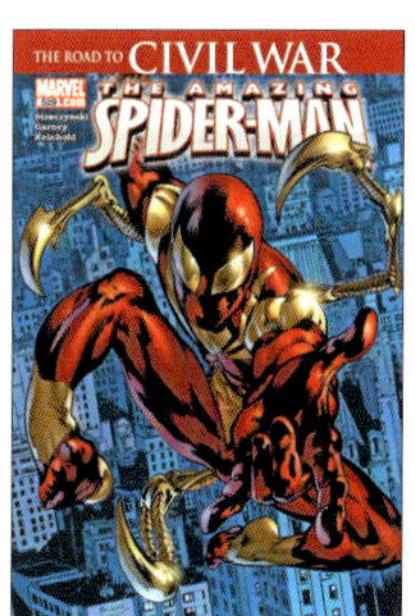

APRIL 2006
Tony Stark gives Peter Parker custom-made armour with the arrival of the Iron Spider. The costume is similar to the one seen in *Avengers: Infinity War*.

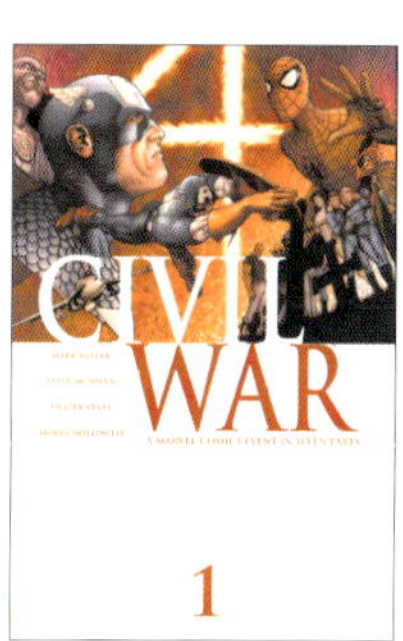

JULY 2006
The beginning of the greatest modern crossover: *Civil War*.

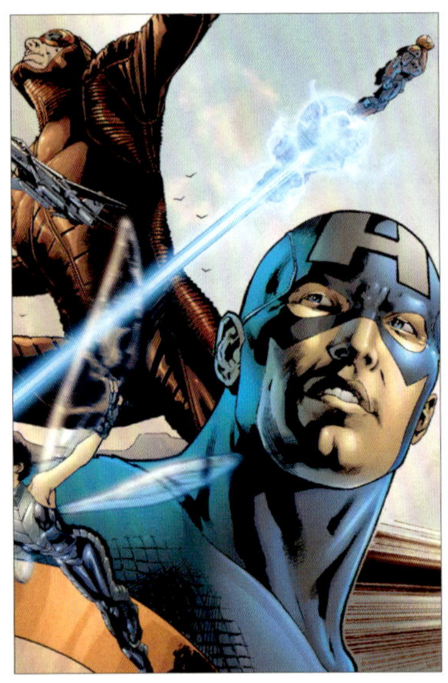

Illustrator Bryan Hitch was known for his spectacular and highly detailed panels that smacked of scenes out of a Hollywood blockbuster film. *The Ultimates* offered an almost realistic approach to Super Heroes, with its sanctimonious Captain America, a cannibal Hulk, and a Thor who was not believed when he claimed to be a god. Standout enemies included Chitauri aliens. More Ultimate series followed, including *Ultimate Fantastic Four*. Ultimate was a survivor alongside the 'regular' Marvel Universe, and had a decisive impact on future styles and themes.

The *Civil War* event (see sidebar, page 141) that would soon follow would change the status quo of the Super Heroes for years, especially the fates of Captain America and

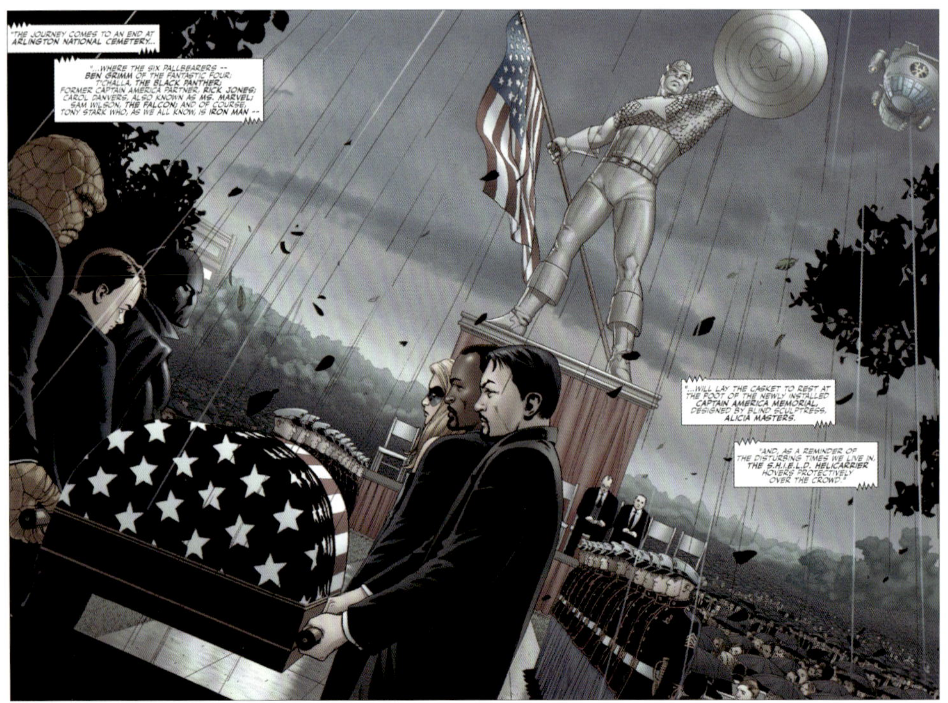

ABOVE
Back cover detail from *The Ultimates #1* (March 2002). Art by Bryan Hitch and Paul Mounts.

RIGHT
Panel from *Fallen Son: The Death of Captain America #1* (dated June 2007, released April 4, 2007). Script by Jeph Loeb. Art by Leinil Yu (pencils, inks), Dave McCaig (colours), Richard Starkings and Comicraft (letters).

OPPOSITE PAGE
Part one of the "Planet Hulk" storyline from *The Incredible Hulk #92* (April 2006). Art by José Ladrönn.

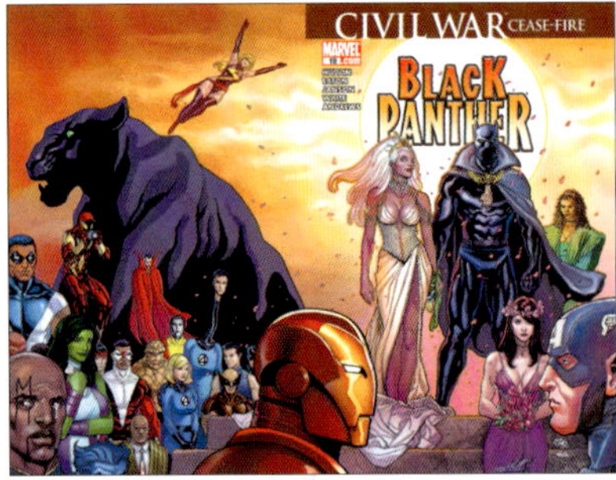

SEPTEMBER 2006
Super Heroes reunite during a truce in their *Civil War*: Black Panther and Storm, of X-Men fame, are married!

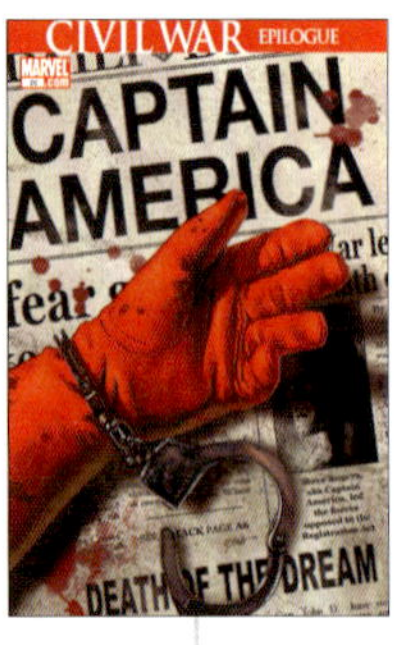

APRIL 2007
At the end of the *Civil War*, Captain America is killed by a mysterious sniper. All part of Red Skull's complex plan.

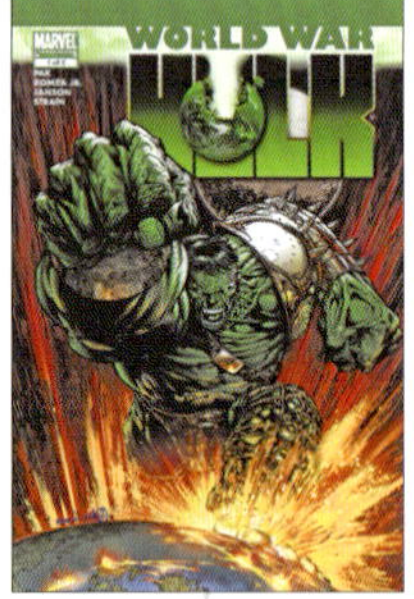

AUGUST 2007
After a year of exile in slavery, as a gladiator and a commander of troops on another planet, Hulk is back on Earth declaring war on the Super Heroes in *World War Hulk*.

Iron Man. The series became the standard bearer for trenchant Super Hero action. Shortly after the end of the Civil War, Steve Rogers was assassinated. Handcuffed, he was hit by a shooter as he walked down the steps of the Capitol. His death would spark repercussions throughout the Marvel Universe! In the months immediately prior, writer Ed Brubaker and artist Steve Epting brought back Cap's old sidekick Bucky Barnes in *Captain America*.

He didn't die on his last mission, but had been captured by the Soviets, who brainwashed him and transformed him into the killer Winter Soldier. Once back with the good guys, Bucky took Steve's place after his death. A few years later Steve came back. He brought his shield with him.

Another character that went through some major issues was Spider-Man. Initially, Peter sided with Iron Man in the Civil War and had publicly revealed his secret identity, before regretting it. In a 2008 story co-written by Straczynski and Quesada and illustrated by Quesada, 'One More Day', Peter makes a deal with the demon Mephisto to save the life of Aunt May. In exchange for which, his marriage to Mary Jane would never have happened. At the end of the saga, Peter Parker is once again single. The bond with Mary Jane was still a lifeline for Spider-Man, who experienced new adventures in 'Brand New Day'. As for Hulk, he gained new popularity in the 2000s thanks to two long sagas—*Planet Hulk* and *World War Hulk*.

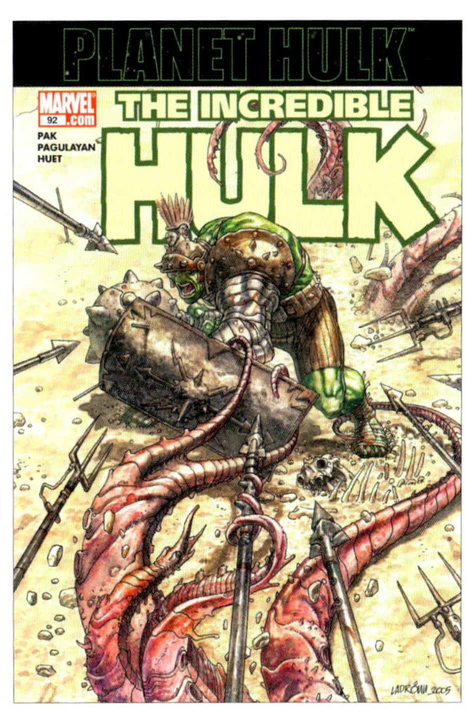

CIVIL WAR

Following the success of Ultimate Comics, Mark Millar went to work on the Super Heroes of the Marvel classic Earth-616. It was an event that influenced all the plots and the many characters to come. In the 2006 *Civil War* limited series, illustrated by Steve McNiven, Captain America and Iron Man went their separate ways over the issue of the government's new law that Super Heroes had to be officially registered. Under the law, Super Heroes had to reveal their secret identities to the government. The question readers and characters alike were asked: "Whose Side Are You On?" Captain America's and the freedom of choice, or Iron Man's and the security option? Heroes split into two factions. Stories focused on characters' choices and the consequences. The Avengers would never be the same... for a few years, at least.

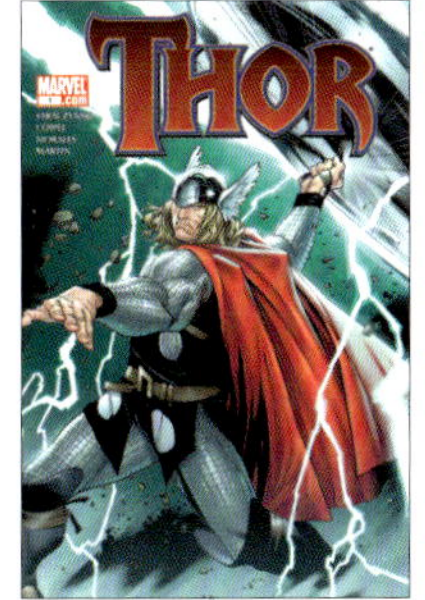

SEPTEMBER 2007
Absent since 'Avengers Disassembled', following the cyclical Asgard apocalypse, Ragnarok, Thor returns in a new series by J. M. Straczynski and Olivier Coipel.

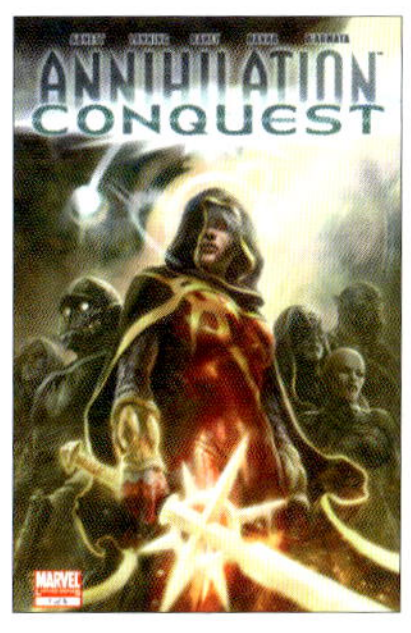

JANUARY 2008
The crossover storyline *Annihilation: Conquest* is the sequel to the big hit Annihilation, upending Marvel's 'cosmic' universe and spelling trouble for the Guardians of the Galaxy.

NEW AVENGERS, NEW HEROES

A team of incredible creators comes together to introduce a new take on a classic team as new heroes come into the fold.

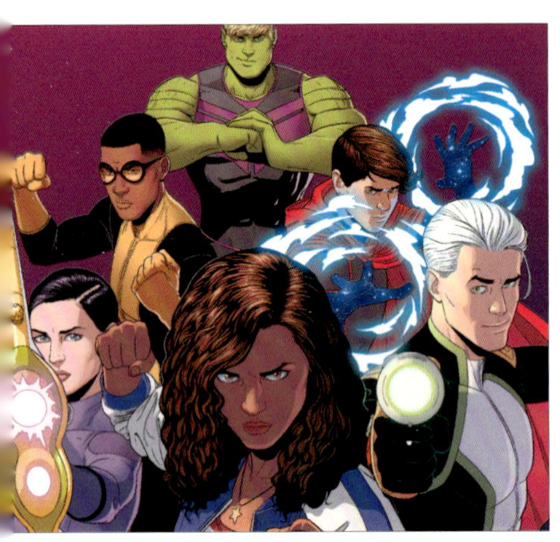

Detail from the cover to *Young Avengers #13* (dated February 2014, released 4 December 2013). Art by Jamie McKelvie.

After the success of *Ultimate Spider-Man*, Bendis was put to work on one of Marvel's flagship series, *The Avengers*. But the question was, if Spider-Man and Wolverine were the most popular characters, why not put them on the team? Bendis's first approach with Earth's Mightiest Heroes saw the destruction of the classic formation in the saga 'Avengers: Disassembled'. Some characters died; others, like Scarlet Witch and She-Hulk, went crazy. Their headquarters was destroyed.

A few months later, in *The New Avengers*, a new team was born, featuring old members like Cap and Iron Man, as well as Spidey, Logan, Luke Cage, and Spider-Woman. The 2000s also saw the emergence of two new groups of young heroes. In *Runaways*,

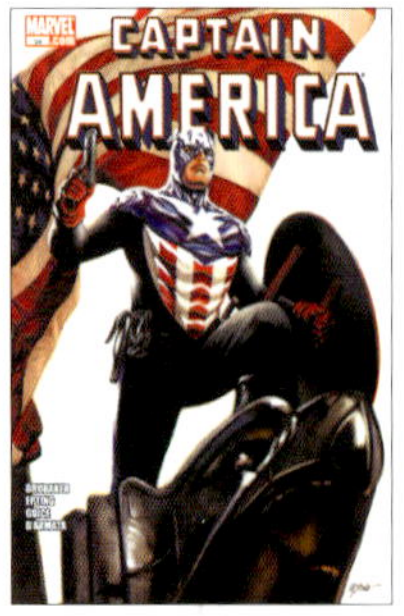

MARCH 2008
Bucky Barnes inherits Captain America's shield in *Captain America #34*, by Ed Brubaker and Steve Epting.

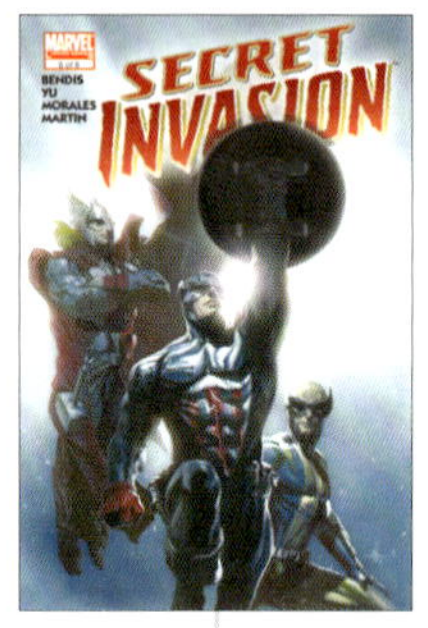

JANUARY 2009
The crossover *Secret Invasion* comes to an end with the discovery that shape-shifting Skrull aliens infiltrate the Super Hero community.

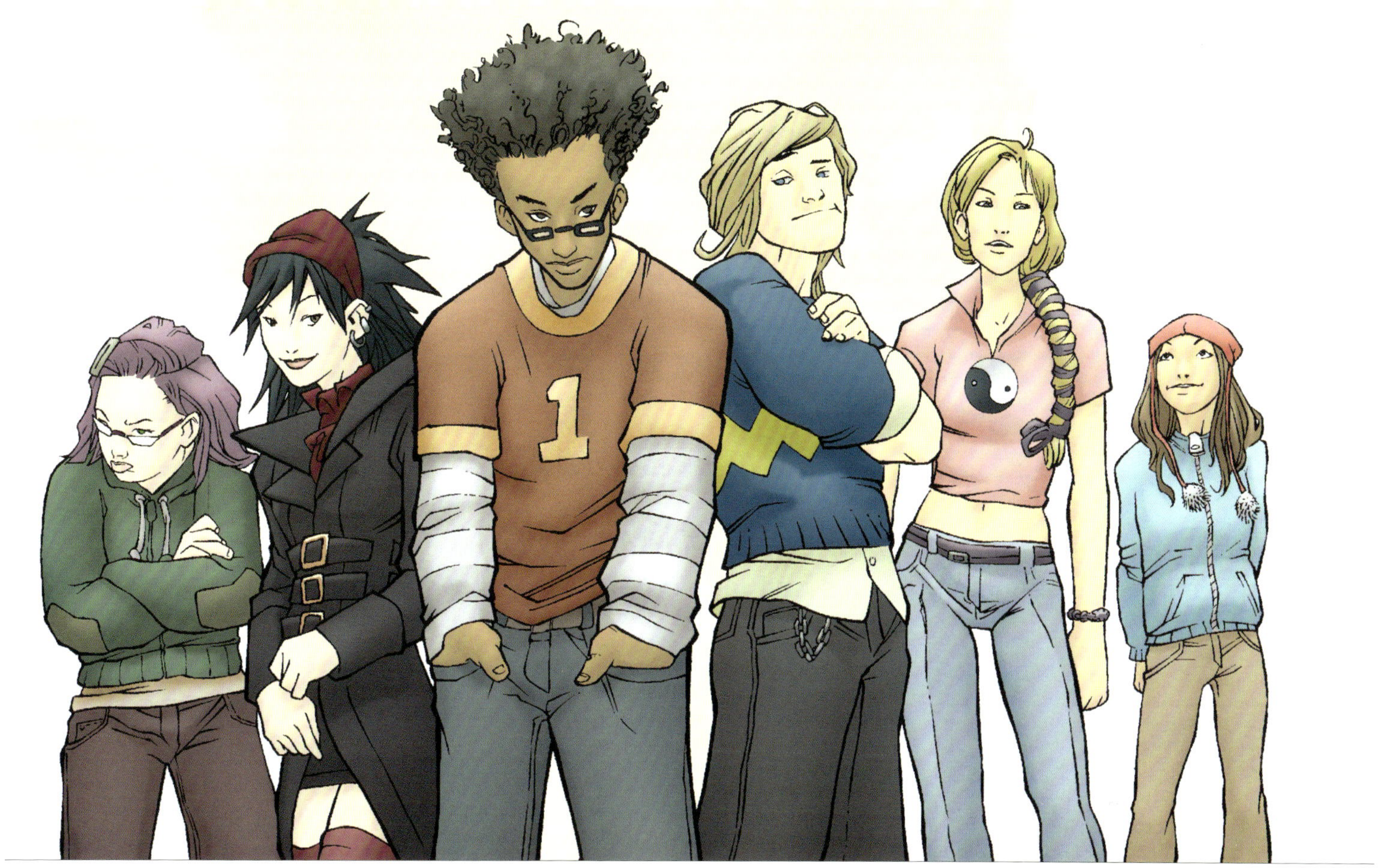

Brian K. Vaughan and Adrian Alphona presented a team of teenagers who rebelled against their parents, who turned out to be Super Villains and mob leaders in Los Angeles. Taking advantage of money from merchandising and their inherited powers, they became true runaways and Super Heroes. Allan Heinberg, who scripted the TV series *The O.C.*, wrote *Young Avengers*, a spin-off dedicated to the young 'heirs' of Iron Man and company. Both soon became cult hits. Remarkably innovative was the project behind Sentry: Marvel Knights hyped him as a character Stan Lee had created in the 1960s who had at last seen the light of day. As for continuity, he was considered outside the realm of collective memory in order to protect his dual nature—heroic Sentry and evil Void.

Cover detail for the *Runaways Volume 1* hardcover edition (August 2005). Art by Adrian Alphona.

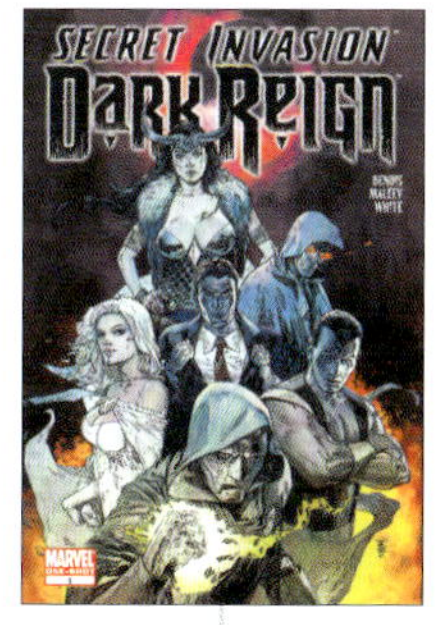

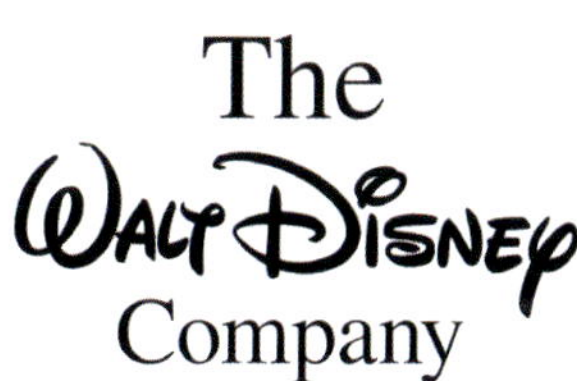

2010

FEBRUARY 2009
Dark Reign is released.
As a result of what happened in *Secret Invasion*, Norman Osborn is charged by the U.S. government to lead the Super Heroes.

AUGUST 2009
The Walt Disney Company acquires Marvel. It's the start of a new era.

THE AGE OF THE WRITERS

An amazingly talented team of writers assembles, making their mark on the mighty heroes and villains of Marvel.

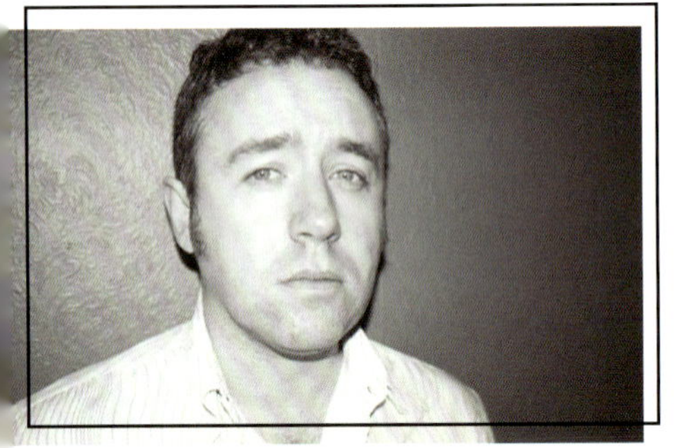

Comics writer Mark Millar.

The 2000s ushered in an era that saw a focus on writers, which was curious at a time when the editor in chief was Quesada, an illustrator. This was thanks to the success of Brian Michael Bendis and Mark Millar.

Ultimate Spider-Man and *The New Avengers* had made Bendis a star. He came back with a long *Daredevil* run, adding new heights in quality, also thanks to illustrations by Alex Maleev, and *Alias*, which opened the R-rated MAX imprint, which also published the new *Punisher* series. *Alias* narrated the adventures of Jessica Jones, a former Super Hero turned alcoholic private investigator.

Mark Millar went on to limited series that Marvel fans couldn't get enough of. Besides *Civil War*, he also wrote the storyline 'Old Man Logan', which featured an elderly Wolverine in a dystopia where villains had beaten almost all the Super Heroes, and *1985*, set in 'our' world, starring a young comic-book reader who meets up with his favourite characters.

His contributions to historical series include an unforgettable *Fantastic Four* cycle illustrated by Bryan Hitch. Less prolific, but fundamental, was the award-winning Neil Gaiman, who wrote two high-quality limited series, *1602* and *Eternals*.

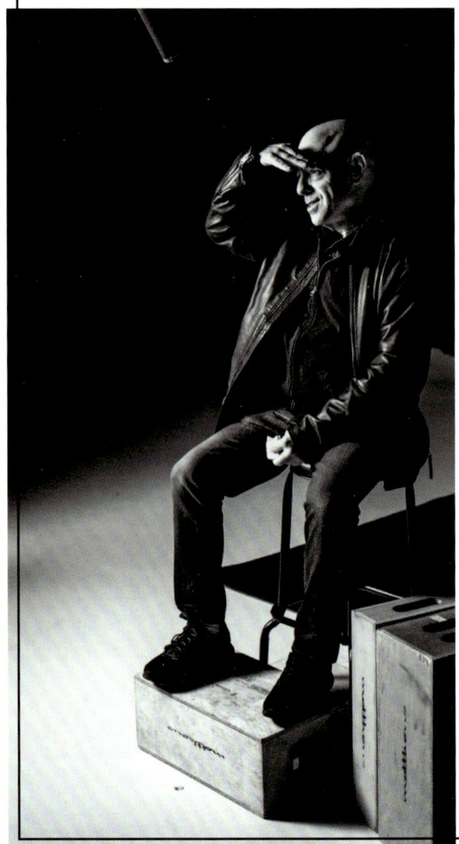

RIGHT
Writer Brian Michael Bendis.

OPPOSITE PAGE
Cover from *Fantastic Four #560* (November 2008). Art by Bryan Hitch.

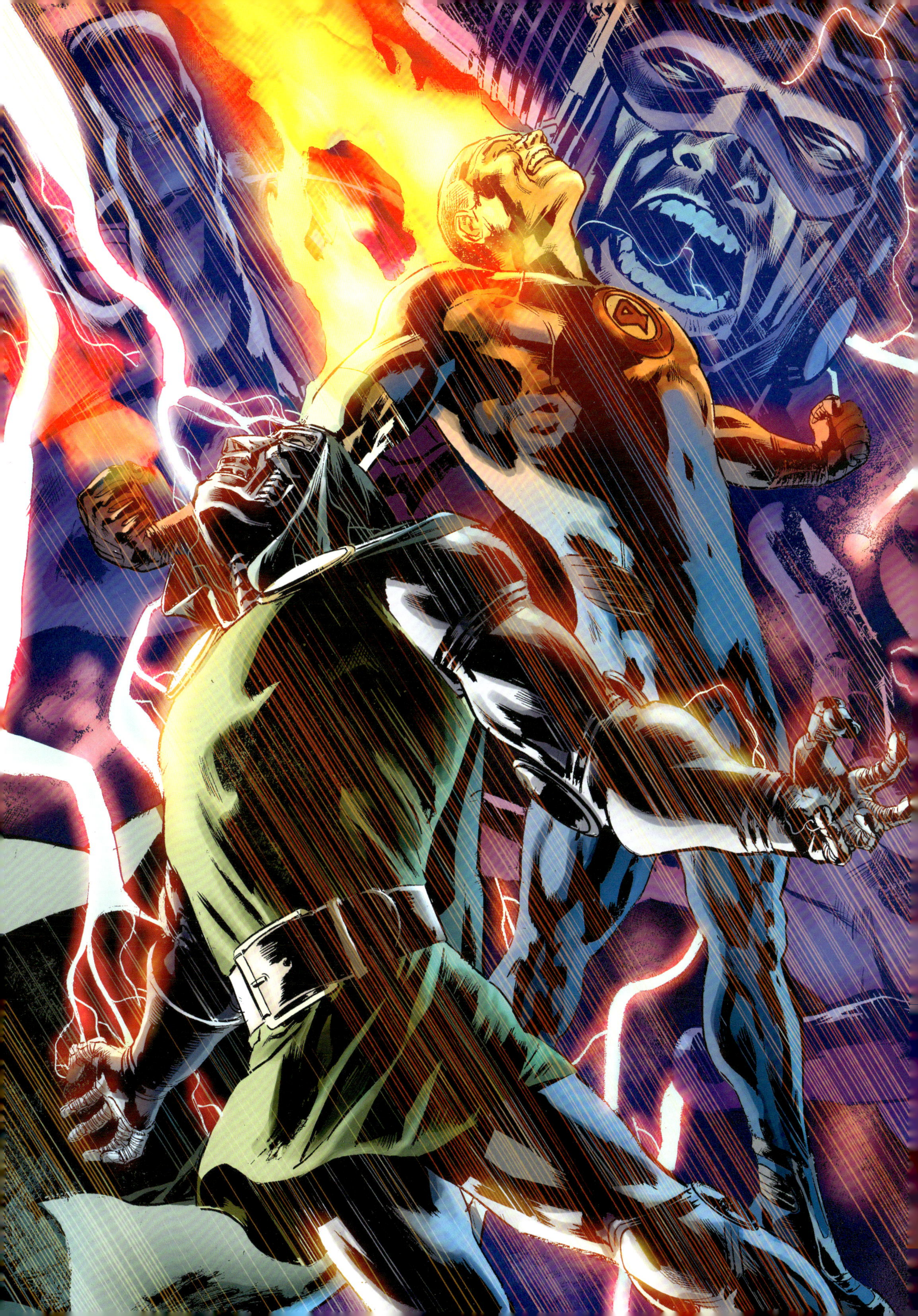

INTO THE FUTURE

Marvel's influence extends beyond comics and into the world of popular culture, growing its audience.

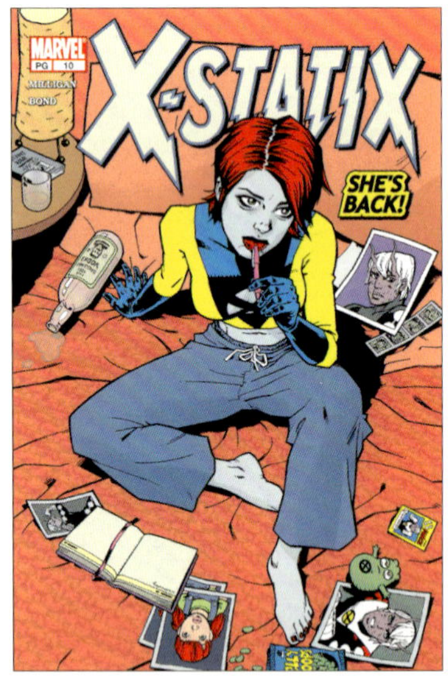

X-Statix #10 (June 2003). Art by Philip Bond.

Marvel readers had grown up. People who read comics in the 1970s and '80s were now adults hankering for more mature stories. Readers young and old found what they were looking for in *Alias*, *Daredevil*, and *X-Statix* by Peter Milligan and Mike Allred (featuring Super Heroes that were depraved, unscrupulous celebrities), and in Garth Ennis's *The Punisher*.

It was time for Marvel to leave the Comics Code Authority behind. Self-censorship hampered creators while hardly affecting sales. Marvel adopted its own rating system. By the end of the 2000s Marvel had legions of new readers and garnered media attention thanks to the Super Heroes' success at the movies. Marvel had become a force to be reckoned with in pop culture.

Characters were quoted and T-shirts sold, as new attention, even by the mainstream media, was lavished on the world of comics like never before. The seeds Stan Lee had planted in the 1960s had sprouted, and Marvel's cross-cultural influence continued to grow.

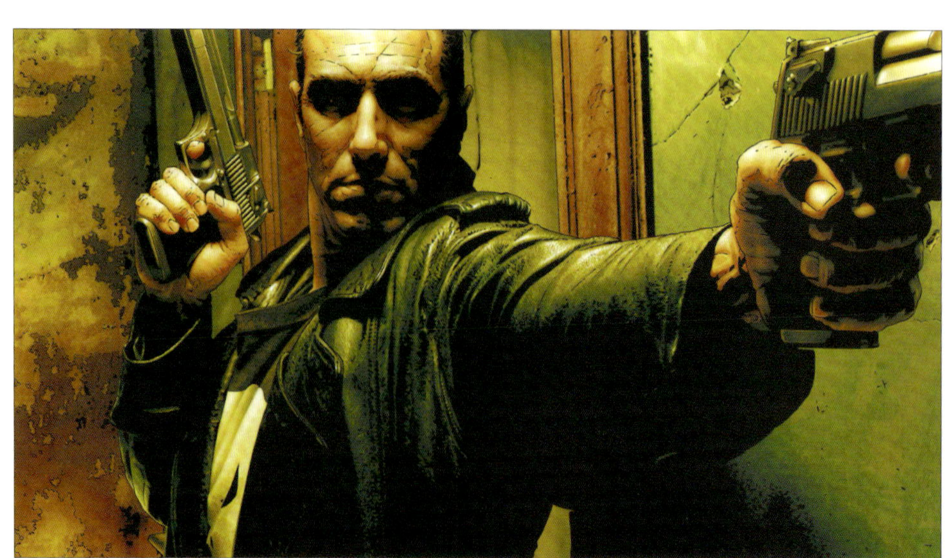

RIGHT
Cover detail from *The Punisher MAX Volume 2: Kitchen Irish* (December 2005). Art by Tim Bradstreet (pencils).

OPPOSITE PAGE
Stan Lee Meets the Amazing Spider-Man #1 (November 2006). Art by Olivier Coipel.

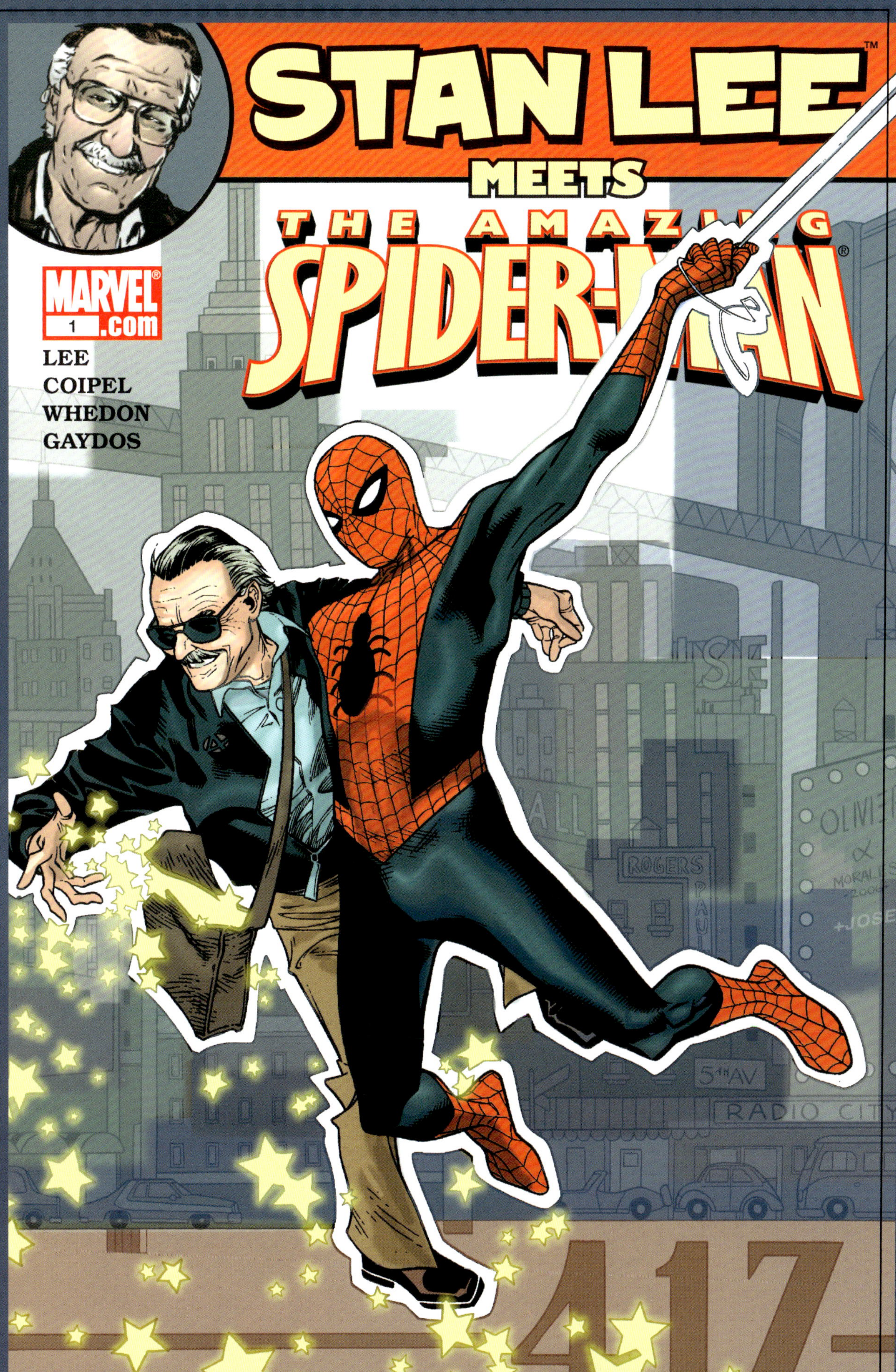
STAN LEE
MEETS
THE AMAZING
SPIDER-MAN
MARVEL
1
.com
LEE
COIPEL
WHEDON
GAYDOS
ROGERS
5TH AV
RADIO CITY
417

The 2010s

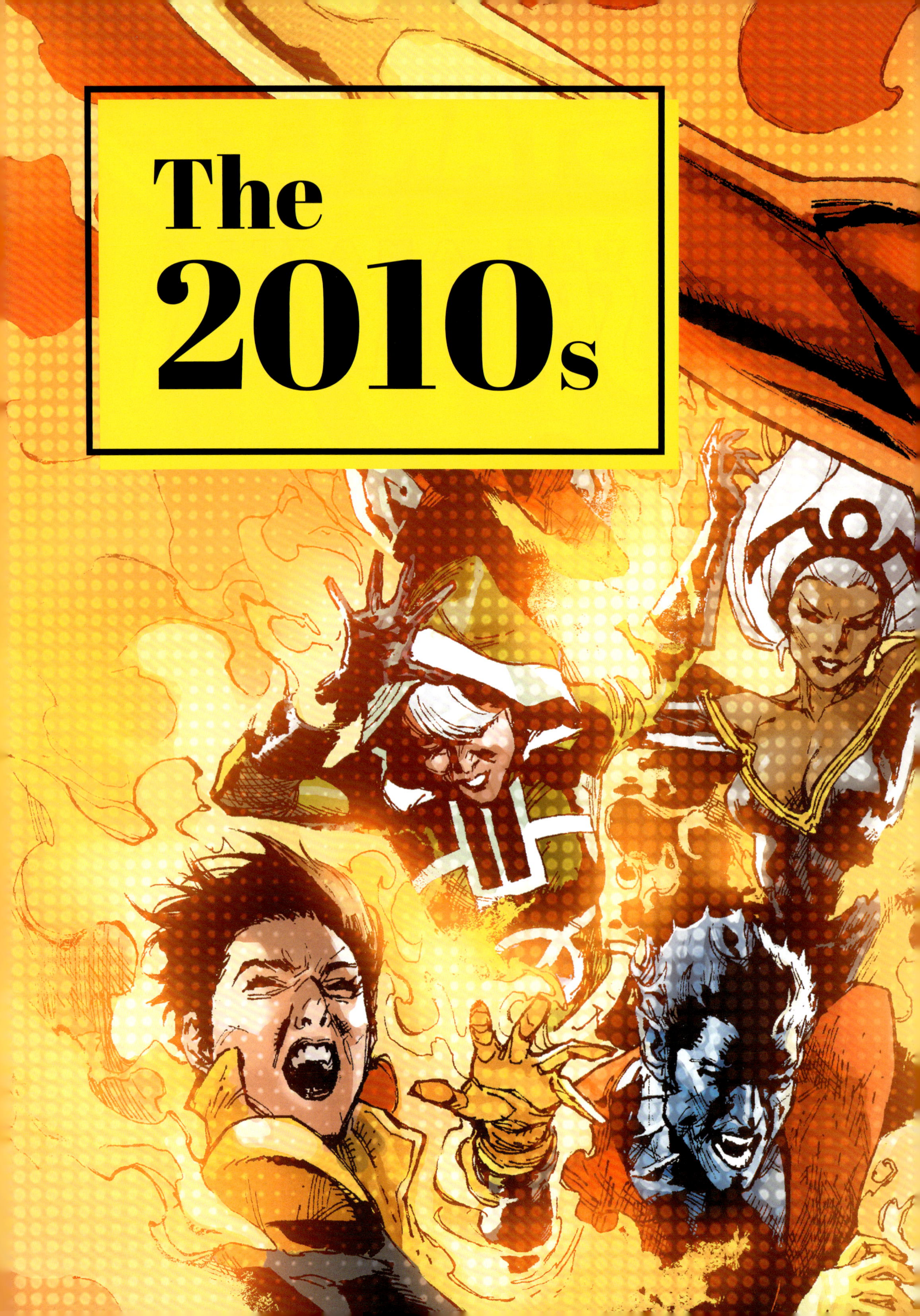

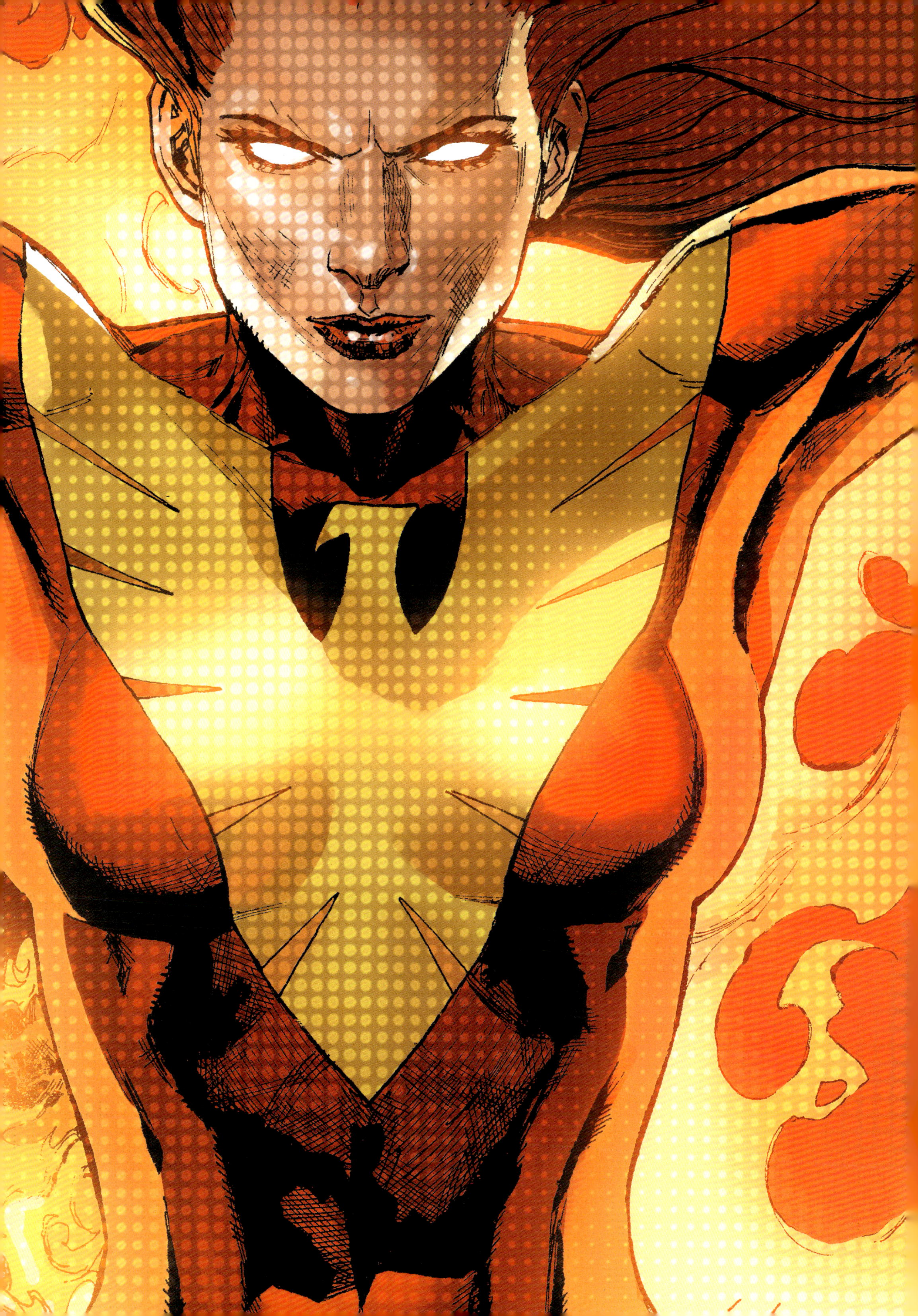

NEW HORIZONS

As the 21st century continued, Marvel adapted even more to the changing demands of both the audience and the culture.

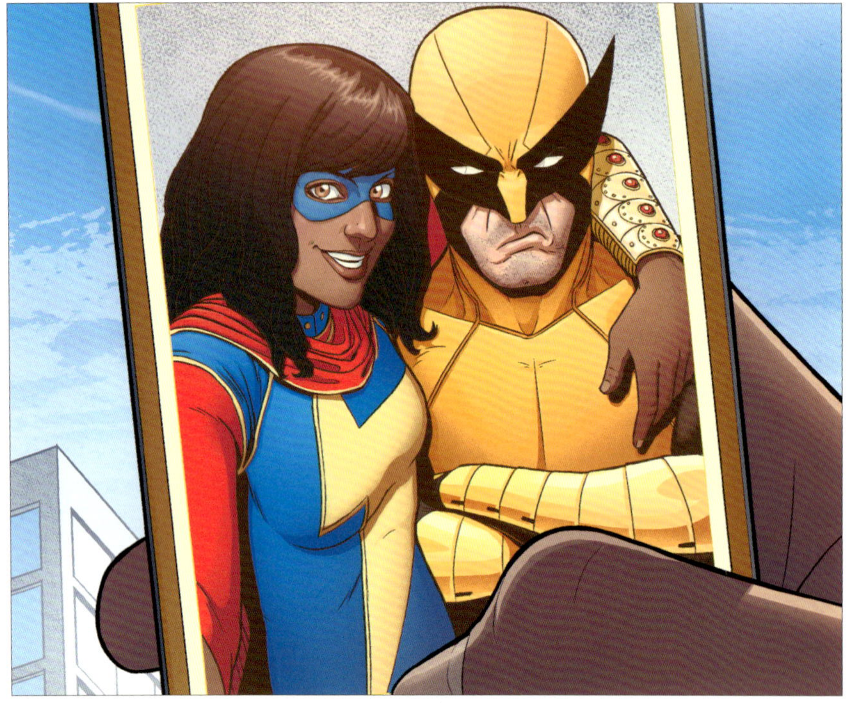

Ms. Marvel and Wolverine pose for a selfie on the cover of *Ms. Marvel* #7 (October 2014). Art by Jamie McKelvie and Matt Wilson.

It was finally happening—what for decades so many artists and writers had worked so hard for. Marvel characters had become part of the world's common heritage, household names, icons of the collective consciousness.

Meanwhile, Marvel wasn't resting on its laurels. Readership was growing, and they were constantly enticing new readers to the fold. The Ultimate line was by now 10 years old and had its own baggage of continuity, while the Super Heroes from Earth-616, the classic Marvel Universe, maintained a strong following. The 2010s thus saw a number of relaunches, with series starting from issue #1, that provided new beginnings as writers carefully crafted their stories so that they would also be accessible to new readers.

These relaunches were usually limited to individual series or to 'families', but in 2012 Marvel took a chance on something much bigger with the *Marvel NOW!* initiative: a new starting point for all the series. It was not a reboot, since continuity would not be altered or disavowed. Simply put, all the series would start fresh from issue #1, with creative teams shifting from book to book. For instance, Brian Michael Bendis, who for years had worked on the Avengers, became the new creator behind the X-Men, while Jason Aaron, the versatile and highly talented writer from

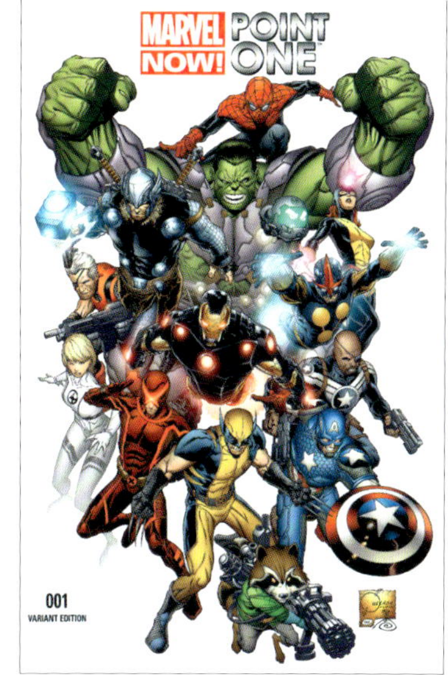

Alabama, moved from Wolverine to Thor. And if this were not enough, new characters would appear as protagonists in the Marvel Universe: a new Ms. Marvel, the young Kamala Khan, a Pakistani-American; a new line-up for the Guardians of the Galaxy; the Korean-American Cindy Moon as Silk, who teamed up with Spider-Man; and others. The audience had grown more diverse, and Marvel along with it.

The world was changing; readers' ethnicity and the places they called home became increasingly diversified. What's more, women were beginning to take a more active interest in comic books, and comic-book creators could not ignore all the progress made in expanding the legal rights and visibility of the LGBTQ+ community. More and more, Marvel Super Heroes would reflect readers' backgrounds and lifestyles, and the world in which they lived.

Formats were also changing. Over the years, new distribution channels came to the fore, and increasingly readers waited for the conclusion of a story arc to read it in its entirety. Like other publishers, Marvel responded with an increasing number of collections in digital, trade paperback, or hardcover form, which

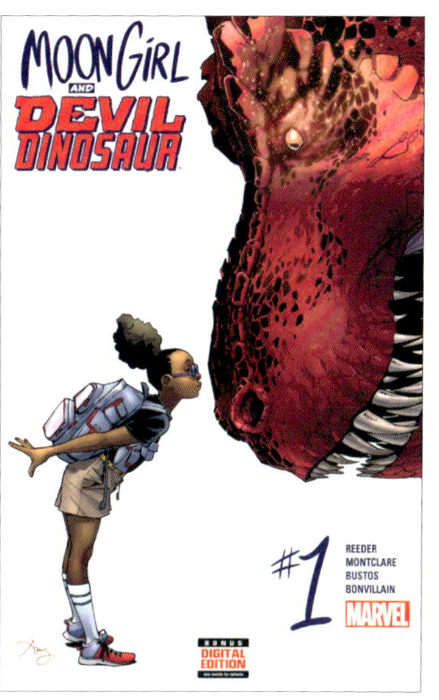

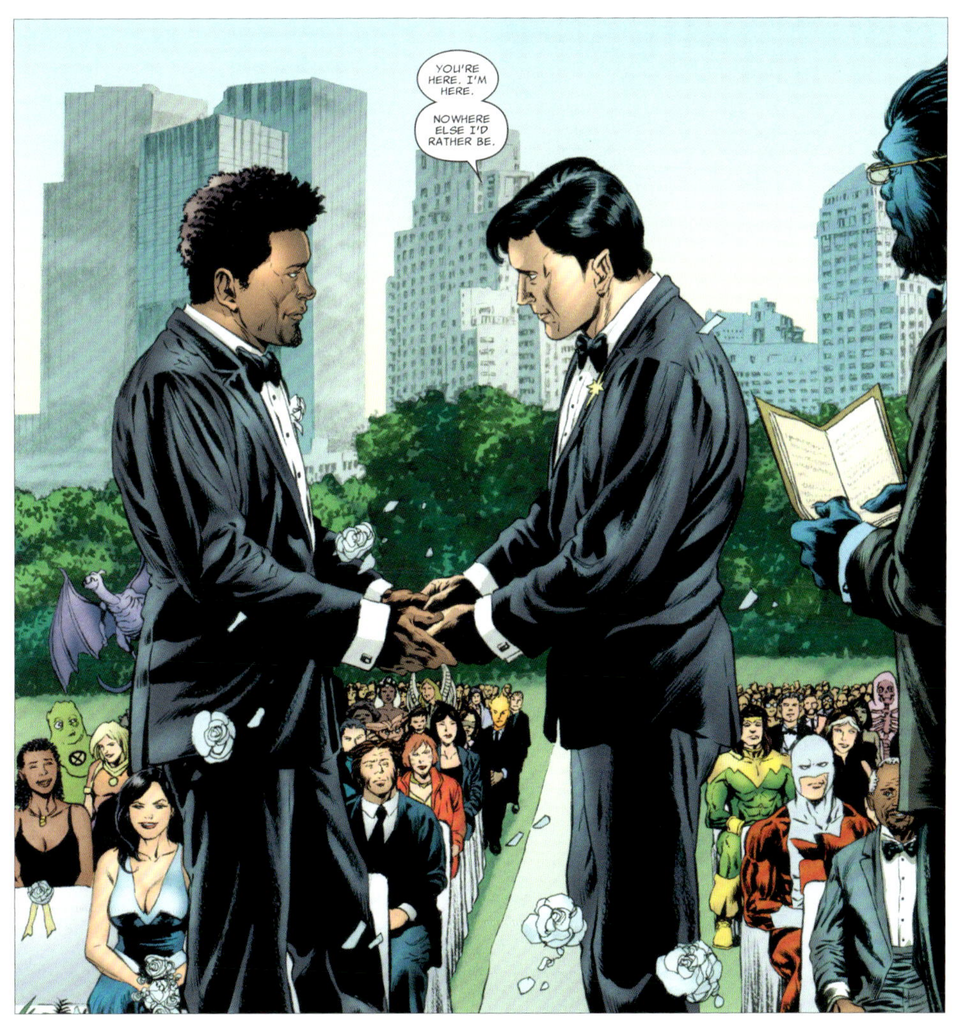

TOP
Promotional image for *Marvel NOW!* by Joe Quesada, 2012.

ABOVE
Moon Girl and Devil Dinosaur #1 (dated January 2016, released 25 November 2015). Art by Amy Reeder.

LEFT
The wedding of Northstar and Kyle Jinadu—the first gay wedding seen in Marvel comics. *Astonishing X-Men #51* (dated August 2012, released 20 June 2012). Art by Mike Perkins (pencils, inks), Andrew Hennessy (inks), Andy Troy, Jim Charalampidis, Rachelle Rosenberg (colours), Joe Caramagna, Cory Petit, Clayton Cowles (letters).

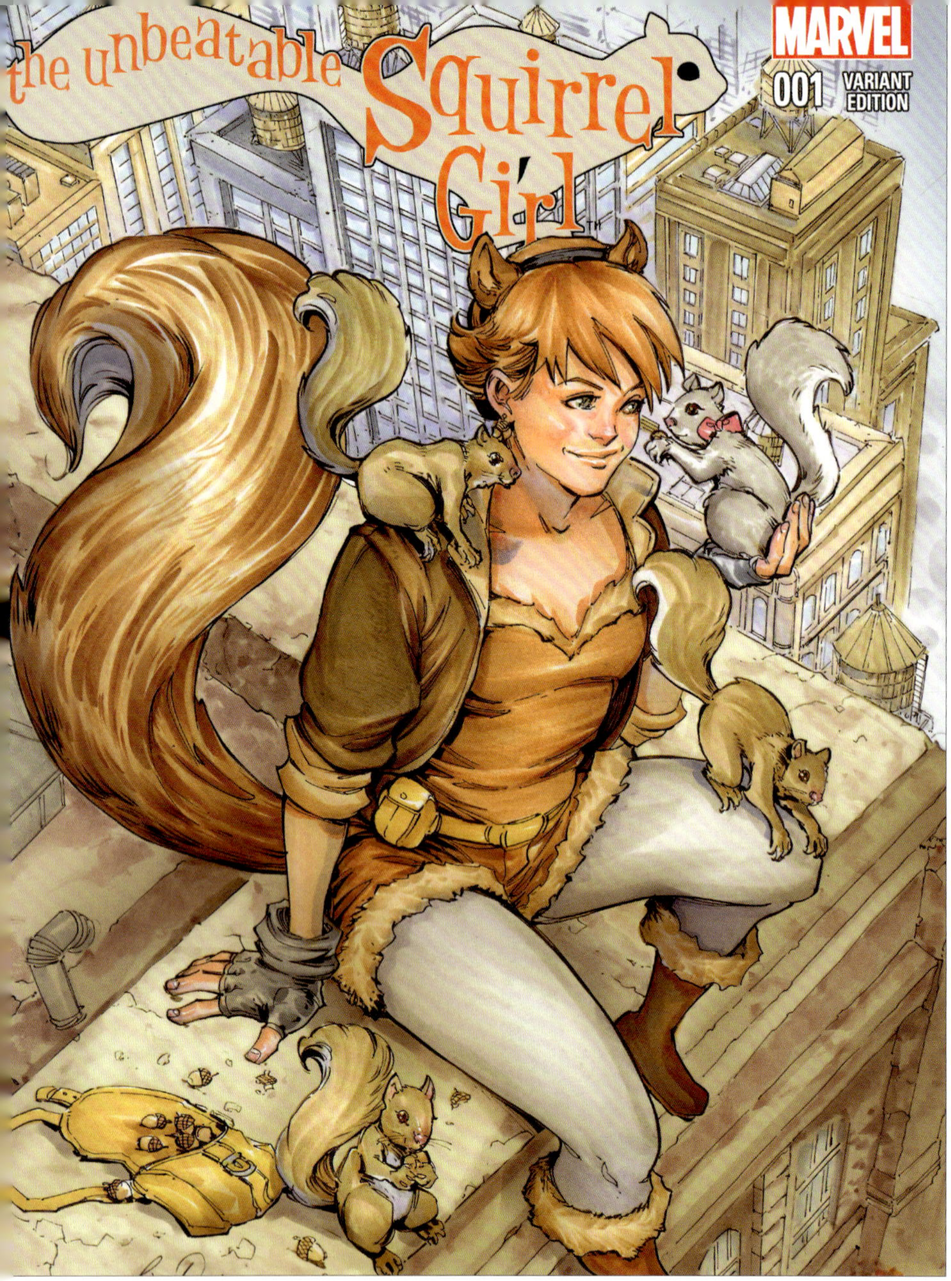

met the needs of both occasional readers and collectors interested in volumes that contained complete story arcs.

As a result, writers often sought out complete cycles within any given series which might easily appear in a single volume. This gave rise to an approach that eventually spelled success for characters that otherwise would have been considered minor. Instead of being relegated to supporting roles in comic books alone, they became stars in their own right, and included characters like Moon Girl and Devil Dinosaur, Squirrel Girl, and, of course, Ms. Marvel.

Toward the end of the decade, new readers and new writers would join in the celebration of Marvel's 80th anniversary.

OPPOSITE PAGE
FF #1 (dated May 2011, released March 23, 2011). Art by Steve Epting.

The Unbeatable Squirrel Girl #1 variant cover (March 2015). Art by Siya Oum.

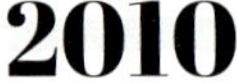

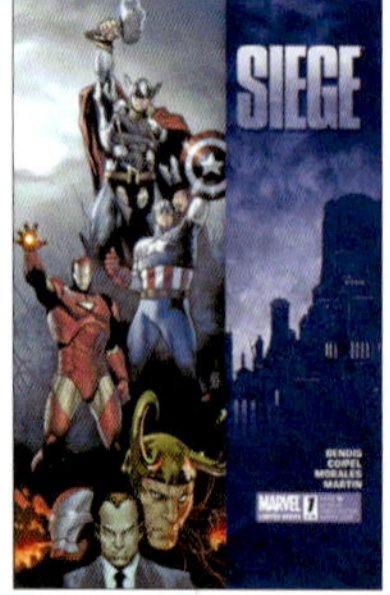

JANUARY 2010
With the event series *Siege*, Norman Osborn attempts to conquer Asgard, and the end to the 'Dark Reign' era is nearly in sight.

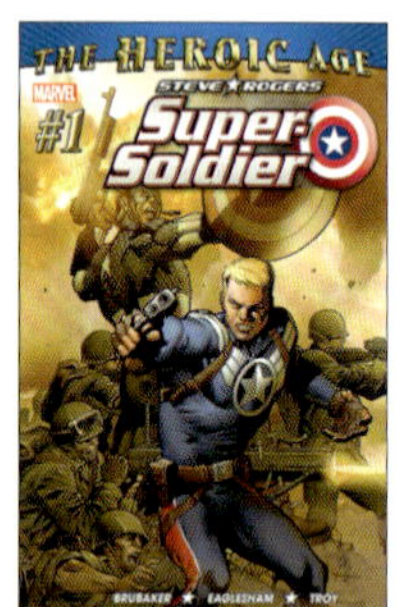

JULY 2010
Steve Rogers becomes the new head of S.H.I.E.L.D. and assumes the identity of Super Soldier.

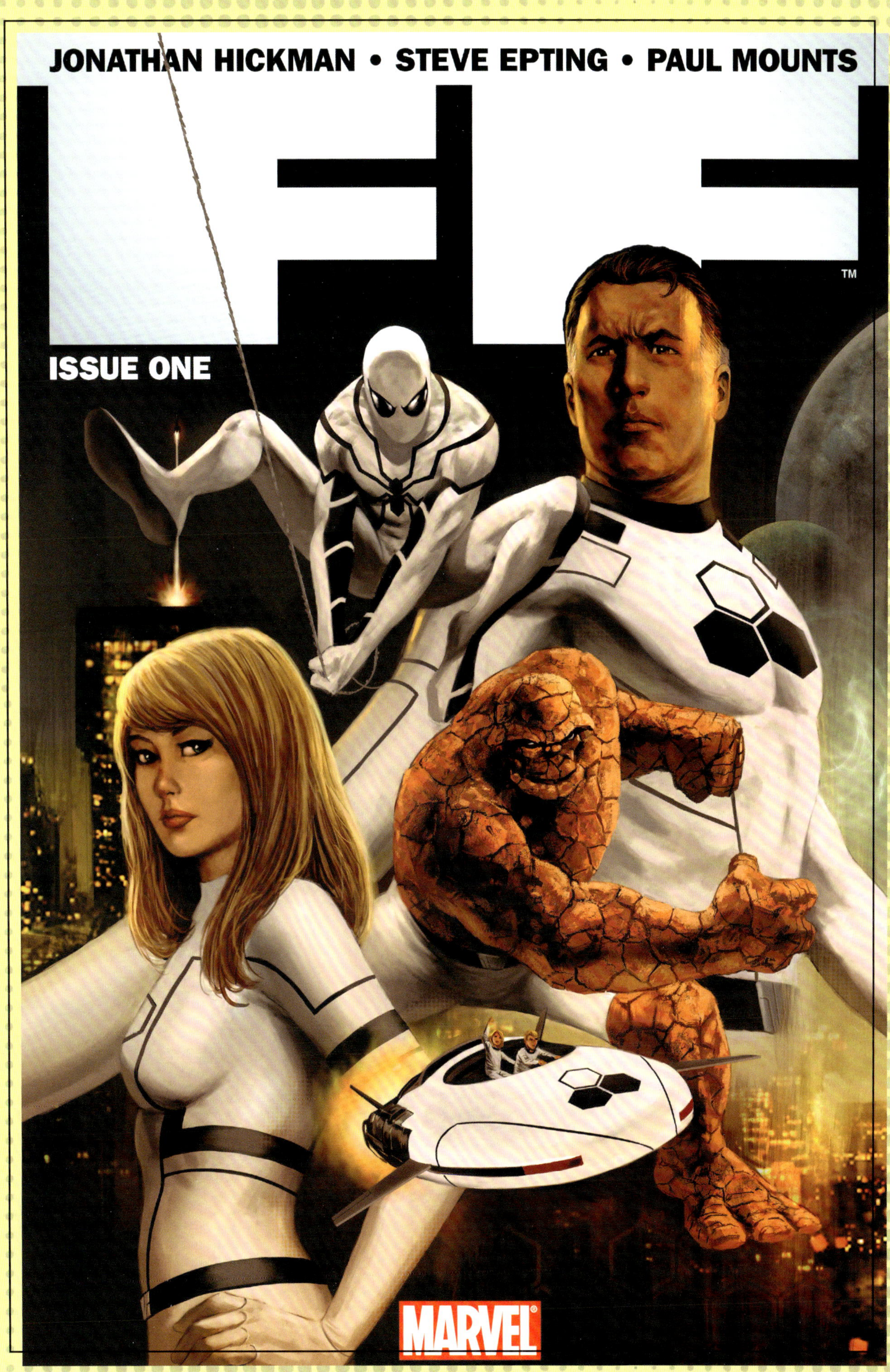
JONATHAN HICKMAN • STEVE EPTING • PAUL MOUNTS
FF
TM
ISSUE ONE
MARVEL

A NEW AGE FOR NEW READERS

2010 began with a bang, as Marvel reunited the trinity of Super Heroes—Captain America, Iron Man, and Thor—and blazed new trails.

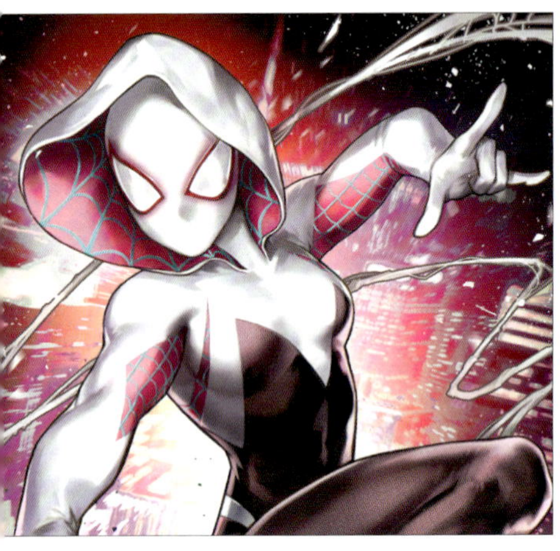

Following the gloom of *Secret Invasion* and *Dark Reign*, crossover events that had an impact on all the series put out at the end of the 2000s, the times were once again ripe for Super Heroes to be portrayed as positive examples of law and order. Marvel kicked off the 2010s with the limited series *Siege*, which laid the foundations for the relaunch of the Avengers family and marked the end of the bleak scenarios commandeered by Norman Osborn.

The core Avengers trinity made their return, now cast in roles that hadn't been seen since the pre–Civil War days: Thor, Iron Man and Captain America would once again be fighting side by side. Tensions within the Super Hero community didn't abate altogether, however, and exploded in a new

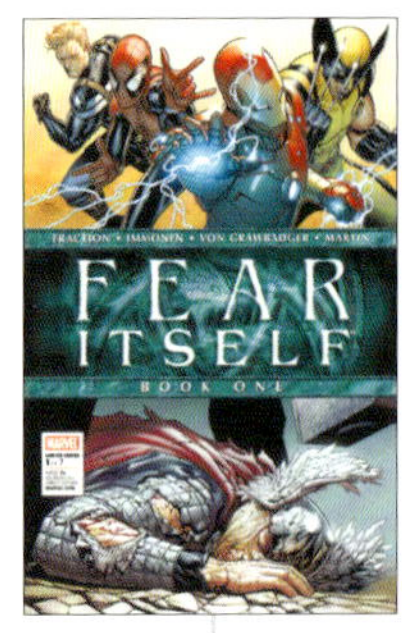

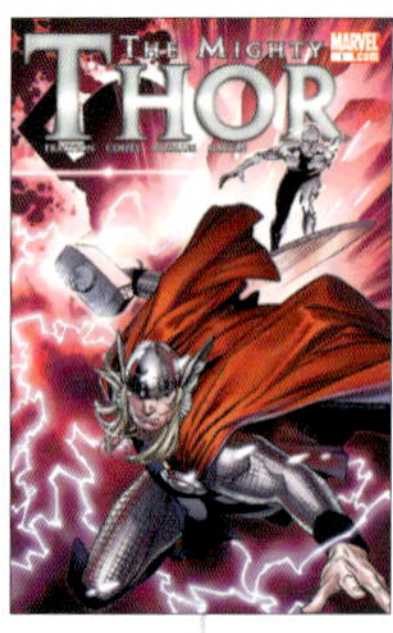

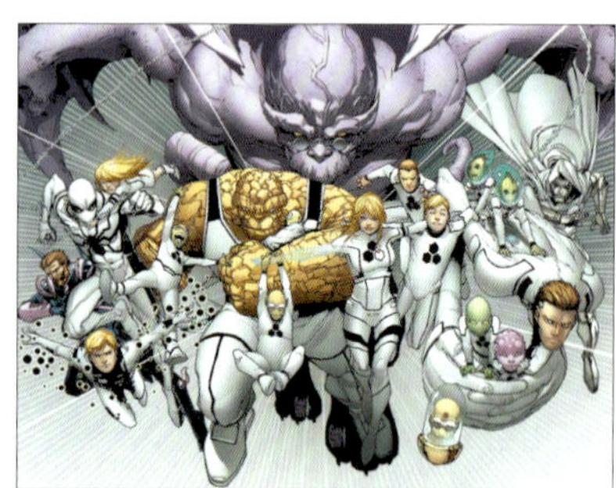

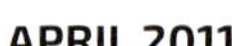

APRIL 2011
The *Fear Itself* crossover recounts the end of the *Dark Reign* and the return of Iron Man, Thor, and Captain America, leading the way for the Avengers.

JUNE 2011
Matt Fraction and Olivier Coipel relaunch the new *Mighty Thor* series with issue #1. His first adversary is Galactus!

JUNE 2011
In Jonathan Hickman and Steve Epting's *FF #1*, with the Human Torch gone, Spider-Man joins the team. The Future Foundation is born.

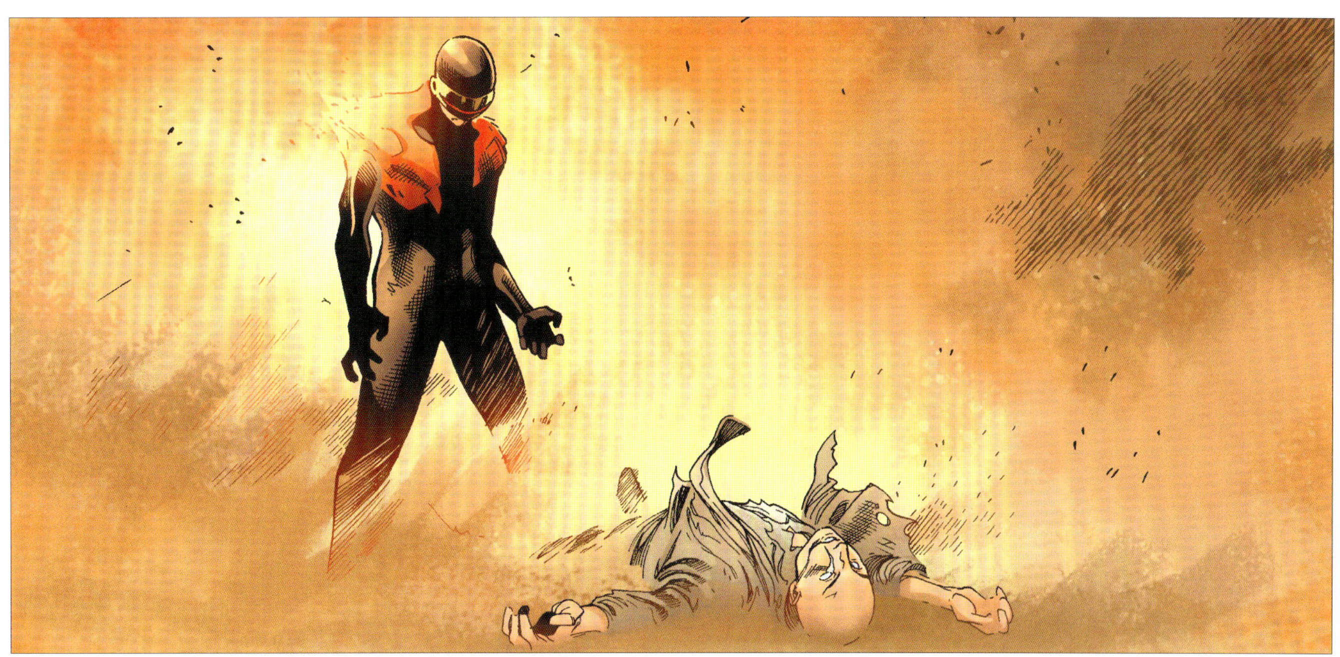

maxi-crossover, *Avengers vs. X-Men*. The two factions clashed over control of the Phoenix Force, heading straight for Earth in the form of a flaming bird.

The devastating war that broke out between the two sides was recounted in a 12-issue series written and illustrated by the hottest names at that time. At the end of the saga, the longtime leader of the X-Men, Cyclops, was corrupted by the power of Dark Phoenix, as had happened many years earlier to his partner Jean Grey.

The mutant family was subject to various acts of vengeance at the hands of this evil Cyclops (he even murdered his mentor, Charles Xavier), although the Avengers wound up with an apparent victory. This event marked the end of a long run of stories that had begun with *Civil War* and proved to be the perfect opportunity for a relaunch, known as *Marvel NOW!* Banners like *All-New Marvel NOW!*, *Ultimate Marvel NOW!* and *Marvel NOW! 2.0* heralded the relaunch of the entire Marvel line and paved the

ABOVE
Cyclops stands over the body of the slain Professor X. *Avengers vs. X-Men #11* (dated November 2012, released 12 September 2012). Art by Olivier Coipel (pencils), Mark Morales (inks), Laura Martin (colours).

OPPOSITE PAGE
Cover detail from *Spider-Gwen: Ghost Spider #1* variant (December 2018). Art by Sujin Jo.

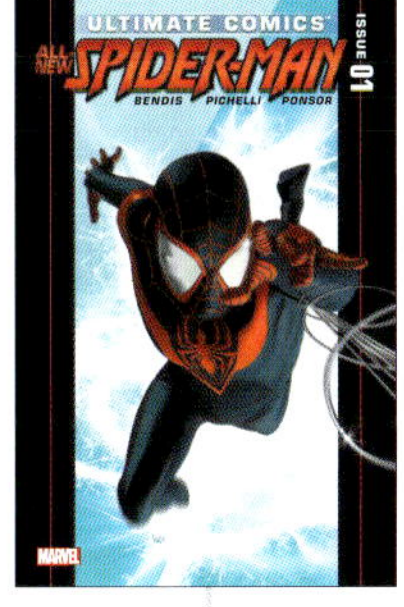

AUGUST 2011
Peter Parker meets up with Miles Morales for the first time in *Ultimate Comics Spider-Man*, by Brian Michael Bendis and Sara Pichelli.

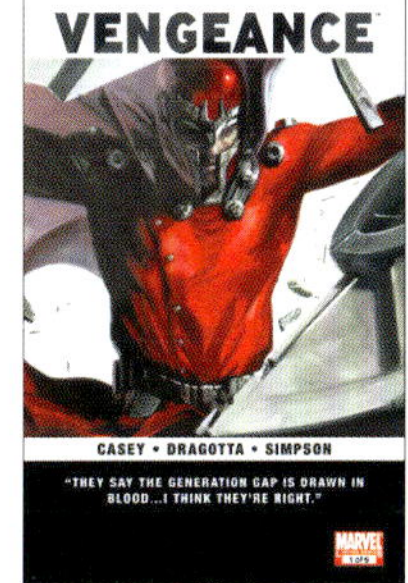

SEPTEMBER 2011
America Chavez, from another dimension, makes her debut in *Vengeance #1*. Soon she would become one of Marvel's top LGBTQ+ icons.

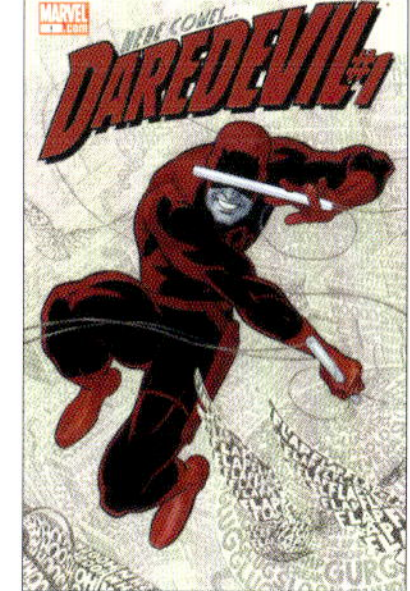

SEPTEMBER 2011
Writer Mark Waid begins his long award-winning run on *Daredevil*, which concludes in 2015. Illustrators: Paolo Rivera, Marcos Martin, and the big gun Chris Samnee.

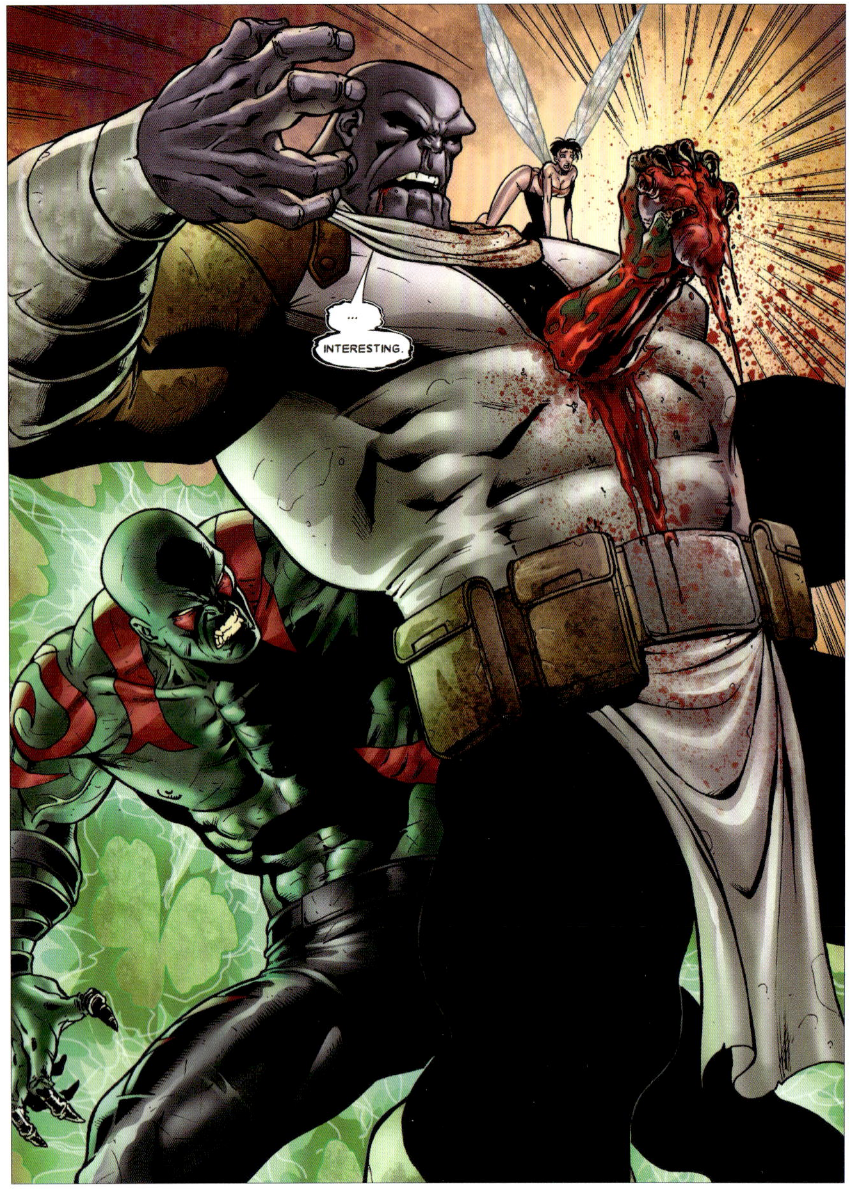

way for all-new series. They included *Guardians of the Galaxy*, which gave readers a taste of what was to come in the 2014 film, featuring characters like Star-Lord, Drax the Destroyer, Rocket Raccoon, and Gamora, in a series written by Bendis and illustrated by Steve McNiven, who did the artwork for *Civil War*.

Each year of the 2010s would see the release of a new crossover event, based on the model of *Secret Wars* from the 1980s. Each event was a chance to reshuffle the cards and serve up starting points for readers new to the comic-book experience, or enjoyed manoeuvring them on PlayStation, Xbox, or their mobile devices. The most important of all these events, beating out even *Avengers vs. X-Men*, was entitled *Secret Wars*, a tribute to the old saga by Jim Shooter and Mike Zeck.

2016 saw the shutdown of all the ongoing series, symbolising the end of the Multiverse, under attack by powerful aliens. They were replaced by various limited series, whose titles echoed the great sagas of the past, such as *Inferno*, *Civil War*,

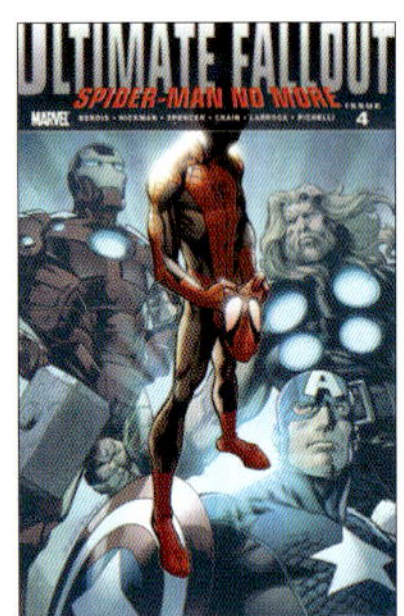

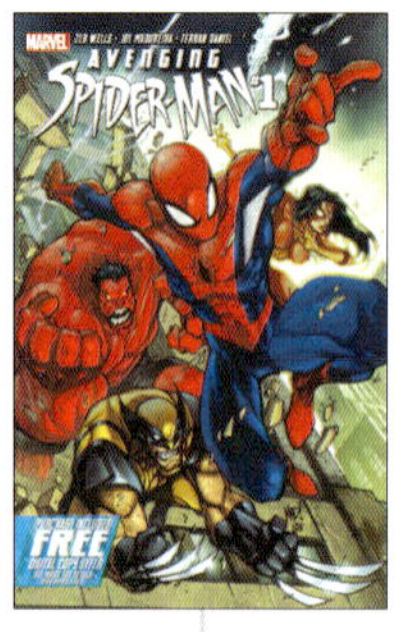

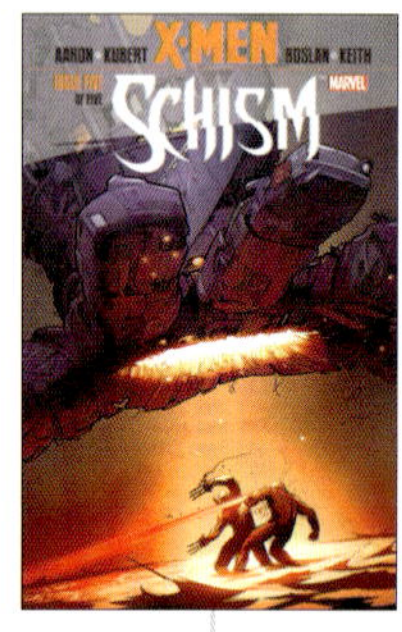

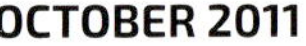

OCTOBER 2011
Miles Morales debuts as the new Spider-Man in *Ultimate Fallout #4*.

NOVEMBER 2011
The *Avenging Spider-Man* series marks the return of artist Joe Madureira, whose work in the 1990s became legendary.

DECEMBER 2011
In the finale of the limited series *X-Men: Schism*, written by Jason Aaron and illustrated by an all-star list of artists, the mutants split into two factions led by Wolverine and Cyclops.

Planet Hulk, and so on. The stories gave readers glimpses of alternative worlds, and ran parallel to the main limited series, *Secret Wars*, written by Jonathan Hickman and illustrated by Esad Ribic. There, Doctor Doom assumes divine powers and re-creates the world in his image after the destruction of the Multiverse.

Once again, an alliance among Super Heroes was necessary in order to bring about his defeat and return the world to normalcy... or nearly so. After 15 years of honourable service, the Ultimate Universe was destroyed, although there were some survivors. Like Miles Morales, who had been the Ultimate Spider-Man in that universe. *Secret Wars* was perhaps the most important of Marvel's new starting points, especially considering the massive amounts of planning that went into the series. The Fantastic Four were left to recreate the Multiverse, keeping them out of action in the main Marvel Universe until 2018.

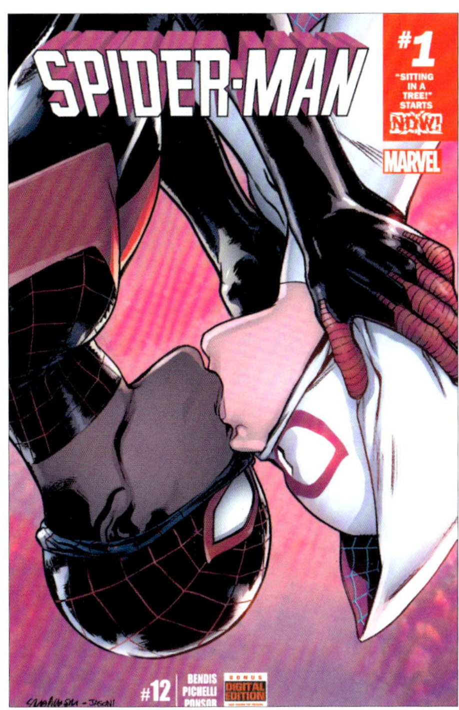

ABOVE
Spider-Man Volume 2 #12 (January 2017). Art by Sara Pichelli and Jason Keith.

OPPOSITE PAGE
Drax destroys Thanos in *Annihilation #4* (January 2007). Script by Keith Giffen. Art by Andrea Di Vito (pencils and inks), Laura Villari (colours), Cory Petit (letters).

MILES & GWEN

As the Ultimate Universe grew, writers and illustrators realised that they could take things well beyond what went on in the classic Marvel Universe. Shocking turns of events soon took place, like the killing of Peter Parker. Taking his place in the role of Spider-Man would be young Miles Morales, the son of an African-American father and a Puerto Rican mother. He got his spider powers much the same way that Peter had gotten them. Conceived by Bendis and illustrator Sara Pichelli in 2011, Miles soon showed himself to be a valid replacement. Following the second incarnation of *Secret Wars* and the destruction of the Ultimate Universe, he turned up alongside the adult Spider-Man in Earth-616. Today Miles is one of the world's best-loved Super Heroes. As is Spider-Woman from Earth-65, better known as Spider-Gwen. In that world it was Gwen Stacy, who received the bite of a radioactive spider. She became a Super Hero who made contact with the Spider-Men of the Multiverse in the 2014 saga *Spider-Verse*.

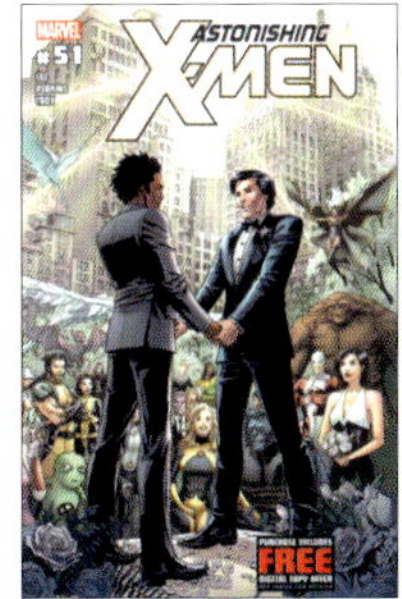

AUGUST 2012
The mutant Northstar marries teammate Kyle in *Astonishing X-Men #51*, written by Marjorie Liu and illustrated by Mike Perkins. It is the first gay marriage in a mainstream comics.

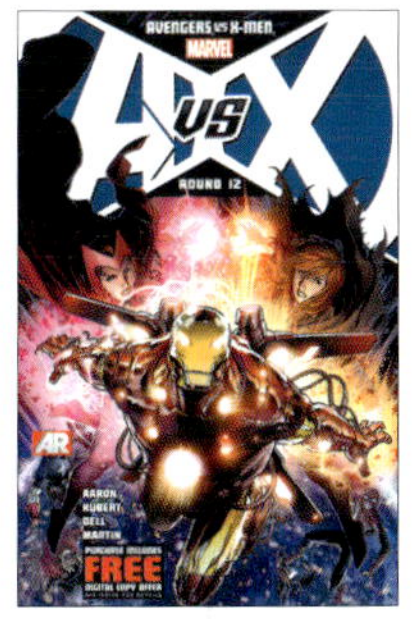

DECEMBER 2012
The crossover event 'Avengers vs. X-Men' comes to an end, paving the way for the *Marvel NOW!* initiative.

ALL-NEW, ALL-DIFFERENT

The classic Marvel heroes were reborn in the 2010s, taking on new forms that spoke to new audiences.

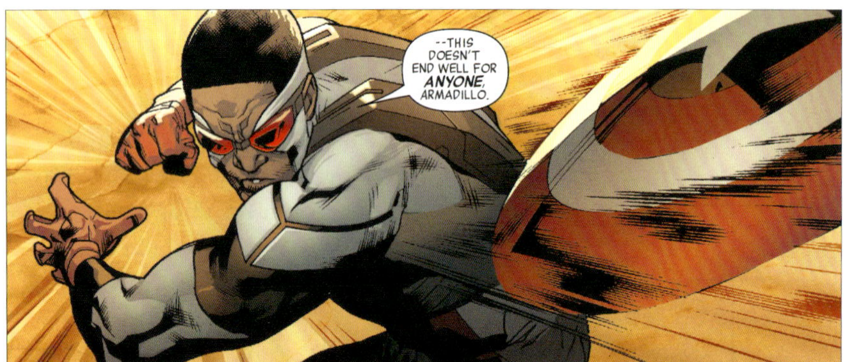

Panel from *All-New Captain America #4* (dated April 2015, released February 18, 2015). Art by Stuart Immonen, Wade Von Grawbadger, Marte Gracia.

Under the leadership of editor in chief Axel Alonso, who followed Joe Quesada after years as a go-to editor, Marvel approached the 2010s hailing diversity. At the same time, Marvel succeeded in consolidating the popularity of its most iconic Super Heroes by making choices that proved to be of watershed magnitude. At a certain point, it almost seemed like the 1980s all over again.

By the mid-2010s, some of the greatest Marvel Super Heroes had once again been replaced. The Hulk was zapped of his strength and apparently dead, until young genius Amadeus Cho assumed his identity, taking the place of Bruce Banner. In a brilliant move by writer Jason Aaron, Jane Foster, Thor's old love interest, took possession of Mjolnir and transformed into Thor after he lost

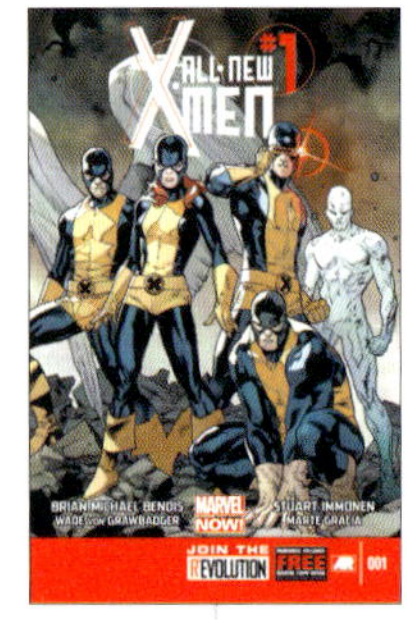

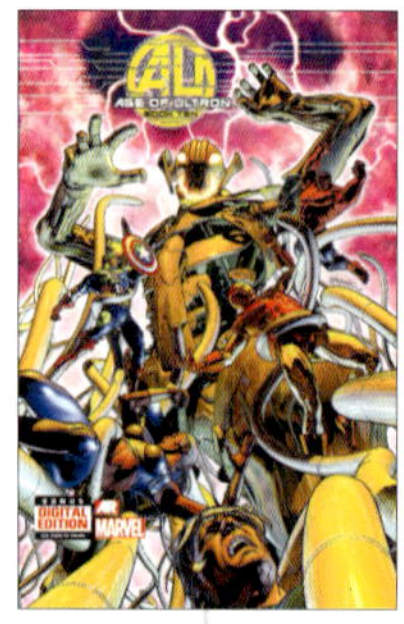

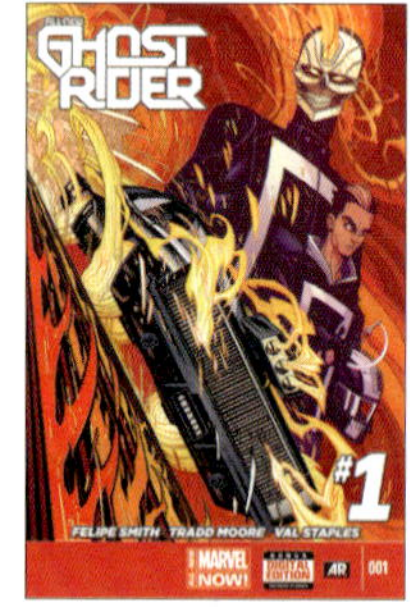

JANUARY 2013
In *All-New X-Men*, by Brian M. Bendis and Stuart Immonen, the five original X-Men travel into the future—the present-day Marvel Universe!

JUNE 2013
The last issue of the *Age of Ultron* event, over the course of which, the evil robot Ultron uses a time travel paradox to take over the world.

MAY 2014
Robbie Reyes becomes the new Ghost Rider. He drives a flaming car instead of a motorcycle.

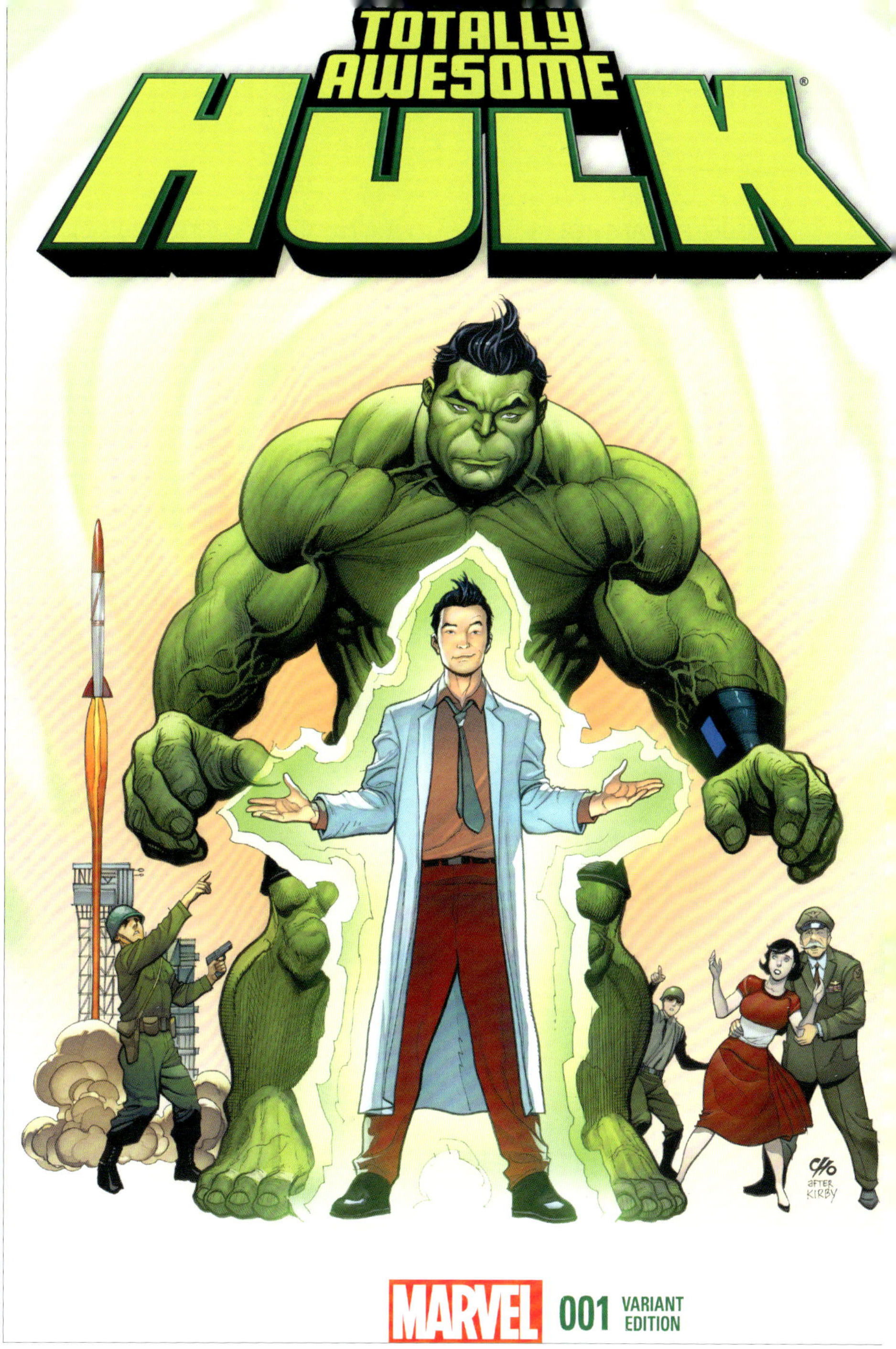

Cover to *The Totally Awesome Hulk #1* variant cover. Art by Frank Cho; Colours by David Curiel.

his ability to use his hammer—a transformation that eased the side effects of Jane's cancer treatment. Steve Rogers lost the benefits of the Super-Soldier Serum and aged suddenly. His place was taken by Sam Wilson, Cap's former sidekick as Falcon, who became a Captain America fighting for civil rights and against racism, putting him on a collision course with the U.S. government.

Steve returned two years later in the *Secret Empire* saga, now a Hydra sleeper agent due to his memories being altered by the sentient Cosmic Cube, Kobik. As for Iron Man, in a cycle written by Bendis, he was replaced by Ironheart, A.K.A. the brilliant young inventor Riri Williams; later, a Doctor Doom in search of redemption would become the third incarnation of Iron Man. Tony Stark, as it turns out, had wound up in a coma after *Civil War II*, the latest clash among Super Heroes,

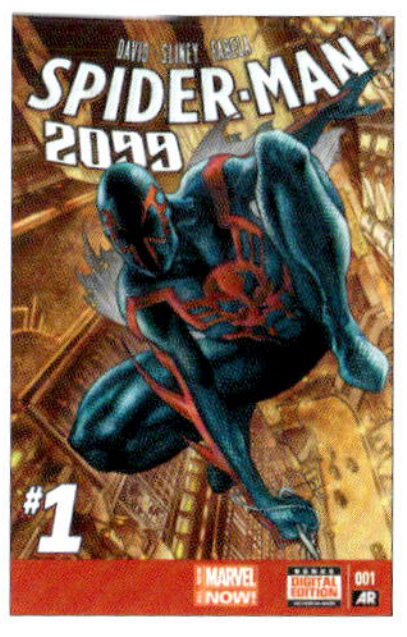

SEPTEMBER 2014
Peter David returns to write *Spider-Man 2099*, featuring the wall-crawler in all-new adventures set in the present.

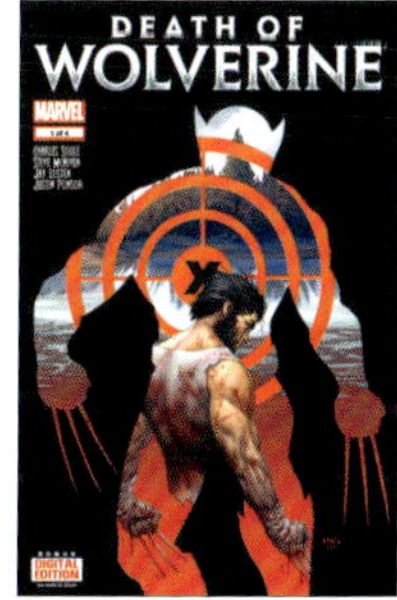

NOVEMBER 2014
Logan loses his final battle in the limited series *Death of Wolverine*. A few months later, X-23 takes his place in *All-New Wolverine*.

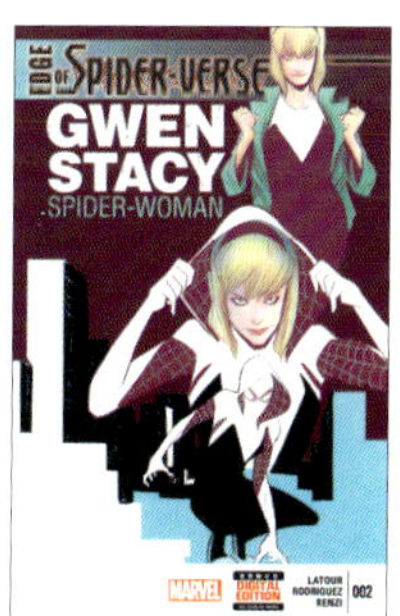

NOVEMBER 2014
Spider-Gwen makes her debut in *Edge of Spider-Verse #2*, the prequel to the *Spider-Verse* crossover event.

RISE OF THE PANTHER

The 2000s had seen the arrival of writers from outside the world of comic books. Following guest appearances by directors and screenwriters for television, in 2016 Marvel opened its doors to author, journalist, and opinion leader Ta-Nehisi Coates. His impressive list of credits includes the memoirs *The Beautiful Struggle: A Father, Two Sons, and An Unlikely Road to Manhood*, and the non-fiction best-seller *Between the World and Me*. Coates was hired by Marvel to relaunch the new *Black Panther* series, illustrated by Brian Stelfreeze. The series' aesthetics had a major impact on the film dedicated to the King of Wakanda. The first issue of the new *Black Panther* sold over 300,000 copies, and the series was a hit with readers and critics alike. Coates' name on the cover catalysed media attention, with reviews and interviews in magazines and on TV. In 2018 he was also tapped to write *Captain America*, and true to form, the series put the spotlight on some of the day's most important issues.

which pitted him against Carol 'Captain Marvel' Danvers. Carol was still in circulation and had earned the right to call herself Captain Marvel, while young Kamala Khan became Ms. Marvel. Kamala had received her powers through terrigenesis, after being caught up in the Terrigen Mists, a mutation causing vapour unleashed by Black Bolt, able to bestow incredible powers on humans who possess traces of Inhuman DNA.

Even if things had pretty much gone back to the old status quo by the end of the decade, the new Super Heroes were here to stay. Many of the younger characters

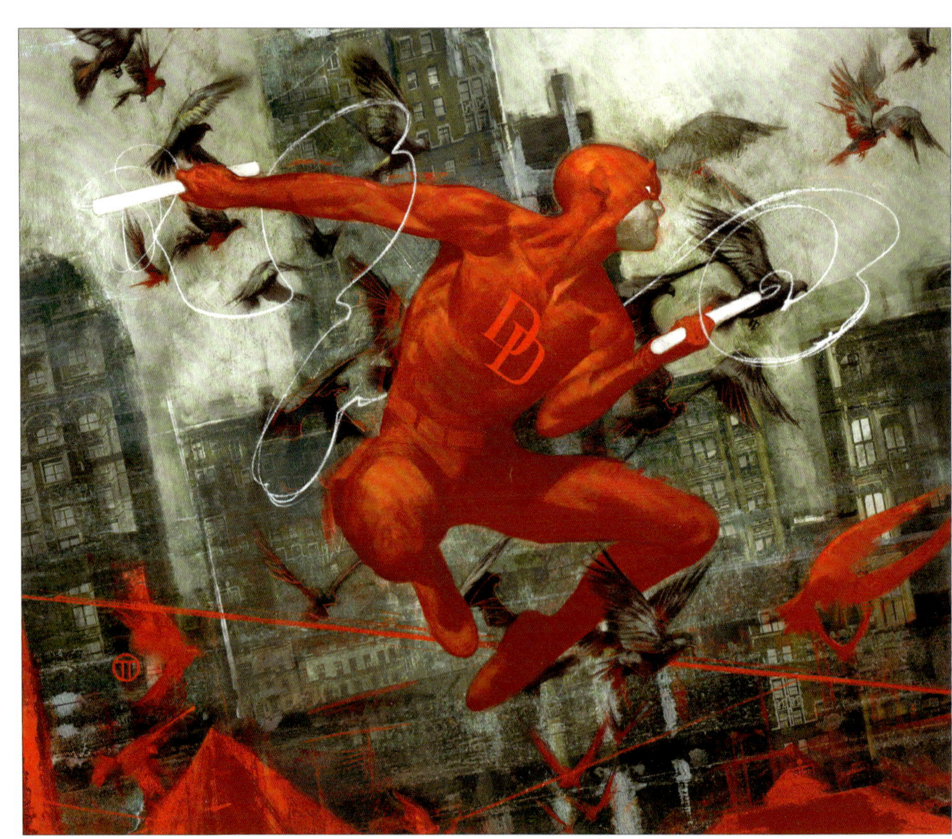

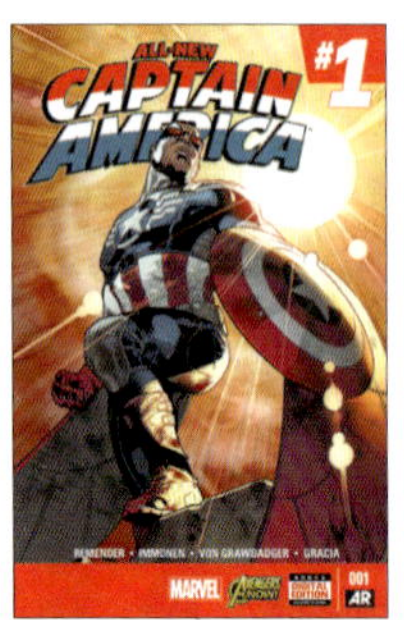

DECEMBER 2014
Steve Rogers, suddenly grown old, taps Sam Wilson, A.K.A. Falcon, as the new Captain America.

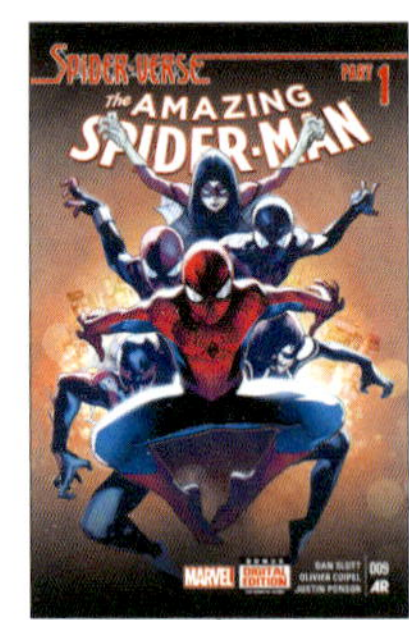

JANUARY 2015
In the *Spider-Verse* event, Peter Parker meets up with Spidey's alter egos from other dimensions.

joined the team known as the Champions, adding a new twist to the old League of Champions from the 1980s.

The spirit of renewal continued with the instalment of a new editor in chief, C. B. Cebulski, in November 2017. Among other credits, Cebulski had lengthy experience as a talent scout, and recruited top young writers and authors from around the world for Marvel. Within a year of signing on as editor in chief, he had relaunched numerous series whose starting points coincided with the arrival of brand new creative personnel.

Relaunches garnered both commercial and critical success, and included *The Immortal Hulk*, a horror-tinged version of the big guy written by Al Ewing and illustrated by Joe Bennett; the return of *Fantastic Four*, written by Dan Slott and illustrated by Sara Pichelli; and the new *Daredevil* series, written by Chip Zdarsky and illustrated by Marco Checchetto.

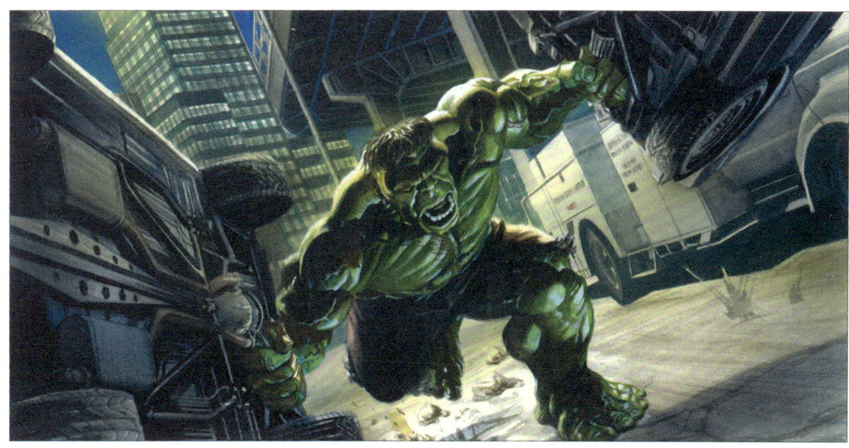

Cover detail from *The Immortal Hulk #4* (dated October 2018, released 1 August 2018). Art by Alex Ross.

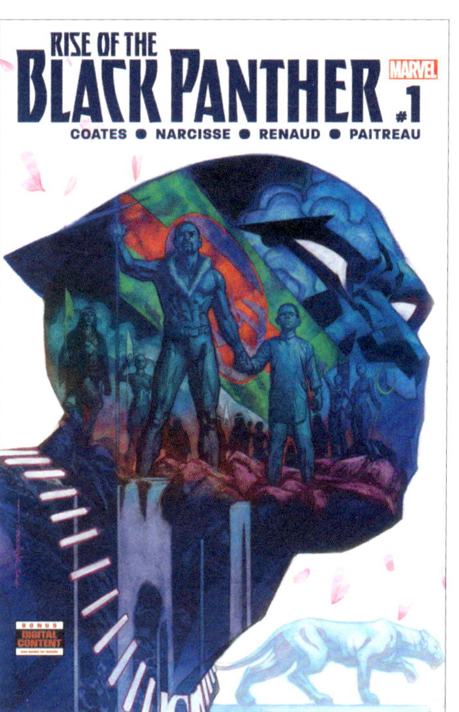

LEFT
Rise of the Black Panther #1 (dated March 2018, released 3 January 2018). Art by Brian Stelfreeze.

OPPOSITE PAGE
Cover detail from *Daredevil Vol. 6, #2* (dated April 2019, released 27 February 2019). Art by Julian Tedesco.

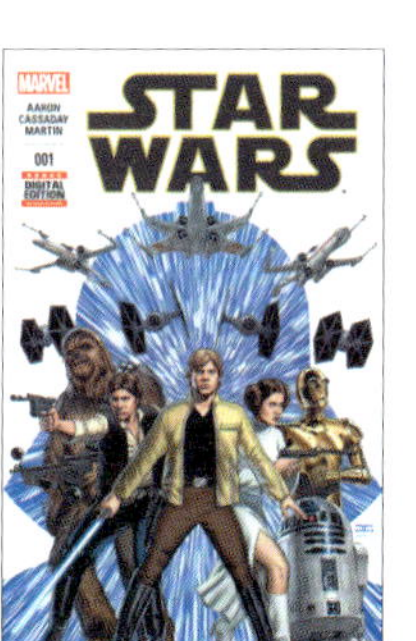

MARCH 2015
The new *Star Wars* series returns to Marvel Comics, and issue #1 sells more than one million copies.

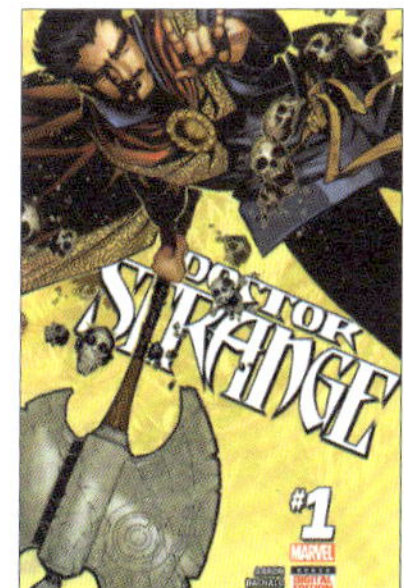

DECEMBER 2015
Jason Aaron and Chris Bachalo create the new *Doctor Strange* series.

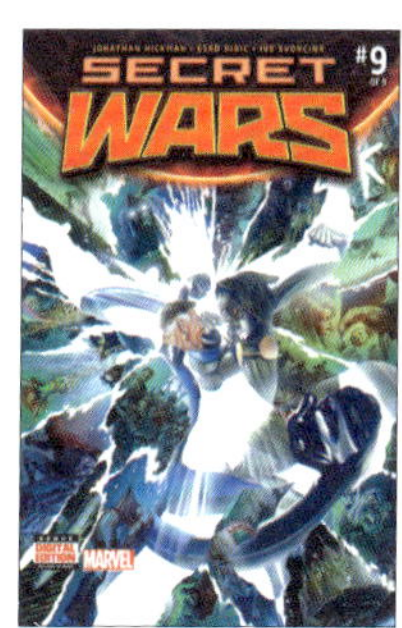

MARCH 2016
The monumental limited series *Secret Wars* brought on the destruction of the Multiverse, including the Marvel and Ultimate Universes.

ARCHITECTS OF THE FUTURE

A new wave of comics creators would rise to prominence in the 2010s, reflecting the diverse audience of Marvel fans.

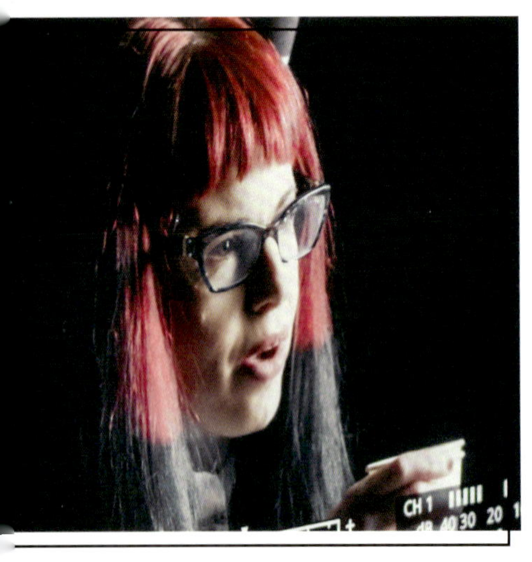

Since the early 2000s, much of readers' attention had been focused on writers. Of course, they were also interested in the artists, but the advent of more complex and detailed artwork meant that any given run might include the work of a team of artists. Writers, on the other hand, tended to stay on for the duration of long story arcs, and thus became stars in their own right, much the way that artists had been idolised by readers in the 1990s.

As far as writers go, Dan Slott is a record holder. From 2010 to 2018, Slott was pretty much the sole writer behind Spidey's adventures, which were studded with electrifying story arcs that kept readers throughout the world on the edges of their seats with non-stop plot twists and cliffhangers—from *Spider-Verse*, featuring alliances among various Spider-Man incarnations in the Multiverse

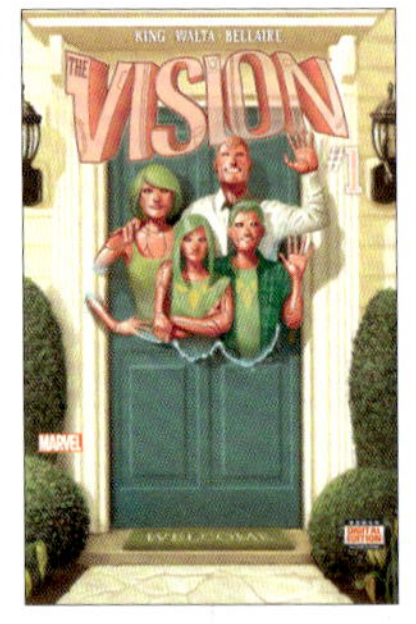

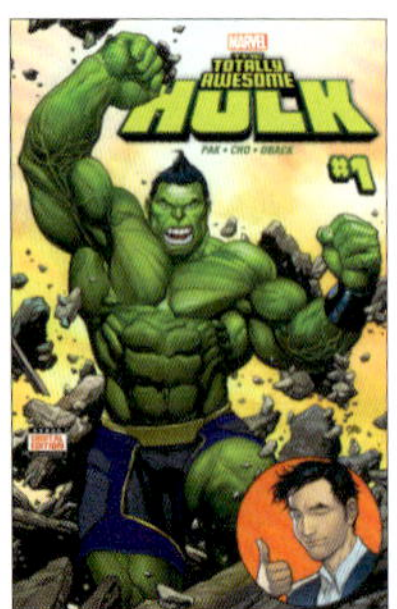

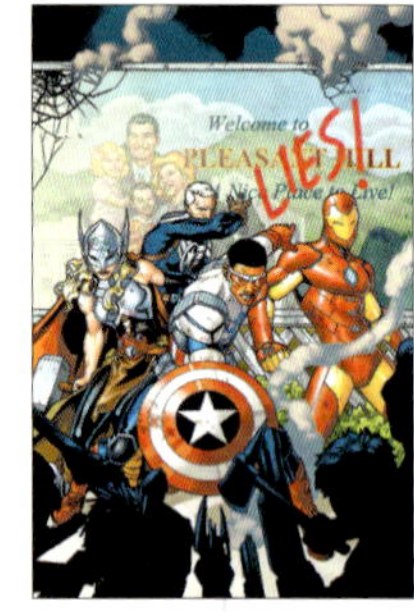

JANUARY 2016
Debut of the maxi-series *Vision*, written by Tom King and illustrated by Gabriel H. Walta. The android Avenger starts a family in a story line that ends in tragedy.

FEBRUARY 2016
In *The Totally Awesome Hulk #1*, written by Greg Pak and illustrated by Frank Cho, Amadeus Cho becomes the new Hulk.

MAY 2016
The *Avengers: Standoff* event gets underway, with unexpected consequences for Steve Rogers and Sam Wilson, who at that time wore the Captain America uniform.

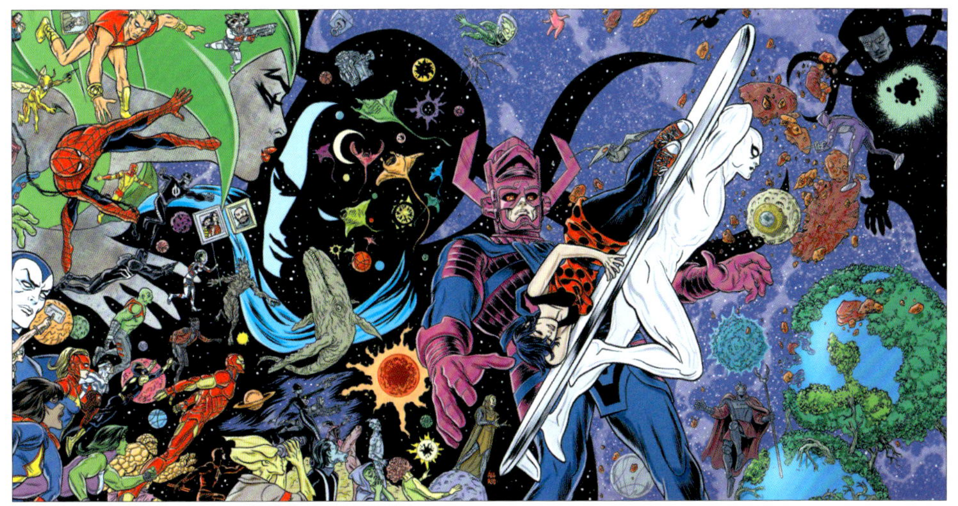

ABOVE
Cover detail from *Silver Surfer Omnibus* (November 2018). Art by Mike Allred (pencils).

OPPOSITE PAGE
Writer Kelly Sue DeConnick.

against common enemies, to the *Superior Spider-Man* series, which sees Doctor Octopus taking possession of Spidey's mind and identity. During his long run he also transformed Peter Parker into a rich industrialist who eventually slipped into rack and ruin, had Aunt May marry J. Jonah Jameson's father, and created Cindy Moon, A.K.A. Silk, a new Super Hero with spider-powers.

After *Spider-Man* and an award-winning *Silver Surfer* series illustrated by Mike Allred, Slott went on to write for *Iron Man* and the *Fantastic Four*. Other big-name writers included Matt Fraction and his wife Kelly Sue DeConnick. In the late 2000s and early 2010s he revitalised *Iron Man*, while she breathed new life into *Captain Marvel*. Fraction's version of Tony Stark was very similar to the one portrayed by Robert Downey, Jr.,

STAR WARS STRIKES BACK!

The Walt Disney Company acquired Lucasfilm in October 2012, just three years after picking up Marvel Entertainment. Fans worldwide hankered for the return of *Star Wars* to the world of comic books, and Marvel did not disappoint them. The initial *Star Wars* series made its debut in January 2015, written by Jason Aaron and illustrated by John Cassaday. The first issue sold over one million copies, making it the biggest-selling comic of the past two decades. More series followed, featuring the work of artists like Simone Bianchi, Stuart Immonen, and others. The limited series *Star Wars: Princess Leia*, written by Mark Waid and illustrated by Terry Dodson, was the first of several series dedicated to individual characters from the saga; *Star Wars: Darth Vader*, written by Kieron Gillen and illustrated by Salvador Larroca, ran from 2015 to 2016. To this day, *Star Wars* comics rank among Marvel best-sellers and feature some of the leading writers and artists, with all-new stories that have become part of the franchise's canon.

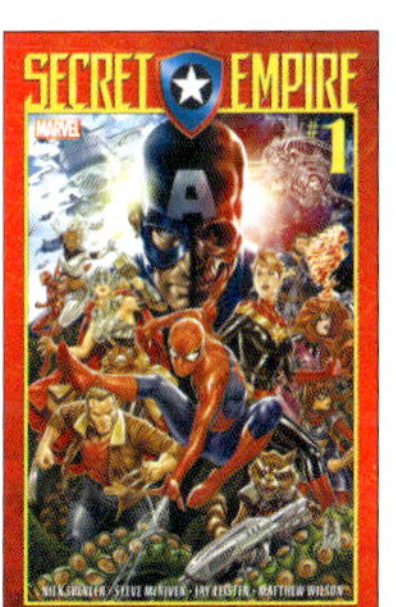

JULY 2017
The beginning of the limited series *Secret Empire*, which sees a villainous Captain America conquer the U.S. thanks to the backing of Hydra.

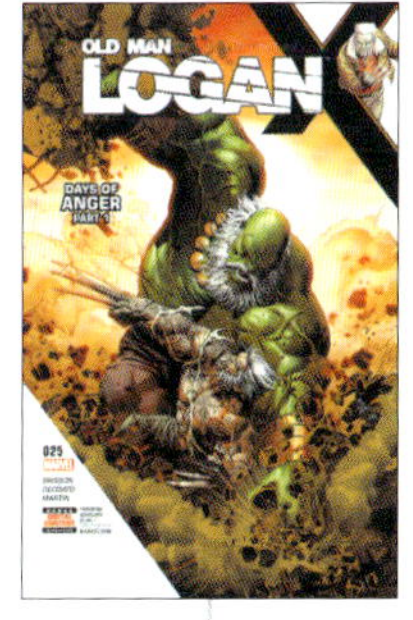

AUGUST 2017
Old Man Logan, the aging Wolverine from a parallel future who took the place of Wolvie, faces off against the Maestro, a mean old future version of Hulk, in *Old Man Logan #25*.

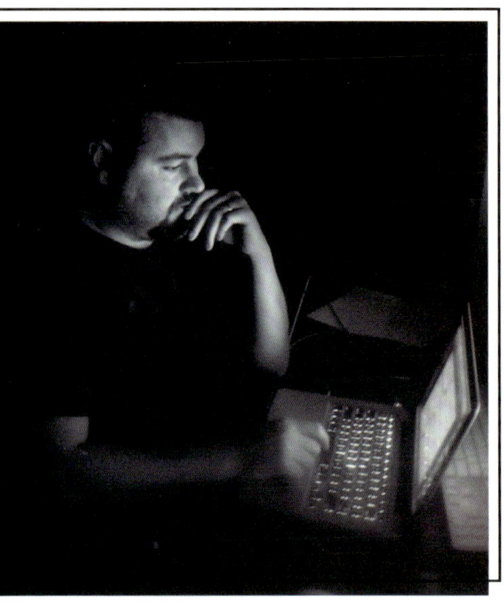

ABOVE
Writer Jonathan Hickman.

RIGHT
Johnny Storm returns in *Fantastic Four #600* (dated January 2012, released 23 November 2011). Script by Jonathan Hickman. Art by Steve Epting (pencils and inks), Rick Magyar (inks), Paul Mounts (colours), Clayton Cowles (letters).

which was a huge hit with fans, for the series *The Invincible Iron Man*, with artwork by Salvador Larroca. DeConnick transformed Carol Danvers from a minor Super Hero into one of the main characters in several recent Marvel sagas and a leader of the Avengers.

G. Willow Wilson was another writer who left her mark. A novelist besides her work in comics, Wilson teamed with editor Sana Amanat to come up with the Kamala Khan character, creating a Super Hero that many would call the Peter Parker of the 21st century, in terms of the way she reflected aspects of today's audience. Lastly, among the great writers in recent years, we can't leave out Jonathan Hickman, who gained fame thanks to several series he created for Image Comics. He is known for his long, complex story lines that crisscross and intertwine before reaching perfect solutions.

Besides masterminding the recent *Secret Wars* series and the spy saga *Secret Warriors*, featuring a team led by Nick Fury, Hickman also wrote a long run for *Fantastic Four*. From 2009 to 2012, in the pages of that old-time favourite, he 'killed' the Human Torch and brought him back to life, transformed the Fantastic Four into the Future Foundation, and made Doctor Doom a reluctant ally. In 2012 Hickman began work on *The Avengers* and *The New Avengers*, leading the teams to a monumental clash with Thanos in the Infinity saga. In 2019 he made his debut on X-Men with '*House of X/Power of X*'.

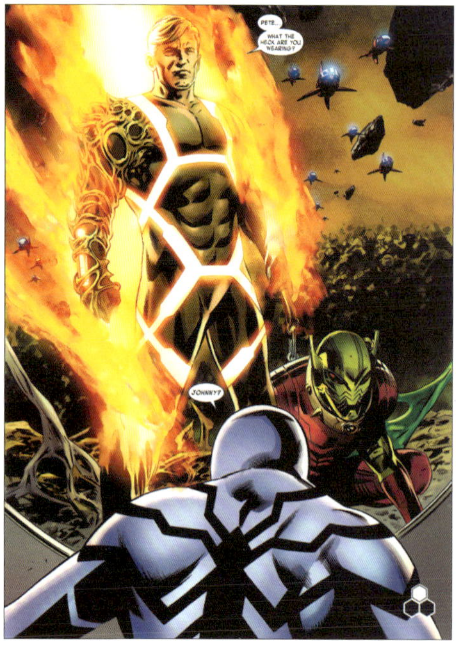

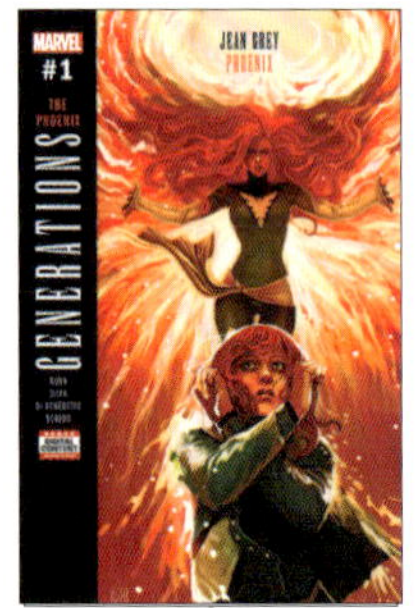

SEPTEMBER 2017
In the anthology *Generations*, Marvel Super Heroes meet their younger counterparts: Wolverine faces his clone Laura Kinney, Kamala Khan deals with Carol Danvers in the past...

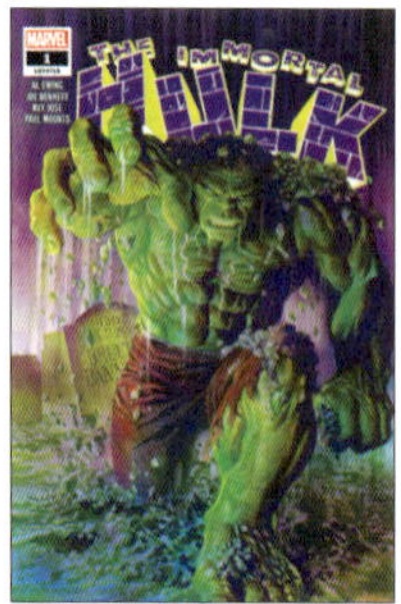

AUGUST 2018
Al Ewing and Joe Bennett come up with an all-new horror version of Hulk in the acclaimed series *The Immortal Hulk*.

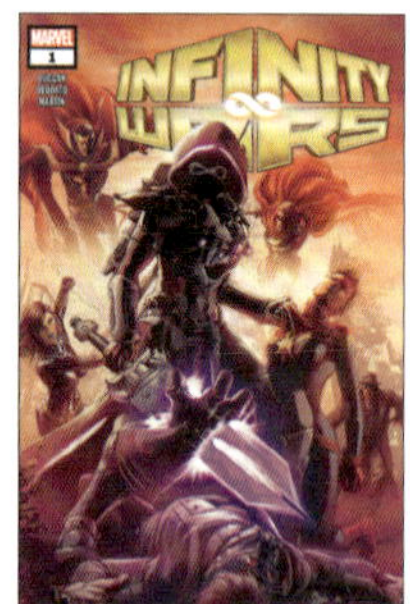

OCTOBER 2018
The Infinity Gems return to the centre of the Marvel Universe in the saga *Infinity Wars*. The first victim of this quest: Thanos!

A NEW GOLDEN AGE

The reach of Marvel extends far beyond the comic-book world, taking global audiences by storm.

After years of television popularity, Marvel Super Heroes had at long last become hits at the movies as well. In just a few years, characters created by Stan Lee, Jack Kirby, Steve Ditko, and others were no longer legends whose fame was limited to a privileged group of aficionados, but had cemented their status as icons of pop culture, recognisable the world over. Today, it's not rare to overhear people not necessarily attuned to comic-book culture discussing the powers of Thor or the dilemmas of Peter Parker.

Today, even the world's most celebrated newspapers indulge in breaking news about the latest developments and disclosures from the world of comics, like *Entertainment Weekly*'s announcement in 2014 that Sam Wilson would take over as Captain America, or recent reporting in the *New York Times* that a new *Captain Marvel* series was on the way. What's more, today tons of merchandising products, which may have been impossible to fathom back in Marvel's early days, invade the homes of not just collectors, but of children and adults that have come to know and love Marvel characters through films, cartoons, and the ever-expanding world of video and

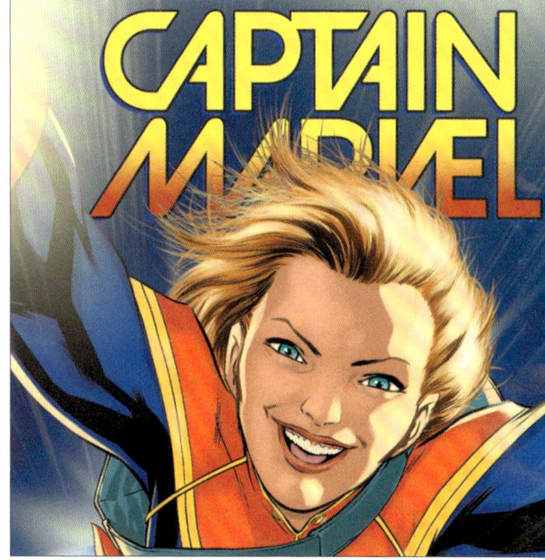

Detail from *Captain Marvel* #2 (dated June 2014, released April 9, 2014). Art by David Lopez.

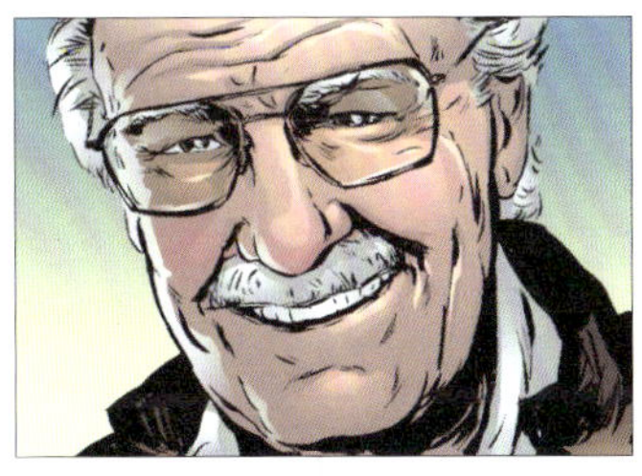

NOVEMBER 2018
On 12 November, fans all over the world mourn the death of Stan Lee.

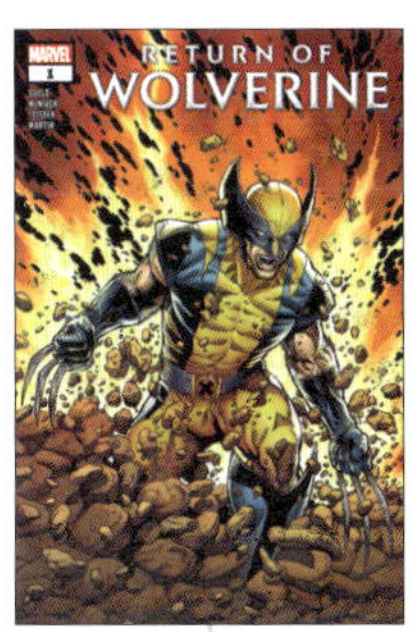

NOVEMBER 2018
Dead for about two years, Logan returns among the living in the limited series *Return of Wolverine*.

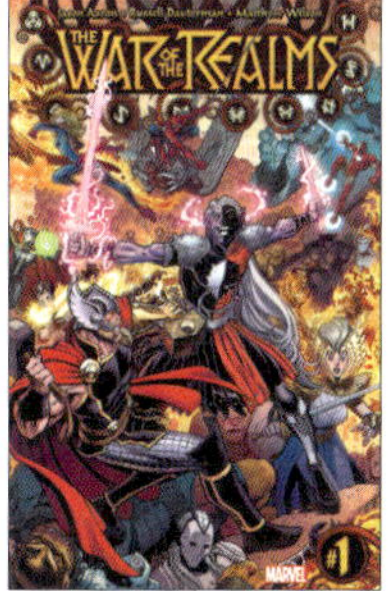

JUNE 2019
Jason Aaron caps his Thor run with the story line 'War of the Realms', which sees the participation of the greatest Super Heroes from the Marvel Universe.

RIGHT
America Chavez gets her own series with *America #1* (dated May 2017, released 1 March 2017). Art by Joe Quinones.

FAR RIGHT
Miles Morales: Spider-Man (Marvel YA Novel; August 2017). By Jason Reynolds (author), Kadir Nelson (illustrator).

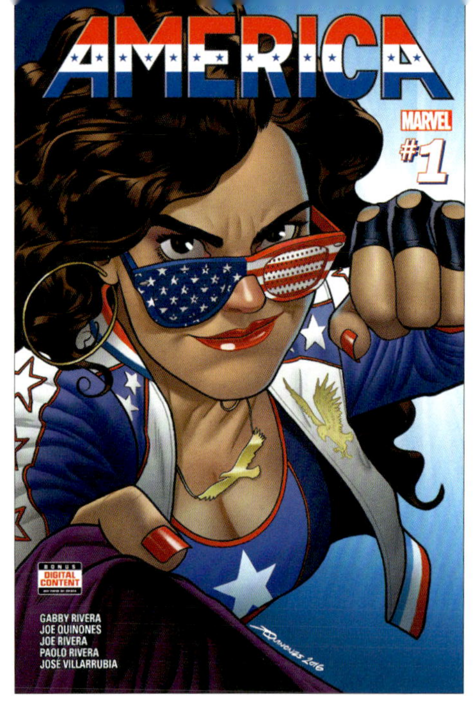

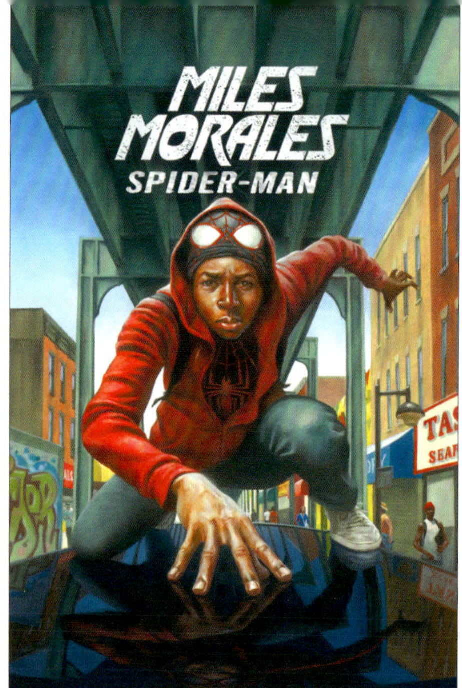

OPPOSITE PAGE
As Marvel looks to the future, its commitment to diversity and strong female characters like Captain Marvel will guide the House of Ideas to even greater heights. Captain Marvel illustration by Jamie McKelvie.

mobile games. The young—and the young at heart—often see Marvel Super Heroes as role models that drive their ambitions and fire their dreams. Today, characters like Kamala Khan, Miles Morales, and America Chavez are idolised by new legions of fans because they reflect their cultural heritage or sexual orientation, the same way nerdy kids in the 1960s could relate to a shy guy by the name of Peter Parker.

Revelling in a glorious past and enjoying the extraordinary present, the future looks bright for Marvel's star-studded cast of Super Heroes. The sad news is that Stan Lee, one of the fathers of so many illustrious characters that populate the Marvel Universe, won't be around to see it. Just as his own popularity and that of his creations reached stunning new heights, Lee left us on 12 November 2018, at the Cedars-Sinai Medical Center in Los Angeles, at the age of 95. Lifelong readers, brand-new fans, and moviegoers who thrilled to his many delightful cameo appearances, all shared in mourning the loss as they relived with one another the slew of memories he left behind.

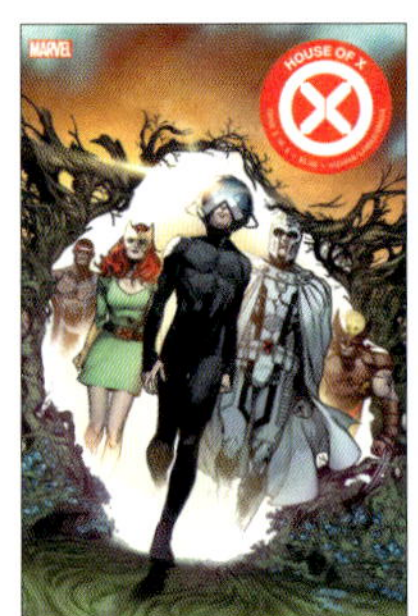

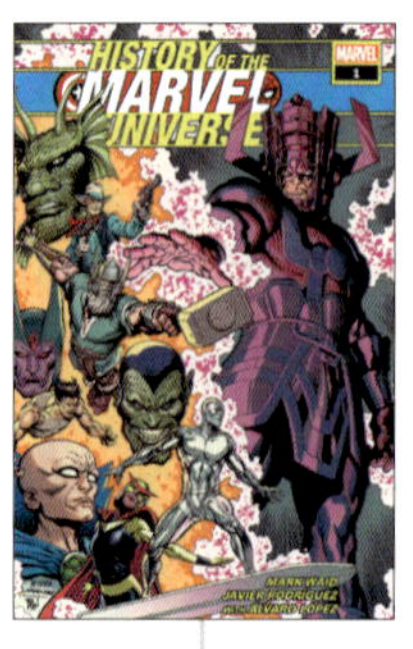

2020

SEPTEMBER 2019
Writer Jonathan Hickman begins work on the X-Men, shaking up the status quo with two limited series, *House of X* and *Powers of X*.

SEPTEMBER 2019
Mark Waid and Javier Rodriguez collect years of story lines to create the ultimate *History of the Marvel Universe*, a new and ambitious limited series.

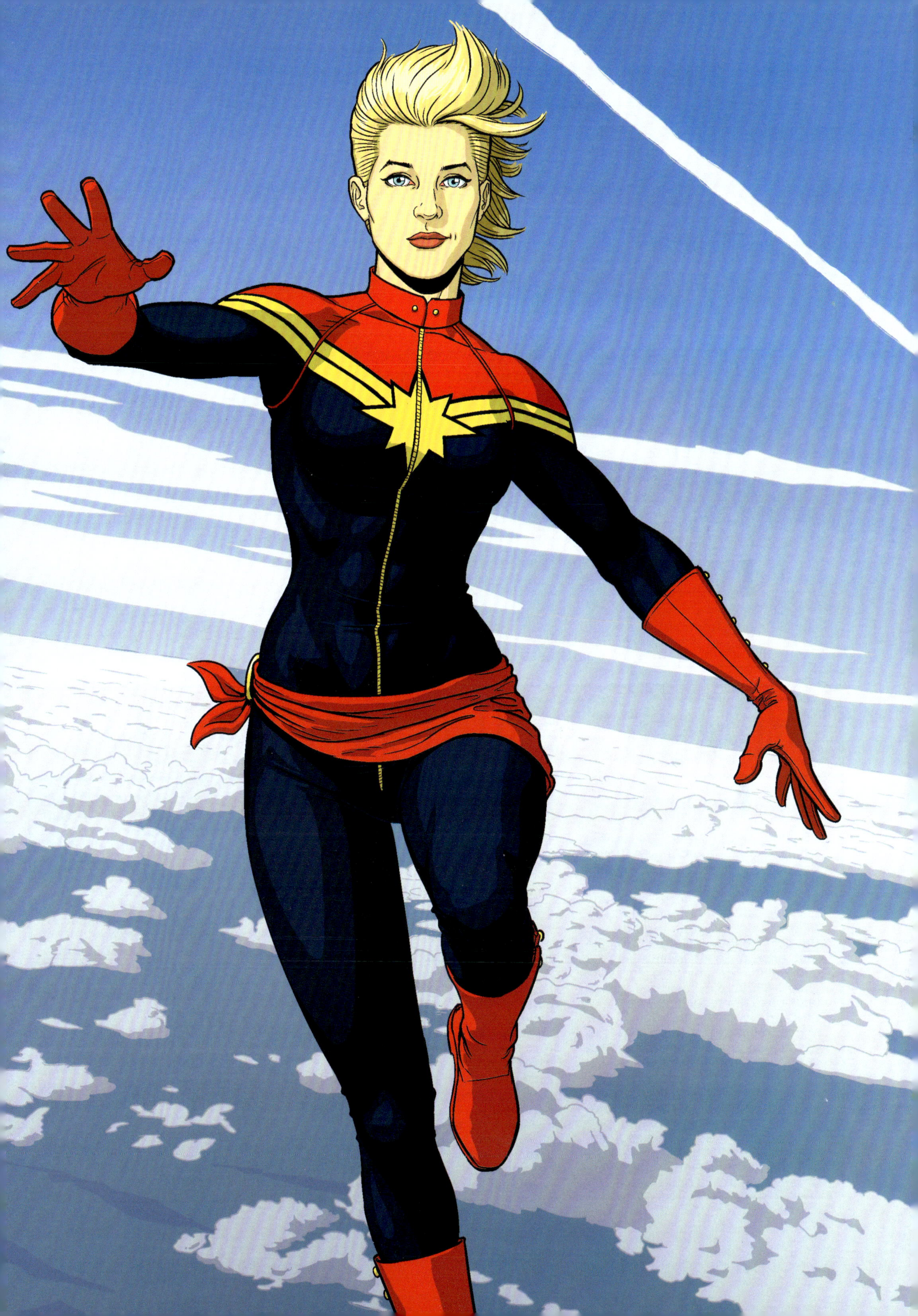

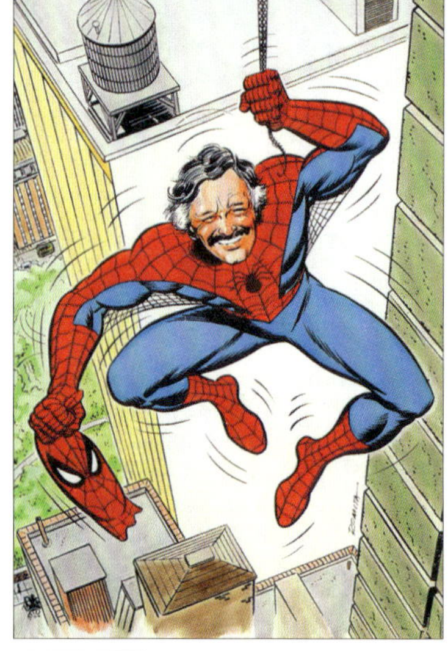

ABOVE
Spider-Man reveals his 'true' secret identity. Art by John Romita, Sr.

OPPOSITE PAGE
Cover art to *Stan Lee Meets Doctor Doom* (December 2006). Art by Salvador Larroca.

Stan Lee's last Stan's Soapbox column from the original run, August 1980.

His death made the front pages of newspapers across the globe; news shows and TV specials paid tribute to him. Although he won't be with us to celebrate Marvel's 80th anniversary, Lee was able to pull off the dream he'd carried with him since his youth—penning the Great American Novel... in his own way, of course. He created a saga that spanned so many of his characters' lifetimes, one destined to last through the ages, and considered by many experts and sociologists to be the annals of modern-day mythology. Few people would ever remember him by the name he was born with, which he was holding in reserve for that novel of his—Stanley Lieber. But many people instinctively link his pen name, Stan Lee, to the flood of quintessential characters seen in today's movie theatres, streamed over the Internet, manoeuvred in video and mobile games, immortalised in statues, their likenesses in action figures, on T-shirts, bags and cereal boxes, and shaped into snack foods, not to mention their appearance on the thousands of pages of comics produced every year by Marvel and its writers and artists.

To this day, the idea of Super Heroes with super problems, living in a world very similar to our own, remains the ingenious driving force behind the latest incredible creations that readers have already come to love. New writers and artists will come, as will new Super Heroes and new readers. And all of them will be grateful to Stan Lee for his masterful insight.

BULLPEN BULLETINS

STAN'S SOAPBOX

Hey, gang, I think I'm in big trouble, and since misery loves company, I might as well let you worry along with me! Y'see, I've got this Soapbox column to write and it's due at the printer tomorrow morning! So, I've gotta wrap it up in the next hour, or else! But, for the first time in about twenty years, I can't think of anything to write about! Oh sure, I could tell you to latch on to the second great issue of EPIC, or one of our many new regular comicbook titles, but I've been trying to avoid the big sell here in the Soapbox. Or, I could give you some gossip about what's happening amongst our batty bullpen bigwigs, but Jolly Jim Shooter and his capricious cohorts usually like to feed you those illuminating items themselves. So here I sit, staring at an emotionless typewriter with fear and panic welling up within my noble breast, while the clock keeps — HEY! Hold it! I thought of something! Wow — saved by the bell! And, best of all, it's something you can help me with!

Ever since I've been out here in Los Angeles, working on Marvel's many magnificent tv and film projects, one thought's been bugging me. I have a feeling that I don't really understand what makes the Saturday morning animated cartoon shows tick on tv! They're so different from the mighty masterworks you find in our mags that they might have originated on another planet. Okay, then, here's what you can do to help me — and perhaps to help the entire world of tv cartoons...

Just send me a short note, no more than 100 words, saying "Here's what I like about tv cartoons: ————", "Here's what I hate about tv cartoons: ————", and "Here's how to make them better: ————". I'll have our staff of thousands (Irving Thousands, the boss's uncle!) read 'em, and tabulate your opinions. Then, we'll print a summary of your suggestions in a future Soapbox (thereby guaranteeing that I'll have another topic for at least one more column)! Remember, what you write may change the entire tv industry — or, at the very least, give us a case of eyestrain! Just address your oh-so-meaningful missives to STAN LEE'S TV SURVEY, 575 Madison Ave., NYC, NY 10022. Culture lovers everywhere will be eternally in your debt!

Till we meet again, stay cool, stay happy, and stay in touch with the EPIC Epidemic! (Might as well get a plug in somewhere)!

Excelsior!

Stan

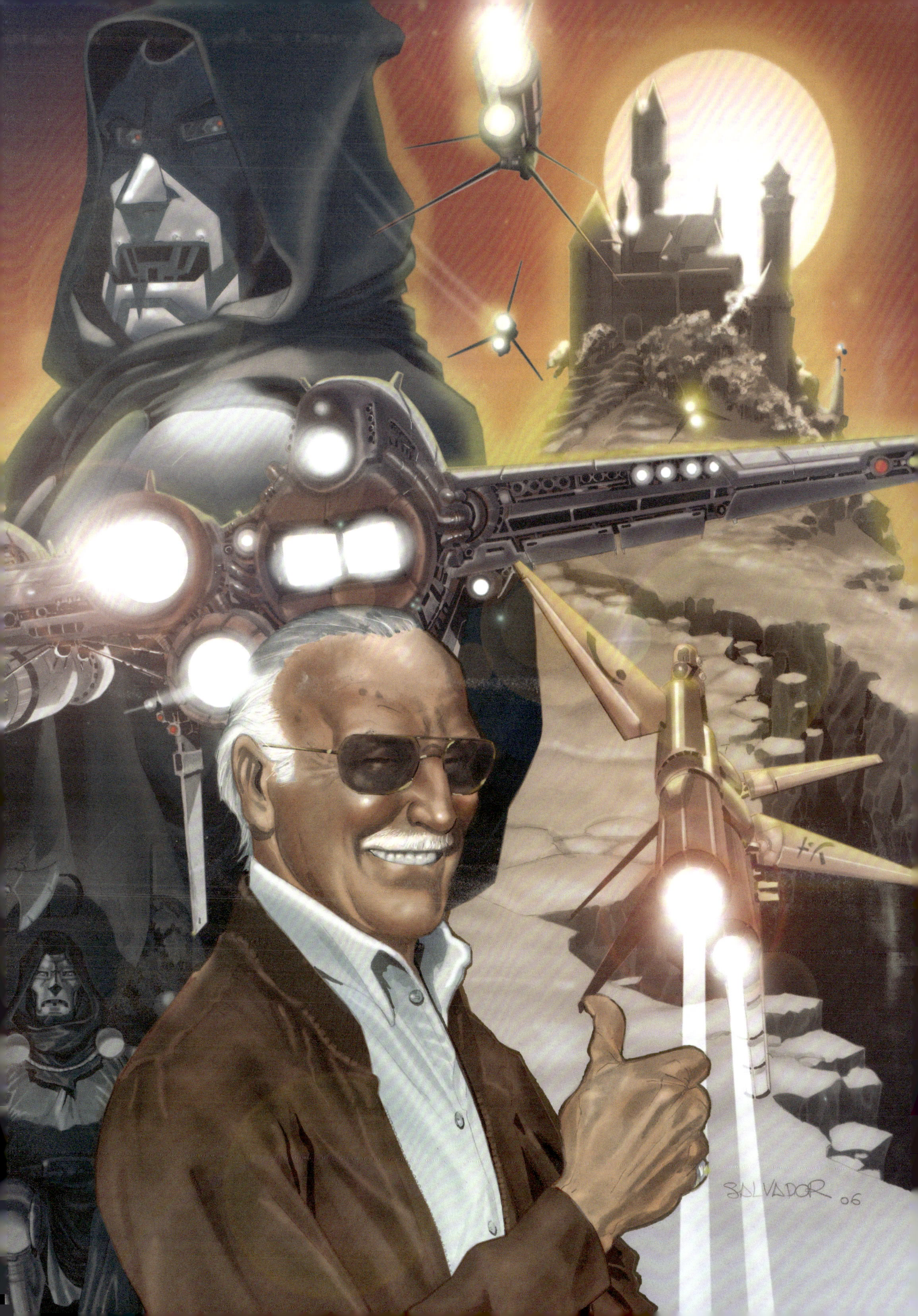
SALVADOR 06

Index & Credits

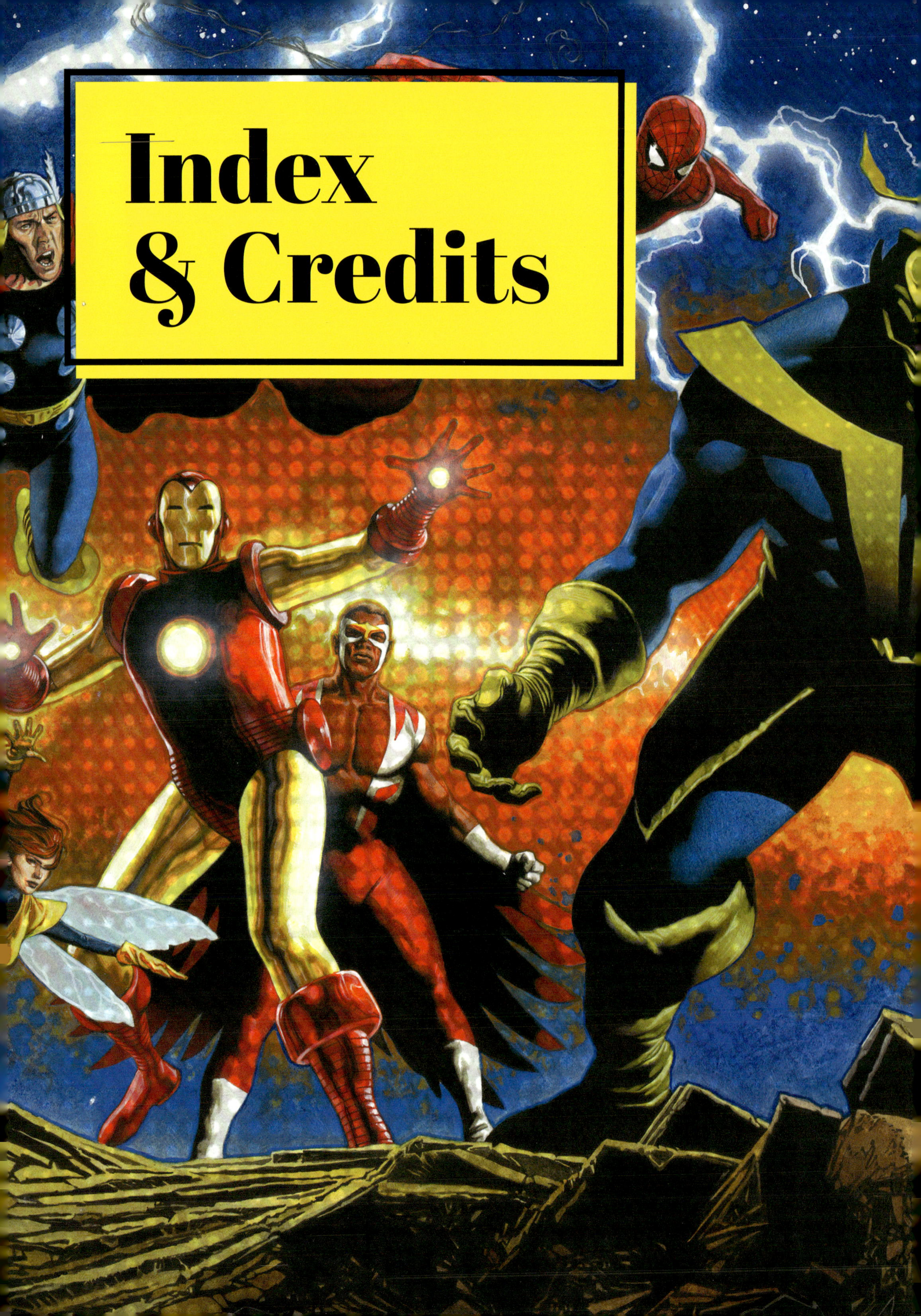

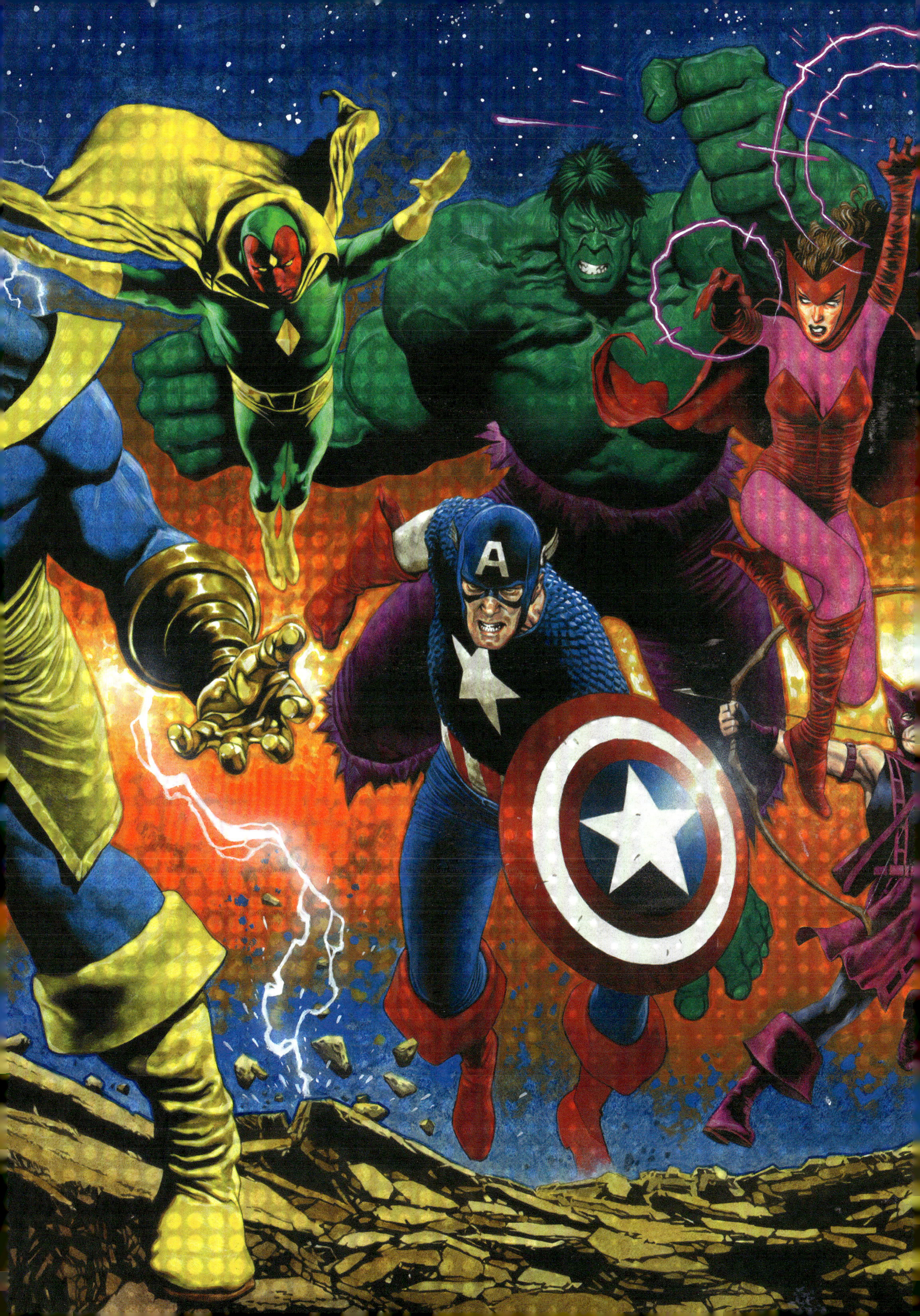

INDEX

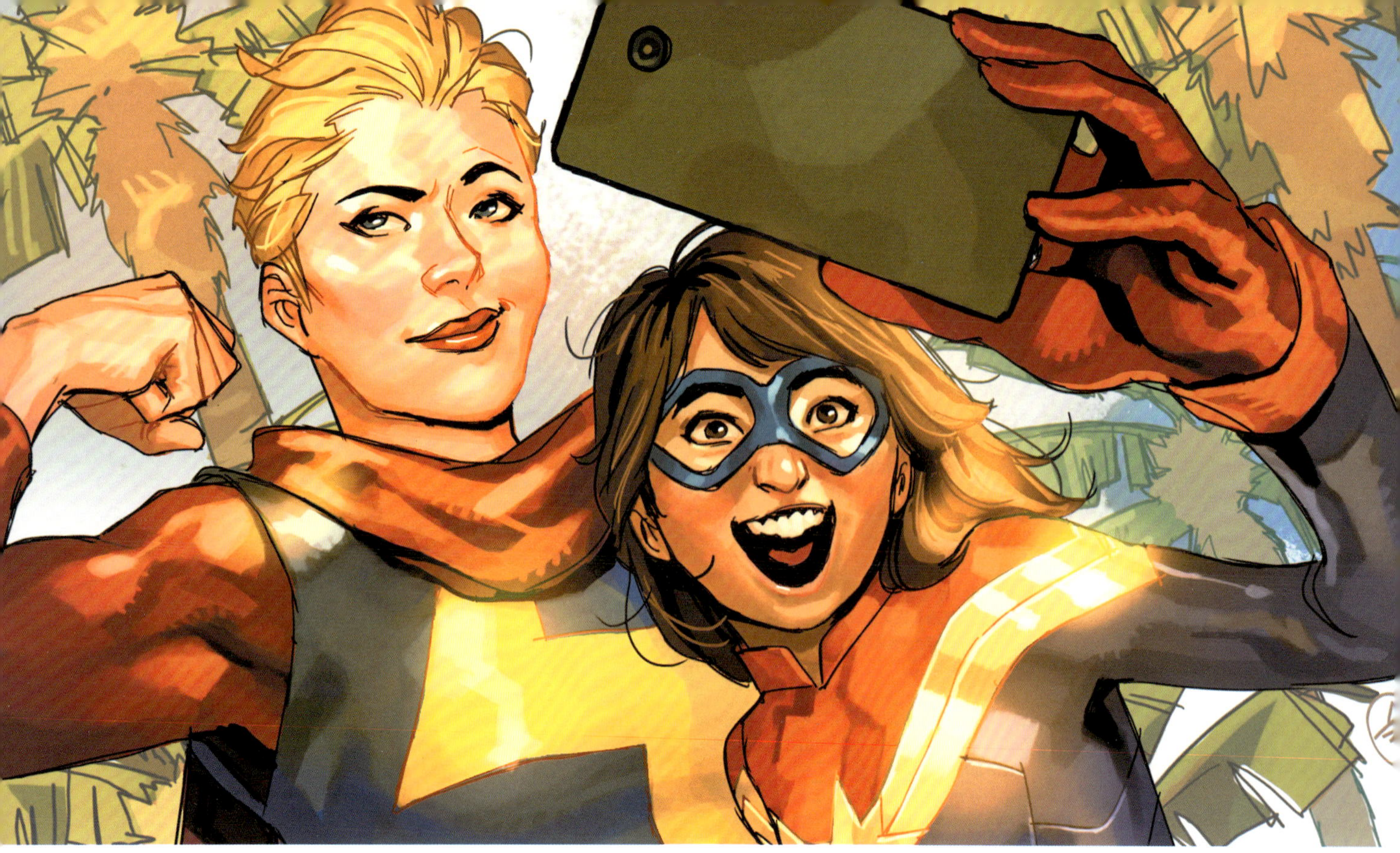

CREDITS

All photos and artwork from Marvel archives

pp. 2-3
The Avengers: David Finch (pencils), Art Thibert (inks), Frank G. D'Armata (colours).

pp. 6-7
Spider-Man vs. the Sinister Six: Alex Ross (painting).

p. 8
Tales of Suspense #94 (October 1967): Jack Kirby (pencils), Joe Sinnott (inks).

p. 11
Promotional image for *Marvel NOW!* (2012): Joe Quesada.

pp. 12-13
Marvel Mystery Comics #13 (November 1940): Jack Kirby (pencils).

pp. 28-29
Journey Into Mystery #1 (June 1952): Russ Heath, Stan Goldberg.

pp. 40-41
The Incredible Hulk King-Size Special #1 (October 1968): Jim Steranko, Marie Severin.

pp. 68-69
The Amazing Spider-Man #80 (January 1970): John Romita, Sr.

pp. 90-91
Wolverine #1 (September 1982): Frank Miller (pencils), Joe Rubinstein (inks).

pp. 108-109
Marvels (trade paperback): Alex Ross (painting).

pp. 130-131
The Amazing Spider-Man #36 (December 2001): John Romita, Jr. (pencils), Scott Hanna (inks), Avalon Studios/Dan Kemp (colours).

pp. 148-149
Phoenix Resurrection: The Return of Jean Grey #1 (February 2018): Leinil Francis Yu, Sunny Gho.

pp. 170-171
The Avengers vs. Thanos: Travis Charest (painting).

p. 176
The Life of Captain Marvel #1 variant cover (September 2018): Yasmine Putri (painter).

DISNEY PUBLISHING WORLDWIDE Global Magazines, Comics and Partworks

Publisher
Lynn Waggoner
Editorial Director
Bianca Coletti
Editorial Team
Guido Frazzini (Director, Comics), Stefano Ambrosio (Executive Editor, New IP), Carlotta Quattrocolo (Executive Editor, Franchise), Camilla Vedove (Senior Manager, Editorial Development), Behnoosh Khalili (Senior Editor), Julie Dorris (Senior Editor)
Design
Enrico Soave (Senior Designer)

Art
Ken Shue (VP, Global Art), Roberto Santillo (Creative Director), Marco Ghiglione (Creative Manager), Manny Mederos (Sr Illustration Manager, Comics & Magazines), Stefano Attardi (Illustration Manager)
Portfolio Management
Olivia Ciancarelli (Director)
Business & Marketing
Mariantonietta Galla (Senior Manager, Franchise), Virpi Korhonen (Editorial Manager)
Text
Fabio Licari, Marco Rizzo

Additional Text & Editing
Steve Behling
Design and Editing
Ellisse s.a.s. di Sergio Abate & C.
Valentina Bonura (Designer)
Tiziana Quirico (Editor)
Translation
John Rugman
Thanks to
Guy Cunningham, Joseph Hochstein, Mark Long, Caitlin O'Connell, Brian Overton, Jeff Youngquist.